DAUGHTERS
of
FREEDOM

DAUGHTERS *of* FREEDOM

AN ALBATROSS BOOK

© Janet West, 1997

Published by
Albatross Books Pty Ltd
PO Box 320, Sutherland
NSW 2232, Australia

First edition 1997

National Library of Australia
Cataloguing-in-Publication data

West, Janet
A history of women in the Australian church

ISBN   0 7324 1012 6

1. Women in Christianity — Australia — History.
2. Women in the Catholic Church — Australia — History.
3. Catholic women — Australia — History.
4. Protestant women — Australia — History.   I. Title

270.082

Front cover photograph: Courtesy of the National Gallery of Victoria
   Girolamo Nerli: born Italy 1860, arrived Australia 1885, died Italy 1926
   Head of a woman
   oil on composition board, 46.0 x 38.1 cm
   Purchased 1960
Printed and bound in Australia by McPherson's Printing Group
   Maryborough, Victoria

Contents

FOR:
Michael, Julia, Catherine and Marcus

Liberis mater
dono dedit
amans amantibus

Foreword

THE NUMBER OF BOOKS on the expanding role of women in the Christian church today is growing. It is a popular subject being studied from biblical, cultural and historical perspectives. Not until this book, *Daughters of Freedom*, has there been a comprehensive study into the history of women's place in the Australian church over the past two hundred years.

It is a remarkable achievement, with its sweeping survey of fascinating historical data, significant development themes and the liberating influences leading to the present day. Thorough-ly researched, it describes church women from a wide range of backgrounds, experience and traditions. It is not only schol-arly; it is inspiring as we consider the convictions of pioneering women, the enterprise of women missionaries at home and abroad, the astounding story of the Roman Catholic and Anglican Orders, the key role of lay women in philanthropic endeavours, the significance of female education in church schools, and the advancement of women in the ordained ministry and church leadership of Protestant denominations.

With its valuable insights, this book will not fail to stir the conscience concerning the waste of women's gifts and the limited scope given to them because of conventional attitudes in the Australian church in the past, but it will encourage all who read it to continue the struggle for women to be acknowledged as equal contributors with men in the church as we come to maturity on this issue.

In these days, there are encouraging signs that more and more women are expressing themselves freely and articulately, and taking their rightful place alongside men in ministry and church leadership without conflict and with mutual respect: men and women moving out in partnership to build the kingdom of God. This has come about through the agency of the Holy Spirit.

I believe that he, the Spirit of Truth, will use this book to bring illumination and greater clarity to the issue, and that today's 'daughters of freedom' will increasingly enrich the life and activity of the Christian church in this land.

The kingdom of God needs all of us, released to serve our Lord and his cause.

General Eva Burrows
Retired international leader
The Salvation Army

Preface

WOMEN'S HISTORY AND WOMEN'S CHURCH HISTORY have only lately become fashionable. When I embarked on this study less than a decade ago, little had been published in this field. Some might argue that the floodgates are now opening, but this is the first attempt at a general history of women in the Australian church.

No doubt some will feel that I have omitted too many of the achievements of these women over two centuries. However, I felt it right to concentrate upon role within a theme of freedom, leaving other aspects to be treated in greater depth by future enquirers.

I must pay tribute to Sisters Moira O'Sullivan and Cathleen O'Carrigan of the Sisters of Charity, Sister McGlynn of the Good Samaritans and Sister Evelyn of the Order of St Joseph. They were ever-encouraging in their assistance to an ignorant Anglican researcher. Also of inestimable help were Elizabeth Burchill, a Presbyterian nurse-deaconess, and Mary Andrews, Dorothy Harris and Margaret Rodgers — all Anglican deaconesses. Mrs Margarethe Warren aided me greatly in contacting women of the Salvation Army.

Progress would have been impossible without the cheerful

assistance of the librarians of the Mitchell, Battye and Mortlock Libraries. The Mitchell, in particular, contains a vast collection of mission records and literature within its capacious depths. My thanks also go to the National Library in Canberra, the Northern Territory Archives in Darwin, to Moore Theological College Library and to the archivists of the Presbyterian Church in Sydney and of the Uniting Church in North Parramatta. The Church Missionary Society and the Overseas Missionary Fellowship in both Melbourne and Sydney are likewise most helpful.

Professor Kenneth Cable and his wife Leonie have been a source of wise counsel and encouragement over the years. Few ecclesiastical historians would strike out without their imprimatur! For generations of students, Ken has been (to adapt Cicero) *vir bonus docendi peritus.*

I must express my appreciation to Albatross Books for their devoted professionalism in what are difficult days for Australian publishers. Ken Goodlet has been an editor of rare quality; no author could ask for more.

As far as illustration is concerned, I must thank the Sisters of Charity for the photographs of Mother Gertrude Healy and of the Long Bay visitation.

Ruth Minton Taylor, Sheila Knox for the photograph of Catherine Hamlin, Nungalinya College for the photograph of the ordination of Liyapidiny Marika and the Parramatta Sisters of Mercy for the photograph of the Mamre Project. The portrait of Eva Burrows was by courtesy of the Salvation Army Eastern Territorial Command and that of Dorothy Mowll was supplied by the Anglican Retirement Villages at Castle Hill. The Good Samaritan supplied the portrait of Mother McLoughlin and of the Manly Industrial School. I am indebted to the Reverend Miriam Howard for the rare portrait of Eva Holland.

Finally, I must express my heartfelt gratitude to my husband Roderick and to our four children and their spouses for their support. My doctors have seen me through severe illness so that I could complete the work. The prayers of many and the hospitality of the Daughters of Charity in Eastwood and the Franciscan Sisters of Mary in Point Piper have enabled me to write in conditions of peace and inspiration.

Janet West

Janet West
Newport Beach, NSW

Introduction

To WEAVE A TAPESTRY OF THE ROLES OF WOMEN in the Australian church has been no easy task. The canvas is broad, the gaps are daunting and archives are disappointingly thin.

Sheer survival was the concern of most women in the first fifty years of European settlement. That is why we know so little of the thoughts and spiritual strivings of the earliest white women on this continent. They did not have time to record them, nor the requisite energy. Some did not have the literacy. . . The rawness of the frontier, its loneliness, its unfamiliar sights and sounds, its shortages, the dangers of the voyage out, the dangers of childbirth and the fear of incessant pregnancy — all conspired to place our women pioneers under pressures that are unknown to us.

For much of our period, women were not considered worthy of the historian's pen unless they were monarchs, saints or consorts of the famous. Thus, to be married to an important figure such as a governor or a bishop merited some attention, but a wife's significance was always assessed in terms of her husband's role and her contribution to it. In the same way, members of female orders were regarded as an essential element of the church canonically without being accorded parity of rank or voice in a male-dominated hierarchy.

The church, it must be noted, was hardly more sexist than the society amongst which it worked. Nor were the majority of churchwomen unhappy with the subordinate nature of their role. However, with the advent of universal education in the late nineteenth century, emancipation of women from fixed roles within the church and society was on the way. Nonconformist churches, with their more democratic tradition, were faster to recognise the equality of women than the more hierarchical churches.

Thus, it was with a strong sense of redress that I approached the subject of women in the church over the first two hundred years of European settlement. Discrimination against women was not difficult to find and the very lack of information was discriminatory in itself. Diocesan archives and Conference minutes were almost devoid of reference to women. Research material had to be gleaned at first from biographies or from chance discoveries of letters and diaries. Elderly women who had begun their ministry in the 1930s were interviewed, but these were a declining band. Women who have been significant in the post-war church were naturally more available for interview. Archives of religious orders were thankfully a fruitful source, as were the records of such bodies as the Women's Christian Temperance Union, the Mothers' Union and the Methodist Dorcas Society.

It was instructive to note that, apart from the sisters' records, the vast majority of material relating to churchwomen resides in secular archives. The great public libraries like the Mitchell, the Mortlock and the Battye have provided a haven for the records of women missionaries and laywomen. Perhaps, this is fitting as it was possibly women more than men who came to reach out to the community on behalf of the church as the period unfolded.

As my research uncovered more and more of the largely unrecognised achievements of women in the Australian church, I felt a sense of exhilaration. Of what were these women *not* capable? Physically building churches, hospitals and schools in India, leading services and preaching in Africa and on the beaches of Western Australia, riding by camel into Alice Springs to open a church and a dispensary, visiting gaols daily to bring hope to desperate inmates, visiting squalid mental asylums and lobbying government for their reform.

Aboriginal women played a largely passive role in churches at first, but those with a gift for language began to help in Bible translation and interpretation of Christian teaching to their own people. By the close of our period, the first Aboriginal women had been ordained into the ministry of the church.

I found great satisfaction in crossing denominational boundaries and treating women as women and not as ecclesiastical statistics. Such women found religion to be liberating and empowering and yet they were restricted by societal norms and by the patriarchal nature of their own church. Although they came to dominate congregations numerically and in terms of labour, they were generally not recognised as being capable of executive power within those congregations.

The main thesis which emerges in this study is that there was a widening gap over this entire period between ideal and reality for women within the church. On the one hand, the teaching and attitude of the Founder of the church conferred freedom and recognition upon women; whereas, on the other, the hierarchy of that church refused to grant women parity of esteem or rank within its confines. Women were an indispensable labour force in the church, but autonomy or power- sharing was frowned upon by the hierarchy, save in the remotest mission fields where male workers were at a premium.

A number of important themes have arisen in pursuing this

study. First, the pioneering churchwoman of the Georgian era grappled with her **solitary environment** and proved herself a resilient leader of her church, *de facto* if not *de iure*. Georgiana Molloy and Myrah White are cases in point. The first churches were by nature derivative as early settlers based their religious experience on British and European models, so the woman's role for a great deal of this study has to be set in that context.

A second theme is the heroic contribution of **the religious orders** to church and society and the resultant conflict with the hierarchy over issues of power and procedure which are of absorbing interest to historians of the women's movement. It is difficult not to conclude that the hierarchy's denial of freedom and autonomy to women's orders was an early factor in the rise of feminism in Catholic circles.

A third theme is that of **philanthropy**. Devout women philanthropists of the Victorian era performed significant feats of social work before governments assumed responsibility for this sphere of need. At the same time, these women were cutting their teeth on such executive functions as committee work, speeches and financial administration — areas which were heretofore the province of men.

A fourth important theme is the advent of **first wave feminism** in the later nineteenth century, especially in its interface with the church. Many laywomen like Eliza Pottie and Mary Colton were associated with militant temperance and suffrage societies while sustaining their church and social work. An adequate supply of domestic help which was available to the middle class in the late nineteenth century was a *sine qua non* for such wide-ranging endeavour.

A fifth theme is the question of **female education** which was undoubtedly the most liberating influence for women by the beginning of the twentieth century. Most churches welcomed the growth of church secondary schools for girls and the opening of universities to women, without realising the ultimate implications of such reforms for a male-dominated church. The Catholic Church, in particular, did not realise what an instrument of dissent they were unleashing when they allowed women's orders to take control of the education of girls, as our final chapters disclose.

A sixth theme which arises even before the twentieth century but reaches its apogee by World War II is that of **missions**. Denied opportunities of leadership and independence in their home churches, many women expressed their vocation by serving overseas and in the outback of Australia as missionaries. They set up schools and hospitals, conducted church services and, indeed, planted churches — options which were, for the most part, closed to them in their own countries.

A final major theme which brings us up to 1988 and beyond is the gradual move towards **equality of opportunity** for women in the present-day church. This trend reflected, however haltingly, an irresistible movement in society at large — the liberation of women from traditional expectations.

Smaller bodies like the Quakers, the Salvation Army and the Congregational church became completely democratic in their attitude towards gender roles. The Presbyterian and Methodist churches limped slowly towards the goal of female ordination which their women finally won in 1977 after these churches were united. The oldest and most hierarchical of churches — the Anglican and the Roman Catholic — remained opposed to such moves as the ordination of women, partly for reasons of tradition and interpretation of scripture and partly for reasons of power.

By ignoring the revolutionary changes occurring in the role of women in post-war society in general, they risked losing the membership of spiritual women of independence.

The journey of Australian churchwomen over two hundred years has been characterised by much patience and hard work. This work has often been lowly in nature and is therefore undocumented. It is largely a *hidden* history, save where independent communities of women like the orders have lovingly preserved their records. The absence of women in church archives must not disguise the fact that there has been much fruitful cooperation between the sexes in the service of the church. At the same time, there has been conflict and pain — especially for women workers — that has brought discredit to the church and a recent attrition of its numbers.

Those who have stayed within the church and yet fought for their view of what is right have done much to work towards the freedom which is their birthright.

1

Women, church and society in Australia in the last two hundred years

AN OVERVIEW

'Church history begins when a few women set out to pay their last respects to their dead friend, Jesus. . .'

German delegate to the
1981 World Council of Churches

T HE ISSUE OF EQUALITY FOR WOMEN over Australia's short history of Western settlement has always been problematic. It is certain that the treatment of underprivileged women in the early years — and in particular convict and Aboriginal women — is a blot on human history.

Nor were free women immigrants sufficiently protected from sexually marauding men on the journey to Australia. Caroline Chisholm was furious at the treatment of many single girls on the boats coming out from Britain. She mentioned Margaret Bolton, for example, who travelled on the ship *Carthaginian* and was permanently impaired by the disgraceful treatment of the captain and surgeon.[1]

Some historians have detected an Australian tendency for

women to have a low view of other women as a legacy of the convict days. Lieutenant Ralph Clark's comment about the women of the First Fleet being 'damned whores' reflected a theological as well as a social attitude which prevailed in Georgian and Victorian days. Women were either regarded as temptresses in the tradition of fallen Eve, or else put on a pedestal and invested with the qualities of an archangel or the Virgin Mary. Catholic medieval theology was particularly responsible for this polarised view of women.[2] Other historians have isolated a masculinist ideology both inside and outside the church which has worked against the emancipation of women. The cult of machismo in Australia which has been so prevalent until recently is a probable descendant of the early colonial days of womanlessness.[3]

An Anglican church submission presented as recently as 1975 to the Royal Commission on Human Relationships argued that many important family concerns are left to the woman, 'not because of the male's greater respect for his partner, but because of his own laziness and unwillingness to accept responsibility. The female isn't given pride of place in the relationship; it's just if she doesn't do it, no-one else will . . .in many cases, she is used merely as an object of sexual gratification.' This is probably an overstatement of the case, couched as it is in emotive language.[4] Further, few females desire 'pride of place' in marriage rather, mutuality of expectation. However, it does express the frustration felt by many women in the past, but very rarely expressed.

Despite the undoubted detrimental aspects in the treatment of women in the Australian colonies, many female settlers like the Bussell women of Western Australia and Jane Henty of Victoria welcomed the good climate of the new country and the opportunity to work alongside their husbands on the land. Most of them mixed happily with women of all backgrounds (apart from Aborigines) which they would not have done in the class-structured country of their origin. 'Fond as I am of home, I do greatly enjoy the lovely climate, good health and the free outdoor life that we have here,' wrote Rachel Henning, the lively clergy daughter who stepped from the pages of Jane Austen into a frontier life in outback Queensland.[5]

There was a steady evolution of a more egalitarian family and class structure throughout the nineteenth century. This was partly due to the freshness of the new environment, where old social divisions were fast becoming irrelevant, partly due to increased education and partly to the advent of the first wave of feminism. By the close of the century, Maybanke Anderson, a leading feminist, commented on a greater appreciation of the worth of women by society in general. Australian girls, she said, were 'confident, open, independent and friendly. . . working class girls refreshingly free of servility'[6]

✠ Women and the Australian church in the first hundred years

Despite the derivative nature of early Australian churches, it was inevitable that colonial conditions would modify British and/or European role models. The vigour and adaptability of such currency[7] lasses as Ann Marsden (later Hassall) and Mary Hassall (later Lawry) enabled them to do the work of unpaid curates — and more — in their father's and husband's parishes. They helped pioneer Sunday schools and Bible Society branches. Mary was the first Australian woman missionary in the South Pacific, gaining greater acclaim for her work than her husband.[8]

Membership of the various Roman Catholic orders became increasingly Australian-born as the century progressed. The Sisters of St Joseph, for example, endured great privation and poverty to build up a vast network of schools and orphanages across Australia under their founder, Mary MacKillop. She constantly stressed her pride in being an Australian: 'It is an Australian who writes this, one brought up in the midst of the evils she tries to describe. . .'[9] Her resourcefulness and adaptability enabled her to outstrip in many respects the older and wealthier orders who had greater support from the male hierarchy.

Although there was greater scope for female initiative in Australia than in the home countries, the church context was to prove scarcely propitious for the fostering of that initiative. Patriarchy reigned supreme in all but three small denominations. The Quakers, some of the Congregationalists and later the Salvation Army proclaimed the equality of women in ministry, both in principle and practice. Winifred Kiek, a Congregationalist of Quaker origins, was the first woman to be ordained in Australia — in Adelaide in 1927.

Catherine Booth, wife of the founder of the Salvation Army, was the most articulate of church feminists over this period and such was her eloquence and spirituality that women were ordained to a preaching ministry on exactly the same basis as the men from the very beginning in her church in both Britain and Australia. Gender equality in ministry was also upheld by the Quakers, a church comprising a tiny group of intellectuals meeting in major urban centres. Their sect had a history of female prophecy dating back to the Reformation and they were not about to abandon this tradition in the Antipodes.

In the words of Catherine Booth:

God has given to women a graceful form and attitude, winning manners, persuasive speech and, above all, a finely-toned emotional nature, all of which appear as eminent qualifications for public speaking. . . I believe that one of

the greatest boons to the race would be woman's exaltation
to her proper position, mentally and spiritually. Who can
tell its consequences to posterity? If indeed there is in Jesus
Christ neither male nor female, but in all touching his
kingdom they are one, who shall dare thrust woman out
of the church's operations or presume to put any candle
which God has lighted under a bushel? Why should the
swaddling bands of blind custom. . . be again wrapped
round the female disciples of the Lord?[10]

It was in the Roman Catholic Church that the greatest
oppression of women in ministry was experienced at the hands
of a male hierarchy. Incident after incident occurred, especially
in the Sisters of Charity and the Josephite orders, in which
nuns were bullied, intimidated, exploited and even excommunicated by clergy and bishops who were often less godly than
they. There were explanations for this in terms of Anglo-Irish
differences, lack of education and manners, and the demands
of a frontier church. However, the basis of this behaviour was
the patriarchal system prevailing in the church which in turn
was derived from the sexist ideology of the day which catego-
rised women according to certain suppositions about ability,
birth and role.

Therefore, on the ground that women were naturally
emotional, non-rational and unable to cope with economic
problems, it was valid to take from them title to property that
their order had obtained; to decree what sort of habits should
be worn and when it was time to buy a new one; when
convents should say prayers; when they should have meals;
when and how they should travel outside their house. It was
correct that they should eat less than men and have less
possessions. Therefore, they needed far less to live on — 30
pounds a year for each Sister of Charity was enough in 1839,
while a priest was entitled to passage and outfit money, a

stipend, travelling allowances and a site for church, school and residence.

As the Catholic Church and the colonies became more established, 'Leave it to the good sisters!' became the familiar cry of the male clergy when sundry tasks arose. No matter that the nuns had been teaching or nursing for nine hours on end, they could always manage evening classes, choir training, making the altar breads, mending and laundering the altar linen, visiting the sick and raising funds![11]

One of the most significant doctrines influencing the lives of Western women for at least a century — from approximately 1850 to 1950 — was the Victorian concept of separate spheres. The man's sphere, according to such ideology, was that of public and business life and here he was expected to reign with little or no female input. The woman's sphere, on the other hand, was the home and here her behaviour was subject to angelic expectations, while the man was out in the marketplace or the bush, as the case might be.

The church through its clergy and later through such conservative women's groups as the Mothers' Union encouraged this doctrine, but they tended to stress the supremacy of the home rather than the family with some important results. Australian church historian, Dr Stuart Piggin, argues that while women were held to be the repository of Christian values as home-makers, no such constraints were placed upon the male in his public sphere. The American theologians, D.P. McCann and C.R. Strain, have demonstrated the disparity which occurs when agapaic love is applied to the woman and the home, but not to the public sphere, where men tend to operate under a different code of morality. This had ramifications for the church — as long as women were at home as torchbearers of morality, the behaviour of male church leaders was somehow sanctified.[12]

The consistently high expectations in church circles of women as chiefly responsible for both home and family had its origins in evangelical belief which was probably the strongest religious strand — certainly in Protestant churches — in nineteenth and twentieth century religion in Australia. Even Caroline Chisholm, arguably Australia's greatest social reformer, was of evangelical background prior to her conversion to Catholicism.

Davidoff and Hall claim that the evangelical revival of the eighteenth century — and this would include the rise of Methodism — made a religious idiom the cultural norm for the middle class by 1850. It was a thrusting religion which was generally passionate about winning others and helping the less fortunate in life. The ideal woman was firstly a paragon in the home like the woman of Proverbs 31. The American evangelical, Sarah Stickney Ellis, gave this exalted view of the home-making role of women:

> In the performance of home duties, women were realising
> a divine purpose; as chaste wives and mothers, they partook
> in a heavenly world. . .[13]

However, evangelical women often adjusted the Victorian doctrine of separate spheres to suit their philanthropic and, later, feminist program. Increasing affluence amongst the middle classes and a plentiful supply of domestic help, together with the strong religious fervour of the day, propelled a growing number of women out of their homes and into society at large.[14] Such early evangelical governors' wives as Eliza Macquarie, Eliza Darling and Jane Franklin were indefatigable in their philanthropic work, as we shall see in the next chapter.

As the nineteenth century progressed, middle and upper class girls in Britain and the colonies were brought up not to follow a career, but to include in their week some aspect of philanthropy. A career was not necessary economically if one belonged to an affluent home, but philanthropy was a duty for one who was well endowed with this world's goods. This view was confirmed by the writings of John Ruskin, who claimed that philanthropy was a woman's duty and was necessary to 'soften the harshness of the male-dominated world'. 'A true woman should be a sister,' he claimed,[15] and his saccharine style found an enthusiastic audience in the late Victorian era.

Upper class women tended to patronise the older charities — a good example of this latter group being Lady Marian Allen, wife of the wealthy solicitor and politician, Sir George Wigram Allen. A devout Methodist, she was vice-president of the Hospital for Sick Children and a committee member of the NSW Benevolent Asylum, the State Children's Relief Board, the Sydney Female Refuge, the YWCA and the Sydney Servants' Home. She had gained such a reputation for generosity that she was reportedly driven from her home by beggars, following her husband's death in 1885.[16]

The ideology of the family as the salvation of the Australian colonies, set out by Caroline Chisholm, found acceptance with evangelical members of the British government, who agreed with her concept of women and children as 'God's police', spreading virtue and good works in a needy and fallen society.[17] Henry Parkes took up her view twenty years later when he told parliament: 'Our business being to colonise the country, there was only one way to do it — by spreading all over it the associations and connections of family life.'[18]

It cannot be denied that the growth of family life from the unpromising beginnings of 1788 was the basis of the country's development. This theme was also taken up by the churches, and such groups as the Mothers' Union were founded to strengthen the family, draw women into active church membership and to raise the birthrate which was beginning to fall in an increasingly prosperous society. The Mothers' Union had a philanthropic strand, but it tended to be an inward-looking body, concentrating on church attendance, the promotion of marriage (divorced people were not allowed membership), and the celebration of home and children.[19] This fast-spreading ideology of the home went hand-in-hand with the increased suburbia and gentrification of society in the late nineteenth century.

✠ Women and the Australian church in the late nineteenth century

As the first century of British settlement drew to a close, two highly significant movements for the emancipation of women occurred in the colonies. The first was the arrival of the first wave of feminism in the country, as typified by such agencies as the Women's Christian Temperance Union (WCTU); the second milestone was the opening up of education at all levels to women.

The WCTU was a significant body in articulating the feminist cause and in providing a vehicle for the ideas of women in the church. It has left behind a considerable store of records which have drawn much attention from scholars. By the late 1870s, it had attracted thousands of members across Australia and was publishing a great deal of literature.

Catherine Spence and Emily Clark of South Australia, Jessie Ackermann of Western Australia, Isabel McCorkindale of Victoria and Eliza Pottie from New South Wales were all women of piety or else had been brought up in devout homes. Suddenly, they became national figures, speaking confidently about the evils of intemperance and the need for female suffrage so that society could be purified and re-fashioned.[20] It was a unique period historically for the church, women and politics to conjoin for an idealistic purpose.

Of great significance for women was the introduction of compulsory elementary education for both sexes from 1866 onwards. Victoria led the way in 1874, followed by South Australia in 1875 and NSW in 1880. This reform brought hope to women of intelligence who aspired to university education and the professions. However, there was much male (and female) prejudice to break down. Australia was still very much a chauvinist society. Women were encouraged to think of themselves only as part of a family relationship — with the associated conventions and prescriptions of the family.

The single woman was often an object of fun. At the turn of the century, the female wage was fifty-four per cent of that of the male. It was safer economically for women to base their existence on their husbands' careers. Fine women writers were constantly omitted from the arts and literary awards. Writers like Mary Gilmore, Ada Cambridge and Rosa Campbell-Praed were forced to adopt pseudonyms until their work was accepted.[21]

However, despite society's lack of recognition for women and their achievements, steady progress was being made towards their social and political emancipation. During the 1880s, large numbers of single women were able to move into the workforce as state public services opened up a range of commercial employment to women.[22] The foundation of four high schools for girls in NSW after 1882 meant that girls in that state could then gain identical education to boys. A struggle then began to open first, matriculation examinations and then, universities to women.

The churches were generally in support of this move, believing that women with higher educational qualifications would make better wives and mothers and also better church workers. Single women were beginning to volunteer for missionary service overseas and, if they were trained teachers or nurses, they were usually accepted.

One of the most ardent spokesmen for women's education in this period was Charles Henry Pearson, the first head of PLC Melbourne who proclaimed:

> [As] women exercise. . . a most tremendous direct influence over children, husbands, lovers. . . ought we not. . . to educate our rulers?[23]

Pearson was convinced that women would benefit from a wider liberal education and so offered afternoon lectures at the school to older women, who responded enthusiastically. Meanwhile, there was agitation in the older colonies for women to enter tertiary spheres. In 1874, the University of Adelaide opened and it began by allowing women to attend lectures; but they were not allowed to receive degrees until 1880. C.H. Pearson and Dr John Madden had worked for nine years for Melbourne University to admit women and this finally occurred after Sydney University's Chancellor, Sir William Manning, declared the principle of women's rights and equality within his university in 1888.[24]

Although some, both men and women, were afraid that a university education would detract from the maternal role, the NSW Minister for Education, in opening the Women's College at Sydney University — which was to be equal to the men's colleges in status — declared:

> We must recognise the fact that women are the mothers of the nation. . . it behoves us to see that we strengthen their judgment.[25]

In the golden decades of the 1870s and 1880s, the pace of progress for women was unprecedented, but every now and then a setback occurred which proved how tenuous was the female hold on equality. In the 1890s depression, when school budgets were severely straitened, it was the female teachers who were the first to be dismissed.[26] (This situation was to be repeated in the great depression of the 1930s. Until 1947, women were forced to resign from the permanent teaching staff of schools and colleges when they married.[27] This scenario also obtained in banks and many business houses.)

Fertility has always been a vexed issue for women, especially those caught between a religious interdiction and their own desire for self-preservation and the preservation of their families. Fear of pregnancy looms large in many of the writings of colonial clergy wives — it was for them literally a matter of life or death. Families of ten, twelve and even fourteen children were not uncommon in the Victorian era, provided that the mother escaped death in childbirth in the first place. Records of colonial clergy — like Archdeacon William Cowper (1778–1858), who married three times — reveal a high mortality rate for clergy wives, as do records of the population in general.

Few women within the church were brave enough to oppose a male hierarchy which decreed that large families and Christian self-control were the only options available to beleaguered women. Contraception was heartily opposed by Catholic and Anglican churches, especially as the birthrate had dropped in the depression decades of the 1890s and again in the 1930s.[28]

However, it would seem that most Australian women began to ignore the strictures of the male hierarchy as to the size of their family by the late nineteenth century, so much so that the government became alarmed and called a Royal Commission into the Decline in the Birthrate in 1903. It was delighted to find support from the churches for large families, but failed to convince women themselves that the birthrate should be raised. The fact that women themselves were not properly consulted for their opinion, and that backyard abortion was increasing because the hospital procedure was forbidden under the Crimes Act, never struck the male judges and advocates as anomalous. However, most Protestant churches by World War I came to agree that families should be limited for the sake of the health of the mother and that contraception was preferable to abortion.

Women and the Australian church, 1900–1960

It was ironical that, having won political and educational equality in the nineteenth century, women seemed to stand back, as it were, and even retreat into themselves in the first forty years of the twentieth century. There was also a gradual retreat from philanthropy by churchwomen as the State took over charities and institutions which they had once administered.

The increasing shortage of domestic help which had been a *sine qua non* of WCTU involvement in philanthropy was beginning to dry up with the widening of industrial employment for women. Those with church affiliations who were mainly middle class worked harder than ever for the churches, whether in teaching or in fundraising. Yet there was no move to challenge men for equality of ministry, except in the small denominations mentioned.

The churches themselves expanded up to and including World War I, owing to the spirit of revival generated in the US, Britain and the colonies after the 1880s. Deaconess movements were founded to enlist the aid of women in parish and social ministries. Many women went out to the mission field where their talent and drive found genuine recognition. Vocations to Catholic and Anglican orders increased.[29]

The outbreak of World War I did not immediately affect women in Australia; only nurses were accepted for overseas service. Cheap female labour for factories was not required as in World War II, as the theatres of war were so far removed from Antipodean shores and conscription never eventuated. Women raised funds, knitted and sent parcels to the troops and worried constantly when sons and brothers were away at the front.

Carmel Shute has pointed out that the mythology engendered by the Great War affirmed the dichotomy of the sexes — man was painted in the media and not infrequently in the pulpit as the warrior and creator of history, while woman had the passive role of giving up her son for King and Country.[30] In its lack of recognition of the war effort of all women volunteers except the Nursing Corps and the Red Cross,[31] society was re-affirming that the only worthwhile task a woman could accomplish in peace or war was to mind the hearth.

The inter-war period witnessed a steady confirmation of the role of women as homemakers. Housewives' associations were formed in each state and the Country Women's Association, later to be an important conservative women's pressure group, was founded in 1922. The state demonstrated its attitude towards the female role when it required women employed by the Federal government to resign permanent positions upon marriage, this situation continuing until 1966.[32] There was a growth in the teaching of domestic science and economy and in the publication of women's magazines. The theme of the family as a refuge from an increasingly harsh and alien world was widely promoted.[33]

After the initial post-war euphoria, the church also seemed to turn in upon itself. Pews were beginning to empty as the motor car offered greater mobility and leisure. This period has been characterised as that of the feminisation of the church. Church activities undoubtedly provided a positive outlet from the ennui of the home. Women dominated the pews and kept Sunday schools, Children of Mary Sodalities, fetes and fund-raising going.[34] They were still, however, excluded from the pulpit and the vestry and synods were closed to them. The exigencies of the great depression and the gathering storm clouds in Europe seemed for once to have dampened their spirit and blunted their quest for equality.

An exception to this trend of withdrawal was to be found amongst educated Catholic women who founded such organ-isations as the Catholic Women's Social Guild in Victoria, which were dedicated to social and political reform. They made a spirited effort to improve the health and working conditions of women, but before long they clashed with the church hierarchy, which sought to check their enthusiasm and limit their autonomy. Such reformers as Anna Brenan and Kate Egan had been encouraged by their convent education to think inde-pendently and to work towards equity in society. Their response to obstruction was to work outside the church framework.

The outbreak of World War II in 1939 meant an extension of employment opportunities for women who were needed to replace the male workforce which had enlisted. This time, women were allowed to join the armed forces, but in a non-combatant role. The churches went out of their way to provide support for servicemen and squadrons of laywomen raised funds, knitted, cooked and waited on soldiers on leave. The industrial, military and welfare experience gained by women in the war years increased their confidence and, although they mostly returned to traditional home-making roles after the war, radical change was not far away. The quiet years of post-war reconstruction and consolidation were to give way to the turmoil of the 1960s and 1970s.

✠ Women and the Australian church, 1960–1988

The opening of the decade of the 1960s found the role of women within the church little altered from that obtaining in late Victorian days. Clergy wives still played an invaluable role as semi-professional workers at the grassroots. Most saw their vocation as to act as a bridge between their husband and his laity.

It was not until the 1970s and 1980s, following the advent of second wave feminism, that some clergy wives began to reject traditional role expectations. Younger wives in particular felt the need to pursue their personal professional calling or else were driven into paid employment by the necessity for two incomes to support their family. Others have kept a stiff upper lip and managed to combine traditional commitments (admittedly reduced from pre-war days) with at least some part-time employment outside the parish.[35]

Church attendance by laywomen also began to decline in this period and with it came a decline in the numbers of women joining auxiliaries and church societies. Older laywomen and clergy wives held the fort in office-bearing positions mainly because there were not enough younger women to take their place. The decrease in female commitment which has occurred in most churches can be attributed partly to a questioning of the relevance of some ecclesiastical teaching and partly to the need for the increasing number of women who work full-time to spend Sunday recovering from the previous week and preparing for the next week.

The closing decades of our period also witnessed considerable change in the part played by women in the Catholic church. The first half of the twentieth century had seen a steady escalation in the number of women religious in Australia — from 3 622 in 1901 to 14 622 in 1966.[36] Thereafter, the numbers of women in orders declined steadily, following Vatican II and a range of socio-economic changes. This has meant increased employment for laity in Catholic schools and hospitals, who have taken the places once held so devotedly by women religious.

Members of women's religious institutes, however, have not withdrawn from contemporary issues and have thoughtfully assessed the role of women in the church, making thorough and far-reaching recommendations on the need for greater equality of the sexes in church and society to the Study Commission on Women, established by Pope Paul VI in 1976. While many of these resolutions have not yet been implemented, the groundswell of support for women's rights in the church has grown irresistibly.[37]

How much the emptying of the pew and convent has been due to second-wave feminism is debatable. Whereas first-wave feminism was largely confined to middle and upper class women of some leisure, modern feminism is a more complex movement, with strong roots in academia. Women's studies now interface with such diverse disciplines as theology, psychology, anthropology, history and literature. Within a generation, both men and women have been faced by radical changes in the status and lifestyle of women and many churches have chosen to ignore them. Control of fertility through the pill has meant greater independence for women and wider freedom of choice for their lifestyle. This is a freedom few women are prepared to surrender to ecclesiastical dictate, but it has implications for male-female relationships and families which have still to be worked out.

Another difficulty for the church of the 1970s and 1980s has been the question of male-female power sharing within the church. Since 1970, many women have encountered resistance to the possibility of female ordination. Many theological arguments have been presented against women priests, but political and social factors peculiar to the Australian scene are thought by academics to be the chief motivation for such opposition. Compared to England, the United States, Canada and New Zealand, Australia has dragged its feet — at least in the Anglican Church.

Despite the presence of ordained women in the Congregational church in South Australia since 1927, the former Presbyterians and Methodists who, with the Congregationalists, formed the Uniting Church in 1977, did not ordain women until that date.

By 1980, moves were afoot to achieve the ordination of women in the Anglican Church. All manner of rearguard actions were fought and theological arguments raised against such a proposal so that it was not finally introduced till 1992 — the year that the Ordination of Catholic Women was established as a movement in Australia.

The ordination of Liyapidiny Marika of Yirrkala, NT, the first Aboriginal woman to be ordained to the ministry of the Uniting Church in Australia: 14 September 1991

It has become increasingly clear that the changes in gender roles which have already taken place in secular society cannot be kept out of the church. Younger women of spirituality appear to be determined to forge a different destiny for the church of their mothers.

Female leadership in spiritual matters has always been strong in Aboriginal culture and so it is not surprising that Christian women in Aboriginal communities emerged as leaders in the 1930s. This occurred against a background of dispossession and racism on the part of Europeans, added to appalling sexual exploitation of black women by white men on the frontier and a heartless government policy of removing half-caste children from their mothers.

Most Christian missions fought to protect Aborigines from the worst aspects of white hegemony on the testimony of the Aborigines themselves, but the way in which they carried out their policies was at times problematic.

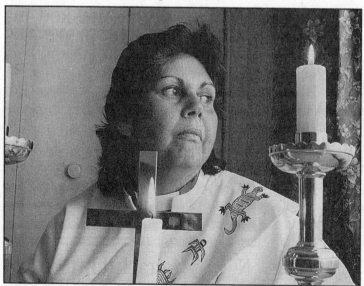

Gloria Shipp, Australia's first Anglican Aboriginal woman to be priested: 21 December 1996 at Holy Trinity Anglican Church, Dubbo, NSW

The turning point for the confidence and sense of autonomy amongst Aboriginal Christians was the revival which broke out at the former Methodist mission on Elcho Island in the early 1980s. Both men and women then began to assume greater responsibility within their churches. No objection was raised by black or white leaders when Nancy Dick was ordained deacon in the Anglican church in Queensland in 1987 or when Liyapidiny Marika was ordained in the Uniting Church of the Northern Territory in 1991. The ordination of Gloria Shipp as Australia's first aboriginal woman priest in 1996 was enormously encouraging not only to aboriginal women but to all church-women across the denominations.

The second half of our period — that is, from the 1890s to the 1990s — has seen considerable changes in the role and status of women, although in the two largest and most conservative churches, women have still not achieved equality of leadership. Apart from the earliest years, women have comprised more than half the membership of the church. Women missionaries and religious have greatly outnumbered their male counterparts, but leadership in the home church has largely eluded them.

However, while it is tempting to portray the history of women in the Australian church as a saga of conflict or the exploitation of cheap labour by the male hierarchy, it must be remembered that the majority of women enjoyed what they were doing and found sacrifice to be fulfilling. Within the church at least till the close of the 1960s, women experienced fellowship with other workers and a positive outlet for their energies. Thereafter, as the majority entered the paid workforce, they found acceptance and status which their churches by and large would not offer them.

2

Women of courage and conviction

PIONEERS OF THE FIRST HALF CENTURY OF EUROPEAN SETTLEMENT

'For in truth, Maggie, I have not time to say my prayers as I ought — but this life is too much both for dear Molloy and myself.'

Georgiana Molloy (1831)

'A perfect pattern of passive piety.'

Walter Lawry, writing of his wife Mary, née Hassall (1820)

'A Bible society has been established lately at Parramatta and a female committee is also formed to act in conjunction with it. I am proud to say, the ladies prosper the best. . .'

Ann Marsden (1820)

THE ROLE OF WOMEN IN THE AUSTRALIAN CHURCH and society in the first years of European settlement was shaped by two main factors: first, the demands of a frontier situation; and second, Georgian attitudes to women.

Pioneering took an immense toll on colonial women.

Outnumbered significantly by men, they battled against a harsh environment, absence of leisure and absence of recognition. The sheer physical labour expected of them meant that they had no time to question accepted attitudes of the day towards their role.

These attitudes were based on a firm belief in the subordination of women in matters social, political and ecclesiastical. Men and also women of this period accepted without query the marginalisation of women in the councils of both church and state. To be a helpmeet to husband or father was the highest duty possible for woman and this concept had the total backing of both church and state. Divorce was difficult to obtain; married women had very limited property rights; access to education for women was restricted. Religion played an ambivalent role here as, on the one hand, it supported the social *status quo*, but on the other, it served to unleash the energies of women of spirit in the earliest days of European settlement.

The lack of specific information about women in the earliest colonial churches, except in the biographies of the wives of men in significant positions, means that biography must be the primary source for creating an analysis of pioneer churchwomen. The situations these women encountered required both flexibility and improvisation. Such untrained women as Mary Burton Johnson threw themselves into teaching or, like Georgiana Molloy, planted and pastored a church in the absence of a clergyman.

The traditional power structures of the home church were temporarily suspended in the interest of consolidating settlement. Thus, women were able to extend their domestic role to one of public leadership in a new and challenging environment. As the colonies developed, men and women found greater freedom of self-expression and greater acceptance of people for what they were, rather than for the rank they would have had in the home society. This was facilitated by the horizontal nature of colonial society, which was based on the economy rather than on an hierarchical structure. However, as soon as it could, the ecclesiastical hierarchy translated itself from one side of the world to the other with little modification. Women were excluded from all church policy in the mainstream churches, with the exception of the Quakers and early Methodists. It was a paradox that religion, on the one hand, determined to a great extent the thinking about women as subordinate in society, but on the other hand, it was to inspire women to break through the restrictions imposed on them.

The second generation of churchwomen in the colonies was able to modify to some degree the church's power structure by their leadership in such new organisations as Sunday school and missions. However, recognition of their vital and sometimes heroic role was frequently tardy and even grudging.

⌘ Mary Johnson, Eliza Marsden and the Marsden daughters

The first settlement at Botany Bay was overwhelmingly male in composition. Of the 725 convicts landed, only 192 were women. Of the 213 people dispatched by the British government to superintend the convicts, 212 were men. There was therefore, officially, one free woman who landed with the First Fleet — Mary Johnson, the wife of Richard Johnson, first chaplain to the colony.[1]

This imbalance of the sexes was to be but slowly redressed; gradually, more female convicts arrived and female children were born to convicts and freed settlers. Moreover, governors, military officers and free settlers began to bring their wives on the perilous adventure to the southern continent. It was to be a lonely life for these women. 'Had we only a few pious friends to pass away an hour with, it would render this colony more tolerable,'[2] lamented Eliza Marsden.

Nevertheless, despite these inauspicious beginnings, early churchwomen were determined to make the most of their lot and, as helpmeets to their husbands, build some kind of Jerusalem out of their unpromising environment. Little is known of Mary Johnson's early life, save that she was a Londoner of Dissenting tendencies from the parish of St Mildred's Poultry, whose maiden name was Burton. Her husband described her as 'half a Baptist and half a Methodist'.[3] With this background, it is likely that she had heard such itinerant women preachers as Anne Mercy Bell, who drew large crowds in the city of London to hear her preach in the 1780s.

Some Baptist congregations encouraged women preachers in industrial communities at this time. The Methodists derived their support from an emergent working class created by the Industrial Revolution, so Mary Johnson was probably working class herself.[4]

Mary was not young, being probably thirty-three at the time of her marriage in 1786, but this maturity was to help her to cope with the vicissitudes of life in the tiny convict outpost. It is possible that she was only semi-literate for no letters from or to her survive, as they do from other early clergy wives.

Her marriage was a happy one, despite the fact that it had been arranged by senior clergy. It was the Reverend John Newton, erstwhile slave trader and by this time notable preacher and hymnwriter, who selected a wife for the new chaplain. Arranged marriages were a common practice for missionary societies, especially in the Americas where

Wesleyan and other groups matched up intending missionaries before their departure for foreign climes:

> So, at last, you have given the good Bishop [sic] of Botany Bay a wife to take with him — a very good thing, if she be a good wife. I pity, and rejoice, pray for and congratulate them both.[5]

Mary Burton proved to be an excellent wife to her unworldly, self-effacing husband. Elizabeth Macarthur found her dull and uninteresting, but Eliza Marsden cherished her company, partly because of their husbands' professional association, but chiefly as a result of Mary Johnson's kindness and hospitality.

When the Marsdens arrived in the colony in March 1794, Eliza was very ill following the birth of her baby on the high seas; it was the older woman who nursed her back to health during a stay of three months.[6] With her Cockney background, Mary Johnson was also able to empathise with the plight of the Londoners about her, as they made up the majority of those detained at His Majesty's pleasure.[7]

She took into her household the young ex-convict Elizabeth Hayward in the hope of saving her from the malignant influence of the older convict women. This thirteen-year-old Londoner was the youngest girl to be transported on the First Fleet. The Johnsons failed to reform her, but it was not an atmosphere conducive to reclamation. Alternately sweltering and shivering in their cabbage palm hut, eking out rations and warding off insects, they found their patience was soon frayed.

Johnson had the girl charged with insolence at the end of twelve months. She received thirty lashes and was sent to Norfolk Island. Whether in spite of or because of this draconian treatment, she later married and lived a reformed life in Van Diemen's Land.[8] In keeping with their evangelical beliefs,

Richard and Mary Johnson sought every opportunity to convert souls. They attempted to befriend the Aborigines,
showed no distaste at their unfamiliar appearance and habits
and took in a little Aboriginal girl, Abaroo by name, both of
whose parents had died of smallpox introduced by the settlers.
Abaroo became quite fond of them and they in their turn tried
to understand when she sporadically discarded her petticoat
and went walkabout.[9]

The Johnsons made a serious attempt to learn an Aboriginal language, unlike most of the early clergy, and where there
was an opportunity they instructed such Aborigines as Abaroo
in English so that they could teach them the scriptures and the
Book of Common Prayer. Their work was very much in the
Moravian tradition as they attempted to identify with the
Aboriginal people as far as possible; for instance, they named
their daughter Milbah Maria when she was born on 3 March
1790, thus making her the first white person to bear an
Aboriginal name.[10]

Mary Johnson lacked sophistication. She was more resilient than Eliza Marsden, but more withdrawn and less
confident than middle-class Sarah Broughton who followed her
two decades later. She shared with her husband the same
evangelical motivation which was contained in two commis-
sions given them by John Newton, their chief spiritual adviser.
One was in a poem composed before they sailed, the other
was in a letter of encouragement written in answer to
Johnson's complaints six years later. The last two stanzas of
the poem read:

> Go, bear the Saviour's name to lands unknown,
> Tell to the southern world his wondrous grace;
> An energy divine thy words shall own,
> And draw their untaught hearts to seek his face.

Many in quest of gold or empty fame
Would compass earth or venture near the poles,
But how much nobler thy reward and aim
To spread his grace and win immortal souls.[11]

This poem spurred Mary Johnson on in her hospitality and
help of the needy. Abaroo was not the only Aboriginal child
cared for in her home. Convention and commonsense, on the
other hand, decreed that she did not go out and mix too freely
with the penal society which surrounded her. Instead, she
provided company and encouragement for her husband in his
lonely work, nursed him with his migraines and listened to his
incessant complaints about the governors. As the years progressed, she gained in confidence in public speaking; she began
to help her husband teach the convict children in the school
he had set up in his church.[12]

The other commission to the Johnsons, also adopted enthusiastically by the Marsdens and later by the Hassalls — a
missionary family which took refuge in New South Wales
from tribal strife in Tahiti in 1798 — was to till the earth and
reap its fruits:

> I wish you to consider your mission, as a whole composed
> of various parts, each of which, in its proper place, has its
> importance. . . You understand the gospel too well to
> confine religion to devotional exercises. . . When you dig
> in the garden, or plant potatoes or cabbages, you serve the
> Lord as truly as when you are upon your knees or in the
> pulpit, provided you do these things in the right spirit.[13]

If immediate fruits could not be found in the elusive souls
of the Aborigines, in the recalcitrant hearts of the convicts or
in the grasping materialism of the settlers, there was always the
earth to which Christian men and women could address
themselves. Richard and Mary Johnson, Samuel and Eliza

Marsden and the wife and daughters of Rowland Hassall planted vegetables and orchards to help feed their families and the colony at large. They were delighted to find a sure and visible return for their labours — trees bending with fruit, healthy children, and growing flocks and herds.[14] Like Old Testament patriarchs, they progressed in a few years from virtual poverty to wealth and prominence in the land.

There was, however, a cost to the women in this transition to material prosperity. All early female settlers found the voyage out from England particularly traumatic. They suffered miscarriage and stillbirth as well as seasickness, bronchitis and dysentery. Mary Johnson was very ill after leaving the Cape with a stillbirth and constant seasickness.[15] Elizabeth Macarthur suffered a stillbirth on the voyage out in 1789.[16] Eliza Marsden was terribly weak after giving birth in a gale off the coast of Australia.[17] Then once the women had landed, they faced the unaccustomed heat, dust, insects, primitive housing and dangers from convicts and Aborigines.

Above all, they felt the isolation from friends and family with whom they had grown up when any bereavement took place. 'Picture to yourself my feelings to have him in health and spirits and the next moment to behold him in the arms of Death,' wrote a heartbroken Eliza Marsden, after losing her eldest son in a carriage accident. Then two years later, another son died by scalding:

> The loss of those I have parted from weighs so much on my mind that at times I am as miserable as it is possible to be. . . happiness and me seem long since to have parted and I have a presentiment that peace will never more be an inhabitant of my bosom.[18]

This foreboding was to come true as Eliza Marsden suffered a stroke in 1811, bearing her eighth child. The absence of reliable birth control methods was a further burden on the women of the Georgian and Victorian eras. Many died at a relatively young age after bearing too many children; others, like Eliza, sank into invalidism in their thirties. She who had once been a formidable horsewoman, riding from Parramatta to Sydney and back in one day, now confined herself to a couch and allowed her vigorous and intelligent daughters to run the household.[19]

There were no curates in those days to help in the parish, so the five Marsden girls, led by the vivacious Ann as eldest sister, administered the household and even the parish while their father was absent at the farm, sitting on the magistrates' bench or out on clerical duties. During her father's increasing absences in New Zealand evangelising the Maoris, it was left frequently to Ann as the most reliable of the children to act as *de facto* curate in all but the conduct of services.[20] She was to display a resilience and powers of leadership not possessed by her brother. In recognising this, her father was being purely pragmatic; it was certainly not done out of any desire to dent ecclesiastical hierarchy.

The Marsdens might not have had curates to help them, but they did have the fellowship and strong moral support of a band of Congregational and later Wesleyan missionaries in their midst by the time the Johnsons left.

It was Eliza Marsden who extended hospitality to eleven missionaries who arrived in Sydney in 1798 in fear of their lives from tribal warfare in Tahiti. These missionaries were members of the London Missionary Society, a Congregational body, and they provided much-needed fellowship for the Marsdens in a non-spiritual society. Amongst them was Rowland Hassall — formerly a Warwickshire weaver — his wife Elizabeth and their three sons. Marsden found a job for Hassall and settled the family on one of his small farms near

Parramatta. A daughter was born to them in 1799 and named after one of their missionary friends, Mary Cover.[21]

✠ Mary Hassall, the first currency lass missionary

Mary Cover Hassall was to be the first woman born in Australia to serve overseas as a missionary. As she grew up, she and her brothers worked hard in the Sunday school at Parramatta which had been started by her father in 1812 and conducted by his son Thomas. The whole family of eight children attended a Methodist mid-week meeting, led by their father until the arrival of the first Wesleyan ministers. On Sundays, they went to morning prayer at St John's, to Sunday school in the afternoon and then to a Methodist worship service at night.[22]

In this constant round of church functions, it is interesting to observe a changing role for the younger women. Whereas their mothers — admittedly worn down by frequent childbirth — confined themselves to hospitality and domestic tasks associated with the church, the currency lasses involved themselves in teaching, organising meetings and even acting as treasurer where needed. For instance, Mary Hassall was the first treasurer of the Parramatta Sunday School — a position that her mother would never have held. It was within the Sunday school movement that women gained their first official leadership roles in the church, although they could never aspire to the exalted rank of superintendent. From its small beginnings in Parramatta, the Sunday school movement was to be strategic in reaching out to illiterate children whose parents could not afford daily school. It was led by men (either Rowland or Thomas Hassall), but was mainly staffed by women — chiefly the Marsden and Hassall girls.

The children of convicts and Aborigines were accepted whatever their dress or state of cleanliness. They were educated and trained free of charge and society thereby benefited. 'We have, I am happy to say, a good Sunday school, about 110 children attend constantly. The little black children make rapid improvement. The girls can read fluently and write and sew very neatly.'[23]   First, the Hassall home and then, the Parramatta schoolroom became too small for the Sunday school and in five years it moved to St John's Church, where twenty-five teachers of both sexes contended with over 150 pupils. Women led the weekly prayer meetings, played the music for hymns, conducted picnics for the children and began to predominate in the teaching staff.

At about the same time, a Bible Society was founded in Parramatta. A committee of women was formed to help the Society and, before long, they were congratulating themselves on raising more money than the men.[24] This was to be a forerunner of later women's auxiliaries in the Australian church — the men seeming on the whole to be content to leave the fundraising to the women. Thus, by 1820 there was a growing band of women exercising a measure of *de facto* leadership in both Anglican and dissenting churches which was acceptable within its limits.

As the nineteenth century progressed, women were to infiltrate further into what had been traditionally male domains. The mission field was a prime example of this. At first, only single men were encouraged to go out to unreached islands in the South Pacific by such societies as the Wesleyan Missionary Society.

The first Wesleyan ministers to arrive in Sydney were two bachelors, Samuel Leigh and Walter Lawry. Both of them proposed to Mary Hassall, but she decided to accept Lawry. After a short ministry in Sydney, mainly among condemned convicts, Walter Lawry was ordered by the Missionary Society to Tonga to pioneer a mission there. Although graphically warned of the dangers involved, Mary decided to accompany her husband there, taking with her a baby son. She was the first Australian-born woman to undertake overseas service of this kind.[25] Their year in Tonga appeared to be one of failure and the Methodist Missionary Society summoned them home. Walter had found the language problem and the lack of help and equipment insuperable difficulties, while Mary was more adaptable and 'seemed to glide through it'.[26] She befriended the Tongan women, invited them into her home and picked up their customs and language more quickly than her husband. Her husband wrote of her admiringly as 'a perfect pattern of passive piety', but in actual fact it was he who was passive and inflexible in his ministry, expecting the natives to flock to his services as if he were back in Cornwall.

When they came to leave the island, however, they were amazed at the genuine sorrow of the Tongans at losing them.[27] Mary Lawry's ministry to the Tongans was more successful than her husband's because she was prepared to meet the women on their own ground, visiting them in their own homes, identifying with them in bringing up their children, in illness and on happy occasions. Therefore, it was all the more hurtful to find that her name had been edited out of her husband's diary accounts of the Tongan work when they were printed in the *Wesleyan Methodist Magazine*. This was galling for a woman of spirit, but a characteristic attitude on the part of churchmen of the day. She whom the Society expected to work unpaid in the island school was considered not fit to be mentioned because of her sex.[28]

However, this was a problem which was endemic in church and society until well into the twentieth century; many would feel it has not yet been eliminated. Attitudes of discrimination against women in ministry, condescension and active ignoring of their gifts (except in the sphere of housekeeping) were encountered by women of the church over the whole two hundred year period.

Mary Lawry's initiative as a missionary was probably due to her colonial background: resourcefulness, friendliness and adaptability were the order of the day in New South Wales and she was to acknowledge her debt to her country in the naming of her last child Mary Australia Lawry.[29]

✠ Georgiana Molloy, the 'Madonna of the Bush'

Georgiana Molloy (1805–1843) became known as the 'Madonna of the Bush' and is revered by many today in south-western Australia. She encountered fearful hardship as a pioneer and indifference to her spiritual and scientific gifts from the patriarchal society of the day. For Georgiana, hand-to-mouth survival was the first imperative, she and her husband Captain John Molloy (always referred to as 'Molloy' in her letters) being amongst the first band of settlers at the Swan River in Western Australia.

From her arrival on 12 March 1830, she battled against loneliness, physical danger from Aborigines and a delicate constitution until her premature death. Nor did she possess the substantial domestic help enjoyed by the devout governors' wives whom we shall be examining next. Her voluminous correspondence has been largely preserved, so that her impressions and spiritual struggle are more closely documented than any of the other religious women of the early years.

Born when her husband was fighting at Trafalgar, she was exactly half his age when she married him at twenty-four. It was to be a supremely happy marriage for the worldly army officer and his earnest Presbyterian wife. Her fervent piety stemmed from the revival which was sweeping Scotland in the early nineteenth century. The Church of Scotland was also influential in the motivation of such colonial churchwomen as

Georgiana Molloy: 'The Madonna of the Bush'

Eliza Macquarie and Jane Barker.

Georgiana was to keep up a lifelong correspondence with her Scottish friends, the Dunlops, and with her friend Helen who was married to Robert Story, the minister of Roseneath, Dunbartonshire. Story's best friend was the Reverend Edward Irving, a fiery preacher, who was minister of the Caledonian Church in London in the 1820s. The Molloys were in the practice of joining such notables as George Canning and Lady

Jersey in the regular congregation there.[30] At this stage of her life, Georgiana was so convinced of her need to convert people that she buttonholed an astonished Jewish saleswoman in London with the words:

> My dear woman, I devoutly pray that the light of the gospel will enable you to see that you are one of Christ's redeemed sinners.[31]

On the voyage out to the Swan River, she made herself unpopular with the soldiers' wives for attempting to proselytise them, but she was soon laid low by pregnancy and seasickness. Captain Molloy was content to go along with his wife's evangelising fervour, but he restricted himself to the reading of prayers night and morning on the ship.

Georgiana was more than a little depressed when she beheld the tent city at Fremantle and even more dismayed when they moved to the outskirts of the settlement at Augusta, Cape Leeuwin. Here, far from the ministrations of a doctor or clergyman, her first baby died in their primitive cottage on the edge of the beach. Despondent, she wrote to her Scottish friends:

> Language refuses to utter what I experienced when mine died in my arms in this dreary land, with no one but Molloy near me.[32]

As with other pioneer churchwomen, lack of companionship was one of her greatest problems; the only other white family near her were the Bussells — a large, self-sufficient group, the four brothers having decided to emigrate together. Old prejudices carried over into the new country; Mrs Bussell senior was formal Church of England and a clergyman's widow to boot, so she did not approve of Georgiana's brand of enthusiasm. With no church to turn to and her husband frequently away in Perth on his duties as Resident, Georgiana flung herself into reading Christian books:

> I am now reading for the third time Henry Martyn's life. . .
> I confine myself chiefly to these books for conscience seems
> to say when reading any others — 'Is your peace made
> with God?'. . . I really long and pray for some faithful
> minister.

None came and her husband when present was obliged to act as clergyman and to officiate at weddings and funerals.[33] Georgiana herself read services which were often conducted on her verandah in the absence of a church. She was the first woman in Australia to take a funeral service, there being no-one else to bury her unfortunate maid, Kitty. She had nursed Kitty through epilepsy and insanity and the last responsibility was to inter her decently while the other servants stood round in the torchlight.

Her own health was ebbing away with each successive pregnancy, but there was worse to come. The Aborigines who hovered about the house could be menacing and one day, when her husband was away, they appeared in the kitchen, shook their spears at her and poked her in the face. She was forced to bring out the pistols to persuade them to go. However, this was an isolated incident and Georgiana maintained a cordial relationship with the Aborigines, compiling a dictionary of local Aboriginal dialects. Her little daughter, Sabina, was totally fearless of the Aborigines and 'danced opposite the native children with great glee'.[34]

In April, 1836, her son John was born, but within a year he had drowned in a well. The shock of the loss of their son and heir made her very ill indeed and she sought solace in the garden, like others before her. She threw herself into the collection and classification of native plants, going out with the

Aborigines to find new species. She corresponded with botanists and entertained them as guests. 'The most charming personage in all South Australia [sic],' wrote Dr John Lindley of her.

Other botanists were not as appreciative of her hospitality or her unique research. They neglected to acknowledge her kindness and her enormous contribution to world botany. Her work was plundered for Edwards' classic Botanical Register of the 1830s and all she received as reward was a mouth organ and some toys for the children. Her scientific contribution was not acknowledged in print. The German naturalist, Ludwig Preiss, shamelessly plagiarised her work after a month's stay at the Molloys. He also not only failed to thank her for her hospitality, but he broke a promise to return valuable specimens to her.[35]

Georgiana died at thirty-seven, bearing her seventh child — but not before one of her dreams had been realised, the opening of the first church in her district. The massive work she had carried out as a botanist was not recognised till years later.[36] Her husband marked her contribution to religion in the colony by having her re-interred under the pulpit of the newly built Church of St Mary, Busselton. The Bussell family, who had once been cool to her, raised no objection to this tribute to her spiritual leadership.

✠ Myrah White

In the early years of the foundation of the free colony of South Australia, it was a woman who established Methodist worship long before the arrival of Wesleyan clergy. Myrah Oakey was born in British Guiana in 1809. She married John Charles White in London and migrated with him to Adelaide in 1837, as members of the first party of settlers. Myrah White somehow managed to combine church planting and nurture with the production of twelve children!

By her conduct and example she contributed largely to the establishment of Methodism upon a firm basis, long before the arrival of any Wesleyan minister.[37]

It is not surprising, therefore, that it was to be in this state that the first woman in Australia was to be ordained exactly ninety years later.

✠ Elizabeth Macquarie

The nineteenth century was an age of philanthropy in Britain and the colonies. Such was the influence of the Evangelical Revival and the Quaker movement in British society, that it was increasingly expected of women of rank that they should engage in philanthropy. It was in the realm of philanthropy that women were to gain leadership experience outside the home.

Governors' wives in the colonies were no exception and had their names placed on the committee to found a female orphan school from 1800 onwards. It was not always plain sailing for the governors' wives, who frequently encountered opposition from vested interests and chauvinistic officials. For instance, Anna Josepha King attracted criticism for what was seen as her dictatorial approach when visiting the school from 1800 to 1807.[38]

The energetic Elizabeth Macquarie received similar criticism in 1821 over the Parramatta orphan school from a more unpleasant quarter, her husband's enemy, the Reverend Samuel Marsden: 'Both profane and sacred history hath taught us that it is very dangerous to offend a Lady in Power. John the Baptist lost his head for this.'[39] Even women of rank encountered male opposition as power structures in the male hierarchy were threatened. The fact that the male opponent was encased in clerical trappings made no difference to his attitude, nor did it seem relevant that he was presumably engaged in the same sort of work. In practice, it often served to heighten unpleasantness, although Marsden's jibe was chiefly rooted in his acrimonious relationship with Macquarie himself.

Not only was Eliza Macquarie very interested in the Female Orphan School at Parramatta, but she also acted as patroness of the native institution founded by her husband in the same town. At the school of thirty pupils, boys learnt gardening and girls domestic work. The school was moderately successful except when the Aborigines went on periodic walkabout.[40]

Elizabeth Macquarie's religious commitment is indicated by her insistence that she and her husband should take communion in St James Church, Piccadilly, prior to their departure for Australia. Her general background was Scottish Presbyterian, but the great influences in her life philosophically were Dr Samuel Johnson and William Wilberforce, not an entirely compatible pair. From the former, she learnt a respect for church and state (befitting a good High Tory) and a belief that Sunday should not be a day of gloom. From Wilberforce, she learnt a passion for the redemption of souls and assistance for the poor.

The evangelical concepts of atonement, absolution and redemption, which she heartily embraced, also influenced Lachlan Macquarie in his emancipist policy. Why shouldn't society forgive the truly repentant, both husband and wife argued — but they had trampled on the corns of Macarthur and Marsden, the latter of whom attacked the well-meaning Elizabeth for giving a St Patrick's Day dinner for fifty-eight convicts and overseers employed at Government House.

This intelligent and compassionate woman had much to bear from the chaplain to the colony.[41]

A tireless philanthropist: Eliza Darling and her children, 1825

⚶ Eliza Darling

Foremost among the governors' wives for her philanthropic work was the accomplished and mercurial Lady Eliza Darling. Born in the evangelical centre of Cheltenham, she was a woman of considerable drive and gifts. She won acclaim as an artist and musician, wrote three books and found time in seven short years in the colony to involve herself in the following good works: she joined the committee of the Female Orphan School like her predecessors; she attended and subscribed to the Benevolent Society, sending gifts of food to the needy; she was an energetic supporter of the Sunday school movement, attending its services and prizegivings.

With her husband, she founded the Sydney Dispensary for helping to cure illness amongst the poor.[42] She organised sales of clothing for the poor.[43] An active and successful hostess, she attracted — and sometimes coerced — a number of women into joining the committee of the female factory at Parramatta where sewing classes were set up for convict women. The Board of Management noted in 1829 that these women evinced a desire to improve their station in life by becoming good servants.[44]   Eliza Darling worked in conjunction with the Quaker reformer, Elizabeth Fry, in establishing a policy towards women and children associated with the penal system. Fry had been responsible for a change in the attitude of governments in Britain towards the sick and imprisoned from the time she first visited Newgate Prison in 1812. From the early 1820s, governors of New South Wales and Van Diemen's Land constantly received letters from the Quaker reformer.

Eliza Darling took over her husband's correspondence with Fry. The result of this interchange between the two women was the foundation of the Female School of Industry in 1826 and the Female Friendly Society the following year. These two projects were Eliza's chief delight. She visited them daily and talked constantly of them to her influential friends.

The Female School of Industry was set up for children of poor parents who wished to improve their children's lot. Pupils could be of any age between five and eighteen years and they were to be given religious instruction and training for domestic service. In that sectarian age, no Roman Catholics were allowed to enrol, but Jews were not excluded.

Eliza modelled her school on one she was familiar with in Cheltenham. To ensure that the school got off the ground, she provided a loan of 258 pounds and from then on she was always fund-raising with the help of her committee.[45]   Every day that the Governor was resident in Sydney saw Eliza walking energetically up Macquarie Street to visit her school. With such oversight, it was no wonder it was such a success.

The Report of the Board of Management for 1829 declared that the children were clean, healthy and well-dressed and that there was a strong demand for places.

Eliza next determined to found a similar school in Parramatta. No matter that her friends complained that they were being elected to her committees in their absence.[46]

A female Friendly Society was a further project; this was an evening class designed to rehabilitate girls with a prison or emancipist background. Before long, it had fifty-two subscribers and served to follow up the work of the Female School of Industry.[47]

Eliza Darling attended church with her husband each Sunday either at St James', if they were in Sydney, or at St John's, if they were in Parramatta. As a woman of the Georgian era, she never contemplated a leadership role in ecclesiastical matters. The best way she could serve God, she reasoned, was to exercise philanthropy. So she set about writing a book to edify her young charges and help them settle into domestic service. In draft form, it was used as part of the curriculum at the Female School of Industry and it was finally published a year after her departure under the title of *Simple Rules of the Guidance of Persons in Humble Life, more particularly for Young Girls Going Out to Service.*[48]

The tone of the book is kindly and concerned; it is laced with exhortations from scripture, but its contents reflect prevailing concepts of class. Being very much a product of her age and class, Eliza reminded the girls at the outset of the duties which ought to be performed by those in that 'station of life in which it has pleased the Almighty to place you'. She could promise them only the joys of a classless heaven:

If you observe the plain and simple rules contained in these pages, you will prove blessings, not only to those with whom you are immediately connected, but to your children's children; and through the merits of your Saviour will be received into his kingdom and hear the joyful sounds, 'Well done, ye good and faithful servants, enter ye into the joy of your Lord.'

In the preface to her little volume, Eliza makes no claim to originality. The first three fictional chapters are cloying excerpts drawn from such manuals as *The Christian Gleaner* and *The Cottager's Monthly Visitor*. No attempt is made to upset the social *status quo* in this or any other dialogue:

> *Mary:* Yes, but mother! Are not the rich happier than the poor?
> *Mother:* I do not think so, Mary. The poor have less cares and are equal in the sight of God.

The next section of the book contains such principles of housekeeping as:

> In a large household, there should be a cook, housemaid, nursemaid, lady's maid, laundress, seamstress, and perhaps a dairymaid and a housekeeper. . . A small household would have a cook, housemaid and nursemaid or lady's maid.

These were ideals mostly unattainable in early colonial households with the chronic shortage of domestic staff and the fact that the best servants usually became (swiftly) the best wives because of the shortage of women. Eliza never allowed herself to be daunted by problems or fears; the book presses on with a series of wage tables, poems and exhortations on acceptable behaviour, accompanied by scripture texts. The housekeeper's duties finish with 'Live under the influence of religious principle. Read the Bible daily and by it regulate your life.'[49]

In many ways, Eliza Darling was the forerunner of Caroline Chisholm, except that one worked principally amongst Protestants and the other was oriented towards Roman Catholics. Eliza had, of course, rank and sophistication on her side and did not have to struggle as hard as Caroline to achieve her reforms. Both women, however, were possessed of boundless energy and tender conscience towards the needy. Both were stoical about illness and personal sorrow — Eliza wrote of the loss of a baby son:

> A few selfish tears will fall, but God knows best and I can say, I hope with resignation, his will be done.[50]

Neither reformer minded manipulating people — the exalted 'end' always justified the means. Eliza niggled at her husband until he decreed that all convicts should attend divine service on Sundays and that Bibles should be sent to penal establishments.[51] Both women tended to neglect their children, and certainly their own health, as they carried out their deeds of mercy. Eliza was constantly pregnant and was obliged to do much of her planning from her sofa.

Yet somehow she managed to orchestrate an ambitious social round at Government House and all enjoyed the delightful parties that she hosted. Following a glittering ball in honour of the King's birthday, a correspondent for the *Sydney Gazette* wrote: 'She appeared altogether happy in the pleasure that her presence diffused throughout the gay and brilliant throng.'[52] Even the fussy Elizabeth Macarthur was charmed by Eliza and approved of her musical evenings and attempts to 'please us all'.[53]

In the case of both Eliza Darling and Caroline Chisholm, their roots went back to a happy childhood and both had been reared in an atmosphere of evangelical fervour. Eliza's family, the Dumaresqs, were extremely close-knit and loving. Eliza corresponded regularly with her brothers, two of whom followed her out to Australia in varying occupations. Eliza's strong religious convictions came from her mother Ann Dumaresq who believed that 'God was in all her thoughts, mingling in her gayest as well as her most serious occupations'.[54]

Eliza was not unscathed in life, but nevertheless she was fortunate not to suffer the extreme isolation of Georgiana Molloy where a burning faith and an enquiring mind were almost extinguished by pain and loneliness. The privileged position of Governor's wife, in addition to the relatively stimulating society of Sydney town, was also an advantage in Eliza's favour.

On her return to England with her seven children, she continued to take an interest in the colonies and philanthropy, especially as her brothers and their families had remained there. First, she stood by her husband at the House of Commons Committee enquiry into his behaviour as Governor until he was exonerated and knighted. Then, she agitated on behalf of the potential of transportation for reforming whole families. She attacked the concept of probationary gangs and proposed instead probationary colonies for families, each having access to a local church and school.

She wrote devotional books like *The Happy Family* and *Young Christian's Sunday Mornings* which she intended for family reading.[55] At every instance, her aim was to redeem the time and to live with one eye firmly fixed on the next world. There is more than a hint of mysticism in her motivation, as she wrote to her brother:

The Communion of Saints has always been to me not a mere vague idea, but a reality — an almost present enjoyment realising to my mind fully the perfect truth of St Paul's definition of faith, 'the substance of things hoped for, the evidence of things not seen'.

She then described her feelings when someone had died in the faith:

> I almost fancy I can hear the hallelujah of the angels and the shout of joy and the triumph with which they are received into heaven.[56]

There can be no doubt that Eliza Darling was a doyenne of British governors' wives in the nineteenth century. Her charm, gifts, unselfishness and philanthropic achievements were not equalled by her ilk, despite the appearance in the firmament of such bright lights as Lady Jane Franklin.

✠ Jane Franklin

Lady Jane, whose husband was Lieutenant-Governor of Van Diemen's Land from 1837 to 1843, was attractive, intelligent and resourceful. She also took a sincere interest in the welfare of female convicts, despite the consistent efforts of penal officers to discourage her. She, too, was spurred on in her desire for penal reform by the great Quaker reformer, Elizabeth Fry, with whom she corresponded regularly. The latter encouraged her with the following charge:

> May the Lord. . . make you a blessing to many poor wanderers and may he grant thy husband sound wisdom and discretion in his very important and difficult situation.[57]

Jane responded by visiting prisons and hospitals in Hobart and especially the orphan school and the female factory. She founded a ladies' prison committee to help rehabilitate prisoners, despite the mockery of the press and of her husband's enemies who called her a 'man in petticoats'. Patriarchal society in Van Diemen's Land felt threatened by her charm and reforming zeal.

They were delighted at the embarrassment suffered by the

Governor and his wife on their first official visit to the Cascades Female Factory. As the chaplain began to preach, the women workers turned round, flung up their skirts and slapped their bottoms. 'If only I had been a Quaker and had [Elizabeth Fry's] majestic mien,' commented Jane later; the incident had brought her near to tears, although her husband had taken it more philosophically. There were occasions, as he well knew, when the deprived in working class society expressed their sense of contempt and alienation by embarrassing their 'betters'.[58] However, she was not to be deterred.

Her next target was the system of assignment of women. She was horrified at the way in which female prisoners and those who had fully served their terms were mechanically doled out to the settlers, without any thought of the suitability of an arrangement which often condemned women to a life of subjugation or concubinage.

As she confided to Elizabeth Fry:

Are women wholly forgotten in England? or is assignment stripped of its horrors, cleansed from its iniquity when applied to them?[59]

She appealed forcefully for more free settlers in Tasmania who would raise the quality and morality of colonial families. Education was surely another answer to the problem and she and her husband attempted to found a boys' and a girls' school, Jane wishing to call the girls' school the Queen's School. However, they were so frustrated in their plans by officialdom and lack of money that she decided to use what funds there were for the establishment of a botanical garden instead.[60]

Like Eliza Macquarie, she encountered problems with male vested interests who did their best to block reform without excessively antagonising the Governor himself. Jane had no children of her own, apart from a stepdaughter by her husband's first marriage, so that her health was not threatened by numerous pregnancies, as was the case with Eliza Darling and Georgiana Molloy. She was able, therefore, to channel all her formidable energies into public life.

She was indubitably a blue stocking. Intellectual life in Hobart soared during her tenure; she travelled widely and was a good mixer in all strata of society. She wrote countless letters and journals. Although some found her overbearing and a 'woman of the world', others, like the new Bishop of Tasmania, found her 'the most amiable, simple and unassuming person he had ever met, and that if her stockings are blue, her petticoats are so long that I have never found it out'.[61]

The truth probably lay between the two assessments. Jane's religious faith was formal and in many ways derivative. She never wrote of a divine relationship as did Georgiana Molloy and Eliza Darling, but she drew strength from her beloved husband and his simple evangelical beliefs. She also sought out the company of clergy and religious men wherever she travelled and she corresponded frequently with such reformers as Elizabeth Fry and Dr Thomas Arnold.[62]

Although not sympathetic to Wesleyan practices, she built a Methodist chapel for settlers in the Huon Valley and had it consecrated by Archdeacon Hutchins. The local people were so grateful that many named their children after her. Others, especially in neighbouring colonies, looked upon her as the best ambassador Tasmania had ever had.[63]

⚜ An assessment of the first half century

The close of the first half century of white settlement in Australia saw the emergence of a strong feminine influence at the head of what was still a firmly masculine society. Eliza Macquarie was a trailblazer, but the mould for governors' wives was irrevocably broken when Eliza Darling and Jane

Franklin appeared on the scene.

Refusing to confine themselves to embroidery and the administration of their own households, as male (and female) vested interests wished they would, they brought about genuine alleviation of misery and ignorance in their husbands' fiefs. Their rank in society enabled them to exercise their intellectual gifts and their charm and religious faith went some way towards breaking down male prejudice. Despite the great talent and strong faith of these laywomen, they made no formal attempt to extend their leadership into the ecclesiastical sphere.

Lady Jane Franklin exercised somewhat of a Lady Mary Vere role in Van Diemen's Land in the encouragement of all the clergy she met and the building of a Wesleyan church south of Hobart.[64] Georgiana Molloy led services and gave homilies in a totally unpromising situation where no clergy or devout layman were present but, even in this, she had to survive the initial disapproval of her neighbour, Mrs Bussell, who was strict Establishment Church. The church itself, having activated these women into works of mercy, was careful not to allow them a share in church policy. Nor did they, at this stage, expect such a role.

The native-born Australians, on the other hand, were more adventurous and resilient in their attitude to church work. The Marsden and Hassall daughters threw themselves into pioneering Sunday School and Bible Society movements. Titular leadership of these bodies was usually denied them, but their work was regarded as indispensable at parish level. The role of Mary Lawry as a missionary in Tonga was a prototype of the future Australian missionary movement when women would predominate in the dangerous and uncomfortable work of preaching the gospel overseas. A small but significant dent had been made in gender expectations both within and outside the church.

The commission of these religious women, whether clergy wives, missionaries or laity, was to reach out and help others for the sake of their faith. However, a large pool of women still remained virtually untouched by the church. These were the proletarian illiterates, many of whom were Irish Catholics, until 1820 denied a priest to minister to them. It would be twenty-eight years before they were allowed their own system of education.[65] Succeeding chapters will demonstrate how this section of society was finally reached and given vigorous nurture.

Education was the key to confidence and then to leadership, as women began to discover. It was also the key to religious understanding. The barely literate scribblings of wives to their convict husbands which have been preserved indicate hearts desperate for love and companionship that were unable to express divine longings or grasp such abstractions as theology, because of lack of schooling and the need for hand-to-mouth survival.[66]

The next generation of Australian was to encounter a better-equipped church and a wider spectrum of educated women who would rise to leadership in society, although not in the church which sponsored them. A subordinate role was to be expected of women in matters ecclesiastical for another century yet, despite the emergence of significant general leadership by churchwomen from the earliest days of the colonies.

3

Paragons of virtue
and industry

CLERGY AND BISHOPS' WIVES IN
THE VICTORIAN ERA AND BEYOND

'The clergyman's wife [ought] to renounce the world
and the things of the world, its fashions, its amusements, its pursuits. . . every moment of the day must
have its appropriate employment.'

Hints for a Clergyman's Wife (1832)

'She speaks, too, simply, tersely, where her support,
comment or encouragement are required. . . An
unusually clear brain enables her to keep many irons
in the fire. And never for a moment does she grow
absorbed in her own enterprises to the exclusion of
her husband's work.'

The Wives of Bishops in *The Lady's Realm* (1899)

T HE VICTORIAN ERA LASTED WELL OVER SIXTY YEARS
and its influence — especially in church circles — permeated
deep into the twentieth century. It was the heyday of the
church, as well as of the British Empire. Following the
evangelical revival of the eighteenth century and the bright

flowering of Methodism, the various Protestant churches experienced substantial growth.[1]

This expansion took place on several fronts: first, in the sheer numbers of adherents attracted to the pew; second, in the burgeoning philanthropy and social reform of the period, spearheaded by the devout; and third, in the growth of an independent women's voice in national and, more slowly, church affairs.

As a derivative society, Australia followed British trends and this was particularly so in church attitudes towards women. An examination of the role of clergy and bishops' wives in the Victorian period, and into the early years of the twentieth century, reveals that they worked principally as indispensable helpmeets to their husbands in their public life and as models up to whom the women of the parish looked. Thus, their role was semi-professional in nature and it was to become increasingly complex and subject to higher expectations as time went on.

In the previous chapter an assessment of the work of the earliest chaplains' wives, Mary Johnson and Eliza Marsden, led to the conclusion that these women were loyal, but generally silent appendages of their husbands' work; their circumscribed education and upbringing in lower middle class Georgian society had not prepared them for a life in any way independent of their husbands' household.

Mary Lawry, on the other hand, having been brought up in a freer society, was able to respond differently to the colonial situation as well as to other cultures; she took up opportunities to teach and evangelise almost as readily as her husband and in many cases more effectively.

Another currency lass, Ann Marsden, was also more confident and flexible in her approach to church work, both as Samuel Marsden's daughter and later as the Reverend Thomas Hassall's wife.

Clergy wives in the Victorian and post-Victorian period

Expectations of clergy wives were extraordinarily high in the Victorian era. Indeed, a clergy wife was expected to be a superwoman in terms of roles — helpmeet, mother (usually of large numbers of children), counsellor and public figure, chairwoman of numerous public bodies and often *de facto* curate if her husband were away.

She acted as a bridge between the hierarchy and the laity and was therefore often the key to a happy parish. She showed little interest in the feminist movement within the church and outside it. Catering for the whims of the Victorian male was in most cases not a problem for her, although her premature death rate last century was far higher than his.

Records of clergy marrying two or even three times are not uncommon, but it is difficult to make conclusive assumptions about the mortality rate of clergy wives, as death in childbirth was a common enough occurrence in society at large. Death-rates for Australian women prior to 1900 reveal little disparity with death rates among clergy wives. Researchers have concluded that life expectancy for the clergy wife was comparable to that of the laywoman, while clergy themselves had a longer than average life expectancy.[2]

What were the models which English clergy wives followed in their work and how were they modified by the colonial experience? In 1832, five years before the accession of Victoria, there appeared an anonymous manual entitled *Hints for a Clergyman's Wife or Female Parochial Duties*.[3] The anonymity of the authorship suggests that its writer may have been a woman, as this ploy or the use of a pseudonym was often the only way a woman writer of the period could find a publisher.

The book advocates a counsel of perfection for clergy

wives, constantly emphasising a subordinate role for women, which was thoroughly in keeping with the expectations of both genders in society at the time. The author states that the clergyman's spouse should be a good wife and mother and a gracious hostess and supporter of her husband. Her family ought to be a model to the parish. She is called to account for every moment of the day, having, of course, 'renounced the world, its fashions and amusements'.[4]

As the century wore on, the paragon of virtue thus delineated was expected to add evangelistic, educational and social service strands to her role and this was particularly true of the colonial clergy wife. Admittedly, household help was more readily available in the nineteenth century, but its quality and quantity were usually higher in the home country where there were more women in the population and social stratification was greater.

Anglican clergy wives were generally in a more comfortable position than their counterparts in the Dissenting churches, who were forced to contend with frequent moves and low remuneration.

However, even in a church so closely associated with the Establishment, there were problems of administration and personnel in the Australian colonies which would not have arisen in England. Very few curates were available for colonial vicars and the parish infrastructure in a church, which usually covered a number of centres, was generally meagre. Thus, the Marsden and Hassall rectories at Parramatta and Cobbitty relied heavily on the daughters of the family to help run the parish.[5] When the rector was away visiting other centres, his wife or daughter was expected to deputise in everything but formal services, where a male lay reader or catechist presided.

Housing was generally more uncomfortable in the Antipodes than in the home country and stipends by the end of the nineteenth century were falling behind those in comparable secular occupations. All in all, the expectations of the clergy wife in the colonies were greater than those of her counterpart in Britain. As the century wore on, the province of female workers in the church steadily enlarged. The concept of the clergy wife as a superwoman was reinforced. Parish visiting, fundraising for missions, church fabric and the poor became part of her expected role. She and her lady supporters or guild undertook cooking, sewing, decoration of the church and the running of fetes and church teas. It was not all drudgery, for the women enjoyed each other's company and experienced a sense of achievement when functions went well and targets were met.

However, domestic help was essential for the mental and physical health of the clergy wife and good labour of this variety was a rare commodity in Australia.[6] Conditions in and near the main cities of Sydney and Melbourne were more civilised for clergy wives, but for those on the frontier there was greater hardship and even danger.

A Western Australian clergy wife: Janet Millett

Janet Millett, wife of an early chaplain in Western Australia, arrived at the Swan River in 1863. Edward Millett suffered from *tic douloureux*, which had caused a morphine addiction he hoped the warm climate of Western Australia would cure. Like many clergy wives, she was the strong one in the partnership. She encountered the usual problems of a pioneer rural wife: isolation, frequent absences of her husband, fairly primitive housing, dust, heat, insects and shortages of supplies.

She was also faced — in her semi-professional capacity as a clergy wife — with ministering to a totally diverse flock. This ranged from the haughtier free settlers to convicts and ticket-of-leave men and, at the bottom of the social ladder, the

Aborigines. These she called 'the Australians' and, like Mary Johnson, she was thoroughly sympathetic to a people whose land was being steadily usurped and who were condemned to work as servants of the white man, often lying about on his verandah until sent on an errand.[7] Demonstrating great patience and sangfroid, Mrs Millett attempted to learn the Aborigines' language. She treated them medically as far as possible, washing their eyes which were frequently infected and arranging for troublesome teeth to be pulled. She tried to help bring up their orphaned children — although she turned a blind Victorian eye to the source of the dislocation of unfortunate Aboriginal families. In the seven years of their ministry to the native peoples, she and her husband earned their affection and respect.

Convicts and ticket-of-leave men were less appreciative of her care, but she also attempted to help them medically and in the finding of work. She sympathised with their having to attend church in a regimented fashion, 'sitting in rows like Crown serfs'.[8]

She displayed all the qualities mandatory in a pioneering clergy wife: ingenuity, organisation, spirituality and an equable, caring temperament. She coped with shortages by encouraging her household — despite the apparent lack of suitable servants — to make shoes and clothes, to grow food and flowers, to grind flour and to cook, and wash for the community.

Mercifully for the historian, she wrote a journal for prospective migrants and in it we are able to read her enlightened comments on most aspects of life in the West at the time. Her graceful prose covers such matters as the geology, botany and zoology of the area and the problems of the Western Australian economy which, in a small population of 25 000 in the mid-1860s, had been based on an unfair barter system. She is always positive in her observations, writing of 'the superb beauty of the climate. . . taken together with the primitive appearance of our carpetless dwelling, conveyed the impression of perpetually living in a garden house for the summer season.[9] The Milletts were, of course, fortunate that they were on an adequate stipend of two hundred to two hundred and fifty pounds per annum paid for by the British government.

No bishop or Dissenting church at that time could offer their clergy such financial security. The vast majority of clergy was dependent on the collection plate and gifts in kind from members of the congregation. Small wonder that Bishop Broughton and his successors found it difficult to recruit clergy overseas — only those of fervent missionary calling felt disposed to take up the challenge (or those who were sick or misfits).

The bishops always encouraged their clergy to marry, realising how difficult parish life was for a bachelor.[10] Dr John Dunmore Lang, the great recruiter of Scottish and Ulster clergy for the Presbyterian Church, also counselled marriage for future colonial ministers.[11] The Wesleyan Methodist Missionary Society, on the other hand, preferred single men for frontier service and both Samuel Leigh and Walter Lawry had to write away for permission to marry after they had served a certain number of years in New South Wales.[12]

Changes in the second half of the nineteenth century

By the second half of the nineteenth century, conditions for clergy and their wives — in all but the less developed colonies of Western Australia and Queensland — had begun to change. The gold rushes brought about a period of unprecedented economic growth which involved a much needed flood of immigration. The pastoral industry continued to expand, secondary industries were set up, trade grew and transport and communications were transformed.

This economic revolution had its implications for the churches who were themselves now in a better position to expand and even to train their own clergy. Only the bishops of poorer, outlying dioceses continued recruiting drives for clergy overseas. The others found that changing conditions in Britain, particularly overpopulation and economic depression in such areas as Ireland, Scotland and Cornwall, were causing clergy to apply to them for positions. It was a happier state to be in.

The majority of these overseas clergy brought their wives with them. Again, there were adjustment problems for these women who missed the familiar customs and comforts of home. Unfortunately, few appear to have kept diaries or journals of their experiences as many of the bishops' wives did. Their education and self-esteem did not match that of the bishops' wives who came from middle to upper middle class backgrounds. The wives of ordinary clergy also lacked the leisure and domestic help to allow them time to assess and write down their experiences. Even the most intelligent felt that their lives were of insufficient interest to posterity.[13]

Clergy wife cum novelist: Ada Cambridge

There was a significant exception to this rule and this was created by Ada Cambridge, the Victorian novelist, who was somehow able to combine a nomadic and high profile public life as a clergyman's wife with a prolific output as an author. She left England three weeks after her marriage to the Reverend George Cross in 1870 and settled quickly into her new country. On her journey to their first parish at Wangaratta, she wrote warmly of 'the smell of rain-washed air, the scent of gum and wattle and the fresh-springing grass. . . and parrots of all colours'.

Although the Crosses moved eight times from one parish to another in Victoria, she never complained, but revelled in building a new home out of chaos: 'I have thoroughly enjoyed it. . . and should like nothing better than to move again tomorrow, provided it were to the right place.'[14] Altogether, Cambridge published thirty novels, five volumes of poetry and numerous esays and stories.

Although dismissed by many male contemporary critics as 'romantic' and 'clumsy', her style was frequently ironic and rebellious. In the poem 'Unspoken Thoughts', she attacked clericalism and the social mores of the day. She wrote on behalf of women and their right to vote and she opposed racism and anti-Chinese sentiment in particular.

When commenting on their time in the parish of Ballan, she wrote ironically:

> I found, if not my level, the level which suited me. . . a
> poor parson's wife, lawful prey and protégé of patronising
> tradesmen's wives.[15]

Ada was able as a writer to supplement amply her husband's meagre income and she battled to make it clear that parish demands were not to interfere with her profession. Thus, she spent considerable periods of time propped up in her sickbed writing furiously, as this was the only place to which she could retreat without fear of interruption. She complained to fellow writer Ethel Turner about the eternal dilemma of the woman artist:

> . . .the many domestic and other affairs which are always
> warring against literary interests of all sorts; (for instance,
> I have just been wasting a whole week making fancy dresses
> for tableaux!).[16]

Therefore in practice, she often put parish commitments

first and assisted her husband by playing the organ and helping generally in the parish, which meant 'squeezing [her novels] into the odd times'.[17]

✠ Prevailing attitudes to clergy wives

Few clergy wives were prepared to pursue their talents and defy convention as Ada Cambridge did, nor did their physical strength and determination match hers. The comparative lack of confidence and independence of the majority was reinforced by the attitudes of churchmen of the period who wrote and edited church magazines and newspapers. These magazines either ignored the role of women in the church altogether or else made patronising statements which jar on the modern ear.

The *Christian Advocate* and *Wesleyan Record* of 1859 quotes at length a sermon delivered by the Reverend Thomas Binney about the role of women:

> Women are not to be men in character, ambition, pursuit or achievement; but they are to be more; they are to be the makers of man, they are to affect for all that is good and great those with whom they are linked in life. . . They may be the regulating power, the animating and inspiring face, the soothing and resuscitating influence by which the mighty engine of masculine life may be aided in its actions, its order and its results.[18]

There was no apparent hostile reaction to this highly chauvinist definition of the female role. Women at this stage seemed to be content to confine themselves in their parsonages and churches to raising funds, decorating their churches with greenery and texts and working in Sunday schools and the Band of Hope (a temperance organisation) in addition to their massive domestic duties.

Perhaps the views of the Reverend Binney (himself a

Congregationalist) were typical of the artisan and lower middle class society amongst which Non-conformism was strongest. The Methodist, Baptist and Congregationalist churches had numerous adherents in South Australia where Cornish miners, influenced by the Wesleyan Revival, migrated to work in the copper mines after 1840.[19]

Methodist and Baptist churches, in particular, managed to opine about women in a way not even evident in the literature of other churches at this time. One later Methodist journal offered the following helpful insight to its readers, which must surely have been tongue in cheek:

> Women are charming creatures, when they content themselves with nursing babies and making puddings, but beware, ye young men, of the women who have opinions and express them.[20]

With attitudes such as this abroad in the churches, it was little wonder that devout women of spirit turned for fulfilment to temperance and suffrage movements outside the church! These late Victorian reformers will be treated in a subsequent chapter where it will be demonstrated that very few of them were clergy wives, the latter being too bowed down by parish duties and expectations to engage in extra-parochial activities.

Recognition for clergy wives of these churches was never in proportion to their efforts. Such journals as the *Baptist Magazine* spoke of the ideal 'shrinking, modest, delicate woman' and yet expected the churchwoman and the minister's wife in particular to work often harder than her husband. Her domestic load, in addition to her fundraising duties, entailed a physical burden which made grave inroads on her health.

Moreover, the Pauline injunction that women were to keep silent in church was narrowly applied so that women were kept off committees as long as possible and mentioned as seldom as possible in ecclesiastical magazines. An example of this 'discrimination by silence' which approaches bathos was an account of the death of the pastor's wife in the Central Baptist Church in Sydney as late as 1924. Elizabeth Complin, wife of the Reverend J. Complin, was playing the organ at the opening of an important church mission when she suffered a fatal stroke. The account of her funeral gave no attention to her life of service, but substituted potted biographies of the important male church leaders present at the funeral. It was even implied that it had been very inconvenient for the church that their pastor's wife should have taken a stroke at such a moment![21]

The wife of the country parsonage was the least well off amongst clergy wives in terms of income and work expectations. She was totally dependent on the collection plate to feed her family; her housing was usually poorer than that of her Anglican sister and, if she were a Methodist wife, she could never put down roots because of the rotational system of deploying clergy.

The wife of the Presbyterian manse did not undergo as many moves as her Methodist counterpart. Her husband had to be 'called' by another congregation before he could move. She was expected to teach in the Sunday school, chair the women's guild meeting, and cook for various teas and fetes. She frequently went out visiting with her husband in order to keep in contact with the congregation which was supporting them. If he were an introverted, bookish man, then it was up to her to learn names and take an interest in the local Presbyterian families, otherwise the family starved.

The manse was often a large house set on a good expanse of land where a cow could be maintained and there was enough timber for firewood, but there was never enough money for repairs or for domestic help. If she had children

— and she often had six or more — the minister's wife waited anxiously for the session clerk to bring round the monthly cheque which was totally derived from the collection plate.

One clergy daughter remembered seeing her normally cheerful mother in floods of tears because she had inadvertently burnt a one pound note (the week's housekeeping) in the fuel stove. This mother, Margaret McIlwraith, wife of the Presbyterian minister in Grafton following World War I, was a graduate of the University of Sydney, yet never had the confidence to charge people for the hours of mathematics tutoring that she gave them. Nor did she complain when she was suddenly passed over for a mathematics post at the local high school when a male of slighter qualifications applied for the job at the last minute. Such a pattern of vocational discrimination was part of the lot of women.[22]

There can be no doubt that Victorian and also post-Victorian society expected an enormous amount from ministers' wives and it is to be wondered why more of them did not break down under the strain. 'She was the sacrificial lamb' was the verdict of the daughter-in-law of Constance Sharpe, a Non-conformist clergy wife who suffered breakdowns in health — and finally premature death — in post-war Sydney, attempting to run a missionary home for her zealous, unpaid husband.[23]

Admittedly, clergy usually received free accommodation, assistance with transport and unofficial medical care; country people often brought in gifts of produce and firewood to their minister as well. But for most, it was a tale of pitifully low income, lack of privacy and lack of recognition for much menial support work.

Mrs Jessie Newth, wife of the rector of the country parish of Lake Bathurst in the early 1890s, often longed for a holiday or even an opportunity to sew or read, but the demands of parish life were such that holidays were impossible:

> After breakfast, James and I got discussing plans about my
> getting away for a change — nothing feasible it seems. It
> simply can't be done. I cooked beefhead pudding tarts,
> turnovers, potatoes, pumpkin. In the afternoon when
> finished, I felt too tired to live.[24]

Added to the normal expectations of the rural clergy wife
of this period were the particular demands associated with
marriage to a man of religious scruple. James Newth kept the
letter of the law when Jessie's stillborn baby was buried outside
consecrated ground because the child had not been baptised.
Jessie was haunted by the memory of this and, four years later,
arranged for the baby's remains to be moved to the churchyard
when her husband was away.[25]

The plight of young clergy in outback parishes who wished
to marry is well illustrated in the diaries of Maude Richardson.[26] She and the Reverend Reginald Smee of the Bathurst
Diocese became engaged in 1892, but were obliged to wait
eight years before a remotely suitable house could be found
for them. A catechist's and even a curate's wage in the country
barely supported one, much less two people. Finally, he was
offered a viable parish at Brewarrina and they were able to
marry.

With eager expectation, she set out for her new home, but
a rude shock awaited her:

> We left before dawn next morning to escape some of the
> heat and arrived in Brewarrina about 2.00 p.m. I must
> add we had emptied our water bags on the journey and
> arrived with bloodshot eyes, cracked lips and covered from
> head to foot with fine red dust. . . our new house was
> built of some sort of corrugated iron lined with hessian;
> there was a sort of lean-to roofed with galvanised iron and

closed in on one side only, which apparently served as a kitchen and washhouse. There was no running water.

> The outhouse stood at the bottom of the yard across bare red ground, with not even a tree to shelter it. . . I could think of nothing but the unrelenting heat averaging 116 to 126 degrees in my first three months there.[27]

Small wonder that Maude Smee lost her first three babies in the heat and privation of 1899 to 1902. At times, she contemplated suicide when her husband was away on his tours of the huge parish and it was only when they moved to the cooler and more established town of Deniliquin that she was able to rear live children. The church finally realised that the outback was too much for women and small children and such missions as the Brotherhood of the Good Shepherd were set up (in 1902) to enable bachelors on a pittance to minister to far-flung people.

Loneliness in terms of both physical and social isolation was a continuing problem for clergy wives in the Australian context. Clergy did not have the respected position in society which was accorded them in Britain. Moreover, the Non-conformist minister and his wife found themselves in a less secure position of tenure than their Anglican counterparts. Once the congregation turned against their pastor, there was no hope of their staying — as there was no bishop in the equation.

✠ Bishops' wives in the Victorian and post-Victorian period

The protection and encouragement of a bishop and his wife, on the other hand, was of inestimable benefit to clerical families in terms of security and friendship.[28] Colonial bishops and their wives had a good record of pastoral care of their clergy. They corresponded constantly with them and visited them as frequently as possible. Bishops' wives like Jane Barker of Sydney and Maud Montgomery of Tasmania took a motherly interest in the clergy wives and children of their dioceses.

The bishop's wife was a significant figure in colonial society, as was her counterpart in Britain. Some of the colonial bishops' wives proved to be the agents of much social and educational reform, especially in matters concerning women. They were not as upper class as many English bishops' wives who were, after all, married to peers of the realm. Nor were they as dynamic or confident as Mrs Mandell Creighton, wife of the Bishop of London in the 1890s, who was an historian of note as well as a tireless philanthropist:

> She is equally at home in a drawing-room meeting, a gathering of factory girls, a church congress, or in the presidential chair of a Congress of Women Workers. Everywhere she makes friends; yet no modern woman is more delightfully unconventional; she forms her own opinions about everything and never minds expressing them under any circumstances.
>
> She has always taken a very special interest in girls and is particularly clever when handling subjects that are found very difficult to manage by the average clergyman's wife.[29]

Equally able and poised was Blanche, wife of Frederick Temple, Archbishop of Canterbury from 1897 to 1902. She shared her husband's Spartan ideals and interest in the poor:

> Her friends from Royal personages to the very poorest of those under her care are legion. And she speaks too, simply, tersely, to the point where her support, comment or encouragement are required in the many branches of work in which she is deeply interested. An unusually clear brain enables her to keep many irons in the fire. And never for a moment does she grow absorbed in her own

enterprises to the exclusion of her husband's work.[30]

There is a sycophantic note about these pen portraits, but it appears that English bishops' wives were superior to their colonial counterparts not only in social class, but also in confidence and influence. The majority of colonial bishops and their wives were drawn from the middle class, yet the record of the latter fell in no way behind in terms of hard work, pastoral care and philanthropy. It was only in the matter of women's rights that Australian bishops' wives were more reticent and this was probably the result of working in a frontier, male-orientated society.

Australian bishops and their wives were also subject to some other factors not encountered by the episcopate at home. First, the church was not established in the colonies, the bishop being elected after 1853 by democratic process in a synod rather than being appointed by the Crown. This meant they were more accountable to their flock than the English bishops. They were expected to work hard and to mix easily with all sections of society.

On the other hand, city bishops resembled English bishops in their rank in society, being acceptable members of the colonial elite on important occasions.

Finally, the greatest modifying factor for colonial bishops was the tyranny of distance. Most Australian dioceses were scattered over a large area and this meant that the bishop and his wife were expected to travel as much as possible over large distances and poor roads. Those bishops' wives like Frances Perry of Melbourne, Jane Barker of Sydney and Mary Thomas of Goulburn who had no children were able to do more to support their husbands ecclesiastically than were Sarah Broughton and Louise Barry who felt obliged to spend much of their time with their children.

A bishop's wife with a low profile:
Sarah Broughton

Sarah Broughton had been brought up in the shadow of the mother cathedral at Canterbury, so that she was well aware of the role and expectations of a bishop's wife.[31] She decided she should support him in both his ecclesiastical and political role (Broughton was an active member of the NSW Legislative Council) and that she and her daughters should represent him in polite society.

Broughton detested small talk and dancing perhaps because of his lameness — so he remained at home in the evenings, immersed in his paperwork while his wife and their daughters went out to various balls and parties.[32] Sarah accompanied Broughton on some of his earlier visitations to the far-flung frontier families, but later, her health was not up to long days of lurching carriage travel, which meant that she often did not see him for three months at a time. She was kind and hospitable to clergy, especially the younger bachelors, and she aided her husband spiritually so that, when she predeceased him, he published a collection of her favourite prayers and meditations as a tribute to her.[33]

Sarah Broughton did not engage in philanthropy, partly because of personal diffidence and partly because she was not an evangelical. She belonged to an earlier rural tradition of Georgian churchmanship in which a lower public profile for bishops' wives was the norm. Her husband had arrived in the colony as an Archdeacon in 1829 and been consecrated Bishop one year before Victoria's accession to the throne. As time went on, there was also not much room for social reform with Eliza Darling and then Caroline Chisholm occupying centre stage. Sarah Broughton might have done more for the needy, but her husband's view of himself as a High Churchman, plus her deteriorating health, meant that she chose not to be involved.

A high profile Melbourne bishop's wife:
Frances Perry

Frances Perry, wife of the first Bishop of Melbourne, Charles Perry (1847–1873), saw her role in a different light. Perhaps this was because she arrived twenty years later, when evangelicals like Hannah More and Lord Shaftesbury had achieved so much in social reform in England. A witty, well-educated woman of evangelical conviction like her husband, she had no children and therefore felt free to accompany her husband everywhere. She was not averse to mingling in polite society in the city as Sarah Broughton had done, but she also mixed freely with gold miners and the lower strata of society.

Her chief love was to accompany her husband on his journeys of visitation and to write endless letters and journals about her experiences of colonial life and landscape. She was perennially cheerful about jolting over execrable country roads, about nights spent in primitive conditions, where the wind whistled through the slab walls, and about the snakes and wild life they encountered.[34]

'Toujours le gum,' she commented about the Australian foliage as they bumped along, her vivacious presence buoying her husband up and winning friends for the church wherever she went. As Perry wrote his sermons, she spent the time composing her journal which she then dispatched to her relatives in England.[35] The discovery of gold evoked some pertinent comments from her about its implications for Melbourne and for society in general:

> Gold! gold! gold! My dear A, we are gone mad with gold and what is to be the end of it no-one knows. . . Melbourne is left pretty nearly under petticoat dominion![36]

Within a month, she and Charles had set off on horseback for the goldfields, taking tracts with them and determined to

*Frances Perry, wife of the Bishop of Melbourne and founder of
the Royal Women's Hospital, Melbourne*

hold services amongst the tents. The bishop took services in
his riding clothes, using a tree stump as a pulpit. She laughed
heartily when both of them had falls from their horses, dusted
herself off, and then went to visit a new Sunday school at Mt
Alexander and a colporteur's cart, which was selling scriptures
apace to the miners.

She called to see the wives of her husband's clergy regularly, encouraging them to make their own clothes in an

expensive society and comforting them in their fears about the bad influence the goldfields might have on their children.[37]

Frances Perry was the first bishop's wife to adopt a philanthropic role in Australia. She was worried about the plight of young female immigrants who arrived in the country without sufficient education for their proposed employment as governesses.

At first, she attempted to find accommodation for them and then a job at the school at St James Church and further afield. Next, she established a Home for Governesses so that these young women would be housed safely on disembarkation until they were assimilated into the community.[38]

Her most lasting memorial was her development of a Lying-in Hospital for poor women. She had observed how many settlers' wives had died in childbirth or had lost their babies soon after birth, so she worked hard to pioneer what is now the Royal Women's Hospital in Melbourne. She acted as President of the Board of the Hospital from 1856 to 1874 when she and her husband returned to England.[39]

Another high profile bishop's wife: Jane Barker

Frances Perry's role as evangelical reformer was to be duplicated, and in some ways extended by, Jane Barker, wife of the equally long-serving Archbishop of Sydney, Frederic Barker, who held that position from 1854 to 1882. Like Frances, Jane was the scion of a loving and lively merchant family; she was also unable to have children. This meant that she, too, was free to travel the length and breadth of New South Wales with her husband and to write up her impressions of their journeyings for the benefit of her family in England.

Life in the colony was to be a far cry from the leisured and artistic life she had known as a child; her father had been an accomplished water colourist and a friend of the Lake poets.

Coleridge's son was deeply impressed by her, but he resented her conversion to ardent evangelicalism as a result of her Scottish aunt's influence:

> Jane is a fine girl, very religious, and her religion is good as far as it emanates from herself, but I am afraid that a few drops of sulphuric acid have been infused into the pure milk of the word by that abstract of ugliness, that incarnation of Calvinism, that strong-minded woman — her Aunt Rankin — with whom I fell in hate at first sight.[40]

On her mother's death, she ran the household for a number of years, finally marrying Frederic Barker in her mid-thirties, and working with him in the Liverpool suburban parish of Edge Hill. They threw themselves into the work there, which was not dissimilar to conditions in Sydney's growing suburban sprawl. However, this did not prepare her for the formidable distances and problems involved in looking after the flock in the vast Diocese of Sydney.

Her heart went out particularly to the isolated wives in settlers' huts and distant homesteads. When visiting the parsonage at Molong on one journey in 1855, she was saddened by the thought of the minister's daughters there not being able to receive a worthwhile education. On her return to Sydney, she decided to set up a school for clergy daughters so that these girls would receive the educational opportunities of city girls and perhaps be prepared for future service as clergy wives.

St Catherine's Clergy Daughters' School was set up first in Point Piper's Road and later at Waverley, within striking distance of Bishopscourt. Jane Barker made no secret of the fact that she was modelling her school on a similar Clergy Daughters' School at Casterton near her home in the Lake District. She visited the school almost every day in its infancy, interviewing staff and children where her time allowed. After an early financial struggle, St Catherine's was firmly established as the first independent church school for girls in the colony.

It was to be nearly forty years before another Anglican school for girls was to be founded in Sydney. Apart from constantly travelling and attending church services and meetings with the indefatigable Frederic, Jane made time to exercise a pastoral ministry of visiting the sick and poor. She was engaged in that ministry the day her final illness overtook her.

She also worked long and hard for the Church Society, the Sunday school at Randwick, the Servants' Home and various ladies' committees.

Her chief love — apart from country touring — was the monthly prayer meeting which she and her husband attended at Millers' Point with leading clergy and laity. Here, they read the scriptures and prayed earnestly for the showy, materialistic city in which they had been placed. It was not an easy time for her as her husband was desperately short-staffed in administration as well as at a pastoral level. Sometimes she lost heart, especially when battling with the 'furnace wind' of the Australian summer or endeavouring vainly to sleep as battalions of mosquitoes attacked them in the night.

The frustration of the early days could be shared only with her husband and her journal:

> We have no flock here and I feel myself put upon the top shelf quite out of everybody's reach and covered with a thick layer of dust and rust. I hope to be taken down one of these days and mingle once more among the kindred spirits.[41]

This depression was replaced over the years by a growing optimism and satisfaction as her 'Daughters' [school] took root. It was her personal project which she oversaw from beginning to end, but this did not prevent her from supporting 'dear F' in all his endeavours as well. Together, they worked fearfully hard to orchestrate the expansion of the church in the 1860s and 1870s, keeping pace with the irresistible growth of Sydney itself.

She died before him, worn out by the relentless pace she had set herself. The tributes paid to her were many: 'a lady of rare gifts and graces. In presence, in culture, in intelligence, in disposition, in command, in aptitude for business, in kindness. . . she had few, if any equals.'[42]

✠ Bishops' wives outside Melbourne and Sydney

Bishops' wives in poorer, less populous dioceses like Goulburn had less to do than their city counterparts, but they had other problems. These were difficulties associated with climate, isolation and shortages. Conditions in Sydney and Melbourne were closer to those at home culturally and in terms of companionship, medical attention and educational opportunity.

The early bishops in Queensland were largely unmarried because of the deleterious effects of the tropical heat there. A bishop's wife was needed at the turn of the century in Brisbane to help with 'a Sisterhood, Orphanage, Rescue Home, Women's Shelter, Industrial Reformatory, all in their infancy', but the search was in vain.

The next bishop, St Clair Donaldson was, unsurprisingly, a bachelor.[43] Already, the intelligence had drifted across the hemispheres that Australia, or at least non-urban Australia, was not a place for bishops' wives. Bishop Montgomery, who had served in Tasmania and was the Archbishop of Canterbury's (Randall Davidson) consultant on Australian affairs, commented about a candidate's wife for the vacant see of Brisbane:

> . . .[She] is too English now to care for the rough and tumble of the colonies . . .[If] left alone for two months in the heat, it would break her heart. You want stiffer

material. The women are an awful difficulty; very few like it. Mrs Harmer [Adelaide], Mrs Clarke [Melbourne], Mrs Mercer [Tasmania] all at this moment would give anything to come home.[44]

However, some bishops' wives were made of sterner stuff — as were many clergy wives — and they refused to allow the climate and other problems to overwhelm them. Mary Thomas worked tirelessly beside her husband, Bishop Mesac Thomas of the new Goulburn Diocese, for nearly thirty years. She, too, had no children and was therefore able to accompany the humorous bishop on his seven tours to the furthest corner of his diocese — the township of Wentworth — which was 600 miles away.

Mary was an idealist and a reformer. After reading Harriet Beecher Stowe's *Uncle Tom's Cabin* in England, she had devoted much of her energy to organising a fugitive slave mission in Canada.[45] When she arrived in Goulburn, she took an active interest in the Church Society which worked amongst the poor. When funds proved scarce in the country diocese, she organised her friends in England to fund an annual sale of gifts for the support of the Society's work. The building of the new Cathedral of St Saviour was her most passionate interest and she and her husband watched with delight as its beautiful design took shape.[46]

Not all effective bishops' wives were, however, childless. Perhaps the most formidable of them all — and the mother of eight children to boot — was Maud Montgomery, wife of the Bishop of Tasmania from 1889 to 1902, and the mother of a future Field Marshal.

As a daughter of the Dean of Westminster, she had some notion of the role expected of her. Despite her early marriage at the age of seventeen, she demonstrated initiative, drive and fierce self and family discipline. In this way, she fulfilled all the expectations which could have attached to her role. Apart from pioneering the Mothers' Union in Australia, she ran her own school in the 1890s in which children of the intelligentsia in Hobart were principally enrolled.[47]

The severe depression of the 1890s caused the Montgomery family much anxiety, but Maud responded by taking charge of the family finances — perhaps not the first clergy wife to do so — and making severe economies. She released the bishop from all responsibility for household accounts, giving him a weekly allowance and enabling him to devote all his time to the diocese. As a result of her leadership, the family was so ordered and the episcopate so effective that the Montgomery family never forgot the happiness of their stay in Tasmania.[48]

Bishops' wives in the twentieth century played a less conspicuous role than their predecessors. Many were reserved like Dorothy Wright, wife of Archbishop J.C. Wright (1909–1933). She was unobtrusive in her chairing of women's meetings and in her hosting of receptions and house guests. Wifely support was supremely important for English bishops arriving in the country. Alfred Barry had been obliged to resign in 1889 because his wife refused to live in Sydney. His successor, Bishop (from 1897 Archbishop) Saumarez Smith was desperately lonely as a widower, coping with a tumultuous diocese from 1890 until his death in 1909.

So Wright nervously watched his wife in the early days after his enthronement later that year, apprehensive lest she also should find conditions in Sydney too much for her:

'O God, help D to like Australia, else I know not what to do. . .'[49] he prayed soon after his arrival in Sydney.

Their marriage was a particularly happy one and this partnership was invaluable in leading the country's largest diocese and denomination through the turmoil of war and economic depression.

What then was the role expected of clergy wives in the colonies, as opposed to that in the mother country? In both contexts, clergy wives were expected to be paragons of virtue and industry, retiring helpmeets of their husbands and matriarchs of a model family, but in no way threatening to the masculine leadership role of the Victorian age. This role model was easier for the clergy wife of the home country to live up to, as she resided in more comfortable quarters, with better household help and higher respect socially in the community.

The climate and sparser provision of medical help in the colonies meant that a number of colonial clergy wives died prematurely. For example, Archdeacon William Cowper of the Sydney Diocese married three times. Other wives in the ministry, like Eliza Marsden, became invalids because of the stress of pioneer conditions. Wives on the frontier like Janet Millett in Western Australia in the 1860s were frequently in danger of their life from natural disaster and dispossessed natives. The lack of curates in the colonies meant that clergy wives and daughters often had to deputise for husbands away on visitation. Non-conformist clergy wives suffered harsh conditions with pitifully low remuneration and frequent moves of household.

By the turn of the century, there were greater creature comforts for the clergy wife; her life expectancy was greater with improved medicine. Yet her role had considerably expanded: philanthropic and mission tasks had been added to her burdens. She was expected to support temperance work and missionary societies, to take part (if not lead) in sewing circles and fetes. Larger church populations meant that the clergy wife was often the coordinator of bands of women workers, a task which often taxed her patience and diplomacy to the limit. For instance, she was usually president of the Mothers' Union branch, the Ladies' Guild or the Dorcas

Society — depending on the denomination — or she was expected to organise work amongst girls in the parish, whether it was the Girls' Friendly Society, the Covenant or the Burning Bush.[50]

The Australian clergy wife generally rose to the level of ecclesiastical expectations. Where she had the health, she enjoyed for the most part working alongside her husband and acting as a bridge between the hierarchy and the laypeople. Finally, the parish and the diocese were undoubtedly the stronger and the happier when her impact was also positive.

4

The price of independence

THE WOMEN OF ROMAN CATHOLIC ORDERS, NINETEENTH AND EARLY TWENTIETH CENTURIES

'So tell Archdeacon R what I propose about the exchange of schools. And don't fear to enlarge on the want of another sister — at the same time letting him understand that I will not give you one until you have more accommodation.'

Mother Ignatius McQuoin (1879)

Caritas Christi Urget Nos .— 'The love of Christ constrains us.'

Motto of the Sisters of Charity
and the Daughters of Charity.

'The bishops and the priests have an awful power and terrible in the sight of God must it be if that be abused.'

Mary MacKillop, after her excommunication (1879)

THE SECOND HALF OF THE NINETEENTH CENTURY and the early twentieth century witnessed an enormous expansion in influence and numbers in the Roman Catholic Church in Australia. Without detracting fom the work of parish priests and male teaching orders, it could be argued for reasons of numerical preponderance alone that women in orders were at the forefront of this explosive growth in the church. They certainly came to outnumber their male counterparts in the church within a few decades.

Beginning with the Sisters of Charity at the close of 1838, a steady stream of women from various international orders arrived in the country which had been designated part of the 'Mission' of Oceania by Rome. Most orders arrived in response to a plea by archbishop or bishop, but one order — in many ways the most unusual — appeared to sprout from antipodean soil unaided. The Order of St Joseph, led by the redoubtable Mary MacKillop, was perhaps to exceed — if that were possible — the heroism of the other orders in teaching and caring. However, there was a price to pay for the extraordinary endeavour of the female religious and this was a pattern of oppression suffered by them at the hands of the male hierarchy.

Conversely, the bishops and the priests had to pay a price for the indispensable support of the Sisters. The latter, especially their leaders, could be dictatorial and expedient in their policy to the extent of outmanoeuvering the hierarchy on occasions. Whatever the power play at the top, the female order, through its democratic processes and system of central government, was able to establish a prototype of the independent woman who as teacher, nurse or social worker had a career in her own right. Such a pattern of female independence was to be passed on through convent education to generations of schoolgirls, many of whom would embrace feminism and reject the authority of the church in the following century.

Until the nineteenth century, the vast majority of female orders in the church were contemplative and enclosed. Such orders as the Carmelites — later to be represented in Australia

— were entirely enclosed, devoting themselves to prayer, fasting and religious exercises. A cloistered woman was able to pursue her own career, rising — if deemed suitable by her sisters — to a position of considerable power and authority within the church.

Following the Industrial Revolution which produced increased population and social misery, devout women were constrained to move outside the walls of the convent and grapple with the problems of the poor.[1] Despite its early repression of Catholicism, the French Revolution with its ideals of freedom and internationalism was influential in the long term in bringing about the re-emergence of religious orders in Europe.

Almost all of these orders were to come to Australia within the next century. First of all, the Jesuits, whose order had been banned in 1773, gathered unofficially before being re-constituted in 1814. Then Madeline-Sophie Barat, brought up in the tradition of the old Italian Order of the Ursulines, founded the religious of the Sacred Heart in 1807 as a teaching order of the highest classical standards. The Sacred Heart Sisters and the Ursulines catered mainly for the middle and upper classes and emphasised the intellectual and cultural development of women. Older orders like the Benedictines, Cistercians and Visitation nuns were also interested in deepening and refining women's education. Their curricula included large segments of instruction in music, drawing and dancing — activities more likely to be pursued by the upper classes.[2]

French hospitals in the care of orders also began to gain a reputation at this time for care of the distressed as well as for a high standard of medical practice. Such was the fame of the medical and educational work of the orders in France that Irish women of spirituality travelled across the Channel to prepare for their life's work. Mother Mary Aikenhead, the founder of Australia's first Catholic order, the Sisters of Charity, had been influenced by the French Loreto Order during her religious training in England and Margaret and Maria O'Brien, who were Australian pioneers of the order, had been educated in France.

Catholic Ireland felt a much greater affinity with Catholic France than with Protestant England, the old oppressor. It is therefore interesting to trace the indirect (as well as direct) French influence on Roman Catholicism in Australia through the Irish.

When Aikenhead founded her order in Dublin in 1815, she adopted the same motto as the older French order, the Daughters of Charity — '*Caritas Christi Urget Nos*'.[3] The latter Order, founded by St Vincent de Paul and St Louise de Marillac in 1633, was dedicated to the relief of the poor and the suffering. It did not actually send its own missionaries to Australia till 1926, but its stress on ministry to the sick poor undoubtedly influenced Irish orders like the Sisters of Charity.[4]

In choosing a constitution for her new order, Mary Aikenhead included the concept of central government — that is, she and her sisters were to be answerable to the central authority of Rome through their own head superior and not to the local diocese.[5] Herein lay the nub of the later disagreement with the colonial hierarchy — indeed, of the female struggle for autonomy within the Roman Catholic Church. The nuns saw their first loyalty through their vows to the heavenly Bridegroom and then to their sisters within the community. They were willing to help the bishop and the local priest as far as possible, but only Rome was permitted to overrule their independence. With the passing of the Catholic Emancipation Act in 1829 in Britain, the right of Roman Catholics to worship and to educate their flock in Ireland and the colonies was finally recognised. A period of unprecedented expansion of the Catholic Church followed over the next half century.

Australia was declared a 'Mission' because of its distance from Europe and the lack of ecclesiastical infrastructure here. An English Benedictine monk, John Bede Polding, was appointed as first Archbishop of Sydney. Polding was a man of scholastic bent and nobility of character. He was, however, a better missionary pastor than administrator. He was frequently away on visitation or else overseas recruiting. His colleagues were men of lesser ability and he generally found considerable problems amongst his Sydney flock on his return. Moreover, the Benedictine hierarchy disapproved of the Sisters of Charity's insistence on autonomy in matters internal and financial. The resultant situation of distrust was exacerbated by Anglo-Irish differences which created suspicion on both sides.

Early difficulties for the Sisters of Charity

Who were the members of the first party of nuns to work in Australia and what problems did they encounter on their arrival in Sydney in 1838? The leader of the five Sisters of Charity was Sister Joan Cahill whom Mother Mary Aikenhead had appointed Superior of the group; under her were sisters Margaret O'Brien, Alicia De Lacy and Sisters Caton and Williams. All of them had had medical or teaching experience in Dublin.

They travelled out to Australia in the company of Polding's Vicar-General, W.B. Ullathorne, a Benedictine monk who had been visiting Britain to recruit for the Sydney Archdiocese. With his usual impulsiveness, Ullathorne upset the sensibilities of the five sisters by demoting Sister Cahill from her position of Superior on the voyage out.[6] He also showed no respect for the Order's constitution when he promoted novitiate sisters three to four years early to the position of formed Sisters. News of these breaches of the Constitution was received with disquiet by the foundress in Dublin months later, but they were not to be the last.[7] Further problems awaited them on their arrival in Sydney.

First of all, it was midsummer and they had undertaken to wear their northern hemisphere clothing — ten pounds of black serge plus guimpe, veil and cap. They found they were quickly exhausted by the heat and tormented by mosquitoes.

Most disturbing of all was their financial position. On leaving Ireland, they had renounced the dowries they had brought to the Order on the expectation of a stipend from the church. Ullathorne had promised they would be provided for, but Polding refused at first to make preparations for their support.[8] 'How they [the Sisters of Charity] will be supported is a secret to me, in the bosom of Providence, not made known,' he shrugged.[9]

Before leaving Ireland, they had chosen to decline the salary of forty pounds per annum which the government paid catechists. This was on account of their vow of poverty and because they did not want to be restricted to teaching once they arrived in the colony. Nor did the church give them a housing or clothing allowance such as priests arriving in the colony were accustomed to receive. Polding finally allowed them thirty pounds per annum from his own purse for each of the five of them, after changing the amount from letter to letter. As a result, they could not maintain a nutritious diet, nor could they afford to replace shoes or clothing.[10]

Soon after their arrival in Sydney, they were despatched to Parramatta to work in the female factory. Existing on the very minimum of food, they visited the thousand odd inmates of the factory twice daily, reading and praying with them and listening to their problems. They persuaded the authorities to change the women's work from breaking wood and stones to laundry and needlework. In this way, the inmates felt they were being trained for the outside world rather than filling their day with soul-destroying work. Within a few weeks, there was a palpable change of attitude in the female factory. Delighted with their work, Polding wrote off to Archbishop Murray in Dublin:

> Their success has gone beyond my most sanguine expectations. A change which seems almost miraculous has taken place. Where heretofore all was noise and ribaldry and obscene conversation, you may now see a quiet and well-ordered family. Not an oath, nor coarse nor brawling word is heard and a general desire to receive the sacraments prevails.[11]

Despite the joy of the hierarchy at the efficacy of the sisters' work, misunderstandings between hierarchy and order continued to grow. The women were genuinely hungry and exhausted at the end of the day and malnutrition was setting in. Their financial worries were exacerbated by the distance from Ireland and their disappointment that Dublin had refused to send them their dowries, having already used them to accept members to replace those who had gone to Australia. Often, communications between the two countries were confused and Dublin found it hard to comprehend the great differences in climate and social and economic conditions prevailing in the colony. The nuns felt spiritually isolated and secretly wished to confess to each other rather than to a priest, but of course it was forbidden.[12]

Suspicion of the hierarchy increased in the late 1840s when the nuns discovered that Polding had gone behind their back in an attempt to nullify the central government of the order. In 1842, he officially petitioned the Pope for the Australian Congregation of the Sisters of Charity to be canonically separated from the Irish Congregation.

Having got his own way on the grounds of distance from the Mother House in Dublin, he did not inform the sisters, but went across to Ireland and showed the Papal Rescript to Mary Aikenhead and Archbishop Daniel Murray, both of whom were under the impression that the Australian sisters knew about the separation and had even requested it. When he returned to Australia, he still did not inform the sisters about the rescript and they did not hear about it till 1846 — four years after it was first drawn up. The occasion of this revelation caused further distress for the pioneer order, especially as the Archbishop himself was away. Polding had left for Europe in 1845, leaving the diocese to the tender mercies of his Vicar-General. Dom Gregory was a headstrong man in his twenties who had received little or no theological education.[13]

He proceeded to alienate all the Sisters of Charity — except Sister de Lacy whose difficulties were to appear ten years later. Upon demanding a constitutional change to the rule of their order, he was met with a refusal from the Superior Mother Catherine O'Brien. Gregory then produced the rescript, read it aloud to the sisters and then posted it on the chapel door as a means of bringing the sisters into line. He then declared all offices vacant in the order, demoting Mother Catherine O'Brien as Superior. When a month had elapsed, he behaved unforgivably as far as the sisters were concerned, taking over the office of Superior, eating with the convent and walking into the nuns' rooms when they were sick.

Dismayed, Sister O'Brien smuggled off a letter of protest to Dublin with the Christian Brothers who were returning home also because of a tussle with Abbot Gregory.[14] At this juncture, three of the pioneer sisters, with Gregory's encouragement, decided to transfer to Van Diemen's Land to work at the Cascades Female Factory in Hobart.[15]   Gregory was on the way to having his wish — openly expressed in the hearing of the sisters: 'I wish that there was not a Sister of Charity in the colony.'[16]

The reasons for the escalating clash between the Charities and the hierarchy are not difficult to find.   First, there was always an element of Anglo-Irish tension simmering below the outwardly calm surface of the early colonial church.   English Benedictines like Polding, Ullathorne and Gregory felt they were superior to new-fangled Irish orders like the Charities and the Christian Brothers.   The Irish, in their turn, found it difficult to forget past ill-treatment at the hands of the English.

Second, harmonious expansion was difficult to sustain in the frontier church when workers were few and isolated and communication with Europe was months away.

Finally, there was an element of sexual warfare which contributed to the conflict.   The Charities were in a unique position to offer a skilled service in the colony and no male, whether bishop or parish priest, liked to be stood up to by a convent sister.   When it was a question of power — either ecclesiastical or financial, perceived or actual — the male hierarchy was determined to have its way.   This was the experience of practically all orders, but most notably the Charities and the Josephites.

✠ Conflict over St Vincent's Hospital

It was over St Vincent's Hospital, Darlinghurst that the last great showdown between the Sisters of Charity and the Bishop occurred.   The Mother Superior of the Order and the Matron of the Hospital, Alicia De Lacy, had long nurtured an ambition to serve the people of NSW from the time of her girlhood in Ireland.   She was a fine administrator and bookkeeper and dreamt of starting a Catholic hospital in Sydney like St

Vincent's in Dublin where she had trained. Although busy running a refuge for the poor in Sydney, she began saving funds through bazaars and other means for land for the hospital.

A narrow strip of land had been granted to the order by the Governor, Charles Fitzroy, just before his return to England in 1855. This was in Darlinghurst but, as this area was not big enough for a hospital and a convent, De Lacy looked further. Archbishop Polding was away when 'Tarmons', the fine Potts Point property of Sir Charles Nicholson, came up for sale. Here at last could be the hospital she dreamed of. She and a committee of leading citizens raised 5000 pounds and the property was transferred by deed of conveyance to Archdeacon McEncroe, Alicia De Lacy and J.H Plunkett (a Catholic layman) in trust for the Sisters of Charity.[17]

On his return to the country in 1856, Polding was furious to hear about the debt of 5000 pounds and that the Charities not only controlled the new hospital, but held the deeds to the estate in their name. Tales were also being whispered about the hospital's dependence on Protestant funding and Protestant doctors. The fact that Dr James Robertson was an Edinburgh graduate and a Presbyterian was stressed rather than his qualifications as the best man available to head the medical staff at St Vincent's.

Although a man of fine character himself, Polding was not an especially good judge of the character of others and those to whom he delegated power — like Dom Gregory and, to some degree, Sister Scholastica Gibbons — were tactless and inflexible at the best of times. Discontent with his administration, especially on the part of his Irish laity, was already simmering and it needed only a major incident to bring it to the boil. St Vincent's Hospital opened in the front rooms of

'Tarmons' with Sister De Lacy on call in the room above. It was an outstanding success from the beginning and Alicia De Lacy began to fulfil her dream of a great hospital serving the people of NSW.

But many trials lay ahead — not least those within the order itself. Some of the Sisters of Charity had expressed their desire to become Benedictines in the mid-1850s, as a result of the pressure of the English Catholic hierarchy who had already set up a small Benedictine convent in the Parramatta area.

Polding decided to ask three of the Charities, led by Sister Scholastica Gibbons, to open a refuge in Pitt Street, called the House of the Good Shepherd, for women in distress. It appears that relations between De Lacy and Gibbons had not been good since they had fallen out in the pioneer days working in Parramatta. Gibbons was something of a martinet and she criticised De Lacy for taking too much advice from 'externs'.[18] As Superior of the order, she made life difficult for De Lacy with petty prohibitions, such as refusing her permission to use the courtyard pump to supply the hospital with water.

Everything came to a head over the Protestant Bible and Prayer Book which Matron De Lacy had accepted as a gift from the Rector of St John's Church, Darlinghurst for the use of Protestant patients in the hospital. St Vincent's had been founded for the benefit of all denominations. The new hospital chaplain, Father Patrick Kenyon, was making his rounds, when he came upon the Bible and Prayer Book which were clearly marked with the hospital's name. He rebuked Matron De Lacy and ordered the offending items to be withdrawn; whereupon Doctor Robertson and the medical staff resigned, as did J.H. Plunkett, the treasurer of the hospital.

There followed a blaze of publicity about the incident in the *Sydney Morning Herald* and the Catholic newspaper *Freeman's Journal*, which put Archbishop Polding under pressure.

He sent Sister Scholastica Gibbons to reprove Matron De Lacy, whereupon the latter decided to give up her dream of a great hospital and return to Ireland. She wrote to her Superior-General in Dublin:

> I could not remain here without endangering my soul by yielding and complying with what is against our holy Constitution. . . The state of this diocese is most deplorable.[19]

Thus, over what appeared to be a sectarian squabble, Sydney lost its most qualified matron, as Lucy Osburn did not arrive at Sydney Hospital till 1868. Polding was incensed by Mother De Lacy's decision to return to Ireland and he virtually excommunicated her, ordering his priests to refuse her the sacraments on the grounds that she had left the convent to take refuge in the Plunketts' house. As soon as a ship was available, she slipped home to Ireland in non-religious dress.

The media had a field day, especially when a large meeting of Catholic laymen gathered in 1859 to pass a vote of no-confidence in the ecclesiastical administration of the diocese and to move for the setting up of a provisional committee to run the diocese. Polding was furious and threatened excommunication of all involved if the motion was not withdrawn. Angry correspondence with Archbishop Cullen of Dublin which followed only served to heighten Polding's insecurity and he received a severe blow when Rome decided to recall Abbot Gregory the following year.

The chief oppressor of the Sisters of Charity was at last removed.[20] As far as relations between the hierarchy and the Sisters of Charity were concerned, they were never to be absolutely healed. Present-day successors of those pioneer sisters still nurse a feeling of hurt at the way in which Polding and Gregory acted. Alicia De Lacy herself was ever-forgiving, if wistful at the lost opportunity to run her cherished hospital:

> Though I felt leaving Sydney, yet my motives were conscientious. . . in heaven, we will know the goodness of our divine Lord in sending us crosses, trials and disappointments to detach our affections from all that is earthly, that we may thus subdue nature which is so apt to rest on creatures. . .[21]

Abbot Gregory had almost got his own way as there were but a handful of Sisters of Charity left in the colony at this point. However, they were to rebuild steadily under the watchful eye of the formidable Scholastica Gibbons. It was this lady whom Polding chose as the linchpin of a new order which would act as his handmaid in the diocese.

✠ The Order of the Good Samaritans

Polding needed fresh people to run the Pitt Street Refuge for needy and distressed women, so he founded the Order of the Good Shepherd in 1854. This order, whose regulations were largely according to the rule of St Benedict, was later renamed the Order of the Good Samaritans, because Polding discovered that there were French communities of the Good Shepherd when he went to Rome to gain permission for the order to begin.

The Benedictine component in the rule of the new order ensured a close relationship with the Australian hierarchy while they were of like persuasion.[22] The new order began to flourish, first of all under the leadership of Mother Mary Scholastica Gibbons who acted as both superior of the Good Samaritans and the Sisters of Charity for a number of years. She was an archetypal figure, retaining her links with her old order and wearing the Charity habit until her death. At the same time, she worked closely with Polding in co-founding the new order.

Girls at work in the Manly Industrial School,
Order of the Good Samaritan: about 1905

The nuns in the new order were predominantly English rather that Irish, so that the Anglo-Irish tension between religious and hierarchy which other orders experienced did not take place. By the time the hierarchy had become Irish in the mid-1880s with the appointment of Cardinal Moran, many of the Samaritan postulants were native-born — the 'kangaroos', as the older sisters used to call them because of their exuberance.[23]

The Good Samaritans were the first Australian-born order in the colonies and their indigenous flavour helped them to expand swiftly to nineteen houses in NSW alone by the turn of the century. Their early close relationship with a hierarchy of Benedictine persuasion was a second factor in their early growth.

A third reason for their rapid expansion can be sheeted home to the leadership of Mother Mary Berchmans McLaughlin who was born to a farming family in the Bathurst district. In her nineteen years as Superior of the order, Mother Berchmans was a dynamo of energy, charm and business acumen. In administering her chain of schools, refuges and orphanages, she experienced her share of conflict with the hierarchy. However, such were her social skills that she always triumphed in such encounters.

On one occasion during World War I, the fiery parish priest at Newtown took a taxi cab to St Scholastica's Convent at Glebe to demand that Mother Berchmans reverse her decision to transfer two personable young sisters from his school to another. He returned crestfallen to his curate:

I was putty in her hands. She turned those eyes of hers directly on mine and said, 'Your Reverence, may I be permitted to ask you in all sincerity with which you are most concerned, the social scenery in your school or the schooling progress of its pupils? I have given you two [other] excellent teachers whom you will soon find are classroom treasures!'

I was dumb, Battle. What a woman![24]

Without gainsaying Mother Berchmans' charm and aura of

An empire-builder, Mother Mary Berchmans McLaughlin,
before taking vows

authority, the sixty years since the foundation of the order had witnessed a change in the attitude of the hierarchy towards the professionalism of women in orders. It is doubtful that Abbot Gregory or Father Kenyon would have tolerated such non-co-operation from a nun in their day, but the frontier conditions of the 1840s and 1850s, which had created such dissension in the Archdiocese of Sydney, were a thing of the past.

Friction between orders and hierarchy seemed to be almost inevitable in the early days, however, even when the order was under diocesan control.

✠ The Sisters of Mercy

The Sisters of Mercy were a great Irish order which flourished in the Australian colonies, and particularly Queensland and Western Australia. This order was also invited by Archbishop Polding to come to his vast diocese.

Polding was extremely wary after his experience with the Charities, but he did not have sufficient womanpower in his favourite non-enclosed order, the Sisterhood of the Good Shepherd (later the Samaritans), to cope with the expanding number of Catholic children in NSW. So in 1865, he applied for recruits to St Ethelburga's Convent in Liverpool which had been established by the Mercies. Besides, there were good reports of the Mercy foundation in Perth where the first Catholic school was set up in 1846 under the new Catholic Bishop of Perth.[25]

The Mercy Sisters had a proud record of financial inde-pendence since their founder, Catherine McAuley, devoted her considerable inheritance to educating the poor and caring for the sick in Dublin. She founded her order of 'walking nuns' (named because of their visits to the poor) in 1833, two years after the Emancipation Act of 1831 which gave Roman Catho-lics in Ireland freedom of worship.

Frontispiece of the original Rule of the Sisters of Mercy (1833),
the largest order to work in Australia

She did not follow the Charities' system of government
which was a generalate, with one superior for the whole
country. Instead, each priory was autonomous, especially in
matters of finances, property, election of superiors and training
of novices. However, there was some measure of diocesan
oversight in that the bishop's permission had to be sought for
matters requiring heavy expenditure and the sisters could be

interviewed and examined by the bishop every three years.[26] Thus, a different style of government was more promising for the future relationship between the Mercies and the hierarchy in Australia. However, it was not long before the strains were felt on both sides.

Polding intended that the Mercies should work in Bathurst, where a tiny group of nuns were trying to educate the large number of Catholic children west of the Blue Mountains. When the Mercies arrived in 1865 from Liverpool, they found that the diocese had been split during the voyage out and that the new bishop, Matthew Quinn, had decided to bring another community of Mercy nuns out with him from Ireland. The three pioneer Mercy Sisters in Sydney were therefore bewildered to find that they had no home and no job to go to. Polding put them to work in the Convent School of St Patrick in inner Sydney, but could not find them a house nearby.

It was a wet summer and the sisters were forced to trudge through the Rocks area several times a day, often drenched to the skin. Their health began to suffer and one delicate novice was obliged to leave the order.

Their disappointment with the hierarchy gradually turned to distrust when a property adjacent to the school was purchased. The Sisters were allowed to move in but, although they attempted to renovate it, they were not encouraged to regard it as their own. The diocese held on to the deed to their Convent property at St Patrick's and so was able to hand it over as part of the whole parish to the Marist Fathers a few years later.[27]

A further baptism of fire awaited the Mercies when they moved to Parramatta to help the Marist Brothers educate primary school children. They began work in an old cottage and numbers of pupils grew from 40 to 200 very quickly. Teaching went on in an old stable and then an open shed in the grounds. The walls of the former were patched with sugar bags to help prevent the wind blowing the books off the tables. The nuns who taught in the shed in summer were close to fainting under the low zinc roof. By contrast, the Marist Brothers 'had the use of a large school' nearby. After six years, a school room was finally provided for the sisters who first of all slaved to pay the rent for it and furnish it, and then set about funding the building of a convent.

The following year, 1883, Co-adjutor Archbishop Vaughan came to lay the foundation stone of the convent, volunteered a substantial contribution, as did the sisters, only to find that their convent was destined by the parish priest to be the new infants' school![28] Thus, where the nuns were too closely subject to the parish priest, their housing was often desperately inadequate and their autonomy was sharply curtailed. Every minute of their day was exploited to the benefit of the parish. They were expected to act as sacristan and organist in the church, train choirs to sing in the church, visit the sick — and all on top of a full day's teaching. So it was no wonder that they had sought a refuge in a quiet part of Sydney where no bishop or priest could disturb them or dislodge them.

With the aid of a small legacy, much desperate fund-raising and a guarantee from a 'Protestant gentleman', they had been able to purchase in 1879 a handsome property on a healthy ridge on the North Shore. The Convent of St Joseph and the Monte Sant' Angelo School were established as a fitting head-quarters of the Sydney order by the late 1880s. From this base, the Mercies could not only educate the Catholic daughters of northern Sydney, but they could set up a fine hospital nearby, the Mater Misericordiae (1905), as their sisters in Ireland and the United States had done.[29]

Autonomous congregations of Sisters of Mercy began to spring up across the Australian colonies, beginning with Western Australia in 1846, until the order became the largest women's religious community in the country. 'The Sisters of Mercy, it can be truthfully said, were the propagators of Catholicism in Western Australia,' declared an early commentator.[30]

A foundation next began in Melbourne under the redoubtable Ursula Frayne, who came across from Perth's community when she could not get on with the Bishop of Perth. As befitting a pioneer missionary, Bishop John Brady was a man of remarkable asceticism and zeal. He did not use a bed, but slept in a chair in his church. His diet was extremely poor and he expected the Mercies to share such conditions. After eleven years, Ursula Frayne gave up exhausted, but not before some excellent work had been done, particularly with Aborigines.[31]

The greatest expansion of the order took place in Queensland which became a new Catholic diocese from the moment Queensland was gazetted a separate colony in 1859. The first bishop of the diocese to be appointed was Dr James Quinn, brother of the bishop of Bathurst, who would not invite the English Mercies to work with him. James Quinn had worked as chaplain to the Mercy convent in Dublin and, while there, had been deeply impressed by the character and work of Sister Ellen Whitty. He urged her convent to release her and finally she arrived as the first Mercy Superior in Brisbane in 1861.

As Mother Vincent Whitty, she laboured mightily in Queensland until her death in 1892. She began acting independently of state funding so that her system of education would not be beholden to the government in any way. Fundraising was chiefly by means of bazaars, which sold everything from imported lace to home-grown fruit and vegetables. Starting with the great College of All Hallows in Brisbane, which was often kept going by Protestant school fees, she began a chain of twenty-six boarding schools throughout the colony. She coped superbly with the vast distances, tropical heat and isolation. Her band of five sisters grew to 222 by the time of her death, most of whom had trained at the novitiate set up by Archbishop Cullen in Dublin.[32]

Mother Vincent Whitty, pioneer Superior of the Sisters of Mercy

The great strengths of her system of education were moral training, art and music so that each convent and school became an oasis of civilisation in the frontier culture of Queensland. However, despite being of a gentler and more conciliatory spirit than her counterpart in Sydney, Mother Ignatius McQuoin, Mother Vincent Whitty also fell foul of the bishop. Bishop Quinn interfered in internal matters of order such as the length of postulancy for sisters. He stopped her working amongst the Aborigines in Rockhampton and he tried to veto on financial grounds her takeover of Ipswich Hospital. Finally, he acted illegally in demoting her as Superior in favour of Sister Bridget Conlan.[33]

Despite her years of seniority in Ireland as well as Australia, Mother Vincent Whitty graciously forgave the bishop this demotion. She did not leave her work as Sister De Lacy did, nor did she fight back like Mary MacKillop or Sister Ignatius

McQuoin of the Sydney Mercies.

When Sister Ignatius McQuoin was treated unfeelingly by the hierarchy, following the death of her dearest friend, Archdeacon McEncroe in 1878, she became ill, tired and dispirited. Polding and his colleagues refused to comfort her, but instead asked her to start a mission in the country forthwith.

She agreed with a sigh: 'I came here not of my own choice, but in obedience to my Superiors, and I expect Almighty God to sustain me.'

'So he will,' said the Very Reverend Archdeacon Rigney, the Vicar General.[34]

The following year, she wrote to encourage one of her lonely sisters in Parramatta and to indicate her resolve to defy the hierarchy if need be:

> So tell the Archdeacon what I propose about the exchange of schools; and don't fear to enlarge on the want of another Sister — at the same time letting him understand that I will not give you one until you have more accommodation.[35]

It must be conceded that many of the mother superiors were intransigent and even imperious in their dealings with the bishops. There were not many positive avenues open to them if they objected to the bishop: they could resign as De Lacy did or they could go to Rome as Mary MacKillop did. Only someone as redoubtable as she was prepared to brave the dangers and difficulties of a solo visit to Rome.

A further obstacle was the notorious indecision of the Vatican. Italian papal authorities were not very interested in Oceania and they often hoped that the problem would go away before a ruling was necessary. If they (the Congregation de Propaganda Fide) did come to a decision — as in the case of Polding and the Rescript of 1842 — it was usually on the side of the hierarchy, especially as the latter had greater resources and time to carry out lobbying. Although female pressure groups were starting to make an impression in Protestant countries, they scarcely carried weight in Rome.

✠ The Presentation and Dominican sisters

As the nineteenth century drew to a close, the influx of orders to the Australian colonies continued — as did the incidents of patriarchal oppression. The Presentation Sisters of the Blessed Virgin Mary came from Ireland to Hobart in 1866 to establish schools in Tasmania. In 1873, they entered Victoria in response to the 1872 Education Act which had introduced free, compulsory and secular education.[36] This order then expanded to Wagga, New South Wales, where the sisters endured an unpleasant relationship with the Bishop of Goulburn, Bishop William Lanigan, for a quarter of a century. The bishop interfered in almost every aspect of their foundation and rule.

On their arrival in Wagga, a leading layman offered them forty acres of land for their convent and school. Unfortunately, the layman never presented them with the deeds to that land and so the bishop was able to divert the estate to a trust 'for Catholic purposes', there being a church, school and presbytery assigned to it, as well as a convent.

As the school and convent buildings went up, the sisters were expected to finance them on land they were never allowed to own. They were continually criticised by Lanigan for their extravagance: 'Unnecessary expenses everywhere. . .', 'My advice slighted. . . ', he wrote in his diary. In 1877, he marked out draconian rules for life in the convent, the most difficult being the enclosure of the convent by fifty feet and the reduction of the sisters' modest back garden by one third. Thus, the Presentation Sisters were never able to relax in their own grounds until 1900 when their tormentor finally died.[37]

Where the female orders had a traditional relationship with an allied male order, such as the Loreto Order with the Jesuits and the Dominican sisters with the Dominican Order, there appears to have been less friction with the hierarchy, one exception to this observation being the treatment of the Dominican sisters in Maitland by Bishop James Murray.

This band of sisters arrived in the new Diocese of Maitland in 1867. As a very old order responsible to Rome and accustomed to enclosure, this group of sisters lacked strong leadership and experience in apostolic work. They soon found they could not stand up to their harsh young bishop.

He criticised them for accepting Protestants into their schools; he sometimes deprived them of the Mass and sacraments in order to discipline them. Amongst their 'excruciating trials' were arbitrary instructions to fast, wretched working conditions and a prohibition on holidays at home. Their mortality rate was high: of the thirty-four missionaries who came to Maitland from 1867 to 1888, fourteen were dead by 1890. Yet the Dominicans battled on magnificently, constantly achieving a higher standard of education, especially in the teaching of the deaf-mute.[38]

✠ The Society of the Sacred Heart

Some orders with financial backing and higher social standing like the Society of the Sacred Heart and the Faithful companions of Jesus were able to ignore the hierarchy and get on with their teaching. The former arrived in Sydney in May 1882 and the latter in Melbourne the following month. Both set up prestigious convents — one at Rose Bay, the other in Kew.

Their exotic origins — French orders — their system of central government and their high standard of classical scholarship and cultural pursuits also helped to ensure the sisters' immunity from clerical attack.[39] The first SSH Superior, a Belgian noblewoman, commented adversely to the Head House on the Irish connection:

> Almost all the priests are Irish and share the common prejudices, alas! One of the most senior leaves out the prayers for the Queen in the public ceremonies and even refused to ask for prayers in his parish for a dead priest because the latter was English. The bishops, Irish to a man, refused to meet Monsignor Vaughan when he first arrived as co-adjutor, because he is English; however by his conciliatory attitudes, he has won them over slowly. . . I tell you these things, Rev. Mother, in order that you may know something of the spirit of the place.[40]

Although the Sacred Heart order was small in numbers, its influence on women and their role in society was very great. It supplied a majority of early Catholic women university undergraduates at the University of Sydney. SSH alumni were active in the foundation of the first Roman Catholic women's university college in New South Wales. They were leaders in the Catholic Women's League, which was founded in 1916 and later known as the Legion of Catholic Women. Finally, it was the first Australian order to send missionaries overseas; this was to Japan, when a group went under the dynamic leadership of Mother Mary Sheldon.[41]

✠ Mary MacKillop and the Josephites

No account of the remarkable flowering of women's Catholic orders in the Australian colonies would be complete without an analysis of the work of Mary MacKillop and the Josephites.

The Order of the Sacred Heart of St Joseph had its origins in the largely Protestant state of South Australia where Mary, the offspring of a Highland Scots family, came from Melbourne to work as a governess in the small township of Penola. There she met an unusual English priest, Father Julian Tenison-Woods, who asked her to begin a school in his small country parish. He and his bishop, Patrick Geoghegan, were concerned lest the small number of Catholics in the state were swamped by the newly introduced secular education system.[42]

She responded immediately, gathering about her a group of women who were willing to work beyond the frontier if needed. As one who was Australian-born, she was proud of her land of birth and was free of the emotional baggage of the Old World carried about by many Catholics of her day:

Mary MacKillop, founder of the Order of St Joseph

> It is an Australian who writes this, one brought up in the midst of the evils she tries to describe. . . Australia is in every sense a dangerous place for Catholics; the poor and their children are torn away from the true faith.[43]

It is difficult to explain the rapid expansion of her work in the seven short years from 1866 in Penola to 1873 in Rome, except in terms of her magnetic leadership, her gifts of organisation and her ability to identify with the poor.

She trained her recruits like an army on the march, the experienced sisters taking charge of the novices. The sisters were to be mobile, as were the itinerant people to whom they were ministering. They were to travel and visit in twos and to be prepared to live away from convent support and the presence of the Reserved Sacrament, or the ministrations of the nearest priest.[44] Other orders would not countenance their sisters living in slab huts with hessian walls or going about begging in order to fund schools and orphanages.

The clerical hierarchy were uncomfortable with Mary MacKillop's unorthodox methods and unfaltering leadership. She was always softly-spoken with them and never bitter when she was excommunicated (by Adelaide) or expelled (by Queensland). But the bishops found that under her sweetness was a will that was diamond hard. One by one, all the colonies but Tasmania accepted the brown-habited Sisterhood of St Joseph. Even New Zealand invited them over. A novitiate was set up in Ireland to train new teachers, but Mary also recruited and trained her own. She always rejected government aid for her schools as part of her policy of living by faith.

No property should be owned by the order was her ardent belief. Indeed, she thoroughly endorsed the rule of poverty followed by St Francis and endorsed by Father Julian Tenison-Woods, with whom she founded the Josephite order. It was a rule which meant enormous hardship for her and her sisters, sleeping on plank beds with straw palliasses, eating bread and dripping — sometimes spread with molasses — wearing threadbare, faded habits and coping with primitive housing.[45] Mary MacKillop remained calm and forgiving during her numerous brushes with the hierarchy. Her sweet obduracy seemed to arouse the greater opposition, but it was nearly always the men who backed down in the end.

The first man to clash strongly with her was Father Julian Tenison-Woods, the mystical eccentric who co-founded her Order. It was he who had drawn up the Rule for the Order of St Joseph, naming her Mother Mary of the Cross. On his transfer to Adelaide as Director of Schools, he invited her to commence a series of schools there, which attracted large enrolments in a matter of months. Within five years, the number of her sisters had risen from ten to 124. An invitation to set up Josephite schools in Queensland followed and Mary left with some misgivings because of Woods' increasingly strange behaviour.

When she returned from Queensland in 1871, she found that Woods had suffered a nervous breakdown and was bankrupt. He had turned against her but, more alarmingly, he was influencing several of her more gullible Sisters of St Joseph's into strange behaviour and hallucinations. She begged him to exercise more restraint in the matter of false spirituality, fearing that it was bringing the order into bad odour with the bishops. However, his relations with Mary continued to deteriorate and he asked her to burn his letters to her.[46]

Her reply softened his bitterness for a little time:

> It is not the will of God. . . that I should burn your letters, Father. Do not ask it, but let us do the will of God — oh, the beautiful, wise will of God, my Father — and you are the only instrument, you know not for what![47]

Julian Tenison-Woods was never to be a support to Mary MacKillop again — in fact, she had only known his support for five brief years. However, she continued to refer to him as 'My first Father and teacher in the spiritual life'.[48]

A greater trial awaited MacKillop in the form of excommunication by the Bishop of Adelaide, Bishop L.B. Sheil in

1871. Within three months, he realised his mistake and sent a priest to absolve her of this edict.

His decision to take such a drastic step is explicable in the following terms. First, her association with Tenison-Woods, who was causing trouble in the order and was *persona non grata* in Adelaide anyway because of his debts. Second, the bishop doubted Mary's ability as Superior to control such a fast burgeoning order without episcopal oversight. Finally, he had to keep a hastily made promise to his advisers to excommunicate her or he would have lost face. Her reaction was to live quietly in virtual disguise while various newspapers took up her cause without her permission. She wrote:

> All I can say and the best I can say is that I have done my duty and the poor dear old bishop has made a terrible mistake. My cares are heavy and my responsibilities great. . . I would fairly sink under them, but for the treasured friends and advisers God has given me.[49]

Her next clash with episcopal authority was over the new rule of central government for the Order which the Pope had granted her following her journey to Rome in 1873. The brothers, Bishop James Quinn of Queensland and Bishop Matthew Quinn of Bathurst, had been brought up in the Irish tradition of tight episcopal control over all orders within each diocese. Irish dioceses like Cork and Waterford were small and isolated from the European tradition of transnational orders, like the Benedictines or the Franciscans. Their cultural background also prevented Irish clergy from attributing administrative skills or spiritual leadership to mere women. [Nor was it only Irish clergy who felt this way: the head of Propaganda and Abbot Gregory had both emphasised the weakness of women in dealing with the Charities].

Bishop James Quinn was violently opposed to the idea of

central government of Josephite institutions in Queensland from the Head House in Adelaide. Despite his attitude, Mary MacKillop went ahead in 1879 with the first meeting of the General Chapter in Brisbane, at which she was elected Superior-General of the order, and Sister Clare the Provincial for Queensland. In a fury, Quinn refused to recognise Sister Clare's appointment and offered to send back to Adelaide those sisters who wished to leave.

MacKillop returned to Brisbane to confront Bishop Quinn. She was made of sterner stuff than Mother Vincent Whitty and she called his bluff, pointing out that the sisters themselves had decided to accept central government. They would remain in his diocese for another year until he could make other arrangements for his schools.[50] Enraged, the bishop threatened her with the police and forcible detention in a convent. He called her an obstinate and ambitious woman. He thundered from the pulpit:

> You are aware that I am the ecclesiastical Superior and judge of the church and anything contrary to it is schism . . . It is impossible for me to accept the government of a woman or to have a community of nuns governed by a lady from Adelaide. I won't allow any woman to make a disturbance in my diocese.[51]

Mary's reaction to this episcopal onslaught was typically courageous and forgiving:

> No words can tell you what a time of suspense and trouble we have had here. The bishop is a terrible man to deal with and yet he can be frightened in the end (by fear of Rome). He is very good, though, and will get on well. . . God alone knows how hard I found it to be firm with him.[52]

The bishop's brother, Matthew Quinn of Bathurst, was even harder to deal with and Mary decided on a more concerted policy. She travelled vast distances each month visiting her convents in his diocese, encouraging her sisters with massive correspondence and detailed administrative instruction. Matthew Quinn was especially paranoid about central government and he told her he had consulted Rome about his rights and forbade her to visit her sisters at the Perthville Convent outside Bathurst. He insisted that she stay with his diocesan order, the Sisters of Mercy, instead. She tried to compromise with him, offering to allow a senior sister to remain behind to train his postulants, but her advisers suggested that she bring her sisters back to Adelaide.

By late 1879, MacKillop had withdrawn all her sisters who wished to leave from Queensland and Bathurst and brought them down to Sydney, where they received a cordial welcome from Archbishop Vaughan.[53]

The following year, encouraged by Vaughan's acceptance of the principle of central government, she moved the headquarters of the institute to Sydney. Finally, she made a clean break with Adelaide when Bishop Christopher Reynolds began to question her jurisdiction over her sisters and institutions, particularly in financial management. She moved her novitiate to Sydney in 1881 and that city has remained the home of the order.

Until full papal recognition of her Congregation's legal status occurred seven years later, MacKillop, by now tired and ill, had to deal with constant opposition to the Josephites from the majority of bishops.[54]

✠ The Catholic orders by 1900

Despite the difficulties encountered both within and without the church, vocations continued to increase in the colonial

Catholic Church. By 1900, nuns had become — among Catholic women — the largest single grouping in the census category 'professional class', with teachers a close second. For instance, the Josephites numbered 458 by that year.[55]

As with Protestant women missionaries, the nuns came to outnumber male religious and clergy by as much as 2:1 in Australian society.[56] Thus, their impact and role in the Australian Catholic Church has been integral in the life of that church and the country as a whole, especially through the education system which they spearheaded.

Orders catered for recruits from all strata of society: the Sisters of Charity and Presentation Sisters attracted middle class women because of the necessity for a dowry on entering; the Josephites and Mercies tended to comprise working class women and their vows were simpler as well; the Society of the Sacred Heart contained a number of upper class French women and its congregations were stratified in European style into choir and lay sisters. Whatever their vows or tradition, it was not difficult for orders to expand in this period because vocation was viewed by Catholic families as an honourable and fulfilling profession; it also meant economic security for single women.

✠ Reasons for the conflict between orders and hierarchy

Why was there hierarchical opposition to so many of the Catholic women's orders in Australia in the nineteenth century? First, it was at base a question of power. Male clergy felt ill at ease with a large body of professional women whose vocation and mandate were voluntary in origin and who could technically withdraw their labour if sufficiently provoked. Ownership of land and resources by these women posed a threat to the male hierarchy, especially if property had been acquired with the help of Protestants.

Second, the church naturally reflected contemporary society's attitudes towards women and authority. A traditional and symbolic monarch who was a woman did not offend them; nor did female leadership of an enclosed convent. However, once the women of the church went out into the marketplace and began running schools and hospitals as happened so conspicuously in the nineteenth century, then male prejudices were often aroused. In their view, women could not cope with financial affairs and administration as well as men. Neither should the orders own property; that should be the responsibility of the church.

Third, the early sisters clearly found the male hierarchy — whether English Benedictine or provincial Irish — to be frequently obscurantist and tyrannical. Churchmen like Dom Gregory and the Quinn brothers, for their part, often found Mother Superiors dragons who consciously or unconsciously undermined bishops and priests.

A modern commentator, Sister Anne McLay of the Mercy Order, believes that the actions of Gregory, Polding and the Quinns — amongst others — in harassing female orders illustrates Engels' premise of the subjugation of women as the first relationship of the oppressor to the oppressed in human society.[57]

Although male despotism appeared to be benevolent, it often proved restricting in practice for men like Polding or Tenison-Woods to write the constitutions of female orders. Their knowledge of ecclesiastical law was greater than the women's, but their writing of the rule gave them too great a proprietorial hold over the order. Nor was it just for bishops or their representatives to assume the role of Higher Superior of womens' orders. The invariable appointment of priests — usually Jesuits — as spiritual directors also reinforced the notion of female inferiority. It is axiomatic that conflict is necessary within a community or institution in order to achieve adjustment and progress. This was especially true of a transplanted church which had its roots in another hemisphere and other cultures. Moreover, a frontier church had its own peculiar stresses and vitality. This was particularly evident in the Sydney troubles encountered by the Sisters of Charity in the 1840s and 1850s.

Confrontation was also inevitable in that the orders quickly developed a high degree of professionalism in their work and 'maleness' in their organisation inasmuch as their relationship was with God, not with husband or father. This relationship gave them a freedom and autonomy which enabled them to rise to extraordinary heights of public service. However, in the process, their independent role cost religious women dearly in terms of health and anguish as they interacted with male authority.

5

Handmaids of the church
— and more

LAYWOMEN OF THE VICTORIAN ERA

'Still women exercise. . . the most tremendous direct
influence over children, husbands, lovers. . . ought we
not . . . to educate our rulers?'

C.H. Pearson, foundation Headmaster
of PLC Melbourne (1875)

'Fetters of iron, walls of stone, gates of brass might
be more easily broken down than to uproot established custom and popular prejudice. . . it must be
softened by current events and die out with the
passing generations.'

Reverend C.P. Wallace, Women's Franchise Paper (1894)

'Besides their other duties, women have now the
burden of the vote, as if wives and mothers had not
quite enough to do without that extra burden.'

Mrs H. Dangar, Vice-President of the
Sydney Mothers' Union (1903)

B Y THE CLOSE OF THE VICTORIAN ERA, women in the
church and beyond it had achieved a measure of emancipation
from previous restrictive roles and assumptions. Whilst re-

maining loyal to their churches, women like Caroline Chisholm, Mary Colton and Eliza Pottie played a wide-ranging part in philanthropic and even political activity.

A number of factors contributed to the changing status and role of women over this period. First, the Victorian practice of philanthropy, which arose out of evangelical motivation as well as the doctrine of the 'woman's sphere', gave middle class women confidence in their ability to handle public life.

Second, the infiltration of first wave feminism into the country after 1870, mainly from the USA, was warmly embraced by many churchwomen, because the feminists supported temperance and the goal of purifying society.

Finally, the growth of education for women in the last quarter of the nineteenth century was responsible for motivating them towards undertaking an active role outside the church. The church's response to this enlarged role for

Master of all he surveys. The traditional role of the laywoman:
Exeter Anglican Parish, NSW

women was not only to found orders to occupy the single woman, but also auxiliaries and devotional bodies like the Mothers' Union which occupied married women mainly at parish level, without embracing too many radical ideas.

Our study must of necessity concentrate on the middle and upper classes in the Australian colonies as it was they who were released by education and economic security to pursue a reasonably independent role in society. Women of all classes were, of course, welcome to enter the pew and contribute to the collection plate, but many of the lower classes chose not to for a variety of social and personal reasons. Others were quite happy to occupy a pew on Sundays, but saw their role as spectator and helpmeet to their husband or father within a narrow congregational context.

A small but active elite — perhaps as small as two per cent of laywomen — went beyond this role and involved themselves in programs of philanthropy and social reform. They were, of course, free to pursue this role because of the ready availability of domestic servants at that time for those who could afford them.

These women were motivated by the church's teaching, but also by the Victorian concept of the 'woman's sphere'. This concept was based, first, on the notion that the private or domestic sphere was the domain of the woman and the public sphere was the province of the man. Its corollary was the obligation of the fortunate woman to extend her influence beyond the home in order to minister to less fortunate women and children. In practice, there was a strong element of condescension in Victorian philanthropy, but — as we have seen — such governors' wives as Jane Franklin and bishops' wives as Frances Perry carried out sterling work for the distressed and needy in accordance with their religious duty as they saw it.

As the century progressed, an increasing number of married women — especially of Non-conformist denominations — began to involve themselves in active philanthropy outside their local congregations.

The single woman was in a more anomalous position: the doctrine of separate spheres had kept her enchained in another's household where she was usually expected to devote herself to the care of elderly relatives.[1] However, if she were a bold spirit, she had greater options: she could insist on joining an order or serving as a missionary overseas.

The church's attitude to the single woman was at best paradoxical. On the one hand, she was treated with condescension by many in the church at home because she had not 'achieved' the married state; on the other, she was able as time went on to receive education at the hands of the church, which liberated her into a life of professional fulfilment and service. For it was not only parish activities like Sunday school teaching and ladies' auxiliaries which increased the confidence of women, but increased professional opportunities were to be found through orders, church schools and hospitals (which were either run by the churches or had religious origins) and later through missionary training colleges.

The Victorian era was one of unparalleled expansion for the British church. The evangelical revival of the late eighteenth century, the spread of Wesleyanism, the fervour of the Tractarians, the labours of Catholic orders all contributed to the growth of congregations and religious practice. Secular factors also facilitated the growth of the church in Australia; increased wealth and population after the 1850s and the increased gentrification of colonial society led to a dramatic increase in church attendance.[2] New churches were built, devotional literature flourished, religious societies were founded and missionaries were sent out. In all these endeavours, women began to play an increasingly active role.

However, it took some decades to overcome male prejudice as to female competence in administration and financial matters. After all, women were excluded from even attending Bible Society annual general meetings in Britain until 1831. The same applied with early Church Missionary Society annual general meetings.

This prohibition did not apply in the Australian colonies where there was greater social elasticity and informality: indeed, Ann Marsden commented on the cooperation between the sexes in the parish branch of the Bible Society in Parramatta as early as 1820. However, despite the superiority of the women in fundraising for this branch, they had no say in the ultimate disbursement of funds at headquarters.

Not surprisingly, it was the Church of England which was the most conservative in its attitude to women playing an active role in the church. A church associated with government and

*Bible study group, St Andrew's Anglican Church,
Summer Hill, NSW, c.1900*

the upper classes is usually the last to disturb the *status quo* and, although the Anglican Church had been disestablished in New South Wales in 1826, it still retained its association with the ruling classes until well into the twentieth century.

An English cleric writing at the beginning of the Victorian age expressed his fear of 'amazonian women who challenge attention and put us upon our defence' and of 'the evils and inconveniences of ladies' associations'.[3] This attitude carried over to Australia where no independent women's organisations existed in Anglican parishes until the 1880s.[4] Women were allowed to clean and decorate the church, teach Sunday school and run fetes and bazaars. However, once they had raised their funds for parish and missions, they were not allowed to disburse them as they saw fit.

Thus, a dichotomy often arose between the role expected of women within the church and the role which the woman of spirit adopted outside the church. The active and intelligent woman often became frustrated by limited opportunities within her church, while at the same time she was privately motivated by the church's teachings to go out into the world and play a more challenging role in society.

The laywoman who chose to serve within the parish framework was usually a married woman of modest education who closely identified herself and her family with her local church. Clergy coming from England to Australia in this period found that Anglican women in the colonies supported their parishes much more vigorously than Englishwomen. Parishes in England were generally more heavily endowed and better furnished because of their older foundations, whereas in Australia clergy stipends were poor and churches were new or makeshift.

Ada Cambridge, wife of the Anglican minister, the Reverend George Cross, was slightly dismayed — if somewhat gratified — at the enthusiasm of the women in the various country parishes to which her husband was posted in Victoria in the 1870s and 1880s.[5]

Sometimes, the established laity in a parish were in a position to intimidate the clergyman and his wife. This was especially the case when the incumbent was new and when the wives and maiden sisters of the most influential laymen in the parish were in charge of functions and groups. If the minister continued to preach unacceptably or to tamper with the liturgy or the church furniture, powerful laywomen often marched their children off to the nearest Wesleyan chapel.[6]

⚑ Opportunities for service within the church

One of the chief social outlets for the laywoman who wished to serve only within her local church was the fete or bazaar. For many, these were an absorbing escape from domestic ennui. Women found companionship and confidence as a result of engaging in fetes and jumble sales. In addition, their household routine was not threatened by periodic Saturdays behind a stall.

By 1880, most churches were holding their own fetes to help with building programs, but their income was modest besides that of the large missionary and church societies. For instance, the Church Missionary Society received 28 000 pounds in England in 1900 — many millions of dollars in today's terms — from the proceeds of fetes and sales of work alone.[7]

The church fete in Australia was necessarily less ambitious, but it was not only helpful to parishes and missions, but also a significant event in the calendar of rural areas in particular. Bazaars were central in funding the expansion of the Catholic Church throughout Australia, although at times they were criticised for their emphasis on raffles and art unions.[8]

Catholic fundraising, 1883

Allied to the fete was the ladies' auxiliary or, as it was known in some parishes, the women's association or the guild of service. Its function was purely fundraising as distinct from such devotional bodies as the Mothers' Union. The auxiliary system arose out of the Victorian era and its leaders were forerunners of the modern organisational woman.

Despite male misgivings — 'for the cure of every sorrow. . . there are patrons, vice-presidents and secretaries. For the diffusion of every blessing. . . there is a committee'[9]— women were not slow to prove their competence. A ladies' auxiliary was formed in 1870 to raise funds for the Sydney City Mission which had fallen on hard times financially. However, it was to be some time before the ladies were allowed full autonomy as the Reverend Mr Webb was given 'special charge of the Ladies' Auxiliary'.[10] The more conservative Benevolent Society, half of whose members were women anyway, allowed a ladies' committee to be founded in 1879, but it was to be at all times subject to a male executive.[11]

Parish auxiliaries in general suffered the same fate: the clergyman was always present at meetings ready to exercise the veto and with one eye on the afternoon tea to come. All funds raised were to be submitted to the male parish council for their imprimatur on disbursement. It was not till 1921 that women were permitted to join parish councils in Australia and, in practice, few women were elected to that position until well after World War II.

Nineteenth century women in the mainstream churches were reticent about speaking in public or chairing meetings so that they did not resent male domination of these roles, but usually welcomed it. They felt happier expressing their philanthropic role in less structured terms: calling in on neighbours in distress, providing Sunday dinners for the bereaved or for deprived children, giving free or reduced lodging to needy friends, or taking in their washing or cooking for them. This was a pattern of caring which was particularly prevalent in rural areas and in such churches as the Methodist, Baptist and Presbyterian.

One son of a Methodist family in Gilgandra, western New South Wales, recalls a network of pastoral care in which his mother was a leader. She did not wait for direction from the minister — whose tenure was brief in accordance with Methodist polity anyway — but immediately swung into action with her team of fellow laywomen, demonstrating practical help the moment a bereavement or an accident occurred.

Help was particularly directed at church members, but it was not always confined to them, for to help those on the periphery was to these women a form of practical evangelism more potent than preaching.[12]

The pastoral strategy of the Salvation Army, which was possibly to excel all others in its speed and universality, will be looked treated later in the next chapter.

No barrier was ever placed in the way of the woman who wished to cook, sew or clean for her local church but, when it came to speaking or administration, she kept or was kept well in the background. This was particularly so in a Nonconformist church like the Baptist Church which generally found its adherents amongst lower middle and working class families. No reference is made in nineteenth century Baptist publications to women except in terms of a feminine ideal of 'shrinking, delicate modesty'. One woman was permitted in the *Baptist Magazine* of 1859 to contribute a poem entitled 'A Mother's Sacrifice', but this contribution was exceptional.[13] The Baptist Ladies' Melbourne and Suburban City Mission held its second annual meeting in 1892, which was chaired by a male judge who congratulated the ladies on their work. Although nine other men spoke during the course of the evening, there is no record that even one woman replied.[14]

The chief reasons for the reluctance of the majority of laywomen to speak in public were societal expectation and lack of education. Despite the advent of first wave feminism into Australia in the 1860s, women were still cast well and truly into a submissive role in society and only a few of the smaller churches such as the Quakers, the Congregationalists and certain of the Methodists were prepared ideologically to endorse a reversal of that role. Most women were too afraid to speak out in public or chair meetings for fear of being laughed to scorn. The attitude of the male dominated press, led by the widely read *Bulletin*, which derided temperance ladies and female philanthropists, further discouraged women from public speaking. Moreover, until women were admitted to tertiary education in the 1880s, they were generally not prepared at school level for debate, oratory or administration.[15]

✠ Opportunities for service outside the church

Turning to those hardy and more adventurous souls who were prepared to go outside parish and denominational boundaries to achieve social reform as an expression of their faith, we are confronted by an inspiring roll call of women. Four of these outstanding laywomen have been selected for particular treatment — Caroline Chisholm, Lady Marian Allen, Eliza Pottie and Mary Colton. These women went beyond the traditional philanthropic role into traditionally masculine spheres of politics and administration.

The practice of philanthropy in Australia, as we have seen, had largely been the province of governors' wives and leading women of colonial society. Such women had been imbued from childhood with the Victorian concept of charity for the needy and especially for women and children. The great model for philanthropic women of middle and upper classes was Countess Angela Burdett-Coutts, the fervent English evangelical, who gave over a million pounds to charity in the first half of the nineteenth century.

One of her most significant acts of charity as far as Australia was concerned, was to help endow the See of Adelaide in 1847, 'in the hope that the presence of a bishop would be instrumental in suppressing irreligion and promoting unity in the Province of South Australia'.[16] There was no woman of comparable wealth in the colonies, but many shared the Countess' evangelical motivation. Not only must an attempt be made to redeem the soul at the same time as reclaiming the body, but — they firmly believed — the injunction of Christ must be heeded: 'Inasmuch as you have done it unto the least of these my brethren, you have done it unto me.'[17]

Caroline Chisholm

Foremost amongst the great evangelical philanthropists of the Victorian era was, of course, Caroline Chisholm. A convert to Roman Catholicism at marriage, she led the way in assuming a role which exceeded that which church and society had assigned her. Her audacity and reforming drive were the more remarkable in one who was ostensibly an obscure military wife. Her life has been well dealt with in no less than four biographies,[18] so that detail is not needed here; but there are four principal aspects of her work which were to influence society and the public-spirited women who came after her.

First, she played a political role in both Britain and Australia when she lobbied governments on behalf of women in general and migrant families in particular. Pamphlets and letters, especially to the Colonial Secretary, poured from her pen as she laid down a policy of family migration and employment for single women before marriage. Women, she argued, would be the leaven to raise the quality of society and they would act as 'God's police' to improve the morality of the population.[19]

Second, Chisholm was not afraid to innovate and act alone if need be. For instance, in 1841 she was virtually single-handed in her rescue of young female immigrants off the streets and in the opening of a female immigrants' home for 600 in Sydney.

Third, she showed great courage and initiative by taking her girls on the empty bullock drays returning from the port to the bush. Once in the country, she set up employment centres where she had great success in finding work for both men and women.

Finally, she was willing to break with convention by accepting help from other denominations in her work: the Anglican bishop, W.G. Broughton, although fiercely anti-Roman Catholic in outlook, secretly supported her work, as did the Presbyterian leader, Dr John Dunmore Lang.[20]

For raw courage and burning vision, as well as intellectual toughness, Chisholm was a fine example to the later Victorian philanthropists. As a devout member of her church, she was a frequent communicant at Mass when in Sydney, but such regularity was impossible on her travels into the country. We are afforded one glimpse into her spiritual journey:

> During the season of Lent (1841), I suffered much; but on the Easter Sunday I was enabled, at the altar of our Lord, to make an offering of my talents to the God who gave them. I promised to know neither country nor creed, but to try to serve all justly and impartially. I asked only to be enabled to keep these poor girls from being tempted, by their need, to mortal sin; and resolved that, to accomplish this, I would in every way sacrifice my feelings, surrender all comfort. . . but wholly devote myself to the work I had in hand. . .[21]

Chisholm's helpers in early orders like the Sisters of Charity were prepared to seek help from Protestant businessmen, but it was rare for the reverse to occur. Sectarian bigotry generally prevented Protestant philanthropists from approaching Roman Catholics for support. It must also be pointed out that Chisholm could not have achieved her magnificent feats without the unfailing support of her long-suffering husband, Archibald. His patience and steady backing, both at family and public level, illustrate the third-wave feminist viewpoint that men generally play a significant role in the achievement of great women.

By the more prosperous late nineteenth century, almost every denomination had its benefactress who donated generously to needy causes in the capital cities and who had been admitted to a seat on various boards in order to help those less fortunate than herself.

Mary Cowper, second wife of the Very Reverend W.M. Cowper, Dean of Sydney, was a member of five different boards, including Sydney Hospital and the YWCA. Helen Hunter Baillie, wife of the wealthy Presbyterian merchant, John Hunter Baillie, was a generous philanthropist — as was Louisa Ardill, an ardent Baptist. Euphemia Bridges-Bowes was one of a number of Methodist activists in the country; she combined the raising of eleven children with running a sizeable ladies' college from her own home.

All of these women were devout churchgoers, but each of them — with the possible exception of Mary Cowper who had extra duties as Dean's wife — found that their local church gave them insufficient outlet for their talents and energies. All of them had supportive husbands who shared a similar spiritual and entrepreneurial viewpoint.[22]

Lady Marian Allen

Lady Marian Allen, wife of Sir George Wigram Allen, a prominent Sydney lawyer and politician, was the colonies' nearest counterpart to Baroness Burdett-Coutts. She was a Methodist of Quaker background and her strong evangelical convictions, allied to the reformist independence of the Quakers, led her to devote all her time to an abundance of charities in New South Wales. These included the State Children's Relief Board, the Children's Hospital, the Society for the Relief of Destitute Children, the Benevolent Society, the Sydney Female Rescue Society, the Sydney Female Mission Home and the Sydney Servants' Home.

Although the mother of ten children, she was able to call upon substantial domestic help to enable her to pursue an independent philanthropic role — and perhaps also to provide her with an avenue of escape from the home! She was also so famous for her personal generosity that, when her husband died, she was, reputedly, driven from her mansion in Glebe by importunate beggars.[23]

Eliza Pottie

One of the most remarkable of the evangelical women philanthropists was Eliza Pottie. A relative of Marian Allen's, her background was also Quaker, so that she was sometimes known as the Australian Elizabeth Fry. She brought up six children, wrote poetry and plied premiers and newspapers with letters agitating for social reform. Her husband was a Scot, but she would not attend the Presbyterian church because of its conservatism. Instead, she went to the Wesleyan church on Sunday mornings at Bondi Junction in Sydney's east.

In the afternoon, she would coax young relatives along to the more unusual Quaker-style meetings at the Unitarian Church in Oxford Street. They found such services excruciatingly dull with their emphasis on meditation, but she seemed to receive from them extra motivation for her week of zealous good works.[24]

Eliza was unable to confine herself to specific church activities, despite an active role serving on the committees of the Sydney Women's Prayer Union and the Sydney Ladies United Evangelical Association. She constantly agitated for prison reform and for improvements in women's working conditions. She campaigned against the Contagious Diseases

Acts, which were demeaning to women in their policy of testing women only and protecting promiscuous men. Nor was she a theoretical reformer; she took needy children into her home for holidays and baked sponge cakes for long-term inmates of asylums and similar institutions. She served on twelve of Sydney's charitable committees.

A *sine qua non* for such relentless activity was a tolerant family plus domestic help — and Eliza was fortunate in possessing both. She was never still and, whenever she had a spare afternoon, she would visit the slum areas with 'a tin of bulls eyes under her arm which she would distribute freely along with her tracts of religious import'.[25]

One of the issues which she took up with the government was that of conditions at the government asylum for the aged and insane at Newington on the Parramatta River. She had been appointed to a government board which was to make recommendations on conditions at Newington.

When she and her friends stepped off the boat laden with sponge cakes for the inmates, she was horrified at the situation which confronted her. Apart from the general squalor, cancer patients, the blind and the insane were lumped together. They were inadequately fed and cared for. Patients were being denied milk and other nutritious food, while money was diverted into huge liquor purchases made on behalf of corrupt staff. She was appalled to see patients dying without privacy in the middle of wards, quite unable to brush clouds of flies from their faces. At the enquiry in September 1886, she was eloquent in her criticism of conditions there and this led to government reform of management at Newington.[26]

Eliza Pottie's social conscience did not stop at asylum and prison reform. She was an ardent member of the Women's Christian Temperance Union and of its associated body, the Franchise League. As President of the League in the 1890s, she made a number of telling speeches in favour of women's suffrage:

> . . .her pen and voice [were] always ready. . . in the cause of peace, temperance and purity. . . her public addresses were always a treat to listen to.[27]

She did not wait for her own church to occupy or encourage her; she played every role open to her — evangelist, social agitator, practical social worker, political debater and organiser. The last role was the most daring for a laywoman of her day, yet she appeared to attract nothing but praise from her family and the public for her 'sound judgment and tender heart [which] were on the side of the helpless and downtrodden'.[28]

Mary Colton

Almost as versatile in her expression of the laywoman's role as Eliza Pottie was Mary Colton. This Adelaide philanthropist and suffragist was also a Wesleyan Methodist. Mother of nine children, she taught Sunday school all her life and, with the help of copious domestic assistance, she was able to undertake an astonishing range of philanthropic and reformist activity.

She founded the Pirie Street Church's Dorcas Society, was Vice-President of the Nursing Sisters' Association of South Australia and treasurer of the Maternity Relief Association, which worked for poor city mothers.

Her husband's business prospered and he was elected Mayor of Adelaide in 1874. Before long, he was Premier of South Australia. This promotion served only to accelerate the work of Lady Colton (as she became) in both philanthropy and social reform. She worked on behalf of the deaf, dumb and blind, the homeless, new immigrants, elderly destitute people and incurables, setting up funds and housing for all these people. In 1879, she began city clubs for young country women and working girls until, in 1884, they merged into the South Australian YWCA of which she remained president until her death.

She was one of the founders of the Adelaide Children's Hospital, which opened in 1876, and she served on the new State Children's Council from 1886. This latter body was particularly concerned with orphans and neglected children.

Finally, she followed a similar pattern to Eliza Pottie and other articulate laywomen in adopting a political role. She founded the Social Purity Society to protect young people and to raise the age of consent. She joined the WCTU and presided over the Women's Suffrage League from its inception in 1892. Within two years, with her political contacts and tactful, friendly manner, she was able to overcome strong opposition and — in cooperation with such activists as Mary Lee and Catherine Helen Spence — bring about female suffrage before any other state in Australia.

Her final post was, significantly, a church one — that of foundation president of the Women's Methodist Auxiliary of Foreign Missions in South Australia.[29]

In conclusion, it must again be pointed out that Marian Allen, Eliza Pottie and Mary Colton — like Caroline Chisholm — were also assisted to a greater or lesser degree by husbands who pursued busy careers, but provided moral and financial support for their frenetically active wives and tolerated their absences and preoccupation.

It is difficult to quantify denominational involvement of women in organisations outside the church, but it appears that Congregationalists and Wesleyans led the way in female involvement in causes and social issues beyond local boundaries. Reformist activism among Methodists was probably influenced by Susannah Wesley's advanced views on the role of women and also by the Arminian emphasis on free will and good works. The Quaker influence on Marian Allen and Eliza Pottie also served to increase their social conscience.

✠ Changes in the later nineteenth century

However, it was not long before more conservative churches like the Anglicans and the Presbyterians began founding organisations specifically for women. The Mothers' Union and the Girls' Friendly Society were established partly in response to perceived social problems and partly as a reaction to such militant Christian organisations for women as the WCTU and the YWCA.

The Anglican Mothers' Union, the Presbyterian Women's Association and, later, the Catholic Women's League, saw as their chief objective the preservation of the family. To many clergy and laywomen, the social and legislative changes which were occurring in the late nineteenth century were a threat to the sanctity of the family. They were alarmed at the passing between 1858 and 1893 of a series of divorce Acts in the colonies. The first Act allowed adultery as the ground for divorce and the last Acts were to allow desertion, cruelty and drunkenness as sufficient grounds for divorce.

Anglican and Catholic bishops reacted angrily to this legislation, ignoring the social evils of domestic violence and deserted wives. They regarded marriage as a sacrament and threatened to defrock clergy found re-marrying divorced persons.

Legislation was also passed at this time to protect the economic rights of women. The Married Women's Property Acts passed in Victoria in 1870 and in NSW in 1879 allowed women to retain their property and earnings after marriage instead of the husband automatically receiving them.

Finally, there was another cause for alarm on the part of government and churches and that was the declining birthrate of the 1880s. Between 1886 and 1901, the birthrate in the colonies declined by one third. Families of three were now more customary than the traditional eight or ten. Fearful of Asian immigration and economic decline, the NSW government held a royal commission on the 'Decline of the Birth Rate and on Mortality of Infants'. The government was surprised to learn that it was prosperity and education that were inclining women towards birth control. Although many of the clergy were implacably opposed to contraception and abortion, it was obvious that most laywomen were ambivalent about birth control and felt that family limitation enabled them to do more for their family and church, not less.[30]

The Mothers' Union

Whatever their views on birth control, most practising Anglican laywomen were happy to support the formation of the Mothers' Union in their parishes in the 1890s. It had been first established in 1876 by Mary Sumner, a clergyman's wife in the Diocese of Winchester. Fourteen years later, it was founded in the Tasmanian parish of Cullenswood by Mary L'Hoste, wife of the vicar. 'It is the essential society in every parish,' she proclaimed and, before long, it had spread to the mainland. It was soon under vice-regal patronage, becoming part of the trappings of empire as branches also sprang up in India, Gibraltar, Malta, Canada and South Africa.

Its aims were threefold: first, to uphold the sanctity of marriage; second, to awaken in mothers of all classes a sense of their responsibilities in training their children; and, third, to organise bands of mothers to unite in prayer and seek by their own example to lead their families in purity and holiness of life.

Ruth Teale argues that in practice most Mothers' Union branches became social clubs in the parishes, which was, perhaps, what Anglican parishes needed at that time.[31] The prohibition on membership of divorcees — but not of single women — was not as noticeable as in later years when divorce was more common. There was a strong element of spirituality and worship in most meetings and some attempt was made to promote social welfare in the wider community. The Mothers' Union was as interested as the WCTU in cleansing society of all that threatened the sanctity of family life, but it was not as open and crusading as the latter body and certainly did not press for women's suffrage. In fact, some of its members regarded the extension of the franchise to women as a burden on wives and mothers, as the statement by a Mothers' Union office-bearer at the beginning of this chapter indicates.[32]

To be fair to the clergy, this condescending attitude towards the role of women was uttered by a woman office-bearer. However, it reflected the conservative standpoint of many members of the Church of England, especially in the realm of gender equality. As an episcopal church, they were naturally influenced by such pronouncements as that uttered in 1888 by the haughty Archbishop of Melbourne, the Right Reverend Field Flowers Goe in relation to the question of female suffrage:

> Many persons thought it was desirable that women should
> have been trusted with political power and that they should
> have the privilege of voting and even sitting in Parliament.
> I have not much sympathy with ideas of that kind. I
> believe that men and women should always work on
> parallel lines, the great virtue of parallel lines being that
> they never crossed one another.[33]

Moreover, Anglicans lagged behind Nonconformists in introducing equal opportunities for women in the sphere of education, apart from Jane Barker's foundation of St Catherine's in 1856.[34] In the meantime, they embraced the Mothers' Union as an instrument for uplifting society from the grass-roots or parish level. Members were asked to supply teachers and funds for teaching scripture in state schools as early as 1899.

Branches grew rapidly and, by 1900, it was thriving in all states except Queensland, which was to follow in 1904. The Milton (Queensland) branch of the Mothers' Union was responsible for starting the first branch of the District Nursing Association of Australia.[35]

Members of the Mothers' Union saw themselves as 'handmaids of the church', while not being a fundraising body. They also regarded themselves as a voice speaking on behalf of the home as well as women in the church.

When Queen Victoria died in 1901, the Mothers' Union, along with most of Australian society, mourned deeply and vowed to set their face — in accordance with the royal example — against anything 'that either directly or indirectly [might] interfere with the sanctity of marriage'. In the same year, Archbishop Saumarez Smith of Sydney told the Annual General Meeting of the Mothers' Union that the Christian ideal of family life was basic to social welfare and 'true national progress'. Archdeacon William Gunther of Parramatta followed this up with the statement that 'in the association of the Christian home, the mother is the morning and evening star and the home should be an earthly paradise'.[36]

Bishops' wives were normally patronesses of the Mothers' Union in each diocese and so the organisation remained as conservative in its policy as the hierarchy itself. Clergy wives often discovered that presidency of the Mothers' Union in their parish was another expectation in their brief. Of the twenty-nine branch presidents in the Sydney Diocese in 1902, eighteen were clergy wives and eleven were laywomen. By

1912, the fifty-six branches in Sydney were presided over by twenty-four clergy wives as opposed to thirty-two laywomen.

The Mothers' Union was entirely different in emphasis to the WCTU which sought to cleanse society by frontal attack; the former somehow hoped to influence the community from its diffuse base in the parishes. One or two delightful if impractical gestures were made, such as sending posies to factory girls in 1903, an echo of the Women's Christian Temperance Union Flower Mission of the 1890s which presented posies and Bible texts to inmates of hospitals and asylums.[37]

The Girls' Friendly Society
The Mothers' Union was, however, most supportive of another Anglican body which was more practical in intent, the Girls' Friendly Society (GFS). This organisation, which began in England in 1874 two years before the Mothers' Union, was designed to support girls working in the city far from their homes.

In its country of origin, the GFS was based on a sharply stratified social structure, whereby the upper-class 'associate' (who was usually older) administered the Society's projects for the benefit of the young working-class 'member'. A whole network of incentives and benefits for members were established from rewards for thrift to training schemes and employment registries. Hostels were built and groups were formed mainly in the parishes to give moral and spiritual assistance to students, factory and office workers.

Like the Mothers' Union, the GFS spread quickly around the empire, the first Australian group starting in Adelaide in 1879. It was particularly effective on the Western Australian goldfields in the 1880s in giving shelter to single girls and encouraging them in habits of thrift, temperance, faithfulness to employers and purity of life, as well as in religious practice.

GFS hostels played an invaluable role in accommodating young women immigrants and country girls seeking employment or education in the cities.

The Australian GFS was a more egalitarian body than its English parent and it was certainly not as elaborate in its organisation, thus reflecting the colonies' smaller population and fluid class structure.[38] Both the GFS and the Mothers' Union displayed the conservatism and political quietism of the Anglican Church at the time. Although some branches were innovative and reforming, most were timid on social issues apart from general strictures on divorce, intemperance and 'impurity'. At this stage, they preferred to reserve enthusiasm — outside specifically spiritual matters, that is — for empire, pageantry and the royal family.

The Women's Christian Temperance Union

For many laywomen of the late Victorian church, especially those of non-Anglican and non-Catholic persuasion, the only way to express a dynamic social conscience was to join the Women's Christian Temperance Union (WCTU). This body, which has been well documented and researched by historians, began in Australia in 1882. Its origins were in the United States, where American women had banded together to fight the liquor traffic in 1874. By 1884, there were 200 000 women members worldwide, all pledged to total abstinence.

Alcoholism was a particular problem in the Australian colonies, where men exceeded women numerically and public houses were often their chief social outlet. Australian churchwomen were opposed to the ready availability of liquor even in hospitals and the fact that it could be purchased at any hour of the day even by children. They often worked with a clergyman to help strengthen their temperance organisation and contacts.

In the case of the WCTU in Victoria, a group of Quaker and Baptist ladies combined with a Congregational minister in 1887 to found the first state-wide branch. It swiftly set about winning converts to temperance, visiting prisons, factories and churches and administering the pledge. The temperance movement soon joined forces with the Women's Suffrage Movement, counting on the female vote as a means of achieving their aims politically: 'To gain victory over the giant, drink, we must have womanhood suffrage.'[39]

It was a period of great buoyancy and fervour for the temperance churchwomen. These Protestant housewives, aged mainly from thirty to fifty, were motivated by an evangelical faith allied with a feminist outlook. They felt that they were peculiarly suited to solving social problems because of their humane and domestic skills. They adopted the emblem of a white ribbon and published their own journal in which they dreamed of the day when 'we shall yet see the *White Ribbon Signal* soaring over the ruined temples of Bacchus'.[40]

Yet they were totally practical in their work for underprivileged women and children when the depression of the 1890s broke. They also demanded a series of reforms which were revolutionary in their day, but are now accepted as basic to the fabric of modern society. First, they asked for equal pay for women — as it was low wages which drove women to immorality. Second, they proposed the introduction of female factory inspectors to protect women workers. Third, they asked for increased career prospects for girls which would promote self-reliance and ultimately 'social purity'. Fourth, they advocated that the age of consent for girls should be raised to sixteen years. Fifth, there should be a program of rehabilitation of female prisoners. Sixth, they saw the need for a children's court, offering themselves as voluntary probation officers. Seventh, there should be supervised playgrounds for inner city children. Lastly, there should be a free kindergarten movement in inner city suburbs.[41]

It was a mouthwatering program of reform which reflected the infectious enthusiasm of WCTU members, whether religious like Mary Colton and Eliza Pottie or humanist like Rose Macaulay and Vida Goldstein. However, the churchwomen who framed it were not primarily thinking of a utopia on earth, purer and fairer though they wanted the world to be. Their chief motivation was eschatological: they wished to help usher in the millennium and hasten the return of the Redeemer to the world.

Doctrines of the 'better time to be' were extremely popular at the close of the century, with evangelical clergymen and women being encouraged in their programs of reform by the current theological emphasis on the second coming of Christ.[42]

The women's suffrage movement

It is clear that women would not have received the vote so early in Australia had it not been for the work of the WCTU and its attendant Suffrage Leagues. 'The women's vote will enable the sacred influences of home to exert their refining, purifying power in the elections, on parliament, on law and the executive,' wrote the Reverend J.C. Kirkby, a Congregational minister, in the *Adelaide Advertiser* on 2 February 1891.[43]

The ubiquitous Eliza Pottie turned up as a member of the Council of Womanhood Suffrage to a meeting chaired by the Premier of NSW nine years later, which was preparing for the vote for women across the Commonwealth.[44] By the close of the century, the cause of the franchise for women had become acceptable to the majority; in Perth the Women's Franchise League received vice-regal patronage at their annual meeting in 1899.[45] Thus, in every state, active laywomen, principally from the various Non-conformist churches, had provided the chief impetus for female suffrage in the colonies.

Herein possibly lies the reason for the delay in granting this reform in Britain and Europe. Established churches were not as interested in upsetting the social *status quo* as were the more democratic congregations from the Dissenting churches.

Further impetus to the cause of the women's vote was supplied by two other church bodies which appeared in the 1890s. One was the quaintly named Labour Church, the other the Women's Social and Political Crusade.

The Labour Church was a *fin de siecle* organisation — made up of Christians, socialists and feminists — which had been founded by the Reverend Archibald Turnbull. It was centred in Melbourne and was intended to allow workers to meet in a spirit of comradeship and ventilate their wrongs. Out of this church came the Women's Social and Political Crusade. Its leader and first president was the Christian socialist, Jean Beadle, who proposed a series of reforms similar to those put forward by the WCTU.[46] She spoke of:

> Justice for all. Our aim is to labour for a higher moral
> life for all, believing that in the diffusion of love and justice
> we are fulfilling the true function of human beings and
> serving the highest ideals of Christ and humanity.[47]

The loose structure, imprecise theology and mixed membership of the Labour Church ensured that it did not survive long into the new century; but Jean Beadle herself continued to promote her brand of Christian labour relations for another two decades.

Catherine Helen Spence

Another controversial figure and a towering reformer in this period was Catherine Helen Spence of South Australia. She took a different religious path, rejecting the predestinarian doctrines of her Calvinist upbringing and finally becoming a preacher in the Unitarian Church. This was a rationalist but socially reformist body, which chiefly originated in the city of Birmingham where Owenite socialism and feminism were also strongest.

The Owenites denied the concept of separate spheres for men and women and much of Spence's life embodied their ideology. She earned her living by her pen and in the process brought up three families of orphaned children. As she wrote in the *Adelaide Advertiser*:

> No one has gone out of the woman's sphere more than I have during the last twelve years and yet I believe I am as womanly as ever.[48]

Spence worked not only for the WCTU and women's suffrage, but she founded with Emily Clark the Boarding Out Society for housing orphaned and destitute children in private homes, was a member of the State Children's Council from 1886, and helped to establish kindergartens and high schools for girls. However, her theological unorthodoxy and her abrasive manner meant that mainstream churches were distinctly wary of her. The Adelaide branch of the Mothers' Union in 1906 declined a request by the National Council of Women, of which they were a member, to subscribe to a fund to establish a Catherine Helen Spence Scholarship.[49]

The achievement of female suffrage was as much due to the work of spiritual laywomen as to any other factor. Had these women not been prepared to move outside local church boundaries to serve God and their fellows, the franchise might have been delayed much longer. Although they failed to pressurise governments into legislating for temperance, these mainly middle aged married women, who were determined to devote their leisure time to helping the less fortunate, helped to create a fairer society by the close of the Victorian era.

The single woman

The single woman of the Victorian church faced a more difficult situation in life than her married sister. Ignominy and a strong sense of failure was frequently attached to the unmarried woman in Australia's chauvinist society. If they stayed at home, single women were financially dependent on the family and were obliged to play the role of drudge or at least carer of elderly relatives. Without education, the single woman was trapped.

Writing to her father at the age of twenty-five, seven years before her unexpected marriage to a Presbyterian clergyman, Clarinda (Menie) Parkes confided:

> If I go on as I am now doing, I shall be that most useless of all beings, a middle-aged woman, dangling about her parents' home and acting as a foil to her growing brothers and sisters. . .[50]

She pleaded with her father for an opportunity to study for a career so that she could be released from the benevolent prison walls of home. Her frustration mirrored that of such notable single women in England as Florence Nightingale and Clara Lucas Balfour, who chafed under the restrictions of a male-dominated society and the tyranny of over-conscientious filial piety.

Some single women managed to escape by entering orders. A few managed to find employment in the secular world, but the majority remained at home, at least till the 1890s. The emphasis on motherhood in Australian society militated against the single woman in that she was often depicted as a frustrated spinster or only half a woman.[51]

The church could be as insensitive as the outside world in its idealising of motherhood and the home, although the single woman was not excluded from any society — even the Mothers'

Union. By the 1880s, enterprising single women were beginning to go off as missionary nurses and teachers to the outback or else overseas, often relying on their own private means.

Education was the key to fulfilment for unmarried women and they thronged to the great hospitals and later colleges and universities to obtain training for a career. Before the arrival of Lucy Osburn and the Nightingale nurses in Australia in the late 1860s, the status of nursing in Australia was somewhere between domestic service and prostitution. Osburn was horrified at the squalid conditions and the frowsy, ignorant nurses whom she first encountered on her arrival at Sydney Hospital. In a short while, she introduced an elaborate training scheme for nurses, carefully choosing her trainees for their refinement and integrity of character.

Nursing training was particularly apt for the spiritual single girl as it was given the overtones of a religious order, such as Florence Nightingale had experienced herself in her training in Germany. The veil and the regimen were part of the mystique of nursing. A vocation was surely necessary as nurses were never paid well and were expected to work very long hours. Their accommodation was usually primitive, the nurses' quarters at Royal Melbourne being known by 1910 as Ratland and those at Prince Henry in Sydney as the Buggery.[52]

The other main profession often taken up by the single laywoman was teaching. In early Victorian days, the governess was a familiar figure, a large number of them arriving in Australia in search of work and, in many cases, a husband. Women predominated in the population of the British Isles because of male migration to the far reaches of empire. Trade was denied to the middle-class woman, so many took up the role of governess both at home and overseas. Governesses were gradually replaced by trained teachers, but they lasted longest in country areas where schools had not yet been established.[53]

With the introduction of compulsory elementary education in the various colonies from 1866 onwards, younger governesses and teachers in parish schools often entered women's teacher training colleges, like the Hurlstone Training College in NSW or the later kindergarten training colleges. By 1902, nearly half the teachers in NSW were women and they were paid half as much as the men. Only a quarter of the principals were women. The figure was similar in other states. Most single women, however, were only too glad to have a job and ignored the discrimination. After all, it merely reflected the patriarchal society in which they had been brought up.[54]

The education of girls

Attitudes towards the education of girls varied amongst the different churches. Despite the fact, as we have observed, that the Anglican Church was the first to found a secondary girls' school in the country — St Catherine's Waverley in 1856 — it proved to be the slowest to found secondary schools for girls thereafter. The Methodists and Presbyterians were most enthusiastic about preparing girls for matriculation, as were many of the Roman Catholic orders.

The Methodist and Presbyterian Ladies Colleges had flourished in Melbourne and Sydney since the 1870s and 1880s. The Methodists were influenced by Susannah Wesley's views on education for girls, as expressed in a letter to her son John in 1737:

> No girl should be taught to work till she can read very well: and that she be kept to work with the same application and for the same time she was held in remedy. . . The putting of children to learn sewing before they can read perfectly is the very reason why so few women can

read fit to be heard and never well to be understood.[55]

Presbyterians have always held a high view of education for women as well as men, going back to their Scottish heritage of rigour in learning. The appointment of the brilliant Charles Henry Pearson, who had been Professor of Modern History at London University, as first headmaster of PLC Melbourne in 1874 indicates the exalted view of women's education held by the wealthy Presbyterians of Victoria.

C.H. Pearson issued a manifesto on female education, entitled 'The Higher Culture of Women', which was the basis of his policy on the emancipation of women when he later served as Minister of Education in Victoria. In his three years as headmaster, he not only prepared girls for tertiary education, but also offered extension classes to older women in a variety of subjects. In giving women equality of opportunity in education, he believed only good could result for the whole of society. He asserted: 'Still women exercise. . . the most tremendous direct influence over children, husbands, lovers. . . ought we not. . . to educate our rulers?'[56]

Both Presbyterians and Methodists were, however, preceded in their advanced views on female education by the Quakers. The Quakers had fought against the Established Church's denial of equal access of girls to education in Britain over the centuries.

In accordance with the Quaker principle of individualism, Quaker schools never attempted to stereotype by gender in education. In 1691, fifteen Quaker schools taught Science and English as well as Latin to girls. By the 1860s, girls at the Quaker girls school, The Mount, were studying algebra, geometry and trigonometry before they were available at such notable schools as Cheltenham.

Catherine Gurney, Elizabeth Fry's mother, insisted that her daughter learn Latin, French, maths, history and geography, natural history and drawing, as well as domestic economy skills.[57] The Friends School in Hobart, founded in 1886, was a pioneer Australian school in its policy of co-education and in its dual principalship of a man and a woman.[58]

By contrast with these churches, the Anglican hierarchy dragged its heels when it came to founding schools for girls. This hesitation was partly due to an innate conservatism about higher education for women and partly to the opposition of synodsmen to state-aided church education on ideological as well as sectarian grounds. There was also a palpable fear amongst both men and women of the Church of England that education might distract women from their chief task in life — to be the linchpin of the home and therefore of society. The Church of England *Messenger* of 12 October 1885 criticised the amount of school work demanded of girls as it 'encroached perilously on home life'.[59]

It was not till 1895 that the Sydney Church of England Grammar School for Girls was founded in Darlinghurst. A long hesitation followed and finally Abbotsleigh and Redlands were taken over by the Diocese of Sydney after World War I from the laywomen who had founded them thirty years earlier. In the other states, the Anglican hierarchy was almost as slow in founding or taking over schools for girls, but they did permit such orders as the Kilburn Sisters to establish Perth College and the Sisters of the Sacred Advent were encouraged to open colleges in Brisbane and north Queensland.

✠ What had been achieved for laywomen

Much had been achieved in terms of gender equality in Australia by the close of the nineteenth century, even in ecclesiastical spheres where change was always slow. Women were now able to enter the workforce and take up a profession, although there was still male ridicule to contend with — as when Julia Bella Guerin, the first woman to graduate from an Australian university, received her BA degree at Melbourne in 1883. The *Bulletin* then expressed the gallant hope that Miss Guerin would in due course attain the title best befitting a woman, that of MAMA.[60]

The Australian churches did not pour scorn on their women members, but they — or at least sections of the Anglican church — tended to stand back and watch their female laity struggle to reach equality and fulfilment through service rather than through education. The Catholic Church felt safe in delegating the education of its girls to the orders, little realising what an agency of liberation this educational system would prove to be.

The role of the laywoman in the Victorian era largely reflected the expectations of society — helpmeet, mother, drudge if need be. However, there was an articulate minority whose faith liberated them into a life of social reform and public service. The Australian laywoman ranged from the mute occupant of the Sunday pew to the enthusiastic parish worker who taught Sunday school, ran fetes or prayed with the Mothers' Union. Many felt that was where the laywoman should stop.

But once released by changing social perceptions and increasing education, others saw their role as lying outside the local church — to do battle for the needy, to lobby governments, to enter the professions, to exercise the vote. These were options which were all open for the laywoman at the end of the Victorian era, but almost non-existent at its beginning.

6

Purposeful undervalued Christian employment

WOMEN IN NON-ROMAN CATHOLIC ORDERS TO 1914

'If feminine influence is to be restricted within families, the equilibrium of society is not preserved, but marred.'

Rev. Mervyn Archdall, founder of the
Bethany Deaconess Institution (1894)

'The others laugh at me for becoming a burning educationalist. The school is my daily delight. . .'

Sister Phyllis, a pioneer Anglican nun,
after three years in Hobart (1895)

'May the Lord, even the just and impartial One, over-rule all for the true emancipation of woman from the swaddling bands of prejudice, ignorance and custom which have so long debased and wronged her.'

Catherine Mumford to William Booth, (1855)

THE MARKED EXPANSION OF THE ROLE OF WOMEN in the Victorian church throughout Australia was examined in earlier chapters. Not only did women begin to assume positions of responsibility within their own church, but they also sought to express their faith as well as their professional aspirations in the wider community.

Increased education as well as an expanding population gave unprecedented opportunities to women, whether professed or lay, whether professionally or domestically engaged. Roman Catholic orders had led the way in providing employment and a consequent sense of fulfilment for their single women members. Many Protestant laywomen — especially those of evangelical conviction — devoted much of their week to philanthropic work amongst the poor and needy.

Following the introduction of compulsory elementary education in the various colonies from 1874 onwards, there was a surge of young women seeking professional training and employment outside the home. A number of these young women followed their Catholic sisters' example and entered Anglican orders or trained as Methodist sisters or Presbyterian and Anglican deaconesses; some were commissioned as Salvation Army officers. In taking up these options, the single churchwoman was able to find professional fulfilment as a nurse, teacher or social worker, while giving practical expression to her piety at the same time.

Some of the organisations under analysis were founded in the British Isles and spread rapidly to Australia. The largest Anglican order to operate in Australia, the Sisters of the Church, was founded in England in 1870 and the Salvation Army commenced in 1878. Both had reached Australia by 1880 and both retained strong administrative links with Britain for some time. However, smaller Anglican orders like the Community of the Holy Name and the Society of the Sacred Advent were founded in Australia. The deaconess movement was also native to Australia, although German and English ancestry must be acknowledged. Both sisters and deaconesses were recruited largely from the twenty to thirty age group and many clergy daughters were to be found among them.

The chief economic reason for the emergence of the female orders across the denominations in Great Britain was the considerable imbalance of the sexes in the population from the 1840s to the 1860s. The half million surplus of women over men as recorded in the census of 1851 was mostly due to the massive migration of single men to the colonies and the United States during that period.[1]

Such a surplus of women who were unlikely to marry highlighted the need of society to accept some kind of autonomous role for women. Single women from the middle classes in Britain had traditionally not been allowed to earn their own living by reason of social taboo, whereas their medieval and Renaissance forbears had held key positions in convents, estates and businesses. Thus, the unpaid work of the orders was an acceptable way out of a life of boredom and frustration for the single woman in nineteenth century Britain.

Their Australian counterparts were not as strictly constrained socially, so they did not rush to join orders in such numbers. Nor were their numbers as great proportionately as recruits in English orders, probably because of the lower female numbers and consequent higher rate of marriage in the Australian population.[2]

✠ The revitalising of female orders in the Church of England

Female orders had been virtually non-existent in Britain since the Reformation. However, they underwent a revival following the emergence of the Tractarian or Oxford Movement in the 1830s. The Tractarians sought to reform the Church of England by emphasising holiness within the church and attempting to return to their concept of the primitive church, whilst embracing aspects of the medieval church such as the monastic life.

From the beginning, these churchmen held an exalted view of an independent role for women in the church. In 1839, Edward Pusey wrote to another leader of the movement, John Keble: 'With N [Newman], I have separately come to think it necessary to have some *Soeurs de Charite* in the Anglo Catholic Church'.[3]

Within two years, the first Anglican sister since the Reformation had taken religious vows before the Tractarian leaders in private. The Tractarians continued to espouse an advanced view of female rights and leadership within the church. The influential Pusey had spoken eloquently on behalf of women's orders as early as early as 1840: 'We, who are admitted to the priesthood, are under vows; we devote ourselves for a whole life; why should not women also for their offices?'[4]

Twelve years later he again argued, this time in front of the Church Congress, in favour of the equality of male and female vocations. Despite stiff opposition from low churchmen who felt that vocations were a denial of the Reformation, recruits flowed steadily to the orders. By 1878, there were at least 660 professed sisters in the Province of Canterbury alone and at least 1300 in the Anglican Church worldwide.

The Sisters of the Church

The first order to arrive in Australia was the Sisters of the Church — or, as they were familiarly known, the Kilburn Sisters, because of the London suburb in which they had their headquarters. This order had been founded by a clergy daughter, Emily Ayckbowm, in 1870 'to promote the honour and glory of Almighty God and the extension of his kingdom on earth'.[5]

The foundress drew her postulants at first from largely

titled and middle-class families, who felt particularly called to care for and educate deprived children. The sisters began setting up children's homes and also convalescent homes. News of their work reached the ears of colonial bishops, starved as they were of reliable workers and funds. Most of the nineteenth-century Australian bishops were Tractarian by persuasion, so they welcomed the thought of Anglican nuns; the large evangelical Diocese of Sydney was naturally opposed to them, especially when they set themselves up within its boundaries without the permission of the bishop.

However, encouragement for orders was officially legislated when the General Synod of 1891 recommended that the church in Australia introduce deaconesses and sisterhoods, because of the need for dedicated women workers and because of the patent success of such communities in England and Europe. The Bishop of Adelaide, Bishop Kennion, wasted no time in issuing an invitation to the Kilburn Sisters to enter his diocese and begin work:

> I write to make an earnest appeal to send one or more
> capable members of your sisterhood to form a branch in
> this city. I turn to your sisterhood with the confidence
> and sympathy which many years of admiration of your
> work have inspired in me.[6]

In 1892, seven sisters sailed for Adelaide, taking with them five orphaned girls and two lady helpers. On the way, they arrived in Hobart,where they were so cordially welcomed by Bishop Montgomery that some disembarked to found a school there first.

The sisters themselves derived enormous satisfaction from their work, although they were untrained gentlewomen rather than professional teachers. 'The others laugh at me for becoming a burning educationalist. The school is my daily delight,' wrote a pioneer sister after three years in Hobart.[7] There was a spirit of joyful commitment about the sisters as they went from Hobart to Adelaide to Perth, setting up schools and orphanages.

However, they found their way blocked in Melbourne, where a new order — the Community of the Holy Name — was on the point of being set up and in Brisbane where the Society of the Sacred Advent had already been founded to open schools and hospitals in Queensland.

Their greatest success was in Perth, where an impressive girls' college — Perth College — was established by them in 1902, as was the Parkerville Orphanage, which especially cared for part-Aboriginal children.

There was an element of naivety about their arrival in the strongly Protestant Diocese of Sydney, where they proceeded to set up a school for poor children in Waverley — named St Gabriel's — without asking the permission of the hierarchy. It was not a diplomatic move, given the Sydney Diocese's antipathy to anything which smacked of Rome or was not tightly controlled by parish clergy.

Bishop Saumarez Smith refused to welcome the sisters in his speech at the opening of the 1893 synod. Instead, he expressed surprise that they should have established themselves in Sydney without his permission:

> I must say that the sudden introduction into the Diocese of members of the Anglican sisterhood bound by vows and rule which have not been subject to my inspection. . . looks like an ecclesiastical intrusion of a somewhat anarchical tendency. . . the sisterhood is associated with the doctrine and ritual of an extremist section of the church. . . which is sufficient reason for my abstaining from approving of their operations. . .[8]

A flurry of letters from sundry clergymen and laymen in the church press followed up the bishop's and synod's resolutions against the sisterhood: 'The deceit practised to mislead unthinking men and women by these Kilburn Sisters'; 'These sisters are notorious for their Romanizing tendencies'; 'They are intruding into a parish against the will of the incumbent. . . promoting schism'.

The sisters never replied to these attacks, but reported to Mother Ayckbowm about 'a little setback' in Sydney. Thus, from January 1893 to November 1893, letters and articles of protest appeared in the evangelically minded newspaper, the *Australian Record*, attacking the intrusion of the sisters into the diocese, which were in turn answered by supporters of the sisters with equal fire. Evangelicals attacked and Tractarians supported the following principle: that a body outside a diocese (or parish) may rightfully establish an organisation in that diocese (or parish) contrary to the wishes of the bishop (or incumbent) and of the synod (or vestry meeting); and that individual clergymen in the diocese may invite them to do so. . . without compromising their character as loyal churchmen. . .[9]

Opponents of the sisters of the church were almost invariably supporters of the deaconess movement which, as we shall see, was more Protestant in practice and easier for a clergyman to keep under control. In the meantime, the sisters went ahead with a touch of *noblesse oblige* and continued to run St Gabriel's for sixty years — much to the irritation of the diocesan hierarchy.[10]

The Community of the Holy Name

The other two orders in the Anglican Church which were flourishing by the turn of the century were the Community of the Holy Name and the Society of the Sacred Advent. The former was a sisterhood set up in Melbourne by the redoubt-able Sister Esther. Born Emma Caroline Silcock in England in 1858, she had been attracted from her youth to the Oxford Movement. She was received into a Community in Dorset and soon afterwards, in 1888, injured her back while working among the urban poor.

She decided to visit Melbourne in order to recuperate and, while there, she was shown the work of the newly founded Mission to Streets and Lanes. This mission worked amongst the waifs of the Fitzroy slums which had been created by the rapid industrialisation of the Victorian economy after 1870. An invitation to direct the work followed and she accepted the challenge. With her drive and magnetic personality, Sister Esther soon made an impact in the inner city.[11]

The question of her status then arose: was she a nun or a deaconess? Although officially a deaconess and recognised as such by the Archbishop of Melbourne — whose diocese was largely evangelical in composition at this stage — she was still anxious to pursue the professed life when the opportunity arose. In the meantime, she proved her worth, ignoring such epithets as 'Popish woman'.

For four years, she and two companions undertook gaol, factory and hospital visiting; they established sewing classes and evening meetings for factory girls, which included Shakespeare readings as well as cookery lessons. They set up soup kitchens for 200 to 500 men each winter as the Depression of the 1890s drew on.

In 1892, following the arrival of the Kilburn Sisters in the country, she finally obtained the archbishop's permission to found the first Australian women's order in the Anglican Church, the Community of the Holy Name. She herself was not professed until 1904 in the Diocese of Ballarat, because of Protestant opposition to Anglo Catholic orders in Melbourne.

A host of good works were carried out over the next forty years until her name became a legend for succour of the poor. The first institution founded by Sister Esther was a splendidly equipped House of Mercy at Cheltenham for wayward girls. Part of the funding for this refuge came from nearby affluent parishes and these tried to assert control. However, the mission council ruled that the House of Mercy should be extra-parochial, thereby adhering to the Tractarian view that Anglican sisterhoods should be centralised and free of interference by parish clergy.

Sister Esther's next move was to open a children's home in Brighton in 1894 for boys and girls. There followed a dispensary and a Ragged School in Melbourne and children's homes in Newcastle, Goulburn, Adelaide and New Guinea — dioceses where Anglo Catholic orders were thoroughly welcome. There was no question of her entering the Diocese of Sydney, but prejudice against her churchmanship was gradually overcome in Melbourne where a new archbishop, Lowther Clarke, who was more sympathetic to the religious life, drew up a charter for her order in 1918 and new members were publicly professed for the first time.

By this time, the climate had changed and Anglican hauteur had moderated in its view of the ministry of women. Sister Esther was ever the pioneer; for instance, she was before her time in her attitude to other races and religious groups in Melbourne. She built up a relationship with the Orthodox churches — whether Greek, Russian or Syrian — offering her hall to the Syrians for their meetings. Her charm, sincerity and galvanising energy overcame the doubts of the male hierarchy and not only helped the poor and needy, but also struck a blow for recognition of the efficacy of female leadership in the church.[12]

The Society of the Sacred Advent

Another Australian-born order which rapidly became indispensable to the frontier church was the Society of the Sacred Advent. This order laboured principally in Queensland. It was founded by Canon Montague Stone-Wigg of the Diocese of Brisbane, an ardent Anglo-Catholic who later became Bishop of New Guinea.

The new townships of Queensland desperately needed schools and orphanages in the 1890s and Roman Catholic orders like the Sisters of Mercy had risen magnificently to meet this challenge. The six Church of England schools existing in 1874 had been closed when the Education Act of that year had withdrawn State Aid and abolished school fees.

By 1890, the Anglican Church was extremely anxious to re-enter the educational field, especially when it was reported in synod that only forty-four per cent of Anglicans were practising their faith. Stone-Wigg was further encouraged in his desire to found an Anglican women's order by the recommendation of the General Synod of 1891 that the church in Australia should introduce deaconesses and sisterhoods.[13]

Not only did the Sisters of the Church in Kilburn respond to this resolution in sending the original seven to Tasmania and South Australia, but two other resourceful English women — Sister Caroline, who had trained in the Community of St John the Baptist, and Sister Minnie, a deaconess — agreed to accept Canon Stone-Wigg's invitation, setting sail for Queensland with the blessing of the Archbishop of Canterbury.

Although they maintained their independence from diocesan control, these sisters rapidly became indispensable to the Queensland church in education and social work. They battled with the enervating climate, regular floods and isolation, but by the end of their first year — 1892 — they had founded their first girls' home, the House of the Good Shepherd in

Brisbane. Two years later, St John's School for primary children was opened; then followed a high school, later to become the notable boarding school of St Margaret's. Next to be established was a rescue home for women and children and in 1901 an orphanage and an industrial school.[14]

With the departure of their warden, Canon Stone-Wigg, for New Guinea and the return of their foundation Superior, Sister Caroline, to England in 1898, the Sisters of the Sacred Advent suffered a crisis. Should they affiliate with a larger community or they should struggle on with their huge workload and retain their independence? Only six professed sisters and three novices remained and funds were desperately short.

After much prayer, they elected Sister Emma as their Superior, a post she was to hold with great distinction till World War II. The community began to grow in numbers, chapels were built in their various Brisbane establishments and the foundation was laid for the heroic expansion of the work in outback Queensland which occurred after World War I.[15]

Sister Emma, Superior of the Anglican Society of the Order of the Sacred Advent, Queensland, from 1898 to 1940

✠ Anglican views on sisterhoods or deaconesses

Anglican women wishing to seek a vocation within the church were often confronted by churchmanship differences which affected their role. Protestant dioceses both in Australia and overseas preferred to introduce deaconesses as their female church workers, while Anglo Catholic dioceses plumped for professed religious. In Australia, this meant that the large and wealthy Diocese of Sydney preferred deaconesses as an expression of its reformed theology and its view of church order, whereas the other dioceses, with the possible exception of Melbourne, opted for a sisterhood in keeping with their High Church standpoint.

Furthermore, the choice of either a sisterhood or deaconesses in a particular diocese — and both options sometimes overlapped as in Melbourne — reflected differing attitudes to the autonomy of women. Church historian Michael Hill argues that sisterhoods were the first sign of incipient feminism amongst middle-class women in that members of an order assumed the right to organise their own activity. Herein, as we have seen, lay the nub of the conflict between the women of Roman Catholic orders and the male hierarchy. Hill further points out that Protestant churchmen — and women for that matter — often accused the orders of undermining the authority of the family because of their autonomous role.[16]

Deaconesses were infinitely preferable to Protestant churchmen as they operated under the parish clergyman's control and direction. Protestants held that the office of deaconess not only had theological justification from precedents in the New Testament, but also broadly conformed to the Victorian male viewpoint on the status of women.[17] This view of the dependent role of the deaconess was enunciated by Dean Howson of Chester in his 1862 pamphlet on the subject and received the imprimatur of the evangelical bishops, Lightfoot of Durham and Thorold of Rochester. Howson argued that the deaconess posed a happy medium between the order and the home. Not only was she under male direction, but the very word 'deaconess' meant 'helpful service' in the Greek.[18] It was difficult for a clergyman to resist such an interpretation!

✠ The founding of Anglican deaconess orders

In her scholarly treatment of the origin of deaconesses, Margaret Rodgers argues against the probability of the existence of the office of deaconess in the New Testament church. It was not until the middle of the third century AD that a viable order of deaconesses appeared in the Eastern church.[19]

The first modern order of deaconesses was founded in 1836 by a Lutheran pastor, George Fliedner, in the village of Kaiserwerth, Germany. Fliedner drew up a detailed House Order and Rules of Service and his wife acted as Superior of the order. This was a uniformed order primarily devoted to nursing — and it was here that Florence Nightingale gained inspiration for her celebrated career.[20]

Kaiserwerth also had ramifications for the Australian church in that Martha Archdall, wife of the founder of the Deaconess Institution in Sydney, was the daughter of a Lutheran pastor. She and her husband visited Kaiserwerth before coming to Australia and were deeply impressed by the work of the order. In addition, Mrs Selma Schleicher, mother of the principal of Moore Theological College in the 1890s, had trained at Kaiserwerth.[21] The influence of Kaiserwerth had also spread across the Channel and the first English deaconess was ordained in 1862.

However, English deaconesses came to be attached to parishes rather than to a mother house and they were more inclined to concentrate on social work than the German prototype. As was customary, the English pattern was adopted in Australia.[22]

The Reverend Mervyn Archdall arrived in Sydney in 1882 at the invitation of Bishop Barker to take up the parish of St Mary's, Balmain. A linguist and scholar of repute, he tutored many clergy in theology, but was not content to confine himself to the training of men for ministry. By 1885, he was able to persuade synod to approve the opening of an institution to train deaconesses. He encountered some opposition from traditionalists who felt that the place of the single woman was firmly in the home. His reply to this was that society needed the ministry of trained single women: 'If feminine influence is to be restricted within families, the equilibrium of society is not preserved, but marred. . .[23]

Finally his dream, and that of his wife, became a reality in 1891 when the Bethany Deaconess Institution opened in a rented house next to his church. Eleven 'probationers' enrolled for training in evangelism, education and social work. None could dispute that it was an appropriate time for the church to enlist the aid of deaconesses, as the 1890s were years of poverty and distress in Australia.[24]

The deaconess order in Sydney attracted as probationers for training mainly middle-class women of education and commitment who were single and aged between twenty and thirty years of age. At the conclusion of two years of theological and practical training, they were 'set apart' for service — the term 'ordained' was not used till 1914. Deaconesses were not bound to lifelong celibacy; they worked in parishes, visiting the destitute, prostitutes and the sick. They often gave religious instruction in schools.

By World War I, they had founded a home of peace for the dying in Petersham and a children's home in Ashfield. There was a brave attempt by Mrs Archdall in 1893 to set up a girls' high school in Balmain which might act as a feeder for

Bethany. The school lasted for some years, boasting 150 pupils at one stage, and four other similar schools were set up under deaconess supervision. However, the growing depression and an insufficient band of graduating deaconesses put paid to these schools.

Archdall also hoped to set up a hospital, but there was insufficient capital for that. However, the deaconesses were asked to take over a Home for Working Gentlewomen in Darlinghurst, where they also ran an employment agency for the numerous unemployed women of the day. It was incredibly exhausting work for Archdall, his wife and their students. They ran a second-hand clothing shop to pay for the rent for a boys' club in Balmain. Unfortunately, the young probationer in charge of the club died of consumption and Archdall himself was broken in health by 1907. He was obliged to move to a country parish, but the deaconess order he had founded remained intact, moving its training house to Newtown.[25]

Deaconess orders were revived by those churchmen who were interested in the possibilities of the employment of women in the church, but who rejected the idea of sisterhoods as either too Papist or too feminist.

The Australian deaconess movement in general followed the English model of parochial attachment — members were to take no vows and to be under the jurisdiction of the bishop or parish priest. This particular concept of the deaconess was most readily espoused by evangelical dioceses like Sydney. It was as much an expression of conservative theology as it was of a conservative view of women and their role. Indeed, the two attitudes appear to be closely associated.

Margaret Rodgers notes that when the Bethany Institute was founded in Sydney, it was begun by churchmen — not women — of strong evangelical views.[26] Support for the

Deaconess Institution also grew by default after the arrival of the Kilburn Sisters who could not obtain hierarchical support — apart from their reputed Romanism and ritualism — because they had entered Sydney without permission. Thus, without discounting the influence of Martha Archdall, men were the creators and controllers of the deaconess movement in Sydney. At no stage was it the result of a feminist movement within the church.

The conservative and somewhat limited nature of the deaconess movement is probably the chief reason for its failure to attract substantial numbers to its ranks. Numbers of probationers were often disappointing and those who entered training often did not reach ordination. In the early years, about a dozen women came forward for training, but only five women who trained at the Institution were set apart as deaconesses in the first eight years of its operation.[27]

The rigidity of life in Bethany and the loss of social prestige incurred by becoming a deaconess (which was the opposite of the reaction of Roman Catholic families towards members choosing a vocation) helped to deter would-be candidates from entering. The commonly accepted view amongst male theological students that the Deaconess Institution was mainly a training ground for future clergy wives also did not help to attract women of initiative.

Finally, the perception that the work of a deaconess was nothing more than 'institutionalised ecclesiastical housework' discouraged women of independent spirit from entering.[28] To be fair to the Deaconess Institution, it did train and produce some first-class missionaries and social workers — as well as clergy wives — but its role and influence would have been greater had the church it served possessed a higher view of female ministry and leadership.

✠ Presbyterian deaconessas

Such was the need for skilled women workers in the depression years of the 1890s that the Presbyterian and Methodist churches also embraced the idea of deaconesses.[29] As Protestant denominations, they considered the idea of a professed order too Romish, but neither church objected to the term 'sister' which had been used loosely by them to describe paid women assistants in local churches.

It was not till 1905 that the first Presbyterian deaconess was dedicated — 'ordained' being too daring a term at that stage — in New South Wales. This was the notable Eva Holland who laboured for thirty-three years amongst the poor and outcasts of Woolloomooloo.

Deaconesses had been set apart earlier than this in the strong Presbyterian Church in Victoria. The pioneer of deaconess work in Victoria was the Reverend W.S. Rolland, who founded the Deaconess Training Institute of Victoria at the turn of the century. Encouraged by his equally indefatigable wife, he proceeded to convene a committee to sustain and direct deaconess work throughout the state.

The Melbourne Training Home enrolled candidates for a minimum of one year, but two years was prescribed for those with no prior educational or nursing training.[30] Some deaconesses left for either medical or teaching service in the Presbyterian missions in Korea and the Pacific Islands.

The great educator and churchman Frank Rolland (the son of the founder of the deaconess movement in Victoria), who served as a chaplain in the South Australian desert, pleaded for trained deaconesses of the Presbyterian Church who were also triple-certificated nurses to come and work amongst Aboriginal women and children. The first deaconess to arrive, Miss E.A. Main, began working in a radius out from Oodnadatta in 1908.[31] A fuller treatment of her achievements and that of the nurse deaconesses of the outback, which merged into the work of the Australian Inland Mission, has been reserved for the next chapter.

The New South Wales church continued to rely on Victoria for trained deaconesses until well after World War I, although there were frequent pleas at the Presbyterian Assembly for a 'Training Institute for Deaconesses and Missionary workers' to be set up in Sydney.[32]

Deaconess Eva Holland was perhaps the most outstanding social worker and innovator to serve the church in Australia this century. She was especially responsible for pioneering the concept of settlement work in Sydney's poor areas and a chapel is now dedicated to her in the inner city where she once ministered.[33] The daughter of a Congregational clergyman, she volunteered for service as a deaconess, probably after a period of training at the Deaconess Home in Melbourne.

Deaconess Eva Holland

She was accepted by the Presbyterian Women's Missionary Association for Home Mission work in a difficult part of East Sydney. On 18 September 1905, she was dedicated as the first Presbyterian deaconess in NSW, at a service in the Palmer Street Church.

She always lived on the job and knocked on 900 doors in her first year. She convened mission services and began a Sunday school. She organised the making of winter clothes and the preparation of meals for the destitute. The unemployed were helped to apply for jobs; refuges, brothels and hospitals were regularly visited by her. Scripture was taught in the local schools.

A self-effacing person with an infectious smile, she soon became known to government officials, police and magistrates as she took responsibility for the needy and wayward in her demesne. She founded the 'Inasmuch Fund' for relieving very distressing cases of need; for example, starving children were fed and surgical supports were provided for the crippled out of this fund.[34]

She set up a women's club in Woolloomooloo which attracted up to fifty women each week; while their children played under supervision, these women were encouraged to sing, sew, knit and read books from the library. She took them on picnics and, where possible, organised holidays for them. She tried to cater for every section of the community, from the prostitutes to restless gangs of boys.

By 1910, the work was known as St Andrew's Settlement and it provided a sanctuary and a place of friendship and learning for the whole community. Eva reported to the Assembly with a touch of pride:

> The Settlement is now known from one end of Woolloomooloo to the other and it has disabused. . . the idea that the Presbyterian Church has little sympathy with the poorer classes.[35]

Eva Holland showed characteristic energy and compassion when there was the trauma of losing members of her young men's class to Gallipoli and the Western Front. 'Nearly all our single men are away and two have made the great sacrifice,' she said.[36] The Great Depression saw her and her fellow deaconesses constantly handing out aid to many in appalling poverty.

By the time she resigned in 1939, there were five deaconesses engaged in social work on behalf of the Presbyterian Church of New South Wales. Moreover, her concept of settlement work had become a prototype for community reclamation in cities throughout the country.[37]

✠ Methodist deaconesses

Methodist deaconesses were preceded by the sisterhoods which came into being somewhat haphazardly in the 1880s. Laywomen were appointed to work — often in an unpaid capacity — amongst women and children in mission areas, like the Central Methodist Mission in Sydney. From 1880 to 1890, the so-called 'Forward Movement' in Methodism provided an impulse for work specifically suited to women.

In 1884, the Central Methodist Mission in Sydney founded a training home for Sisters of the People, in which hundreds of young women received some form of training in evangelistic and parochial work.[38] Sisterhoods were also emerging in the other states and church men and women gradually overcame strong prejudice against independent women's work on behalf of the church.

The fact that women were already travelling overseas to dangerous foreign missions in an independent capacity did not register with the parochial minds who rejected the first Sisters of the People.

It was a little easier for those sisters who had a strong clergyman to champion their cause, such as the Western Australian sisters whose patron, the Reverend G.E. Rowe, set up a sisterhood in the early 1890s in Western Australia. This group of thirteen trained nurses worked on the goldfields, where social problems were acute, and also ran a home for women and children in Perth. Branches of the sisterhood were also established in such other centres as Fremantle and York and they were maintained by voluntary contributions from local churches.[39]

Although a 'Wesley Deaconess Order' was founded by Dr T.B. Stephenson and a United Methodist Church Order of Deaconesses began — both before the turn of the century — there was no concerted attempt to give deaconesses parity of training with men or to ordain them until 1935. Consequently, their numbers remained small and they were sketchily trained. Gifted single Methodist women with a strong vocation generally preferred working in church schools or overseas mission stations.[40]

❊ Women workers in interdenominational organisations

Apart from the deaconesses and sisters, there were also small groups of women workers in this period who were paid by large interdenominational societies like the Bible Society and the Sydney City Mission to evangelise and relieve social problems amongst the poor. Mrs Ellen Ranyard had pioneered in 1857 a group of women evangelists in Britain, known as the Biblewomen. These women worked in the slums of the large cities, selling Bibles to the poor, counselling them and even nursing them during cholera epidemics.[41]

The success of the Biblewomen in Britain prompted the Sydney City Mission to employ women in a similar capacity in Sydney in the 1890s. Lucy Gordon, the first Biblewoman to be appointed by the Sydney City Mission, acted as a colporteur of the scriptures, a missioner to prostitutes and a house-to-house visitor.[42] It was incredibly taxing work and the pay was meagre, but at least the single woman missionary was not taken for granted, as was her married sister. Wives of male Sydney City Missionaries were never paid and barely acknowledged for their many hours of visiting and working as Biblewomen.[43]

Although it was recognised by the 1890s that women were desperately needed in social work — especially as the state had not yet assumed responsibility for social welfare — the churches made scant provision to pay these women, speaking soothingly of them as the 'heart' of the church and men as the 'head'.[44] Such truisms were convenient not only financially, but also theologically and politically: why acknowledge or pay women when their labour could be exploited? They were surely better off married anyway.

✠ Salvation Army women

It is a refreshing change to turn to the women of the Salvation Army and to find — even last century — an egalitarianism in gender ratios at all levels which is barely equalled in other churches today. The chief reason for the emancipation of Salvation Army women resides in the personality and intellect of Catherine Booth, the wife of the founder.

Catherine as a child demonstrated great precocity of thought, a talent for debate, as well as a warmth of feeling for the down and out in society. As a young girl, she had walked beside a drunken man being frogmarched to prison through a jeering crowd.[45] Later, she wrote long, reasoned letters of up to 2 500 words in length, partly to set out her own views on ministry and partly to keep her mercurial husband's spirits up. These letters, which take up twelve folios, are a manifesto of Christian faith and social equality and they reveal her tact, intellect and burning sense of fair play. Before she married William Booth, she made her position clear:

I believe woman is destined to assume her true position

and exert her proper influence by the special exertions and attainments of her own sex. . . May the Lord, ever the just and impartial One, over-rule all for the true emancipation of woman from the swaddling bands of prejudice, ignorance and custom which, almost the world over, have so long debased and wronged her.[46]

Soon after marriage, she was moved to express her indignation at attitudes towards women in the church. William Booth was working as a Methodist minister in 1858 in the north of England. One of his colleagues had publicly dismissed women as the weaker sex. William, to her mortification, had agreed with him. She raged:

Oh, prejudice, what will it not do! That woman is in any respect, except physical strength and courage, inferior to man I cannot see cause to believe, and I am sure no one can prove it from the word of God.[47]

Booth replied bravely:

I would not encourage a woman to begin preaching, although I would not stop her on any account. . . I would not stop you if I had the power to do so, although I should not like it.[48]

Within two years, he was obliged to modify his views when Catherine announced in front of a one thousand-strong congregation that she had been shown by divine revelation that it was woman's right and duty to preach as well as man's. She entered the pulpit that night and the Salvation Army principle of gender equality in the church was initiated.

Naturally, there was opposition in Methodist circles to the Booths' ministry and in 1865 they began an independent congregation among the London poor at Mile End. Despite her frail health and her six young children (she did, of course, have domestic help), she began visiting with her husband some of London's 100 000 public houses and preaching in the open.[49]

In 1878, the Salvation Army was officially founded and, within two years, it had spread to Australia, commencing at first in Adelaide.

From the beginning, Salvation Army women officers worldwide enjoyed equal rights with men; Orders and Regulations ceased to distinguish between 'he' and 'she'. Women could hold any rank and officiate at all services; they could speak and vote at all meetings.[50] Booth was soon to boast that 'the best men in my Army are the women'.[51]

The first meetings of the Army in England and Australia were conducted in an atmosphere of mockery and even hostility. A barrage of insults and missiles greeted the 'Hallelujah Lasses', as the women officers were often called.[52]

The early women Salvation Army officers who came from England found it difficult at first to convince Australian women that there was a role for them in the Army, not only as members, but as leaders. Mrs Alice Barker was a dynamic leader of the early work in Victoria, as was Mrs Adelaide Sutherland in Sydney — both of them migrating from England and working alongside their officer husbands.

The first Australian woman to 'go into the work' was Emma Charlesworth who became a soldier in Adelaide in 1883. The first to be promoted was Elizabeth Warrington who went from Adelaide to take charge of the Balmain Corps. Some women officers were sent by reactionary magistrates to gaol for 'offensive conduct' (preaching in the streets). For example, Captain Jessie Belvers was gaoled at Castlemaine for 'unseemly conduct' — that is, preaching in the streets — and Eva Le Cour was imprisoned for marching in the streets of Ballarat. However, opposition to the Salvationists gradually subsided as the genuineness of their social work became apparent.[53]

Women continued to have a high profile in every aspect of Salvation Army work. The Salvationist journal, *War Cry*, devoted an issue in 1895 to the liberation of women:

> There are millions who imagine that women were created for hardly any higher purpose than to cook the food, look after the household affairs, and gratify the wants and wishes of the other sex. She was created equal in dignity to man and intended to be his intellectual and moral associate. . . Society cannot make rapid advances in knowledge and religion until the true dignity of woman is fully recognised.[54]

Despite the feminist viewpoint of its founders, the Salvation Army did not always display an egalitarian attitude towards its women recruits in the early days. First, there was unnecessary segregation of the sexes in the training school for officers in Melbourne; for example, male and female cadets were obliged to use the library on separate days. Even after

An equal calling: Salvation Army officers about 1900

The Salvation Army officer: social worker and evangelist

graduation, women for a time ran separate homes and food depots to the men.

Second, women officers were paid less than the men. Third, married women who 'were officers in their own right were looked upon as their husbands' assistants rather than as equals who had been ordained side by side. Fourth, a woman officer, however senior or experienced, always took her husband's rank upon marriage — no matter that this rank might be inferior to hers. Finally, while more women than men trained as officers, comparatively few were promoted to administrative positions before 1914.[55]

All but the last of these anomalies were eliminated after

World War I, but the last problem — being particularly endemic in society at large — remained with the Salvation Army until mid-century. However, in no other ecclesiastical organisation, with the possible exception of the Quakers, has the principle of sexual equality been so fully proclaimed and implemented. For it has been enshrined from the beginning in Article XII of the Army's Constitution:

> As is manifest from the scriptures of Old and especially New Testaments that God has recognised and sanctified the labours of godly women in his church, godly women possessing the necessary gifts and qualifications shall be employed as preachers — itinerant or otherwise — and as class leaders. . . and they shall be eligible for any office and speak and vote at all official meetings.[56]

⌗ Changing attitudes towards the single churchwoman

The close of the Victorian era and the years leading up to World War I witnessed changing attitudes towards the role of single churchwomen in particular. Roman Catholic and Anglican orders had never been stronger in numbers as large nineteenth-century families provided surplus women, who increasingly wished to take vows and follow a vocation of service outside their families.

Roman Catholic orders were differently oriented in their philanthropic and educational work to their Anglo Catholic counterparts. Their motivation lay in *poenitentia*, the doctrine which implied that the primary motive for philanthropy was the justification of the soul rather than the relief of the poor *per se*.[57]

Protestant deaconesses as well as Anglican nuns were free of guilt-driven motivation in their service, but they lacked the sense of autonomy, strong bond of community and often the reward of recognition enjoyed by their Catholic counterparts. They were allowed to undertake purposeful Christian employment without comparable esteem. Almost all their work was carried out under the supervision of a clergyman, be he parish priest or chaplain. They were utilised and sometimes praised by their churches but, in contrast to Catholic religious, were generally considered to have failed to achieve a higher role — that of marriage.

When one Sister did marry a clergyman, she was commended for 'going to the yet higher dignity of a parsonage helpmate'.[58] The Anglican deaconess magazine of 6 June 1894 commented on the supposed dichotomy between the male 'head' and the female 'heart'.[59] It was not the language of Catherine Booth.

Small wonder there was such a drop-out rate amongst deaconesses. Esteem for their work and position was not adequately expressed, especially when the highest goal for them was so often pointed out as marriage to the nearest clergyman. Recruits were hard to find in Anglican orders in this period because working-class women could not be accepted because of the Victorian view that the middle class must minister to the working class. Then there was the almost impossible task of combining professional competence, a nurturing role and a certain image of ladyhood — all without the strong support of the religious community which Roman Catholic sisters enjoyed. Women of great character like Sister Esther, Sister Frances and Deaconess Pallister did flourish with minimal support. But they were exceptions.

Lingering male attitudes of superiority continued to exist in clerical circles at least until World War I. In 1914, Canon Hensley Henson asserted in the *Church Times* in Britain that 'unmarried women can never be accepted as the true or best representatives of womanhood, however brilliant their intellectual powers or astonishing their actual achievements'.[60]

There is no record of any Australian cleric making such a cruelly ludicrous statement as this. However, most Australian men and women would have agreed at this point with the English clergyman, who told a women's meeting in 1902 that it was all right for a woman to serve on boards, but 'your real influence does not lie in public life and never will. It lies in the power you exert over men, individually and personally.'[61] In other words, influence and manipulation were the preferred approach for the Christian woman instead of service side by side in a spirit of freedom and self-esteem.

Against such a scenario, the contribution of the pioneer sisters and deaconesses in the late nineteenth and early twentieth centuries is all the more remarkable — given also that they did not enjoy the strong community support characteristic of the Roman Catholic orders. Still more liberated was the role of women officers in the Salvation Army; they enjoyed a degree of emancipation as they worked side by side with the men officers which was previously unknown to professional women in the church. Nor were they as restricted in their recruiting, as candidates were drawn from both middle and working classes, like most of the Roman Catholic orders.

The nineteenth century was a time when women began to challenge and leave behind the traditional role which was assigned to them as their function in life. Instead, they began to seek education and subsequently employment in society. There were three professional roles open to the single independent church woman: the most radical was to enter an order where she could organise and supervise her own activity with the help of her fellows. The second was to become a deaconess — a more dependent role where she was subject to the supervision of the male hierarchy. The third option was to enter a normally male workforce where she was allowed equality of role and opportunity, provided she remained single — as in the Salvation Army.

Thus, the Anglo Catholic orders, sisterhoods and deaconess order which arose at this time were part of a wider trend of repidly expanding public activity for women. These women received but modest encouragement from the male hierarchy, but gradually overcame prejudice against the leadership of single women by the genuineness of their work.

7

Undreamt-of fulfilment

THE ROLE OF THE WOMAN MISSIONARY TO WORLD WAR I

'It is a privilege to be living in China, because we feel that our life here resembles the Lord's on earth. We are followed by huge crowds. . . they call after us 'Jesus!' or 'foreign devil!', often throwing stones at us, sometimes cursing us and even pushing us rudely.'

Mary Reed (1888), the first Australian missionary in China.

'I do not see the slightest bit of romance or sentiment about it, but plenty of hard work, discouragement, fever, ague, cholera, disagreeableness, privations and such-like. . . But I have not the slightest bit of fear.'

Ellen Arnold (1882), pioneer Baptist missionary in India

'Women first entered missions in any numbers under the cover of excellent ideology, both evangelical and feminist, which mobilised organisations and funds and made women's work acceptably orthodox.'

Sarah Potter (1974), mission historian

IT WAS THE EXPANSION OF WOMEN INTO the exotic and hazardous field of missions which revealed a growing if un-expressed feminism within the ranks of the church in the

second half of the nineteenth century. Women had traditionally played an active role in missions as fundraisers and
publicists since the 1820s. A significant number, especially in
Wesleyan missions, began to serve as missionary wives and,
although their contribution was frequently of incalculable
benefit to their husband and the mission, it was rarely recognised by the missionary society.

After 1880, the single woman missionary began to depart
these shores in appreciable numbers, experiencing a freedom
of expression and ministry which she lost only on her return
to the home church. On her arrival home, she was never
invited to preach as she had done so freely 'on the field'.
Rarely was employment in the home church awaiting her, as
it usually was for the male missionary. The warmth with
which many women of the church embraced the opportunity
of missionary service arose out of the woman's movement of
the 1880s and 1890s as well as out of the religious revivals of
the period.

As has been already demonstrated, the nineteenth century
witnessed an astonishing expansion in numbers and activity on
the part of the Western church. The influence of evangelicalism on church and society as one of the chief causes of this
expansion has already been remarked and nowhere was this
influence so manifest as in the expansion of overseas missions.

Dr Eugene Stock, the influential mission historian, in
examining the ideology of missions, contrasted the attitude of
puritanism with that of evangelicalism: 'If puritanism was
more fruitful in theological literature, evangelicalism was infinitely more fruitful in works of piety and benevolence; there
was hardly a single missionary and philanthropic scheme of
the day which was not either originated or warmly taken up
by the evangelical party.'[1]

The warmth and flexibility of the evangelical movement,

which transcended denominational and national boundaries, was the key to the rapid acceptance of the ministry of women in overseas mission work as the century progressed. The reluctance of sufficient numbers of men to volunteer for overseas service also led missionary societies to countenance the enlisting of women. Furthermore, the relative peace in the second half of the century caused by the dominance of the European powers worldwide made travel for women a safer prospect, although imperialism had its problems in that missionary work could be associated with condescension and even aggression in indigenous minds.

As the effectiveness of women in philanthropic and evangelistic roles at home had been demonstrated, so it became apparent that they should take up similar roles overseas, provided they felt called to do so. This enlargement of horizons for women was further consolidated by educational training and feminist ideology so that, by the final decade of the century, the trickle of women candidates leaving for the mission field had become a torrent. Overnight, women missionaries had outnumbered their male counterparts.

The early missionary societies, the Society for the Propagation of Christian Knowledge (founded in 1697) and the Society for the Propagation of the Gospel (founded in 1701) made no attempt to appeal to women or enlist their aid in the evangelisation of the world. Missionaries were not prevented from taking wives with them, provided they were not a burden on the sponsoring society, but their role as anything beyond helpmeet was steadfastly ignored.

It was the strongly evangelical London Missionary Society (LMS) and Church Missionary Society (CMS), founded in 1795 and 1799 respectively, which were the first societies explicitly to appeal for feminine help. At the Annual General Meeting of CMS in 1811, the general secretary openly encouraged women to adopt at least a vicarious role in the great cause of missionary outreach:

> Christian matrons! What more laudable ambition can inspire you than a desire to be the mother of the missionaries, confessors and martyrs of Jesus? Generations unborn shall call you blessed. Ye wives also learn to rejoice at the sound of battle. Rouse the slumbering courage of your soldiers to the field and think no place so safe, so honoured, as the camp of Jesus. Tell the missionary story to your little ones, until their young hearts burn and they cry, 'Shall not we also be the missionaries of Jesus Christ?'[2]

The following year, CMS founded its first auxiliary, which enabled more laity and inevitably more women to become interested in the work. LMS had already founded an auxiliary five years earlier and the British and Foreign Bible Society had done likewise. I have already noted that an auxiliary to the Bible Society was founded in New South Wales in 1820 in which, it was said, 'the women did better than the men'.[3] The auxiliaries not only raised funds to support missionaries; they also created a propaganda machine which promoted interest in and information about missions, which inevitably led to recruitment.

Missionary wives

The first women missionaries to prove their worth in the nineteenth century were, of necessity, the missionary wives. Although their role as independently effective workers was scarcely recognised by missionary societies — witness the ignoring of Mary Lawry's work in Tonga in the 1820s by the Wesleyan Methodist Missionary Society[4] — yet most societies encouraged their candidates to take a wife for companionship and assistance in an alien and isolated environment. They did not go as far as the early American Wesleyan societies, which literally arranged marriages between candidates of the opposite sex (though such unions as that of Botany Bay's first chaplain to Mary Burton just before he set sail were all but arranged marriages).

One of the early role models for English and Australian missionary wives was Mary Williams, wife of John Williams, the pioneer LMS missionary in Oceania. Having no children, she was able to travel from island to island with her husband, encountering all manner of receptions and enduring all manner of privation.

After arriving in a hostile Tahiti in 1822, they worked for seven years until the islands were peaceful and clear of idolatry and immorality. Then, they sailed in turn to Tonga where she brought up three children while he was frequently away in Samoa, the Cook Islands and Fiji, evangelising each over the next fifteen years. Like Mary Lawry, Mary Williams attempted to pursue a policy of cultural identification with the native people.

She next settled in Samoa where she instructed the island women in vegetable growing and the making of bonnets, as well as instructing in the scriptures. Each sabbath, she read to the assembled natives in their own tongue, unless there was a ship in port when her husband (if he was home) preached in English — no doubt to the mystification of the majority of his listeners.

Great sadness, however, awaited this devoted missionary wife when her husband attempted to win over the fierce people of the New Hebrides. The Melanesians were more depressed and recalcitrant than the Polynesians — especially as they had had unpleasant experiences at the hands of European traders — and John Williams was clubbed to death at Erromanga in 1839.[5]

Although unpaid and often officially unrecognised (Methodist Overseas Mission registers up to 1916 do not list wives, although they are often mentioned in the column headed 'Remarks'),[6] most missionary wives were extremely conscientious. They set out to learn the language and culture of the people amongst whom their husbands were working. They identified with the women and children especially; they kept virtually open house; they employed local women and sometimes men to help them domestically and in the mission station. They took services when their husbands were away and most of them wrote long journals and letters when their children were asleep.

The journal of Esther Thomas, wife of the veteran Wesleyan missionary John Thomas who worked in the South Pacific for thirty-three years, reveals a woman of mystical piety and depth. She coped well with homesickness and the insecurity of a nomadic existence, but she shrank from such earthy tasks as midwifery and surgery which were often required of missionary wives.[7]

More down-to-earth in her attitude was Janet Cosh, wife of the Presbyterian missionary in the New Hebrides (now Vanuatu), James Cosh. Her letters reveal a kindly woman who battled with malaria, worried over her children's health and tried to overlook the deficiencies of her mud hut residence. She was a firm believer in hospitality as a sounder weapon of evangelism than preaching. She often invited the old men and women of the village into her home for tea and biscuits and was pleased when they smacked their lips and asked for more:

> Preaching is all very well in its way, but they have stomachs to be satisfied as well as souls to be saved and, when you do manage to make them feel you have an interest in them and a strong desire for their good, you have thus taken a great step in gaining their confidence.[8]

Another role model for missionary wives was the gifted Agnes Watt who worked for twenty-five years on the island of Tanna which was also part of the New Hebrides mission. While her husband translated the New Testament into Tannese, she compiled and translated a large scripture history into that language. She wrote hymns and collected games, legends and folklore from Tanna and used them to help reach the islanders. When on deputation in Scotland and Australia, she attracted many to public meetings: 'Her mellow voice, interesting content and singing of Tannese hymns made her addresses very popular.'[9]

Her chief concern was to hear the women of the village being struck by their husbands for very trivial offences. Like Mary Williams, she had no children and so was able to devote her entire day to the people in a teaching and supervising capacity:

> April 22nd [1870]. This has been a busy day. First, I had to bake, then followed cooking, painting, scrubbing, carrying the water, killing fowls, re-boiling jam. . . besides feeding and paying a number who came to work. Each day by two o'clock I feel as wearied as if I had done everything myself, while very often I have only overseen.[10]

Missionary wives won increasing acceptance from mission boards and colonial bishops as the century passed; however, they stood very much in their husbands' shadow as far as missionary authorities were concerned and their work was recognised only by their families, fellow-missionaries and the people to whom they ministered.

✠ Single women

Mission boards were to prove even more tardy in their recognition of the possible role of the single woman on the mission field. Social pressures and expectations in Georgian and early Victorian Britain and Empire were such that single women were regarded as unsafe or a nuisance without a husband and had to be chaperoned at all times.

When writing to the Secretary of LMS about their decision to send a party of single women missionaries to Tahiti via Sydney as early as 1810, Rowland Hassall is almost neurotic in his concern for their safety and chastity. He issued a series of instructions for these women as they prepared to embark. Admittedly, the ship contained a complement of convicts, but his strictures left nothing to chance. He began:

> You will be required during your voyage to adopt the most rigid attention to rule.
> (1) Rise and retire very exactly — this will prevent much confusion.
> (2) Have your own family prayers very exactly. . . be very short and speak very low in the women's cabin. . .
> (5) Do not be hasty to reprove swearing or papism — only look pained — watch for a time. . .
> I commend you to God. Study his will, consult not the flesh. Crucify it. This will prove that you belong to Christ and are fit vessels to contain his treasures. . .[11]

Single women missionaries were still regarded as hazardous, if not unscriptural, as late as the 1840s. Bishop Daniel Wilson, the bishop of Calcutta, declared:

> I object in principle to single ladies coming out unprotected to so distant a place with a climate so unfriendly, and with the almost certainty of their marrying within a month of their arrival. . . The whole thing is against apostolic maxim, 'I suffer not a woman to speak in the church.'[12]

Until thirty years later, the practice of missionary societies (apart from some American boards) conformed to this view, especially in countries like India whose climate and sanitation had made them a graveyard for Europeans.

Zenanas and mission policy towards women

However, it was the Indian situation, paradoxically, which brought about a change in mission policy with regard to female candidates. Increasingly, male missionaries found themselves frustrated in their work of proselytising because they were not allowed in the *zenanas*, the separate apartments where upper-class Hindu and Muslim women were confined within each household. Missionaries were able to speak to lower-class women who were not confined, but such women were powerless within the family structure. Upper-class women, on the other hand, had the power to veto or approve conversion of the whole family to Christianity.

Zenanas ranged from the squalid to the luxurious; women were either expected to work like drudges in them or to lounge about gossiping. When the first Christian women came to visit them, they welcomed them as a relief from boredom. The *zenana* women enjoyed Bible stories and songs and appreciated being taught to read and being treated like human beings.[13]

In the late 1860s, just as the women's movement was gaining strength in Britain and Australia, the plight of Indian women in *zenanas* gained much sympathy from feminists. At the same time, Baptist circles who always regarded India as their special sphere of interest after the pioneer work done by their great preacher and scholar, William Carey, decided to change their policy. In 1869, they founded the Zenana Missionary Society which was administered entirely by women and sent out its first woman missionary in 1874.[14]

The principal aim of the Zenana missionaries was to

educate women thoroughly and to provide literacy for children also. Anglicans joined the Baptists in this work when they founded the Church of England Zenana Missionary Society in 1880 and this was a further occasion for women to apply to missionary boardrooms. In this case, a ladies' missionary committee was set up with male advisers. Wesleyan Methodists, the London Missionary Society and the Church of Scotland Zenana Mission likewise involved themselves in work amongst Indian women.[15] The new mission ideology was strengthened by the Christian feminist view that the plight of the *zenana* women living useless, parasitical lives echoed the plight of the Victorian woman spinster without a career, condemned to a life of uselessness. There was much evidence to support the efficacy of the *zenana* work. As a friendly Hindu once told a LMS missionary:

> We do not greatly fear your schools; we need not send our children. We do not fear your books, for we need not read them. We do not much fear your preaching; we need not listen. But we dread your women and dread your doctors, for your doctors are winning our hearts and your women are winning our homes, and when our hearts and homes are won, what is there left of us?[16]

Australian women were not slow to take up the *zenana* challenge. The gifted Presbyterian missionary, Mary MacLean, volunteered for service in India following the visit to Australia of Mrs Longhurst of the Church of Scotland Zenana Mission in 1891. An experienced teacher with the NSW Department of Public Instruction, she was the first missionary to go out under the aegis of the Presbyterian Women's Missionary Association (PWMA).

Like the Methodist Overseas Missions Board, the Presbyterian Board appeared reluctant to handle women missionaries and so delegated this task to the women themselves. The PWMA was allowed to work alongside the male Heathen Missions Committee and it soon proved the more vital body of the two under its dynamic organising secretary, Jean Forbes. Before long, it was supporting a Chinese mission church in Sydney, work among Aborigines in Queensland and the New Hebrides mission. When Mary MacLean returned from India after five years with the Scottish Zenana mission, the PWMA decided to found its own mission at Sholinghur, sixty miles north of Madras. She returned to lead the work there for twenty years, building a large school there in memory of her mother.[17]

✠ Ellen Arnold and the Australian Baptist Missionary Society

If Mary MacLean was the great Australian Presbyterian missionary in India, then Ellen Arnold was the great Baptist leader. An Australian branch of the Baptist Missionary Society (BMS) was founded in Adelaide in 1864, following the visit of one of the Carey missionaries from India, Rev. James Smith. Branches of the BMS spread to other states and, by 1882, more women than men were volunteering for service overseas. Ellen Arnold left her native Adelaide in that year and was to labour in Bengal until 1931. From the beginning, she was a realist. She wrote on the eve of her departure:

> I do not see the slightest bit of romance or sentiment about it, but plenty of hard work, discouragement, fever, ague, cholera, disagreeableness, privations and such-like. . . But I have not the slightest bit of fear.[18]

She and her fellow volunteer, Marie Gilbert, arrived in Bengal without language, accommodation or any form of acclimatisation. Within eighteen months, she returned with her health broken.

*'The Five Barley Loaves': Ellen Arnold's
Baptist Missionary Society team in Bengal*

In 1885 she set out again, this time with four other women — Ruth Wilkin and Maria Fuller from Victoria, Alice Pappin from South Australia and Martha Plested from Queensland. She christened them 'the five barley loaves' and the two male volunteers 'the two fishes'.

This trend for women missionaries vastly to outnumber men was to continue up to World War I and to remain with some modification thereafter and an attempt will be made to ascertain reasons for it. A total of fifty-five Australian women went to the mission field with BMS up to 1914, as compared with sixteen men. A large number of women above this also applied and were not accepted — many not passing the stringent medical examination of the mission doctor in New South Wales.[19]

Ellen Arnold was the bright star in the missionary firmament in Bengal. Her energy, drive and magnetic leadership knew no bounds. She built a large brick mission house for her rapidly increasing staff by leasing a claypit and making her own bricks — after organising the transport of coal to help fire the bricks, by means of boats plying from West Bengal.

On a whirlwind crusade across Australian states in 1885, she founded the Ladies Zenana Missionary Society to work amongst upper-class women in Bengal. Five *zenana* workers were recruited to the field to visit schools and *zenanas* and to take scripture classes. In 1888, she founded a girls' school for orphans (of whom there were many in a land of plague and child marriage) and staffed it with some of the scores of women she had recruited whilst on her hyperactive furlough. After 1900, her missionaries opened a widows' home and a child welfare centre.[20]

Though trained as a teacher, she saw her work as threefold: evangelistic, medical and social. On the social side, she helped pioneer good sanitation and hygiene in the region; her leadership appeared to reduce crime and brigandage in the area.

Medically, she encouraged vaccination, the boiling of drinking water and the use of mosquito nets. She had gained medical experience at Adelaide Hospital, so she knew how to dispense quinine and other drugs to the fevered villagers. Hers was a holistic approach to evangelism. 'If I were a heathen,' she wrote, 'I should give no ear to a person who came and preached religion at me, leaving me to cough my strength away at night, or to burn my vitals away in fever, or to drink poison in my water.'[21] Ellen Arnold received criticism for her unconventional behaviour. Some called her a Baptist nun because of the ascetic strain in her remarkable personality.

Her character and achievements are certainly reminiscent of Mary MacKillop, although perhaps she lacked a little of the charm of that other famous South Australian. Like St Paul, she 'buffeted' herself and her health was so reduced that she had to be carried off the ship on her last furlough. She insisted on returning to the field in old age, spurning a pension and without the sponsorship of the missionary society.

She was passionate about preaching, paving the way during her crusade of 1885 for women preaching at home as well as abroad. The words most on her lips during her last days were 'Preach, preach, preach. To one and all, the message is preach'.[22] After fifty years of service, she died in her beloved Bengal and is buried, appropriately, by the side of a road where crowds pass her grave each day.

�֍ Women missionaries and the English Church Missionary Society

Not only was there a rapid expansion of women recruits to Baptist missions in the last quarter of the nineteenth century, but the Church Missionary Society (CMS) also experienced an unprecedented growth of involvement on the part of Anglican women. Two revivals, the Anglo Scottish Revival of the 1850s and the Keswick-George Grubb-led revival which burst upon Australia in the early 1890s attracted a large number of women — many of them well-educated — to the ideal of missionary service.

Middle-class women of private means soon found themselves particularly acceptable to boards of cash-strapped missionary societies. Although CMS was not officially opposed to the despatch of women missionaries to the field prior to 1880, it had, in fact, sent very few. The first CMS woman missionary was Mary Bouffler, who was sent to Sierra Leone in 1820 and survived only five months.[23]

So for reasons of health and the ninety per cent marriage rate of women missionaries when overseas, it was unofficial policy to hold single women back. The *zenana* issue, together with improved education for women in such fields as nursing, changed this attitude and CMS threw its weight behind the Church of England Zenana Missionary Society when it was founded in 1880.

Even though the need for women missionaries was by this time being recognised, male attitudes could still be extremely condescending, as when Bishop Hannington of East Africa asked London in 1884 for some 'strapping old maids' to work in his diocese.[24] Possibly, his subsequent martyrdom was at the hands of a feminist in disguise!

The Keswick Convention, which had begun in a Lancashire rectory in 1875 for the purpose of deepening the spiritual life, had an important part to play in promoting the missionary role of women. Evangelicals from the USA and the Empire attended this annual convention which actively encouraged young people, many of whom were graduates, to support missions. In 1887, a CMS missionary in Palestine sent an appeal to Keswick asking specifically for young women to come as missionaries to the Holy Land where Muslim women were mainly in purdah:

> Are there not Christian ladies of private means who are attending the convention who would come out here and work among the Muslim women? Cannot ten come this year?[25]

There was an immediate response which reverberated in Australia as women offered to serve in the Middle East — *gratis* if need be. It scarcely occurred to them that the men alongside whom they would be working would be paid while they would not. The following year, a missionary movement began at Keswick and four of the chief speakers were women. In 1889, a Keswick fund for 'missioners' was set up which despatched George Grubb, the talented Irish preacher, on his world tour.

The Grubb Mission had a marked imprint on Australia. Large crowds attended his missions, churches reported over-flowing congregations and many volunteered for ordination and missionary training. Ordination was closed to women, so they volunteered for missionary service in larger numbers than the men.

✠ Women and the Australian Church Missionary Society

Up to this point, the Australian branches of CMS in Victoria and New South Wales had re-iterated its oneness with London, but by 1891 there was a greater desire for independence. In the heady days following the economic boom of the 1880s and the subsequent Grubb mission, the Australian church had raised considerable funds for overseas missions. They now sought autonomy in sending out their own missionaries. In response, a deputation from CMS London arrived in Australia the following year. These church leaders not only created a great deal of missionary interest, but they also officially loosed the various states' Church Missionary Associations — as they were known — from imperial control:

> Take your own share in the evangelisation of the world; send out your own missionaries and support them; and if they are appointed to CMS fields, they will there have all the privileges and opportunities of CMS links.[26]

Miss Eliza Hassall (seated left) and the first missionary training college for women: Ashfield, 1892

A further result of this deputation was the establishment of formal training for women missionaries. Miss Eliza Hassall, a grand-daughter of Samuel Marsden, who had herself trained at the new Bethany Deaconess Institution in Balmain, offered her house in Ashfield as a training home for women candidates for the mission field.[27]

Eliza Hassall was appointed first superintendent of the Marsden Training Home, as it was known, and remained there for ten years. She lectured her students in the Acts, Revelation and Missionary Geography; they included her own niece Amy Oxley, who went out to China as her first graduate. It kept going till 1903 when training for women missionaries was transferred to the Deaconess Institution, which by now was in Newtown.

Training of Victorian women missionary candidates began at the interdenominational Missionary Training Home in East

Melbourne. By 1902, evangelical Anglicans had opened their own training home for women at Fitzroy, which was known as St Hilda's Training Home.[28] Co-educational institutions for missionary training were as yet unknown. From 1892 to 1895, CMS from NSW, Victoria and New Zealand sent out two clergy and their wives, three unmarried laymen and eight single women to a wide spectrum of mission fields.

The first volunteer to be accepted was Helen Plummer Phillips, a graduate of Bedford College, who had been headmistress of St Catherine's, Waverley for seven years. She had established a reputation at St Catherine's for having raised morale, numbers and the academic life of the school. She had followed the lead taken by South Australian and Victorian schools of entering her girls in the public examinations for matriculation and the civil service.[29]

In 1890, she resigned to take up a position as tutor to women students at the University of Sydney, but within two years she was on her way to Ceylon as a CMS missionary. Here, she was able to bring her considerable professional experience to bear in setting up an educational system in Ceylon over twelve years. She opened an industrial school for girls at Dodandura in 1893, a girls' English high school at Chandicully in 1896, the CMS Ladies College in Colombo in 1900 and a girls' English school at Cotta in 1903. She appointed staff, supervised curricula and travelled constantly to her schools which were spread across three quarters of the island. When she retired in 1905, she devoted herself to writing a book about work amongst Cingalese women.[30]

Despite the fact that the vast majority of CMS candidates departing for overseas in the 1890s were women, no women were represented on mission councils — whether at state or federal level — until well after World War I. However, in 1897 in Victoria a Women's Missionary Council was established to oversee women missionaries. It also founded and sustained Gleaners' Unions, information and fundraising bodies set up to promote missionary interest amongst the laity, and Sowers' Bands, which also operated at parish level, but concentrated on interesting children and youth in missions.[31]

In NSW, a Ladies' Committee had already been formed, not only to raise funds, but also to examine and equip women candidates who wished to proceed to the field. It was a wise step at this stage, given the flood of female applicants; the CMA board in each state relied heavily on the recommendations of its ladies' committee before accepting candidates.

The first members of the ladies' committee were leading clergy wives and laywomen, presided over initially by Eliza Hassall. They set up a depot in the Strand Arcade containing a library, and a tearoom to provide income and missionary displays. So well did they administer their affairs that, by the 1920s, women were finally admitted to the general committee of the CMS and the ladies' committee was no longer needed in its original form.[32]

✄ Women and the China Inland Mission

Perhaps the mission that most clearly welcomed women workers and treated them with total parity of esteem was the China Inland Mission. This remarkable organisation had begun as early as 1853, when the visionary Hudson Taylor was burdened with what he saw as the spiritual darkness of China's millions who numbered nearly a quarter of the human race. He decided that his mission should rely entirely on God for workers, finance and guidance. The principle of the faith mission was born: no salary was ever offered to missionary workers and only the Almighty was ever asked for money.

This principle was taken up by many other missions thereafter and it was a principle which seemed to appeal particularly to single women as it was they who responded most enthusiastically to the challenge of the China Inland Mission. Of the 337 Australian missionaries who sailed to China up to 1938, 193 were single women and 144 were men — some of whom were married. The proportion of women was even higher up to 1918, 198 single women going out with CIM and 122 men, a number of whom were married.[33]

Nor was the female preponderance confined to the turn of the century: the parent council had reported in London in 1889 that of 268 missionaries on the field, 181 were women and 61 were men. Single women numbered 120, so every man at this point must have been married. Hudson Taylor was totally egalitarian in his attitude to the sexes. Although careful about whom he accepted for service — three out of four applicants were turned away — he never rejected a candidate on grounds of sex alone, a policy which earned him criticism amongst some clergymen.[34]

The earliest Australian missionary to serve with CIM was Mary Reed, a young Tasmanian, who applied in England and went out to China in 1888 before the mission was established in Australia. She arrived in Yangchow where she stayed a few weeks with other young women missionaries, learning to wear Chinese dress, aspects of Chinese culture and some vocabulary, as part of the mission's policy of enculturating its workers. Then, she set out with three other ladies and a Chinese guide on a houseboat north up the Grand Canal towards Peking.[35]

Boat travel was often the safest for missionaries — as pioneers in Oceania and the Northern Territory discovered. It not only minimised opportunities for acts of violence and theft, but it also meant less infection and contaminated food. Nevertheless, Chinese boats were dirty, uncomfortable and easily overturned; it was also impossible to stand up inside them because of their low roof.

A sense of adventure, as well as underlying nervousness, is unmistakable in Mary Reed's account of her first journey:

> **27 April 1888:** Just before dark we embarked. Miss Murray and several others prayed to our heavenly Father. Undid our *pukais* (Chinese bedding). Quiet time of prayer, each one alone and then all together each morning. When the boats stopped, went ashore with tracts and gospels to sell and distribute. Chinese women very receptive... Often a large crowd of noisy men surrounded us. . .
>
> **28 April:** Arrived at small hamlets. . . found the women more eager to examine our clothes and feel us than to listen to the gospel. Returned covered in mud and, as we had not a change of garments with us, Miss MacFarlane and I had to spend the rest of the day in bed while our things were being dried.[36]

A good sense of humour helped the pioneer missionary as well as profound *sangfroid*, especially when the Chinese rocked the gondola-style houseboats 'to see if the missionary ladies would scream. But we didn't appear frightened'. Despite the amiability of the Chinese women who were not enclosed in *zenanas* like their Indian and Muslim sisters, danger was not far away:

> **29 April:** We moved for the night on the outskirts of the city. Crowds of men came down to the boat and stared in, in mute amazement, as if we were some marvellous species of wild beasts. Miss McKee and Miss MacFarlane went out, but got so pelted with mud and knocked about in the large crowds that would follow them that, after selling a number of books, they returned. . .[37]

After eighteen months, Mary Reed was invalided home, but she returned to China in 1890 with the first Australian party of twelve. She was the forerunner of a number of exceptional women who worked with the CIM up to 1914 and beyond.

Some met martyrdom, like Mary Heaysman from South Australia during the Boxer Uprisings of 1900–1901. Some died of disease, like Mary Sorensen of Tasmania. Some worked for over thirty years, totally identifying with the Chinese people in language, dress and custom, like Alice MacFarlane (nee Henry) from Victoria and Emma McIntyre (nee Spiller) of Queensland.[38] Members of the same family served with the CIM, like the five Trudinger sisters from South Australia who volunteered along with their brother, Augustus Trudinger. Two sisters, Annie and Susie Garland from Victoria, spent nearly forty years teaching the blind in China and produced a form of Braille for Chinese script.[39]

Florence Young

One of the earliest Australian women to sail with the China Inland Mission was Florence Young of Queensland. She was to be the first Australian woman to found her own mission — indeed, she founded two.

Florence Young was born into a well-to-do Brethren family in 1856. After being educated in England, she returned in 1882 to live on her family's sugar cane plantation at Bundaberg. Here, she took pity on the Kanakas who had been brought from the Solomons and New Hebrides and brought to work as cheap labour on the Queensland cane plantations. She found that most white people in the area regarded them as little more than animals who could not be educated. So she began schools for them, making the Bible the basis of the curriculum.

In 1886, she established the Queensland Kanaka Mission, targeting the 10,000 islanders who were already in Queensland.

She asked often reluctant planters if they would release the Kanakas for a daily lesson run by her workers in each district. This was possibly the brightest spot in the Islanders' day as photographs reveal these unfortunate people chained together in gangs under the hard eyes of armed overseers.[40]

At its peak, the Kanaka Mission had nineteen missionaries working from eleven centres. Also, a positive response from the Islanders was becoming noticeable to employers as well as evangelists.[41] Florence Young attended Hudson Taylor's missionary rally in Brisbane in 1890. His first words to his hearers were, 'Isn't it "*All*" in Christ?".' She was immediately moved to serve in China and, at the age of thirty-five, found herself working mainly with Swedish CIM missionaries in Kiangsi, China. The seven single ladies were supported by Chinese pastors and evangelists in opening schools, a home for old women and thriving native churches.

By 1894, her health was beginning to deteriorate. Boils, infections and malaria had appeared — and a new posting to a difficult village, where she was living in an old house wedged between an opium den and a pigsty, made matters worse. News then came through that the Kanaka Mission was having problems in her absence. Hudson Taylor counselled her to return.[42] After two years of hard work in 1895 and 1896, she was able to restore the Kanaka mission to a proper footing. She returned fresh to China the following year and worked there till the outbreak of the Boxer Rebellion.

This uprising was complex in its origins; social and economic distress had brought discontent against the Chinese government as well as Western intruders to a head. Missionaries in China were often viewed as agents of wealthy, white imperialist countries who would not hesitate to use gunboat diplomacy to protect their nationals. Moreover, the record of Western traders and businessmen who had engaged in such choice occupations as gunrunning and the sale of opium prejudiced indigenes against foreign missionaries.

The Boxer rebels did not hesitate to attack mission stations and thirteen CIM missionaries were murdered. Florence Young and many of her co-workers were evacuated to the coast, escaping the fate of the total of 188 Protestant missionaries who were killed by the insurgents.[43] When she returned to Queensland to consolidate the Kanaka work further, she found that the new federal government of Australia had adopted a White Australia Policy, decreeing that all Kanakas must return to their islands by 1906. News began filtering in of the martyrdom of some of the converts from the Kanaka Mission as they returned to the savagery of their own islands.

In 1904, at the Katoomba Convention — the Australian counterpart of Keswick which met annually in her brother's family mansion in the Blue Mountains — Florence asked for prayer for her Kanakas. As a result, the Solomon Islands Mission, later to be known as the South Sea Evangelical Mission, was begun. Like the CIM, it was a faith mission, interdenominational and evangelical.[44]

Florence herself sailed to the island of Malaita where cannibalism was still practised and was the first white woman to land there. Owing mainly to internal strife, the islanders there were diseased and degraded — in contrast to the neighbouring Maluans who had been evangelised by the members of the Kanaka Mission on their return from Bundaberg and were experiencing a time of joyful revival. However, within two years, the SSEM had established six missionaries, three stations and thirteen outstations on Malaita. The wild island was changed as a result of one woman's vision and it was not the last island to be transformed in this way as a result of her leadership.[45]

❈ Florence Buchanan

Another remarkable woman to work amongst the Kanakas and the Torres Strait Islanders in particular was Deaconess Florence Buchanan. Although frail and crippled in body, her indomitable spirit enabled her to evangelise Melanesians and Japanese alike during her period of service on Thursday Island from 1895 to 1905. During this time, she gained First Class Honours in Theology from the Australian College of Theology. She so impressed the Bishop of Carpentaria, Gilbert White, that he invited her to be ordained deaconess and minister solo to the islanders of Moa. He wrote of her:

> It was impossible to be in her company without being drawn to her. The mobile, pain-drawn face, the great spiritual eyes, the frail little body dressed in plainest uniform were some of the outward marks of the tremendous energy, unconquerable will and ever-present purpose within.

She was carried ashore to the island of Moa in 1908 and set up a well-ordered and happy community amongst the Kanakas who had not been deported, but had married Aboriginal women. From her two-roomed grass hut, she directed the people, her larger room serving as chapel, school, hospital, council chamber and adult classroom.

'She was teacher, priestess [sic], doctor, councillor and friend,' wrote an observer. She survived only three years of this regimen, dying soon afterwards at the age of fifty-two, universally mourned by her islanders.[46]

❈ Women who worked with Aboriginal people

Although few women worked as missionaries to Aborigines before World War I, there were one or two significant exceptions. The wives of two Moravian missionaries to the Cape York area — Matilda Ward and Mary Ann Hey — were sisters.

These women worked in dangerous conditions, despised by white people and distrusted by the dispossessed Aborigines. The latter were disillusioned and wary of white people who had taken their land, and in some cases wives, and who had given them diseases and a taste for alcohol in return.

As these two women tried to help the Aboriginal women and children, they gradually won over their menfolk, so that they were asked to mediate in family disputes. When her husband died in 1894, Matilda Ward was adopted by the Presbyterian Women's Missionary Union, who supported her work and the building of a church as a memorial to her husband. In 1897, the Queensland parliament appointed Mrs Ward and the Heys as Protectors of the Aboriginal people in the region. It was an appropriate title, as they had protected the indigenous people from the depredations of the pearling industry and other white frontier interests.[47]

One of the most effective women missionaries to the Aborigines was Retta Long, who was born in Sydney in 1878 to Baptist parents. Through the interdenominational youth organisation — Christian Endeavour — Retta Dixon, as she then was, first befriended Aborigines living in La Perouse. In 1899, she became a resident missionary there attached to what was known as the NSW Aborigines' Mission. This body later separated into two large missions: the United Aboriginal Mission (UAM) and the Aborigines Inland Mission (AIM). She also travelled to the Hawkesbury River and up and down the NSW coast seeking camps of Aborigines.

After six years, she resigned and went to live in Singleton where she founded, with a group of church people, the Aborigines Inland Mission. The following year (1906), she married Leonard Long who became a co-director of the mission. The work began to expand: Aboriginal churches were formed and their own pastors were appointed. Each church was independent, members being allowed to control their own affairs — an unusual step in times when Aborigines had no rights and it was thought they might die out anyway.

The Aborigines Inland Mission gradually spread to the other states, except Western Australia. When her husband died in 1928, Retta again resumed sole control of the mission, founding a large children's home in Darwin, and a Bible training institute for Aboriginal young men and women.[48]

Unfortunately, despite her worthy and unselfish motives, Retta Long did not bring happiness to many of her little charges in the children's home. This was not only because of the cruel but generally well-meaning policy of the government in separating half-caste children from their mothers, but because the children found the mission's approach too rigid and paternalistic.[49]

Women missionaries and the Methodist church

Turning finally to Methodist women missionaries, it is disappointing to observe that this church was the most patronising in its attitude to women workers — and single women workers in particular. Like the Presbyterians, the Methodists separated mission administration so that women's work was partially run by the Ladies' Foreign Mission Association in each state. No woman was allowed to sit on the Methodist Overseas Mission Board until 1922 and it was not till 1915 that a Register of Missionary 'sisters', as single women missionaries were called, was drawn up.[50]

The term 'sister' had its origins in the first Wesleyan expansion into Europe and North America and, although it was outdated by the late nineteenth century, the Methodist Overseas Mission Board refused a request by the South Australian Ladies Auxiliary to review the name in 1903.[51] On 8 April 1918, the district synod moved that the name 'woman missionary' be substituted for that of missionary sister; nearly two years later, the synod board rejected that request.[52] Subsequent attempts to change the name to a more egalitarian title were consistently rejected. It would appear, then, that the Mission Board was a reactionary body when it came to dealing with women missionaries. It was certainly bureaucratic with its advisory committee and its executive committee — all without female representation.

When commenting on the lowly status of the missionary sisters, an experienced LMS missionary reported to the Methodist Overseas Mission Board in 1918 that Methodist women missionaries were accorded too lowly a status: 'I think you should give your women missionaries the same status as the men. It may not be possible — the principles of Methodism may be against it; but after all, Christ's kingdom comes first; Methodism second.'[53]

It is difficult to reconcile the progressive attitude of the Methodist hierarchy towards secondary education for girls, as summed up in their foundation of the excellent Methodist ladies' colleges throughout Australia, with their conservative mission policy. There seems to be an ambivalence in their attitude towards women in this period. For instance, outdated articles on this subject appear in Methodist magazines at the turn of the century. For example, in a magazine published in 1905 Tennyson is revived: 'Woman has a distinct sphere all of her own. It is not in the public thoroughfare, fighting for supremacy with men.'

Or an even more sickly apotheosis of women:

Not learned, save in gracious household ways;
Not perfect, nay, but full of tender wants;
No angel, but dearer being, all dip't
In angel instincts, breathing Paradise. . .[54]

Small wonder so many Wesleyan women volunteered to go out with CIM! However, there were some missionary sisters of extremely independent spirit, like Hannah Dudley, who did not allow the Mission Board to dominate them. Hannah Dudley was a fully qualified teacher from the outback of NSW who went out with the British Methodist Missionary Society to northern India in 1891. She became proficient in Urdu, working mainly amongst orphans and lower caste children. Her village school was set up in an old mud hut which the people re-plastered and roofed for her; there were no desks, so the children wrote in the sand. After five years, she returned home broken in health.

It was not long before she volunteered to live among the poor Indians who had been shipped to Fiji to work on the plantations there. She opened a school, teaching in Urdu as well as English. Without consulting the Mission Board, she adopted six orphans and at one stage took them to India for three years. When she was finally invalided home in 1913, the Indians mourned the loss of their *Hamari Mataji* — Honoured Mother.[55] Most Methodist missionary sisters were expected to be low key in their approach and work under the married women, even if they were doctors. Harriet Bromilow, wife of Rev. W.C. Bromilow, who pioneered the Methodist field on the island of Dobu off the coast of New Guinea, is described in the following way in the *Christian Weekly Methodist Journal* of Adelaide (16 October 1898):

> Mrs Bromilow oversees the work of the sisters and nurse and, in the absence of her husband, she takes divine service, preaching to the natives with charming ease.[56]

The ten women missionaries who worked under Harriet Bromilow — visiting the villages two by two and teaching and caring for the sick — did not seem to mind the term 'sister' in the 1890s. But as the new century progressed, women missionaries became increasingly restive about it.

The patriarchal climate of Methodist missions is further reinforced by the attitude of mission historians from James Colwell, who published in 1914, to A.H. Wood, who published as late as 1975. The former manages to devote half-a-page to the missionary sisters, while the latter generously gives up one chapter in his four-volume history to Hannah Dudley and the missionary sisterhood — despite the fact that single women missionaries in Methodist missions outnumbered male missionaries in 1915 by 198 to 148.[57]

A growing opportunity for women missionaries

The nineteenth century witnessed a slow and sporadic involvement by women in overseas missions, at least until 1880. There had, of course, been proselytisation in Oceania by Irish, English, Australian and French female orders, as has already been demonstrated. The small band of women sent out to New South Wales by LMS in 1810 was virtually intended for marriage with the single male missionaries in the colony — a purpose which was rapidly fulfilled.

Intrepid missionary wives became an essential part of the campaign to win souls, often sustaining a ministry of their own to the natives, as well as supporting their husband's work. However, there was no concerted effort by missionary societies to send out single women until the *zenana* dilemma confronted missionaries who were endeavouring to evangelise Indian families after 1860.

The success of the *zenana* missionaries, allied to the appeal in the Keswick letter of 1887 for women to go to Palestine, brought about a change in missionary thinking. In the years 1888 and 1889, CMS sent out thirty-one single women missionaries all told and yet, in the next decade, 409 went out.[58] From

1890 to 1914, the departure of women missionaries from Australian shores outnumbered that of men by two to one. If married women are taken into consideration, the female preponderance on overseas mission stations was even higher.

In searching for reasons for the predominance of women missionaries after 1890, social and economic factors must be taken into account. First, there had been an educational explosion for women: universities were open to women in Australia after 1880, as was free elementary education. Church schools and a few high schools were offering matriculation to girls. The feminist movement, spearheaded by such bodies as the Women's Christian Temperance Union, was agitating strongly for the vote for women. Women were actively looking for professional occupation and there was generally a lack of opportunity for this kind of fulfilment at home.

Many women identified with the oppressed women of more primitive societies and the challenge of transforming the lot of fellow women appealed to those who were service-oriented. Ruth Rouse, in her paper entitled 'The Ideal of Womanhood as a Factor in Missionary Work', argues that the woman's movement was an offspring of Christianity and that it found three aspects of missions were congenial to its outlook.

The first was the internationalism of missions. Overseas missions were a means of working with like-minded women of many nationalities to bring Christianity to less fortunate women and children. The fellowship enjoyed by Australian CIM missionaries with colleagues from England, Sweden and other countries, not to mention the internationalism of such Catholic missionary orders as the various Marist Missionary Sisterhoods, are cases in point.

The second was the missionary's concern for morality. The reclamation of alien cultures from such practices as child marriage, temple prostitution and self-immolation of widows chimed in with home movements like the WCTU working for women's rights and the purification of society.

The third was the mission ideal of service.[59] Raised with Victorian concepts of helping the underprivileged and imbued with the attitude of one who said 'I am among you as one who serves,' women missionaries gained not only satisfaction in their work, but also a sense of freedom and independence.

Finally, it is clear that the affinity of the woman's movement with missionary work was strengthened by the providential opening up of such professions as medicine and education to women just when such skills were needed on the mission field. Such a woman was Laura Hope, the first female medical graduate of Adelaide University (1891), who worked with her husband for forty years amongst the poor of India, ignoring indifferent health.[60]

As far as motivation is concerned, Australian women missionaries also relished the sense of adventure and the opportunity to work alongside men in a situation of equal danger and challenge. Suddenly, an opportunity of ministry and leadership was opening up which was denied them in the home church, at least as far as an ordained ministry was concerned. Apart from the chance of serving human beings from another culture, there was the mystical aspect: total fulfilment in a limitless relationship with Jesus the Master was closer in the mission situation.

'We are here for him and with him and he cares for us,' exulted Florence Young in the isolation and squalor of a Chinese village.

At her farewell in Sydney in 1899, Edna Bavin, daughter of the Methodist minister at Ashfield, outlined her motivation in going to China:

> Love to Jesus simplifies everything. Questions about whether we should go or stay — all are answered by our

love to Jesus. When we love Jesus fully, it is easy to do
his service. We go anywhere — suffer anything — when
we are full of love to him![61]

Added to a profound sense of spiritual devotion, which had
its roots in the Keswick and Katoomba Conventions and in
the writings and example of Hudson Taylor, was a strong sense
of *fin de siecle* in the theology of the day. Millennialianism
dominated the thinking of the devout, especially Brethren
families like the Youngs who influenced evangelical leaders in
the Anglican Church like Nathaniel Jones in Sydney and H.B.
Macartney in Melbourne. Not only was the old century
coming to an end in a secular sense but, for the majority of
missionaries, both male and female, events were moving
quickly towards the second coming of Christ, the climactic end
of history to take place once the gospel had been preached to
all people.[62] It was an advent that these women missionaries
were determined to hasten, while at the same time helping to
transform the lot of the less fortunate of the earth.

The role of the single woman missionary in this period,
whether she was married or single, was principally to diffuse
or preach the gospel, but in practice the married woman
concentrated on the role of helpmeet to her husband and
exemplar to indigenous families.

At first, her status was higher than that of her single sister
because of prevailing Victorian domestic concepts. However,
by the end of this period the single woman was coming into
her own as an unexpressed feminist ideology merged with
evangelical fervour gave her undreamt-of fulfilment in her
work at home and abroad.

8

A worthy use of gifts of leadership

WOMEN MISSIONARIES BETWEEN THE WARS

'Do you still have people on pedestals? Mine have all fallen off. . . Today, I preached at the evangelistic service on the Great Supper and have been taking the Sunday school story (as well as) prayers every morning at the clinic.'

Narelle Bullard (1931) in Tanganyika

'The Presbyterian Church has for years had a woman preacher in the outpost furthest in all Australia from the sea and if men have always preached so well nearer the coast, we have cause for deep satisfaction.'

John Flynn (1914), founder of the
Australian Inland Mission

IN THE YEARS FOLLOWING WORLD WAR I, women continued to comprise the majority of Australian missionaries working overseas. Some were gifted young doctors like Mary Glowrey and Adelaide Gault, who were denied opportunities at home in a male-dominated profession. Almost all women missionaries were now trained for teaching or medical work or else for evangelism, unlike many of their pre-War sisters.

231

Male leaders in missionary work like John Flynn and Bishop George Chambers showed no gender bias, believing that women could perform as well as, if not better than the men. Indeed, women missionaries were often more acceptable to Aborigines than the men. It was in missionary work that women were able to experience freedom from the limitations of the patriarchal church at home.

The inter-war period of foreign missions must still be viewed as part of the colonial era which had its origins in the late eighteenth century. Assumptions about the superiority of Western culture still prevailed on mission boards and in the minds of many older missionaries. Every year, CMS missionaries were still issued with diaries featuring maps of the world splashed with the red of Empire. They contained geographical details, but were innocent of cultural information about the various fields.

However, World War I was to prove significant in the gradual breakdown of concepts of Western superiority. Britain and the major European powers had been weakened economically and politically, and nationalist movements were beginning to emerge in China and India where so many missionaries were working. This not only made life dangerous for them, but it forced the wiser amongst them to change their policies and work to expedite the transition from mission to indigenous church.

While the war was still on, British missionaries in East Africa were meeting to discuss a reformist agenda which centred on the education and status of African women. However, when the war was over, most mission boards continued to follow traditional goals which were based on the assumptions of the colonial era.

Anthropological studies were still not offered at missionary training colleges, although they were coming in at university level, usually with an anti-mission bias. They criticised missionaries for imposing Western ways on indigenous cultures, citing demoralisation in such fields as inland Australia and Hawaii as the fault of mission paternalism. Most missionaries were aware, however, that they must review their old methods as they returned to where they had left off when war had broken out.[1]

Although the thrust of missions in the inter-war period was increasingly institutional as more hospitals, schools, orphanages and churches were built, women still provided a larger part of the evangelistic vanguard, pioneering in areas where Christ had never before been preached. New areas were opened in Africa, China and New Guinea and suitable women were encouraged by bishops, mission directors and heads of orders to seek appointments in these areas. A particular study will be made of Australian women missionaries in Tanganyika at this time, as so many of their private papers have survived, compared with other mission areas. The Tanganyika field also provides a valuable case-study in that it reflects a broader and deeper role for women within the framework of a traditionally hierarchical church.

The inter-war period also witnessed a concerted attempt by the churches to reach the Aboriginal people of Australia. The greatest shame of European settlement was white treatment of defenceless Aboriginal women and children. The churches at last realised it was necessary to make amends and who better to lead in reconciliation than women workers themselves?

The Aboriginal response to women missionaries was far more positive because of their gentler approach and their image of non-exploitation. There were, of course, some exceptions to this rule, where certain women were excessively authoritarian in administering children's homes. However, gradually Aboriginal women themselves began to play an independent role on mission stations, assisting with Bible translation and worship.

✠ The effects of the outbreak of war: 1914

The outbreak of war in 1914, without at first greatly affecting the population of Australia, had considerable implications for international bodies like missionary societies. Donations to the work fell sharply and budgets had to be pruned. For example, the income of the China Inland Mission fell alarmingly from 8 633 pounds in 1915 to 4 802 pounds the following year. The improvement thereafter was only gradual and the 1915 level was not regained till 1920.

As far as the recruitment of personnel for CIM was concerned, very few men were able to go to the mission areas, partly because many had enlisted in the forces, partly because travel of male civilians of military age was virtually forbidden. From 1915 to 1919, six new men went out, compared with twenty-two women. Thus, women predominated in the CIM fields more than ever — by almost 3 to 1. This ratio improved post-war to 3 to 2.[2]

Apart from financial and recruitment concerns which were common to all areas, missionaries in China and India were not as severely dislocated by the Great War as were those in the Middle East and East Africa, where the Turkish and German presence were stronger. Missionaries in these areas were either interned or exiled or else went in fear of their lives. The war diaries of Katie Miller, an Australian CMS missionary in German East Africa, have survived to give us a picture of the trials faced by an interned missionary.[3]

The German occupation forces in Tanganyika were on the defensive from 1915 onwards against sporadic British incursions from the sea to the east and more concentrated Belgian attacks from the west. Thus, the British and Australian

missionaries in Tanganyika, who numbered approximately
fifteen, were subjected to severe shortages of food and supplies
and received no communication from home for more than
three years. There were constant rumours about their fate,
while German soldiers continually moved them on before
their final internment in the garrison town of Tabora near the
Belgian lines.

In the early stages, the missionaries kept themselves in good
spirits with prayer services, singing and afternoon teaparties.
The fastidious Katie Miller was always 'turning out' her room
in order to deal with unpleasant members of the insect
kingdom, but chiefly to expunge the omnipresent African dust.
The rumours and uncertainty were unnerving, but finally there
came the command to move:

> **4.20 p.m.** Got the order to pack up and leave in half-
> an-hour. Left with Herr Dornedoff and *asikari* [local
> soldier] (drunk). No meal. Walked all the way to
> Kikimba, reached 7.40, very tired. . . we were all locked
> in the magazine, 49 Europeans, 44 natives, 2 *asikari*; we
> lay on sacks or boxes. Very little sleep. Great row middle
> night. Herr D ordered *asikari* to shoot anyone who spoke!
> Both he and *a[sikari]* were drunk.[4]

When they reached Tabora, thirty women and a baby were
crammed into a school dormitory and seldom had privacy
from soldiers marching into their quarters at will. Katie
occupied herself with sewing, brushing up her Swahili and
doing the inevitable 'turning out' of her room. She suffered
attacks of malaria. The noise of gunfire grew louder as the
Belgian forces approached:

> I unstitched the lining of my helmet and pasted the pieces
> together. Prayer meeting at night. Helped sew a Union

Jack in readiness for the advent of our army. Another
German buried. Red Cross permitted on the roof of the
Native Hospital.[5]

Finally, after six months of internment, they were released
and dispatched north to freedom. On the way, they passed
through country scarred with rifle pits and burnt-out camps.
Finally, they crossed the trenches where German bodies still
lay unburied. Even today, this journey to the border is
lengthy and difficult; how much more taxing it was in the
aftermath of war. What joy it was to be reunited with their
fellow missionaries in Uganda and to receive three years'
supply of letters from home!

✖ The aftermath of war: 1918

Although World War I had caused considerable turmoil for
missions, as well as straitened circumstances, it also brought
about fresh ideas and strategies, many of which touched on the
role of women missionaries. In the secular sphere, women
nurses and voluntary workers had proved their mettle behind
the lines. Likewise in the missionary sphere, women had kept
most fields open with reduced help from men and under
increased difficulty caused by war.

Thus, missionary societies were more disposed than ever to
treat their women workers in an egalitarian fashion. The war
had not even ended when what was designated 'The United
Conference of Missionaries in British East Africa' was held in
Kikuyu, Kenya.[6] Men and women delegates representing the
various missions operating in East Africa debated an enlightened agenda in which women's issues were placed side by side
with men's.

Such difficult questions as polygamy were aired by field
missionaries who were more understanding in cultural matters
than were mission boards in London. For example, they

pressed for education for African girls, theological training for Biblewomen and medical training for nurses. Christian marriage and divorce and the status of African women and girls were thoroughly debated. At no time was the education of women regarded as less important than that of men.[7]

Thus, it was a matter of policy that, when an Australian Anglican episcopate was set up in Tanganyika ten years later, the education of girls at Mvumi High School was regarded as significant as that of the boys at Kongwa College. Bishop George Chambers, as we shall see, did not need any prompting in pursuing an egalitarian policy towards the sexes, especially as the majority of his colleagues turned out to be women.

✠ Australian missionary colleges and women

Such egalitarianism was slower to spread within the home church, where returning women missionaries were asked to address missionary meetings for ten minutes, but never to preach or lead services as they had been accustomed to do overseas. They were scarcely ever invited to join missionary boards or lecture at co-educational training colleges, even though the majority of candidates for the field were women.

At first, missionary colleges were single sex. Anglican women missionaries trained at Deaconess House in Sydney and St Hilda's Training Home in Melbourne, while Presbyterian trainees went to the Deaconess Home in Melbourne. In New South Wales, the Methodists trained their women candidates in the George Brown Training Home, while the men were trained a few miles away at the George Brown Training College. The inequity of this nomenclature must have been apparent even in those days.[8]

One of the most prestigious of the interdenominational missionary colleges was the Missionary and Bible College which was founded at Croydon, NSW in 1916; however, this was strictly for men. A strong Puritanism prevailed on its campus: no woman missionary on deputation set foot inside the college till 1921 and it was not until 1926 that wives of students were permitted to reside on the property. Finally, in 1927, the Board gave way to pressure and agreed to open a women's department the following year — provided, of course, that it was on separate premises.[9] A tradition of separation continued until well after World War II whereby women always sat at the back of lectures and ate at separate tables to the men.

Co-education for missionary candidates, however, was steadily introduced in the 1920s by the Angas College in Adelaide and the Melbourne Bible Institute, which was founded by Rev. C.H. Nash in 1921. Nash introduced women from the beginning and this helps to account for the large number of graduates which his college produced — over 2 000 by 1963.[10]

✠ The male-female ratio of missionaries

Following World War I, the trend towards female predominance in the missionary candidature of Australia was steadied as men of military age returned to the mission field. However, it was never reversed, as increasing numbers of women looked to overseas service, finding that their talents were being more fully used — and appreciated — outside their own country.

The male-female imbalance is also explicable in terms of the option of ordination: men wishing to pursue full-time ministry were able to choose parish work as ordained clergy and this avenue was far more popular than service far from home.

Thus in 1921, of the 136 CIM workers on the field from Australia and New Zealand, forty-seven were men and eighty-nine were women. By 1938, of 166 Australasian missionaries, sixty-three were men and 103 were women.[11] As the flagship of the interdenominational faith missions, CIM reflected volunteer patterns occurring in the smaller missions. It is also one of the better administered and documented missions of this type for later students of the women's role to look at.

The founder of CIM, Hudson Taylor, received much criticism for his acceptance of women to work in such a dangerous field as China.[12] However, the effectiveness of his mission and the glad cooperation of CIM female workers answered most of his critics.

The Australian Home Committee was quite prepared to accept a majoirty of female workers, but not to allow them executive power on the field. The question of female executive power was particularly acute in CIM/OMF because whole areas in China had been opened up and developed by women on their own. In the Kwangsi River area, for example, church planting had been conducted solely by women *ex nihilo* from 1885 onwards. By 1915, there were ten central stations, sixty outstations and 2200 church members and only local pastors and Biblewomen to help the women missionaries.[13] Thus, a gulf between policy and praxis arose as the home council steadfastly refused the request of the field director, D.E. Hoste, to include women in administration overseas. The home council met in the Collins Street Baptist Church between the wars, their meetings being chaired by the son of the veteran Anglican evangelical, Dean MacCartney, the Reverend H.B. Macartney, Rector of St Mary's, Caulfield.

Members frequently discussed the recommendation that women should at least share in field administration, but each time — as in the case below — conservative elements, most of whom were Brethren, extracted one or two Bible verses to reject the proposal:

The question of the wisdom of women taking a seat on

the Shanghai Council was again discussed. . . and it was pointed out that women would not be invested with any ecclesiastical authority, but the suggestion was that they should take a seat on the advisory council where it was not considered they would exercise authority over men.[14]

Lengthy discussion and prolonged prayer accompanied these deliberations throughout the 1920s, but no unanimity could be reached, the council being divided between a church and a mission party. All agreed that women should be accorded 'thankful appreciation' for all they had done, but that:

> We desire, however, to affirm our conviction that the teaching of the Apostle Paul in 1 Timothy 2: 11–14 determines as a matter of principle the limitations set to the authority of women in the church, and to ignore and violate this and cognate scriptures would be so far as to depose the New Testament from its acknowledged position as the final regulative authority in matters of church order.[15]

The issue then dragged on for the next two decades, despite a further plea from the field director that 'these councils are advisory in character and therefore women would not be exercising authority over men'.[16]

▓ Female missionaries in China

In the inter-war period, this danger became more acute as the political situation deteriorated. The centuries-old Manchu dynasty had been overthrown in 1911 by Dr Sun Yat-sen and his Kuomintang party. However, the Kuomintang were not able to establish control over such a vast and populous country. Civil unrest broke out and warlords and brigands roamed the country. Missionaries and Chinese Christians often went in fear of their lives in this uncertain political climate, especially as many nationals viewed Christians as agents of Western imperialism.

Then, to crown this litany of problems, came the invasion of China by the Japanese, beginning with the Manchurian Crisis of 1931. Japan thereafter infiltrated, bombed and invaded China until, by the close of 1938, the whole of coastal China and much of northern China was in their hands.

The experience of Christina Shaw, who escaped death in 1914 at the hands of a particularly notorious bandit known as the White Wolf, was an encouragement to other solo Australian women missionaries in China. She wrote of her capture:

> They were anything but desirable company; their conversation for the greater part was recapitulating, for my benefit, the awful atrocities they had committed at the various places they had visited. . . I had no fear, none whatever; the Lord took away all fear of man; that fact alone saved me. . . A gun was held at my heart and I was told that I would be immediately shot. I prayed the Father to help me speak. . . I said, 'You may shoot me, but you cannot harm me. As soon as you shoot me, my spirit will go straight to heaven.'
>
> 'Why are you not afraid? You are all alone and I mean to shoot you,' he said.
>
> 'You are mistaken,' I said. 'I am not alone. My Father is with me; I am his child and he will not allow any harm to come nigh me.'
>
> 'Where is he? I cannot see him.'
>
> 'No,' I said, 'he is a Spirit, but if you were his, you would know he is here. Do you know he loves you and if you are willing. . . ' The robber unlocked the door and fled.
>
> The White Wolf told his men to allow Christina Shaw to go free and, after walking for two days, she reached safety.[17]

Posing an even greater threat to missionaries at this time than bandits were various forms of disease and fever. These were caused by an absence of public hygiene and by mosquitoes. Matilda Way, a missionary from Victoria, wrote of an unpleasant experience which casts light on the lack of public health in China at the time:

> I had not gone far when it rained heavily. I was unable to cross the river, it was so high; it was sweeping down everything that came before it. I had to stay at any wayside place. My native made up a bed of coffin boards for me on two forms. Alongside this was a coffin with a corpse in it — the smell was almost unbearable. I spent a day and a night in the place.[18]

Small wonder that six Australian women missionaries with CIM died of typhus and other diseases in the 1930s.[19]

Another hazard to public health was the frequent presence of cesspools by the side of Chinese roads. As the weary traveller thumped along in a springless cart, he or she could often be catapulted out if the porter were careless. The future Archbishop of Sydney, Howard Mowll, found himself reposing in a cesspit because of a negligent porter. So did Annabella Parsons, wife of a Tasmanian missionary, who was thrown into the mess with her little baby. Unfortunately, the baby later died as a result of his immersion in such filth.[20]

Often the greatest trial facing married women missionaries was separation from their children once they reached school age. If the children went to boarding school in another country, it meant parents often missed seeing their children growing up. Hudson Taylor was especially concerned about this problem and he was able to obtain some land at Chefoo on the northern Chinese coast, where he built a hospital and sanitorium as well as a school for the children of CIM missionaries. Parents were now able to visit their children at least once a year and know they were in good hands educationally and spiritually — as well as relatively safe from marauding soldiers and bandits.[21]

Some missionaries like the redoubtable Queenslander, Emma McIntyre, whose husband died prematurely on the field in 1920, kept her five children with her as long as possible on evangelistic tours, trying to teach them herself, but this was not a practice normally recommended as mission policy. Mission work was difficult enough without children being exposed to the civil strife which existed in China. Eventually, she sent two to Chefoo and three to Brisbane for schooling. Her eldest son, Herbert, returned to China to help her evangelise forty towns in the Onei area from 1931 to 1935.[22]

Australian women also went to China with the Church Missionary Society in this period. There was a desperate need for orphanages in such a war-torn country and three Tasmanians, Adeline Nisbet, Ethel Kingsmill and Emilie Stevens, did magnificent work with orphans in the Fukien area of China.[23] Victorian CMS had always taken a keen interest in the Fukien mission since the martyrdom of the sisters Nelly and Topsy Saunders at Hwasing in 1895.[24] The girls' mother had gone in an honorary capacity to work in their place and she was followed by a number of others, including Alice Kendall who served for thirty-two years, Isabella Hughes for forty-one years and the twins, Mina and Elizabeth Clark, who were to spend part of their forty years' stint in a Japanese internment camp.[25]

Orphanage and hospital work were also the destiny of a youthful Mary Andrews, future principal of the Anglican Deaconess House in Sydney, who arrived in Beijing in 1938 to find wartime conditions already prevailing. A Chinese family kept her alive in a house where she was interned alone, by hiding the day's food under the back door. She had to eat it all at one sitting in case the Japanese guards should suspect her friends. She was able to escape to a safer area and spend the war years nursing and teaching large numbers of underprivileged children.[26]

Katie Miller

A study of the Australian mission in Tanganyika, which was established in 1928, is especially instructive for the student of women's history in that an excellent resource of diaries and letters from women missionaries has been preserved.

The diaries of Katie Miller, which have already been touched upon, give a fascinating — if cryptic — account of life in a primitive society from 1905 onwards. She is almost totally self-effacing and her bravery and achievements must be deduced from brief entries which centre upon actions rather than feelings.

For example, her battle to save a small baby's life over a period of three weeks in 1919 emerges among her other entries about services, language classes, cooking and cleaning. Finally,

Katie Miller on safari in Africa

she is 'Up all night with wee babe, she passed away at 6.50 a.m. unable to get her breath, Mr Deekes baptised her Hefsi. The old father came and carried her to her grave.' Katie's reaction was 'Rested nearly all day. Had a bad headache.'[27] Again, she disguises her anguish when the small orphan boy she has fostered is difficult to control. . . 'Wee Meshak caught stealing.'[28] She continues to care for him until CMS guarantee his education to the age of eighteen.

Basically her health was good, but 'fever' — usually malaria — was always lurking: 'Sam sick, donkey lazy, I, old and tired.'[29] A sense of humour was a *sine qua non* for a single woman missionary; otherwise, she collapsed under pressure or tension broke out between workers.

As she became a senior missionary, her workload grew until she was taking five services or classes on a Sunday — first the 'Old Folks' Service', then the children's service; then the women's class, then the Sunday school and finally an enquirers' class.

There were never enough helpers. The dispensary also had to be opened every day and domestic chores always had to be 'seen to'. The congregation at her beloved Berega numbered at least 400 souls.[30] In all, she spent twenty-five years at this particular station building up the faith of her 'dear, dark friends'. She cared for their health and she travelled on her donkey Possie all over the countryside, planting new churches and helping to encourage and train native ordinands for the work. 'She was the founder of the church at Berega' is the opinion of one authority on missions.[31]

Such an experienced leader was invaluable to Bishop George Chambers when he arrived in Africa in 1928 to take over the new Diocese of Central Tanganyika. A man of dynamic energy and irresistible leadership, he did not hesitate to utilise the gifts of his predominantly female strikeforce. He quickly perceived Katie's rapport with the Africans, as well as her facility with the Cigogo and Swahili languages, and decided to take her away with him on safari visiting the people in their villages.

The diminutive Katie in her turn was delighted with the reinforcements from Australia and the expansion they brought to the work. But she was never happier than when she was working quietly at Berega among the people who called her 'Bibi'.[32]

✠ Narelle Bullard

The other two women missionaries from Central Tanganyika, whose papers have survived from this period, are Narelle Bullard and Ruth Minton Taylor.

Narelle Bullard had cherished a desire to become a missionary since her days as a Sunday School pupil in George Chambers' parish of Holy Trinity, Dulwich Hill, in Sydney's inner west. After leaving school in 1917, she systematically prepared for overseas service: first, membership of the Young Peoples' Union Missionary Band, then teacher training with the Anglican Board of Religious Training, attainment of the rank of Staff Captain with the Girl Guides (1924) and a St John Ambulance Certificate for first aid.[33]

In 1925, she entered Deaconess House to train for missionary service and applied to CMS. With the post-war stress on professional training, their response was that she should pursue a nursing course with full obstetrics and then come back to them. In the meantime, she graduated with second-class honours in theology and was set apart as a deaconess in March 1928.[34] As soon as her nursing training was complete,[35] she was accepted by CMS and sent out with multitudinous instructions, including exhortations to cultivate a sense of humour and to avoid criticism of other workers. It was mission policy for her to be on mandatory probation until she had completed language study. Above all came the advice:

> Let nothing interfere with your early morning hour for prayer and Bible reading. . . It was to a woman Christ said, 'Great is thy faith, be it unto thee even as thou wilt.'[36]

On arrival in Tanganyika, Narelle found a sense of humour even more necessary than she had imagined. First, she was desperately homesick, craving for letters from home and missing her father and sister, who did not write as often as she. Then, she found she missed her music: 'I'd give anything to hear a piano.'[37] She chafed under the demands of language study, squirmed under her mosquito net to escape the attention of a scorpion and trimmed up an old topee to protect her from the sun — 'It looks as if I came here in 1888!' Then, she went off visiting to ask people to come to church — 'church being a service on our verandah taken by two ladies'.[38]

Finally, after six months in the country, she was able to commence her public health and mothercraft program, work for which she was finally awarded the MBE in Tanganyika:

> Tomorrow I start mothercraft classes and hope to teach hygiene and sewing and try to get Christian women to be leaders in that direction. I want them to be a sort of club, each trying to live up to the ideals they have heard about.[39]

Narelle Bullard had two main problems in building up a medical infrastructure in a primitive society — since she saw this as complementary to her mandate of spreading the gospel. The first was to establish a pattern of outpatient care; the people must be weaned off the native witchdoctors to whom they took their sick children before bringing them half dead to her. She had, as well, to battle to prevent people going home when not sufficiently cured:

> The other mother said, 'Give my baby medicine.' I said, 'I have given it sufficient.' She said, 'I will go home then.' I talked to her like a dutch uncle! Quietness then reigned . . . A father arrived — he said, 'Did you give my child medicine?' I said, 'Yes'. He said, ' We shall return to the *kaya* [village]. I then turned on him . . . what patience one needs with them. . . it is the fifth child they have lost. . .[40]

The second problem facing Narelle Bullard was the building up of a *corpus* of native nurses to take over the work in the long term. It was difficult to train young girls who had no concept of a profession or of care of anyone outside the family. Furthermore, the African concept of taboo forbade girls to take up nursing on pain of never being able to marry and, indeed, bringing upon themselves a general curse. Thus, on Narelle's first arrival, nursing was left to elderly illiterate Christian women.

However, as she established her training hospital at Kongwa, prejudice was gradually broken down and, after two decades, there was a waiting list of girls anxious to train as nurses.[41] By 1938, she was able to report that Kongwa Hospital had twenty-eight beds and ten cots. During the year, there were 252 in-patients and 10 976 outpatients. 'We have tried to do all the work to the glory of Jesus Christ' was her comment.[42]

Apart from her sterling medical work, Narelle Bullard also pursued the roles of pastor, evangelist and preacher. In October 1930, she went on safari with a fellow missionary, Deaconess Louis Wilmot. At the village of Nhambi, they held a three day mission:

> Louis took the children and I the adults and the church was full both times. I preached from 'Jerusalem, Jerusalem who killeth the prophets, how often etc.' and I tried to

plead with all those Christians, some of whom had been away from their teaching for some years; we had silent prayer after and the atmosphere was rather wonderful.[43]

Narelle Bullard experienced a distinct call to preaching as well as nursing:

Today, I preached at the evangelistic service on the Great Supper and have been taking the Sunday school story and taking prayers every morning myself at the clinic.[44]

However, this gift could never be exercised in her own country because of attitudes in church and society at the time. Although she did express disappointment about both this and also the home church's habit of giving credit to male missionaries for much of her medical work,[45] retirement was to mellow many of her frustrations.

For a time, she ran a community of spiritual healing at her home in Wentworth Falls in the Blue Mountains of NSW, but her preaching and, to some degree, her pastoral gifts were allowed to fall into desuetude.

One day at a CMS function, she met an African bishop whom she had known as a boy and instructed as an ordinand. He was very excited to see her and paid tribute to 'Bibi' Bullard: 'She should be up on the platform with me. She is our mother.' Her comment was: 'There was not a chair available. I stayed where I was, feeling very humble at the honour paid me. . . I said later, "Bishop, we were many who were there. . ."'[46]

✠ Ruth Minton Taylor

The final member of the trio of women who have left diaries and letters detailing their experiences in Tanganyika in this period is Ruth Minton Taylor.[47] A woman of spirit and sensitivity who stood up even to Bishop Chambers at times, she was one of the early graduates of Waverley Kindergarten College and her gifts and training were used to the full in the villages of East Africa. Born in Tasmania, she had met Bishop Chambers at various CMS summer schools and been challenged to missionary service.

However, it was something of a shock to receive his characteristically high-powered invitation to join the Australian team in Tanganyika. He was determined to enlist her and so offered her any position from kindergarten teacher at the new Mvumi School for Girls to that of assistant at the teacher training college for men at Kongwa. Like Hudson Taylor, Chambers was refreshingly egalitarian in his attitude towards the women workers in his diocese.

The letter concludes with a typical exhortation:

Do take this letter as the expression of a divine call, for Tanganyika needs you so much. You can fulfil that need so well. May God guide your way.
Yours expectantly and sincerely,
G.A. Central Tanganyika.[48]

Ruth Minton Taylor and her sewing class: Tanganyika, about 1930

She went. Nor was she sorry, as she found she loved the life. In particular, she came to love the school at Mvumi, which was headed by an outstanding administrator from Perth, Avis Richardson. Ruth Minton Taylor made long friezes illustrating the Bible and African life for her classes; she used the gramophone for lessons and services. Sometimes, she would carry it over to the neighbouring hospital where she taught the nurses the quickstep, much to the hilarity of the African patients.

Her superb sense of the ridiculous emerges in this description of teaching the African girls the elements of housekeeping:

> They think we're quite mad in many ways — all our food and fuss, pots and sauces; and little bits of clothing and absurdities. Really, I begin to feel we are, too — specially when I'm housekeeping, or when I get holes in my stockings, and split dresses and things. . .[49]

Like the other women missionaries in Tanganyika, she found the Africans a gentle people and felt quite safe when alone. She was not so fond of the vermin — scorpions, tsetse fly, rats and mosquitoes and the odd snake which sidled in when the door was left open. More disturbing was the deep breathing of the hyenas at the windows at night. They could never be seen by torchlight, but occasionally one of the locals sleeping outside found his little toe being removed during the night!

An assessment of the Australian work in Tanganyika

The Australian team in Tanganyika had an enviable record of happy cooperation and achievement from 1928 through to World War II and beyond. By 1938, George Chambers had gathered a team of twenty-four Australian missionaries around him, seventeen of whom were women. He was always able to get the best out of his workers, partly because he didn't discriminate against women missionaries in terms of tasks allotted and credit given. Katie Miller and Narelle Bullard were encouraged to go on safari to plant and build up churches — a task some missions would have reserved for men.[50]

The achievements of the team in such a primitive area were manifest after ten short years — a vast cathedral, a village school of over 100 students and a kindergarten of comparable size, a large hospital with maternity block and many departments, including a leprosy unit; and a college in Kongwa training African teachers and pastors to spread Christianity, as well as literacy to all the surrounding villages. A conscious attempt had been made to establish a self-supporting church rather than a paternalistic mission, but only time would show the permanence of the work.[51]

❊ Women and the Baptist work in Bengal

Women continued to play a major role with the Baptist Missionary Society in Bengal. Between 1914 and 1938, fifteen new men and forty-three new women went to the area. This meant that the Bengal mission by 1938 had a total ratio of twenty-four men to sixty-nine women.[52] Many Baptists also worked with interdenominational missions in Africa and China and they were particularly active in the Aborigines Inland Mission, founded by the pioneer Retta Long, whose work has been treated in the previous chapter.

One of the reasons for the predominance of Baptist women missionaries in India was the resounding leadership of the great Ellen Arnold. Like the founder of a Catholic order, she gathered a team of devoted women about her and she did not die till 1931. It was not easy for some men missionaries to work under such a powerful woman. The sexual imbalance in Baptist missionary ranks can also be laid at the door of the home church where it has been demonstrated that women were excluded from leadership roles, thus resulting in the stronger female personalities choosing overseas service.[53]

✠ Mary Glowrey

The inter-war period witnessed a growth of missionary service overseas by Australian-born Roman Catholics. This form of Christian service had not been normally chosen by Catholic women up to this point. Those with a strong vocation tended to join an order which concentrated on education, healing and social work among the Australian poor. The Vatican prohibition on women in orders being able to pursue a profession or engage in such activities as midwifery was not relaxed until 1936, so that Australian Catholic work overseas did not really take off until after World War II.

There were, however, two women who blazed the trail for later Catholic missionary work. They were Mary Glowrey and Mary Sheldon.

Mary Glowrey was born in the backblocks of Victoria, where she felt a call to serve in India after meeting poor Indian hawkers who camped on her father's farm. A brilliant student, Mary Glowrey won an Exhibition to Melbourne University where she studied both arts and medicine, graduating in 1910. In accordance with the patriarchal system of the day, no position was available for her at a Melbourne teaching hospital, so she was obliged to do her residency in New Zealand. On returning to Melbourne in 1914, she set up practice in Collins Street.[54]

By 1916, she felt a strong vocation to an order and this call was further strengthened by the publication of a pamphlet about the medical dilemma of Indian women. The pamphlet contained an appeal by a Scottish missionary, Dr Agnes

McLaren, who had converted to Rome at the age of sixty-one and gone to India eleven years later to found a Catholic hospital for women.[55] Dr McLaren pointed out the desperate need for Indian women to be treated medically by qualified women — as their culture prevented them from going to male doctors. Five hundred Indian women were dying each day in childbirth for lack of attention.

Mary Glowrey responded to this need by sailing to India in 1920 and joining an order of Dutch nuns who were doing medical work in the See of Madras.

Two barriers now lay in her way before her ambition to provide Catholic women doctors for the women of India could be fulfilled. The first was that she would have to found an order if she were to get these doctors into India and the second was Rome's caveat against women taking vows while practising a profession.

She paid five visits to Rome, in between healing Indian women in the villages, until finally the Vatican changed its mind about orders and professions and especially the profession of midwifery.[56] Thus, when the news came in 1936 that the papal ban had been lifted, Sister Mary Glowrey of the Society of Jesus, Mary and Joseph was now free, like her Protestant counterparts, to open a medical college. She began training Indian nurses and doctors at St John's College in Bangalore and finally died there in 1957, having never returned to her home country.[57]

❇ Mary Sheldon

The other great Australian Catholic missionary of the inter-war period was Mother Mary Sheldon of the Society of the Sacred Heart. Her field was education which was not under Vatican caveat. Born in Armidale, NSW, in 1876, she was sent to the SSH Convent at Rose Bay, Sydney, where she was influenced by the principal, Mother Alice Power. On her twenty-first birthday, she decided to enter the order, training first of all in London.

After working in Melbourne and Auckland, she was appointed Superior of the Tokyo Convent of the Sacred Heart in 1917. From the outset, she was influenced by the great missionary encyclical, *Rerum Ecclesiae* (1659) , which declared:

> It is not the custom and the rites of any European country that the missioners come to implant, but the faith which does not reject the customs of any land, unless they are evil, but, on the contrary, desires that they should be kept up.[58]

Thus, she set about mastering the Japanese language and determined to make her girls more Japanese and not Westernise them. She appointed a Japanese directress, Madame Hirata, and the two worked in total harmony for twenty years. A training college for teachers was opened in 1920 and then a convent in the Osaka Diocese. In 1923, the catastrophic Tokyo earthquake took place; many Westerners returned home from a city engulfed in flames. She refused to do so and salvaged what she could of her ruined school, reopening classes almost immediately. In 1926 she became provincial of a new SSH province, which included Shanghai.

She and her sisters respected Japanese traditions, but they found themselves in opposition to the fascist and communist movements of the 1930s in Japan and China. Despite poor health, she survived internment and was able to resume her educational role and, like Mary Glowrey, never returned to her home country.[59]

Women and Methodist mission work

Methodist women missionaries maintained their tradition of

educational and medical work in India and the South Pacific during this period. They continued to outnumber men clearly, 141 of them going out between 1915 and 1938 as compared with eighty-two men.[60]

The terminology referring to these women is ambiguous: sometimes they are called by the old name 'missionary sisters' — sometimes 'missionary nurses', sometimes 'trained teachers', sometimes 'doctors'. The term 'missionary sisters' was a useful one for those women without particular professional training who worked in such primitive societies as New Britain. Here, women wore a uniform and worked in pairs for protection; they received praise for their 'devotion and service' in difficult jungle conditions.[61] Women missionaries in the Fiji area, however, petitioned the totally male Methodist Overseas Mission Board for a change of name to 'women missionaries' in 1920. Their request was turned down, but the term 'missionary sisters' is used less and less in the mission board minutes as if members realised its unpopularity with most women.[62]

The Methodist Overseas Mission Board received more than it bargained for when it asked a leading LMS missionary, Florence Garnham, in 1918 to report on the work of the Australian missionary sisters. She began by praising their achievements in Fiji and she then turned her guns on the board:

> Your women missionaries are being given tasks which are overtaxing their strength. I went into schools where some of your women were attempting tremendous tasks. One woman managing a school of eighty-five boys — with one Indian boy to help.[63]

Florence Garnham did not comment on the princely salary of 100 pounds per annum paid to missionary sisters, as her own salary as a missionary in India had probably been as low,

but she objected to the meagre preparation of women missionaries: some were sent out without educational training. Nor
were women given as much language training as the men, so
they could not achieve cultural identification as quickly as the
men. She then made a stinging attack on the paternalism of
Methodist missions vis-a-vis their female staff:

> I am not a suffragette. . . but it strikes me that your women
> missionaries are not given the status that should be given
> them. There is no opportunity to see the work as a
> whole. . . or to think broadly or largely.

In the LMS, she claimed, every woman had the same status
as the men. She had been on the district committee and had
an equal voice with the men. The result of it had been that
the women realised they were truly missionaries as much as
the men — preachers of the gospel — and their responsibility
was equal to that of the men.[64]

It is not hard to detect Florence Garnham's hand in the
subsequent request from the Fiji synod to change the name
'missionary sister'. Her report ends with an impassioned
recommendation:

> I think you should give your women missionaries the same
> status as the men. It may not be possible — the principles
> of Methodism may be against it; but after all, Christ's
> kingdom comes first; Methodism second.[65]

The reaction of the mission board was largely to ignore
this report, although they did establish the George Brown
Training Home to improve the training of women missionaries. Membership of the board continued to be almost
exclusively male for the whole inter-war period, despite the
numerical predominance of women in missionary work.

The reason for this problem of apparent discrimination lay

partly in the Methodist Church's choice of a dual form of administration of missions. The mission board and its executive consisted largely of clergy who delegated the selection and support of the missionary sisters to a women's auxiliary in each state — known as the Methodist Women's Foreign Missionary Auxiliary. The mission board then rubber-stamped the various WFMA's recommendations and left those auxiliaries to take a close interest in their candidates.[66]

Inequities in the Methodist system did not prevent outstanding women from volunteering for service overseas, amongst them Dr Adelaide Gault. While a student at MLC Hawthorn, she had heard Dr Ida Scudder speak. The latter was an American missionary who had founded the great hospital for Indian women at Vellore, South India. Adelaide Gault studied medicine at Melbourne University and, although she gained honours in both medicine and surgery, she shared Mary Glowrey's experience of being unable to obtain a resident's post at a Melbourne teaching hospital.

She therefore decided to proceed to India in 1924, where she discovered for herself the medical impasse facing Indian women. Encouraged by an entrepreneurial missionary, Rev. J.H. Allen, she founded the Christian Hospital for Women at Azarugarh. Conditions were primitive at first, operations were carried out by hurricane lamps and a primus stove was used for sterilising instruments and dressings. Adelaide was exhausted after four years of such pressure and isolation and was forced to return to Australia; but she left a well-established hospital behind her.[67]

Women and Presbyterian mission work

Although the Presbyterian Church used a similar dual system of mission administration to the Methodists — with a central executive mission board and a Presbyterian Women's Missionary Association, which selected women candidates and then made arrangements for their support — there is less evidence of a paternalistic attitude towards women missionaries than obtained in the Methodist Church.

As we have seen, the attitude of the Rollands, father and son, towards the training of Presbyterian deaconesses for ministry at home and abroad helped to raise the status of women in that church. Rev. William Rolland had founded the Deaconess Training Institution in Melbourne in 1898 and his son, Frank, also a moderator of the Presbyterian Church, encouraged graduates of that institution to work in the out-back; he even worked as a 'deaconess' himself later on to confirm his solidarity with women in ministry.

Presbyterian women missionaries, who trained at the Melbourne Deaconess Institution, went to the New Hebrides, Korea and inland Australia. One of their graduates, Nurse M.A. Latto Bett, served first of all at the Oodnadatta Hospital for three years; she then went to a new hospital at Vila, New Hebrides in 1915. Finally, she married a medical missionary in Korea, so she had experienced the whole range of Australian Presbyterian missions![68]

Perhaps the most outspoken 'feminist' of all churchmen at this time was the Reverend John Flynn, founder of the Australian Inland Mission in 1912. In his lively journal, *The Inlander*, which was published four times a year initially, he praised the work of the deaconess sisters of Oodnadatta who ran services, Sunday school and scripture classes in addition to their medical duties:

> The Presbyterian Church has for years had a woman preacher in the outpost furthest in Australia from the sea and if men have always preached as well nearer the coast, we have cause for deep satisfaction.[69]

Sister Jean Williamson, Australian Inland Mission:
a pioneer nurse at Alice Springs, c.1919

The inland work was lonely and taxing for Sister Bett and her successors. Small wonder they did not stay long in the outback — the average stay until 1920 was two years. She once wrote to Flynn in the searing heat of January:

I am sorry I had to omit answering your letter last mail, but my patient died early Monday morning at 3.15. I had been up most of Saturday night. I was too tired to think. Besides, I had all the funeral arrangements [including conducting the burial service at the graveside], wires, registrations, as well as fumigation, to attend to.[70]

Sister Bett was replaced by Sister Jean Finlayson who was soon afterwards posted north to open up the work at Alice Springs. It was a 400 mile journey by mail buggy and camel. So welcome was she that the Alice Springs police officer met her at Heavitree Gap to escort her into 'town'. She was shown a hut where she could open the first dispensary and surgery in the region. She also conducted Sunday school there and took Alice Springs' first regular church services.[71]

Nursing sisters continued to go out with the Australian Inland Mission till 1929 when the twelfth nursing home opened at Innamincka. This hospital — the Elizabeth Symon Home — rose out of the desolation of the Simpson Desert which had defeated the explorers Burke and Wills.

Two young Melbourne nurses, Elizabeth Burchill and Ina Currey, staffed this outpost of civilisation for three years. They coped with such disasters as the bubonic plague epidemic of 1930 and nursed patients in temperatures of 120 degrees. They taught Sunday school, pulled teeth and brought cheerful company to the outback of north-eastern South Australia. It was only with the introduction of wireless and the Flying Doctor Service based in Cloncurry from 1928 that these nurses became less indispensable.[72]

�֎ Women and the Bush Church Aid Society

Almost as active as the Australian Inland Mission in reaching outback whites and Aborigines was the Anglican Bush Church Aid Society (BCA). This mission, which was founded by

Bishop Arthur Pain of the Gippsland Diocese in 1917, concentrated on the south and west of the continent.

At first, it was thought that female participation in the mission was out of the question because of the isolation and type of population. Gradually, however, it was realised that the women who lived in the outback could best be reached by their own sex. 'For the work of the BCA, the ministry of women soon came to be recognised as a complement, not a supplement, to the ministry of men,' wrote Bishop S.J. Kirkby in his slim history of the BCA, which significantly devotes three chapters to the ministry of women.[73]

The BCA came to rely on three categories of women for its outreach: nurses, deaconesses and hostel sisters. These women served as far afield as Gippsland and Wilcannia, the Darling River basin and the Nullarbor Plain. They set up hostels for children from remote areas and a hospital in the Nullarbor. They visited outback people, ran services and conducted a Mail Bag Sunday School which contacted up to 4 000 children of remote areas by means of personal letters and weekly lessons. The mission could not have survived without its female staff and it was the first to admit it.[74]

✠ Women and Aboriginal work

The inter-war period witnessed a great expansion in attempts by the churches to reach Aborigines. European settlers and governments realised by this time that the Aboriginal people as a race were not going to die out and they also felt varying measures of contrition for the manner in which Aborigines had been treated since 1788.

When the eccentric Daisy Bates wrote to the Commonwealth government asking to be considered for the position of Chief Protector of the Northern Territory, she argued:

The Aborigines question is really a woman's question; it

is the Aboriginal women and children we are called upon to protect instead of the men. Native men can take care of themselves at all times, but native women and children have never had a chance in the 100 years of Australian settlement.[75]

There can be no doubt about the shameful treatment meted out to Aboriginal women by white men, particularly in remote areas where few white women lived. One Northern Territory official even found religious sanction for white exploitation of Aboriginal women, declaring that God meant Aboriginal women to be 'used' by white men 'as he had placed them wherever the pioneers go'.[76]

Hence, it is not surprising that amongst the most effective missions to Aborigines were those that were started by or chiefly staffed by women — the Aborigines were less terrified of them. These were the Aborigines Inland Mission, founded by Retta Long, and the United Aborigines Mission.

An Aboriginal training home was set up by UAM in Quorn, South Australia, when Annie Lock was given five young part-Aboriginal girls to care for. She was followed by Ruby Hyde who ran the training home, known as the Colebrook Training Home, assisted by Sister Delia Rutter for nearly thirty years. These loving and maternal women succeeded in winning over a large number of part-Aboriginal children, taken from their mothers by government fiat. Their warm and accepting attitude was in stark contrast to the situation in most government hostels in Western Australia in particular, where the state after 1915 systematically placed half-caste children away from the church as well as their mothers.[77]

The Church Missionary Society also attempted to evangelise remote Northern Territory tribes after 1911, using an increasingly female workforce. When their first mission station opened at Roper River, the customary proportion of three to one obtained — two single women and a married couple, Alfred and Mary Dyer. The latter was known to the people as the 'White Mother' for her unselfish care of them. For example, at the Oenpelli Station which opened in 1913, she clothed and fed up to 200 people, apart from her teaching. Her husband was away for long periods, leaving her to run the mission at Oenpelli. It was no wonder she became exhausted and fell victim to cancer by 1934.[78]

Some missionaries, like Rev. Harold Warren who pioneered the mission which opened at Groote Island in 1921, found their wives' presence doubly valuable in pioneering new fields. On his first river and coastal trips, Harold Warren took his wife and young child. The tribes they encountered had never seen a white woman before and the novelty attracted them out of the bush. Ellie Warren wrote:

> **19 April:** When they saw me, the women hid their faces with paper bark or their hands, because they had never seen a white woman before.
> **20 April:** I allowed myself to be patted and prodded and I even patted their horrible snarling dogs. . . made 'johnny cakes' to win over the terrified children.[79]

Her presence also helped to allay their fears; they were extremely apprehensive at first when Warren gathered them for the first service to be held on Groote Island. When he produced a camera tripod to take their photo, the whole congregation vanished! However, they gradually reappeared, encouraged by her smiles and tea and johnny cakes. She could not believe their responsiveness: 'These are the people reputed to be cannibals and whom the missionaries were warned not to approach without a band of armed men.'[80]

By the close of the 1930s, Aboriginal women on mission

stations were beginning to develop independent roles in the religious life of the community, which flowed on post-war in the Aborigines' own churches. For instance, they contributed greatly to the translation of the Bible into their own tongues and also led in the interpretation of scripture to their own people.

Grace and Bidigainj on the CMS station at Roper River helped to translate two New Testament books into the Nunggubuyu language. Then, Grace asked the mission if they could do Genesis next:

> I told her it was a very big book, but she said she only wanted the first three chapters. 'They are about the beginning of things,' she said. 'You have seen our dances about how the fish came, how the kangaroo came. . . we are interested in the beginning of things.'
>
> So we translated the first three chapters of Genesis and I read them to the people one afternoon. They were very keenly interested. Next morning, everyone was bleary-eyed. I asked Grace if she had slept. 'None of us slept,' she said. 'We talked all night. I told you we were very interested in the beginning of things.'[81]

The period from 1914 to 1938 witnessed a further extension of the work of Australian women missionaries overseas and in the outback of Australia. Women continued to dominate the mission stations numerically — and where there were no men, they were *in loco viri*. When they returned, they were not allowed commensurate leadership in the home church.

By the outbreak of World War II, the executive boards of missionary societies at home were still exceedingly light in female membership — if it existed at all. Yet the majority of candidates being dispatched away were women. This was not a problem to members of Catholic teaching orders like Mother Mary Sheldon, who rejoiced in the autonomy of their order.

However, prospective medical missionaries like Mary Glowrey were frustrated for some years by Vatican opposition to women in orders practising a profession.

Women missionaries between the wars played a number of roles, whether professional — as doctors, nurses or teachers — or evangelistic and pastoral — as church planters, teachers and preachers. Usually, it was a combination of roles. They demonstrated special gifts with languages, often being called upon to interpret for bishops or visiting clergy.

Some adopted children where no-one else would take them, as Katie Miller did in Africa and Annie Lock did in South Australia. They demonstrated a special gift for winning over a shy and alienated people like the Aborigines — although some, of course, were too prescriptive culturally in this work.

Missionary wives generally found great satisfaction in working alongside their husbands in foreign climes. Those who had not married found total sublimation in a life of service:

> Isn't it wonderful what faith in God's will being done in us brings? Whatever comes and whatever God wills for me is the best, it is wonderfully comforting and has been the secret of my happiness.[82]

Whatever the motivation and rewards of the single woman 'on the mission field', it proved to be a place where her talents as a church leader could be amply fulfilled. Once she returned home, she was expected to discard her gifts of leadership and preaching and resume the subordinate role expected of women in the church at home. In her own country, full expression of her accustomed role was impossible.

9

Paving the way
for recognition

WOMEN IN ORDERS BETWEEN THE WARS

'The contribution of the women in orders has been
largely unsung by both civil and ecclesiastical society,
for these religious women do not really belong to the
official institutions of "state" or church.'

Sister Anne Maclay, RSM (1984)

'We must secure for our children, as fast as we can,
an education which relates all subjects to the greatest
event in history, the incarnation of God. If that is in
its right place, everything else makes sense. . .'

Sister Alice, SSA, in north Queensland, (1918)

'Nuns may look rather odd, but the costume is like
a flag, a flaunting banner which proclaims, almost
with drums and trumpets, that Christ is worth more
than all the world.'

Sister M. Declan Ruffles, RSM (professed 1930)

THIS PERIOD CONTAINED MANY PARADOXES for women
seeking to play a role in the church. On the one hand, it
was largely a time of stagnation as far as leadership for women

in the ecclesiastical hierarchy was concerned. On the other, the local church became increasingly feminised as laywomen took over almost all fundraising, education and social work within the parish structure, apart from comprising sixty to seventy per cent of the congregation. The male hierarchy after 1918 appeared to be even more firmly entrenched in power as a result of wartime ideology and of the strictures of post-war reconstruction, followed by the Great Depression.

Yet this was also a period of expansion in women's orders, the members of which made a great professional impact in education, social work and medicine. Membership of orders doubled in the period 1910 to 1930 and, in the case of the small Anglican order, the Society of the Sacred Advent, vocations increased fourfold in answer to the challenge of the need for girls' church schools across Queensland. Women in orders, especially in the Roman Catholic Church, entered the field of tertiary education and, as we shall see, encountered strong opposition from some sectors of the male hierarchy.

However, by the close of this period, they had gained a measure of recognition within the church for the indispensable role of the professional woman in Australian society. Although World War I did not affect the social fabric of Australia as much as it did in Europe, it nevertheless appeared to cause a setback in the progress of women's emancipation. The mythology promulgated in the Great War affirmed such traditional gender roles as man as 'the warrior and creator of history and woman as the mother, the passive flesh at the mercy of fate. . .'[1]

A 1917 issue of the *National Leader*, an organ of the Returned Services and Patriots' League in Queensland stated that: 'The mother who gives her son in war is noble, sublime . . .the noblest thing on earth today.' Marilyn Lake points out that the Great War confirmed man as central to the national culture as never before. The Anzac myth as interpreted by some early commentators made the nomad and the scoundrel a national hero. Such masculinist myths tended to socialise men and women into macho and passive roles respectively. They were arguably a natural corollary of the bushman legend of Lawson and Archibald.[2]

This attitude towards gender roles was reinforced by government policy towards women serving in the War. Although women served in great numbers in voluntary agencies for the war effort, only nurses and those in the Red Cross were permitted to wear uniform. None were allowed to enlist in the services as such. When the war was over, few women were publicly thanked for their work or awarded any medals for their contribution to the war effort. Women were expected to return to their homes and allow their husbands to keep them in a state of economic dependency — and often boredom or quiet despair.

Active laywomen were able to join women's organisations like the Mothers' Union or the Catholic Women's Association or they could raise funds, help with parish chores or with visiting. They were frequently taken for granted — 'not sufficiently appreciated, a silent majority without voice in the church' is the recollection of one Western Australian nun who worked in the 1930s.[3]

For the single woman anxious to play an active role in the church which gave her some independence, the call to a vocation was often irresistible. 'If a woman wanted something above menial service or semi-skilled labour, she had little choice but to be a nun or a teacher.'[4] Orders offered a sense of community, economic security and stability of purpose which was not always available in the outside world.

Secular culture was unsympathetic to the single woman, the Royal Commission into the Basic Wage of 1920 declaring that the single life should be discouraged.[5] The unemployment and economic stress caused by the Great Depression meant that large Catholic families were obliged to encourage some of their children to enter a novitiate in order to feed them.

Thus, there was a marked expansion in recruitment to the orders in the inter-war period. Numbers of professed sisters in the Good Samaritan Order, for instance, rose from 251 in 1910 to 479 in 1930. By the outbreak of World War II, numbers had reached 580.[6] In the Loreto Order, numbers increased nationally from 168 in 1913 to 270 by 1925 to 308 professed by 1930.[7] The Sisters of St Joseph in NSW increased from 228 in 1900 to 500 by 1918 to 634 by 1930.[8]

In the North Sydney Congregation alone, the Sisters of Mercy increased from 148 sisters in 1910 to 187 by 1930. As a diocesan order, the Mercies were by far the most numerous group on a national basis, comprising well over half the total number of the 10 000 women religious working in Australia by 1940.[9]

❊ The situation for those entering Catholic orders

On entering an order, Catholic women found their roles firmly defined for them. Attendance at university was at this stage denied them. They could not enter a profession apart from teaching. They could administer a hospital, but they could not nurse in some fields or practise medicine themselves. Obstetrics were forbidden them until 1936 when the Pope decided that they might not be sexually aroused delivering babies after all.[10]

This was yet another instance of the failure of the Catholic hierarchy to deal with the whole question of female sexuality. The conclusion of the medieval schoolmen that women were rendered unclean by childbirth and menstruation provided a philosophical basis for male insecurities and authoritarianism in this sphere.

As postulants entered into the full life of the order, they often found the gap between mythology and praxis disconcerting. First, some felt uncomfortable with the division between nun and lay within the order; others questioned the teaching that the sisterhood was higher in status than the married state. Second, many felt resentment at the control of the male hierarchy over so many aspects of their daily behaviour and dress. Others resented the mental and physical oppression which often existed within the order itself. They were usually unable to express openly their frustration at that time, but subsequent interviewees have not been slow to do so:

> The option to remain single has always been a dubious one for women in the church. They can act as sacristans, church cleaners or flower arrangers and, if old or unattractive enough, as priests' housekeepers. . . they are second-class citizens whose function is, it seems, to provide a cheap and docile workforce as teachers and nurses.[11]

Ten out of fourteen Catholic nuns who were professed in this period affirmed in a recent survey that they had found the church too male-dominated and that they had experienced genuine frustration at the role expected of them in the church — whether by the parish priest, bishop or Mother Superior.[12] Two out of three Anglican deaconesses also admitted difficulty in this area: 'I accepted that the church was male-dominated. If they tried to offload their work on me, I refused.'[13]

✠ The Catholic Church's view of women

Before examining the role of Catholic religious, it is necessary to look at the church's view of women at this time. This view was an odd mixture of chivalry and judgementalism and had its origins in rural Ireland. Respect for the Virgin Mary meant more politeness and kindliness towards women in practice than that displayed in Protestant circles. However, the priesthood were convinced of the basic fallibility of women, believing simplistically that women were either a model of purity like the Virgin Mary or else were temptresses like Eve, who were likely to bring men to their destruction. Archbishop Michael Kelly of Sydney warned in 1925: 'Don't let Catholic women be as other women — anaemic creatures, filled with lustful desires and thoughts. . .'[14]

This neurotic view of women flowed over into an opposition towards their playing any public leadership role. Indeed, the Archbishop of Adelaide, John O'Reily, had announced his opposition to the franchise for women even when it had been a fact in Australian life for two decades: 'I am an utter disbeliever in woman suffrage. It unsexes and vulgarises those to whom every chivalry is due.'[15]

The hierarchical view of the ideal role of women not in orders was similar to that of the Protestant churches :

[She belonged to] the woman's sphere. . . where she reigned, surrounded by her loving husband and little children. All the good that was in a man was due to his mother, for to her God entrusted the moulding of the mind as well as the safeguarding of the infant intellect.[16]

As far as the role of the woman religious was concerned, the church regarded them as an elite force 'consecrated to Christ'. It constantly encouraged the 'good sisters' to work as missionary shock troops: 'Be sheepdogs to the people, rather than shepherds' was the advice of Bishop James Murray to the Dominican sisters of the Maitland Diocese in the late nineteenth century — and this was an attitude still prevailing amongst the hierarchy in the inter-war period.[17]

However, in the twentieth century, nuns gradually began to seek greater individuality and independence of expression.

They chafed at their lack of training and refreshment and the opportunity to seek higher education. Poorly educated as much of the priesthood was, it did not believe that further training was necessary for the orders; indeed, it might be downright dangerous because of the secular nature of the universities. Our survey of fourteen nuns working in the second quarter of this century reveals considerable frustration on the part of the majority at the lack of encouragement shown them by authority and at their frequent inability to take initiatives or exercise individual gifts.[18]

Priests requested many favours of teaching nuns in the way of printing and typing, but were reluctant to acknowledge the professional skills of many women in general. Some clerics were actually patronising.[19] Perhaps if clerical requests had not come on top of a very hard day's teaching, they might not have grated so much:

> The only frustration felt in those earlier days was the long hours spent in teaching, hours stretching from 8.15 a.m. to 6.00 p.m. without a break. Until the Catholic schools received financial support, this burden had to be borne.[20]

✠ The Daughters of Charity

Not only did numbers expand in Catholic female religious orders during this period, but fresh orders were established like the Daughters of Charity. This order arrived in Australia in 1926 from Ireland, where it had been transplanted from France with the associated Order of St Vincent. Its members did not take perpetual vows, but renewed their decision to serve each year. They carried out a wide-ranging ministry to the poor, assisted by committees of lay men and women. Lay participation helped them to do much effective work amongst the intellectually disabled, single pregnant girls, the homeless, Aboriginal people and refugees.[21]

Gaol visitation by the Sisters of Charity

The expansion of Catholic orders and their schools and hospitals was heavily dependent on the fund-raising efforts of the sisters, especially in the first half of the twentieth century before State Aid was introduced. Exhausted as they were by long hours in overcrowded classrooms, they were still obliged to devote any spare time to running fetes, bazaars, art unions and raffles.

The Sisters of Mercy in the huge All Hallows convent in Brisbane held an annual bazaar which was patronised by the great names of the city. Delicate lace from France and woven goods from Ireland were imported especially for the occasion, which was a highlight of the city's calendar as well as a valuable source of income for the school. As the frontier days receded, fundraising became more sophisticated and genteel in its methods. Gone was the unvarnished begging of the early days and there was increasingly less emphasis on gambling as part of fundraising.

The Sisters of St Joseph continued their notable work of welfare and teaching in this period, determined to maintain their record of independence as far as possible. Some of their early spontaneity might have faded, but their record in elementary education, based as it was on Mary MacKillop's carefully graded curricula, was a proud one. Furthermore, the opposition they had encountered from the hierarchy in the early days had evaporated as the bishops realised they could no longer afford to battle with an order which produced so many of the teachers the church needed, at so little cost.[22]

In the medical sphere, which was of less interest to the hierarchy, the Sisters of Charity had so built up St Vincent's Hospital in Melbourne by 1910 that it became the first hospital in Australia run by religious women to be recognised as a university teaching hospital. In 1923, St Vincent's Hospital in Sydney received the same distinction.

However, neither hospital at this stage could provide full medical training until they were able to offer a course in obstetrics. A papal ban prevented women religious from engaging in such work, as well as a general prohibition against nuns adopting a profession outside teaching and general nursing. The redoubtable Mother Gertrude Healy, the Hospital Administrator of the Sisters of Charity, set about working to reverse that ban. Called by Sir Herbert Schlink, himself a noted hospital superintendent, 'the greatest hospital administrator I have met', she was concerned not only to widen the training offered by St Vincent's, but also to help poorer mothers in need of pre- and post-natal hospitalisation.[23]

She issued a formal paper for the benefit of the clergy in

1923, which argued cogently for the setting up of a maternity hospital:

> The risks attendant upon the birth of children are common both to mother and child. . . it follows that the mother in those difficult and dangerous hours of her life is also an object of that charity, to exercise which is the proper business of Sisters of Charity who nurse. Hence. . . it is hard to see why such women should be excluded from the all-embracing and Christ-like charity it is the aim of our nursing sisters to exercise.[24]

In the same year, Archbishop Mannix of Melbourne and Bishop McCarthy of Bendigo gave permission to the Sisters of Charity to conduct maternity hospitals, but it was twelve years before the Pope changed his mind (modifying Canon 139#2) and officially allowed nuns to engage in obstetric nursing *per se.*

At this news, the Sisters of Charity were galvanised into action and, within twelve months, they had opened a new maternity hospital attached to St Vincent's in Melbourne. Sister Gertrude's dream was fulfilled.

Mother Gertrude Healy of St Vincent's Hospital, Sydney

✠ The Sisters of the Good Samaritan

Information is not always readily available as to the type and origin of candidates entering religious orders, but the Good Samaritan archivists have researched thoroughly into the pattern of application into their institute in this period.

Most of the Good Samaritan sisters working in Australia in the nineteenth and early twentieth century came from Ireland, where there was overpopulation and unemployment as well as strong religious fervour. By the inter-war period, there was a strong increase in Australian-born applicants, many of whom were better educated than their Irish predecessors.

Of those sisters professed between 1885 and 1937, 277 had at least one parent born in Ireland, compared with fifty-four of English stock and fifteen of Scottish parentage. Of these, only thirty-four were themselves born in Ireland, three in England and two in Scotland; the rest were born in Australia. Applicants often presented themselves from a particular country town. For example, the tiny settlement of Moruya, NSW, produced seventeen Good Samaritan sisters by 1937. Charters Towers, Queensland, was even more prolific in its production of postulants, producing forty-four sisters for this order by 1937.[25]

The chief means of recruitment was through personal contact with the sisters in their boarding and day schools and by recommendations from priests with whom the sisters were associated.

St Scholastica's College in Glebe, with its high standard of education and cultural activities, attracted many to the order. Family relationships were also important in attracting recruits to the institute. Between 1857 and 1937, the institute received: two sets of five sisters, five sets of four sisters, twenty-one sets of three sisters and sixty-four sets of two sisters — a tribute to the piety as well as the fecundity of Catholic families at that time![26]

The McDowell family, who were Scottish converts from the Northern Rivers of NSW, contributed five Sisters of Mercy, one Sister of Charity and six Sisters of the Good Samaritan in two generations. The greatest influence in their vocations they attributed to the happy boarding school education provided by the Good Samaritans. Most postulants in this period entered the institute before they turned twenty-five; some were as young as fifteen. Some died in their twenties, mainly of tuberculosis, but most survived to their sixties or seventies in this century.

Nuns leaving their orders for one reason or another have not been specifically documented. The general impression from these statistics is of steady recruitment to female orders in this period and of support from Catholic families for those daughters who wished to devote their lives to Christian service in the context of the independence provided by an order.[27]

Catholic orders and tertiary education

The question of tertiary education for young women of the fold was one which vexed the Roman Catholic hierarchy in Australia after the turn of the century. The widespread growth of female education and the granting of female suffrage in the 1890s meant that the church was constantly obliged to address itself to the question of the role and status of women within its ranks. The days when Catholic women formed the majority of domestic servants in the country (the latter were still seventeen per cent of the workforce at the turn of the century) were fast coming to an end.

Events at the Second Australasian Catholic Congress in 1904 showed that women were seeking a voice in church affairs. Miss Annie Golding put forward a paper supporting the enfranchisement of women on the grounds that Eve was Adam's companion, not his subordinate. She showed great courage as women were not allowed to address a church congress then, so her paper was delivered by a priest. It met a cool response, ranging from 'some things. . . though lawful, are hardly expedient' to 'It is a matter of grave doubt whether the extension of the franchise adds to the exaltation of woman, or whether such power is within the compass of her life and duties.'[28] Not all Catholics were opposed to female suffrage in the early decades of the twentieth century, many seeing it as a valuable weapon in the then-raging sectarian war. However, most favoured an unobtrusive domestic role for women as opposed to 'the indelicacies of the so-called up-to-date woman, who moves about like a man and has no proper sense of decency'.[29]

The march of female education and the gentrification of Catholic laywomen proved to be irreversible as the century progressed. However, such processes were not without difficulty. For example, the twenties were to witness a *cause celebre*, which brought about friction between order and hierarchy before a solution was reached.

As female enrolment increased at the university, the Society of the Sacred Heart was approached to set up a college in the environs of Sydney University. As has been noted in chapter 4, this order, with its largely French and English leadership, had been educating the daughters of wealthy Catholics at Elizabeth Bay and Rose Bay since 1885.[30] A considerable number of its alumnae had attended the university, were not happy with the secular nature of the Women's College which was fully enrolled anyway, and so were anxious for a community for Catholic women students to be set up.

Such women as Odillo Maher, Constance Le Plastrier and Kate Egan petitioned Archbishop Kelly to do something about this matter, rather than procrastinate and hope the problem would go away.[31]

The hierarchy for its part was terrified of secularism and even Protestantism invading the church through contact with the university. There was also a perceived need for nuns studying at the university to have accommodation which preserved them from secular contamination. Kelly was supported in his fears by the rector of St John's, the Catholic men's college, the Reverend Maurice O'Reilly, an able but complex man. O'Reilly urged that that nuns and girl undergraduates had 'an indefensible right to be protected by the church from the dangers of university infidel teaching'.[32]

Kelly was not interested in university education *per se*, but he was interested in pleasing the Catholic aristocracy whose daughters were now agitating for a university women's college. Such a college might also help preserve the traditional ideal of purity for Catholic women.

He continued to lay down his views in this matter in such pastoral letters as the one for January 1922, entitled 'On Women's Dress and Clothing'. 'Clothing,' he wrote, 'was given for our necessities not for our vanities.' God gave human beings clothing 'to hide the shameful members'.[33] The decision of the Catholic Church in Melbourne to set up a university hall of residence in 1918 also probably influenced Kelly in his decision to allow the college to go ahead.[34]

Finally, Kelly had also received encouragement in 1918 from the Catholic Women's Association, who promised to raise funds for a university hostel for women students.[35]

In August 1919, Kelly called a meeting at St Mary's Cathedral Presbytery to discuss the foundation of the college. Present at the meeting was the Rector of St John's and four leading Catholic laywomen, most of whom had been educated by the Society of the Sacred Heart. At this stage, O'Reilly did not foresee a conflict with church feminists, however aristocratic. He had already one month earlier asked the Sacred

Heart nuns to take charge of the proposed women's college which he envisaged as part of his preserve at St John's, not as an autonomous institution.[36]

O'Reilly was to underestimate the liberalism and intellectual autonomy of the Sacred Heart sisters, as well as their determination to run their own venture. The Superior of the new college, Mother Margaret MacRory, who had been headmistress at Rose Bay from 1910 to 1923, proved to be more than a match for him.[37] Although she did not possess O'Reilly's university education, she had prepared children for matriculation for many years; furthermore, she was temperamentally suited to leadership, helped on by a network of her Sacred Heart alumnae. The latter had decided to sponsor an inaugural meeting of the University Catholic Women's Society which proclaimed the following objectives:

(1) To bring Catholic University women, graduates and undergraduates together for the proposal of strengthening among them the Catholic corporate spirit that they may form a tangible body that will act as a leavening influence on public life.

(2) To inculcate Catholic ideas and ideals among the members so that each may be influential in spreading these ideals among her proximate and immediate associates.[38]

These were aims which would hardly have been formulated by Archbishop Kelly or Cardinal Moran as they contained no mention of such themes as secularism, modesty or domesticity, but these were clearly not foremost issues with the Society of the Sacred Heart, either. Its ideals had been forged in the philosophical and social turmoil of the French Revolution and its educational policy as a European order was more sophisticated than that which obtain in rural Ireland.

The new women's college opened as a hostel in a hall in Darlington and there was immediately a *contretemps* between Mother MacRory and Father O'Reilly as to its nomenclature. O'Reilly had proposed the name of St John's College Women's Hostel for the new venture, but the Reverend Mother rejected the brass plate he had inscribed with that title and the name 'Sacre Coeur' prevailed as accepted usage. Further clashes between Rector and Mother Superior were inevitable once the archbishop announced his decision to set aside part of the St John's College grounds for the new women's college.[39]

Although relations between Kelly and O'Reilly were uneasy at the best of times, the Rector was given the task of drafting the Archbishop's Pastoral Letter commending the drive for funds for the new college. The letter was to be read in parish churches throughout the state as Kelly felt 'Catholic women could, without feeling the strain, raise the requisite funds'.[40] Kelly also wrote to Sacre Coeur alumnae, Lady Sheldon and Kate Egan commissioning them to 'organise your sisters in the name of Catholic education' to raise the 20 000 pounds necessary to begin the college. The letter refers to the necessity of protecting 'these undergraduate girls educated so far in Catholic schools, so that none may be endangered by university conditions affecting piety and virtue'.[41]

Cosgrove points out that when Sheldon and Egan reproduced this letter of authority in the Catholic press and elsewhere, the reference to the university's threat to piety and virtue were omitted. These women did not share their archbishop's view of the ideal Catholic woman![42]

From the beginning, the women on the Advisory Council of the new college planned for complete independence from St John's College, despite the proximity of the two institutions. O'Reilly protested to Mother Amelie Salmon, Superior of the Sacred Heart:

A committee appointed by the archbishop to collect for the women's college. . . ignored St John's Council altogether and was secretly working for the complete independence of the women's college.[43]

Although the rector and fellows of St John's claimed they were not opposed to the independence of the new college, they still claimed that under their charter — and as far as the senate of the university was concerned — they were legally bound to exercise control over the new college until it received its own Act of Incorporation.[44]

These technically legal rights were exercised by O'Reilly on 26 March 1925, when the foundation stone of what was to be known as Sancta Sophia Hall was laid. The name was chosen by MacRory — with dubious linguistic validity — to commemorate both holy wisdom and the foundress of the Society of the Sacred Heart, Madame Sophie Barat. An assemblage of church and university notables gathered to watch Archbishop Kelly lay the foundation stone.

It bore a controversial inscription — organised by the Rector to impose his own authority — *In honorem Sancti Joannis Evangelistae* — *not*, as could be expected, *In honorem Sanctae Sophiae*. As soon as MacRory moved into the new building, she planted creepers and roses to hide the offending stone and there it remains to this day, a mute testimony to an incident in feminist church history.[45]

O'Reilly did not interfere further in Sancta Sophia's development, but he nursed a strong sense of grievance at what he felt had been a usurpation of power by the nuns. He watched with bitterness as the college's Advisory Council finally achieved incorporation for Sancta Sophia in 1929. He refused to attend the opening of the new wing of the college, writing a letter of unmitigated sourness in response to his invitation:

As rector of St John's, I am also the head of Sancta Sophia Hall. Permission to erect the Hall was granted by the Senate only on that understanding; and this position was well-known to the Sacred Heart nuns. Neither the council of St John's nor myself had ever submitted to us the plans of the new wing; I have no idea of the disposition of the rooms which it contains, or of the accommodation which it provides. It looks, therefore, like adding insult to injury to give me a formal invitation to the blessing, which I am compelled to decline, if only to protest against a gross irregularity, which has been followed up by equally gross discourtesy. . .

I cannot forget (and here let me claim your indulgence) that in acting as the committee of Sancta Sophia Hall. . . and thus inviting to a public function, you are, I am willing to believe unwittingly, usurping a position that properly belongs to the council of St John's.[46]

The success of Margaret MacRory in gaining autonomy for her college was not to be enjoyed for long as she died the following year, but her steadfastness as well as the distrustful relationship between Kelly and O'Reilly meant that the order prevailed.

At no time did she give way to the rector's bluster, yet she had retained her dignity in the encounter. He had sought to establish a women's college which would be under the control of the male hierarchy, whereas she and her female supporters (and male, for that matter, as husbands of alumnae like Sir Mark Sheldon played a significant part in legal matters) had successfully challenged an entrenched power structure within the church.

All this in an era when women in general had been returned to a position of relative quiescence in society.

Anglican orders

An examination of Anglican orders in this period reveals that they, on the whole, did not experience as marked a growth in numbers as their Catholic counterparts. An exception to this trend was provided by the Society of the Sacred Advent, the small but dynamic Queensland order whose professed sisters rose in number from six in 1905 to thirty-four in 1930 — an increase of more than fivefold. The inter-war period, nevertheless, was one of quiet consolidation for the other two orders, the Sisters of the Church and the Sisters of the Holy Name.

The Sisters of the Church had founded Perth College in 1902, following the arrival of three pioneer sisters. The school moved to a more roomy site at Mt Lawley in 1915, where its handsome chapel was finally completed in 1928. It was by this time one of Perth's most outstanding schools. The sisters received many requests to found other schools, but the only other one they were able to staff was a small school in Kalgoorlie. They did, however, keep their orphanage work going at Parkerville throughout the Depression.[47] The Sisters of the Church continued to visit the sick and poor in inner-city Sydney and to run St Gabriel's School for girls, despite lack of encouragement from a hostile Protestant hierarchy.

Vocations to their order increased from twenty-six sisters in 1910 to thirty-two in 1930, the order being still administered from London and a majority of sisters being English-born.[48] The failure of Anglo Catholic orders to attract Australian candidates was historical in origin; the largest pool of single women of missionary orientation resided in the large cities of Sydney and Melbourne, which were overwhelmingly Protestant. Most Australian women who were Anglo Catholics were countrywomen who married young. If they were single, they tended to move to the cities for work.

Two rural sisterhoods were founded inter-war, but both failed to survive. Anglo Catholic orders were welcomed by bishop and laity, but poverty, isolation and overwork caused by meagre numbers of vocations meant they were always embattled. The Sisterhood of the Holy Cross survived only three years after its foundation in Rockhampton in 1922. The Order of St Elizabeth of Hungary was of longer duration because it operated in the smaller, more settled Diocese of Bunbury and was able to draw more support from the mother house in England. It lasted till 1957 after doing valuable hostel and pastoral work in the Margaret River area.[49]

The Sisters of the Holy Name operated largely in Victoria; it was an order which was larger in numbers containing more Australian-born members. Led by the redoubtable Sister Esther in her latter years, these women worked alongside the Brotherhood of St Lawrence in offering aid to the unemployed and distressed in Melbourne — a city where 36% were Anglican.[50] All told, they ran seven institutions in Melbourne in this period in addition to three in Goulburn and Newcastle.

This order was more fortunate in its financial support than the others as it could draw upon the work of auxiliaries of neighbouring well-heeled Melbourne parishes, like St Andrew's Brighton. It also published a quarterly magazine, entitled *In Our Midst*, which publicised the sisters' work and helped with fundraising.

The sisters staffed schools, children's homes, hospitals and reformatories. St Ives Private Hospital and St George's Hospital flourished under CHN supervision, the latter becoming the third largest training hospital in obstetrics in Victoria.[51]

Their chief work was in children's homes, where they served with great devotion but only moderate success because of their old-fashioned methods, stemming from a lack of training in social work.

What the sisters lacked in education they made up for with their enthusiasm and hard work, which arose from their community and spiritual life. They loved nature, animals and children and found relief in the garden after a day of dealing with difficult children. Retreats as well as the offices of the church continually encouraged their spirituality. But it was never plain sailing, as Sister Eleanor who worked in the Children's Court wrote, in terms familiar to the female religious:

> I know that peace cannot be got without pain — maybe a submission so complete that it humbles to the dust. . . perhaps I may be given a vision of the Blessed Presence that I now cling to by faith — but go on I must, as bravely and cheerfully as I can — and some day, light will break through and light it all up for me. . .[52]

✠ Sisters Alice and Rosa of the Society of the Sacred Advent

It was the far-flung Queensland order, the Society of the Sacred Advent, founded in 1897, which achieved most in opening up North Queensland to Anglican church education for girls. Operating on a shoestring budget — indeed, on a perpetual overdraft — these dedicated sisters moved north from their Brisbane convent and school, the acclaimed St Margaret's College, to the frontier in north Queensland.

They braved the tropical heat and pioneering conditions to found first of all St Anne's School in Townsville on 21 July 1917. The founding headmistress was the redoubtable Sister Alice Mary and she also pioneered several other church schools in north Queensland. She and her sister, Rosa Philpott, were typical of many Anglican nuns in background, being upper middle-class Englishwomen, but basically amateurs as educationists.

The Mother Superior of the order during the inter-war period, Sister Emma, was also an Englishwoman of great nobility of character, but she seldom left the Brisbane mother house. At the age of fifty, Sister Alice arrived in Townsville clad in her habit, which drew many stares from the populace. She would have heartily agreed with the view of one Sister of Mercy expressed a few years later that 'the costume is like a flag. . . which proclaims. . . that Christ is worth more than the world'.[53]

Later, Sister Alice looked back:

Well, we did get our schools, and each school's life centres at the altar, and everything arranges itself in relation to that, becoming clearer, more intelligible and more hopeful all the time. And so it is that, in the whole of our education, every other science pays its tribute to theology — the Queen of the Sciences.[54]

St Anne's quickly became a school of outstanding reputation in north Queensland. Girls achieved excellent academic results in History, Music, Mathematics and Drama. Sister Vernon established a tradition of Shakespearean productions in the garden at St Anne's.

Once St Anne's was on its feet, Sister Alice turned her attention to Charters Towers, the gold city on the tableland behind Townsville. There in 1921, she started St Gabriel's School, again largely on 'tic'. Her comment was, 'We of the SSA are accustomed to overdrafts; we shall pull through.'[55]

Before long, enrolments were flourishing at both schools and she was being co-opted to help fully establish a boys' school, All Souls Charters Towers, which was floundering financially. Her energy and devotion were exceptional: she and her staff survived the pneumonic flu plague of 1919 by turning St Anne's temporarily into a hospital. She also survived bullets which were fired in industrial strife between police and unions adjacent to her premises.[56]

Of like calibre to her sister was Sister Rosa — also barely five feet in height — who became the founding headmistress of St Mary's Herberton in 1918. This isolated school set in forbidding hills laid waste by mining was for a time the largest girls' boarding school in the diocese. It catered for the children of farming and mining communities and it worked in perfect harmony with the Mercy Sisters, who ran the large Catholic school opposite.

Somehow, it survived despite its overdraft, having given its own funds — in company with the donations of Sister Alice — to help start the boys' school in Charters Towers. Sister Rosa was also a skilful fund-raiser and somehow managed to buy pianos, typewriters, blankets and crockery for her rapidly mounting numbers. The bishop commented about St Mary's: 'The SSA was behind it, so far as a society with no funds, but only consecrated human lives, can be behind a financial venture.'[57]

By means of fetes and bazaars, housekeeping for the nearby Brotherhood, plus a stream of appeal letters, Sister Rosa managed to consolidate her school. Her humour and energy were boundless in all situations:

> We are here on the roof of the world and we must be prepared for a few inconveniences. . . People say to me, 'What a funny building!' I say to myself: 'What a heroic building!' And I say the same about every detail of St Mary's estate and equipment, brought into being under constant pressure of need on the most inadequate financial basis.[58]

However, the toll on the health of these two pioneer sisters was such that they did not survive the 1920s and this would appear to be a situation where the bishop could have intervened and ensured that such hard workers took regular furloughs. Lack of reinforcements — the perennial problem facing Australian religious orders and Anglo Catholic ones in particular — was the chief reason for the failure to relieve the troops in the frontline.

✠ The deaconess movements

The deaconess movements in the Anglican, Presbyterian and Methodist churches continued their steady, often unspectacular work during the inter-war period. Numbers of candidates were maintained and even increased during this time, the Presbyterians going mainly to inland Australia, India and Korea as missionaries, while some like Eva Holland worked unobtrusively and effectively at home.[59]

Methodist sisters were still small in number and were not actually ordained as deaconesses until after the general conference of 1941. In the meantime, uniformed but scantily trained 'sisters of the people' continued to operate as social workers with Methodist missions or else as overseas missionaries.[60]

Anglican deaconesses increased slowly but steadily in numbers over the inter-war period. Training either at the Deaconess Institute in Sydney or at the Deaconess Mission House in Melbourne, these deaconesses worked in various Australian states. Forty of them were ordained in this period, joining the twenty-six who were ordained between 1900 and 1917. Of both these groups, only six joined the Community of the Holy Name, so the role of deaconess was clearly preferable to that of professed sister for devout Anglican women in the 1920s and 1930s.[61]

Such was the structure and operation of church hierarchy, however, that deaconesses were dependent on the encouragement of specific bishops and church leaders to launch out into a lonely life of sacrifice. Pay was extremely meagre and the pension was all a deaconess could look forward to on reaching sixty years of age.[62] Very often, a parish clergyman would leave much of his work to his unfortunate deaconess.

'Deaconesses in parishes in Tasmania have been doing the work of clergy for years' was the comment of one senior deaconess. She also added, 'If they tried to offload their work on to me, I refused.'[63]

However, most senior churchmen in this period recognised the value of deaconesses, especially archbishops J.C. Wright and H.W.K. Mowll of Sydney and the Bishop of Gippsland, Geoffrey Cranswick. Episcopal encouragement was vital for the morale of these hard working churchwomen and it also enabled them to have some measure of autonomy in parish work.

Following World War I, deaconesses continued their work of indoor relief for needy women and children, but they also branched out into children's court work after 1920. At the express invitation of Bishop Cranswick, they went to his diocese in Gippsland, travelling through the outback in ancient vans, taking Sunday school and women's meetings and often doing bush nursing.[64]

Some of their number went as missionaries overseas, like Deaconess Lora Claydon to the Middle East and Elizabeth Robinson to Tanganyika. Dorothy Harris (ordained in 1932) was one who experienced most facets of deaconess work, showing great flexibility and devotion and yet independence of mind in her years of service. She began her ministry with three-and-a-half years in the industrial suburb of Pyrmont at the height of the Depression. Her main task there, apart from taking Sunday school, visiting and women's meetings, was to maintain the self-respect of so many poor families. She would go to large stores like Grace Brothers to buy or scrounge the cheapest food and clothing, then she would return to her weekly meeting to dispense this, often feeding as many as fifty women and forty children for afternoon tea.

Two of the letters sent to her from barely literate mothers, whose husbands had lost their jobs at the local CSR factory, reveal the desperation of many of the people amongst whom she worked:

> Please Sister, have you any dress you could give me.
> *Mrs Simon, Pyrmont mother*

> If you have any sox (for the boy) as he has none.
> *Mrs Oakes*[65]

Dorothy Harris' next assignment was two years with the Bush Church Aid Society, driving a primitive van in the wilds of the Burragorang Valley to reach miners' families on behalf of the church. The years 1935 and 1936 were spent as warden of the Wilcannia Hostel for outback children, followed by a spell in the Cann River area of frontier Gippsland.[66]

She next volunteered for overseas service and, while waiting for CMS to dispatch her to orphanage work in India, she carried out children's court work and spent some time in a Sydney orphanage. Arriving in Lahore after the outbreak of war, she was impressed with the egalitarian relationship between clergy and deaconesses in the diocese, a contrast with her Australian experience.[67]

Deaconesses played an important role in the Protestant churches between the wars, although their numbers were not as great as their sisters in Catholic orders. They lacked the ecclesiastical autonomy and sense of community experienced by their professed sisters and also the protection offered by enclosure. Hence, they developed as very strong individuals whose achievements are all the more noteworthy:

Some deaconesses took up parish work that men had given up in despair, some laid foundations that a male ministry was later to build upon. . . They were often expected to accept rebuke and criticism with tolerance and grace and bear patiently the negative attitudes of those who disapproved of feminine initiatives or gifts of wisdom. . . They were often considered to be, and treated as if they as women were born to be, second to men, despite their obvious call from God.[68]

Thus, the Anglican and many of the Non-conformist churches appeared not to value sufficiently the contribution of professional churchwomen. This might have been due to societal attitudes of condescension towards the single woman, but it was also because, in this period, most parishes had an army of willing laywomen, usually led by the clergy wife, who were more than willing to support their parish clergyman in keeping the local church going in an honorary capacity. Unpaid female labour was difficult to resist, especially when it was offered so freely by the shut-in housewife of the inter-war period.

✠ The Salvation Army

As has been noted in chapter 6, it was in the Salvation Army that the greatest equality of ordained people — whether male or female — was apparently demonstrated. Women officers had existed in the Salvation Army since 1865. Yet even in this branch of the church, anomalies occurred.

'The church was able to provide sufficient outlet for female talents, but it was not always overwilling to do so' was the comment of one woman officer of this period.[69] A woman officer, however senior or experienced, always took the rank of her husband on marriage and women officers of this period were still often regarded as their husbands' assistants rather than equals.

Yet for the single woman, promotion was always on equal terms with the men. After World War I, Australia gained its first woman divisional commander, Winifred Horsley, who was placed in charge of the Western Australian Command.[70] Colonel Olive Allitt, a schoolteacher who was commissioned in 1930, worked amongst the unemployed of Bankstown and Burwood at the height of the Depression from 1931 to 1933 — earning the princely sum of two and sixpence a week — before commencing nursing training.[71]

She and other women officers were delighted when the Salvation Army appointed Gladys Calliss to the Army's highest rank, that of commissioner in 1975, following distinguished service as a missionary in Indonesia and Sri Lanka.[72] Clearly, this church was more anxious than most to offer its women in orders a sense of freedom and partnership in terms of work and gender roles.

�֍ The Church Army

A similar body to the Salvation Army was the Church Army, which was founded in Australia with help from the parent body in Britain by certain Anglican bishops and the Bishop of Newcastle in particular. It was a society of male and female evangelists who worked particularly amongst the poor, on virtually no salary at all. They ran hostels for neglected and isolated children and developed a mission amongst Aborigines in north Queensland, a number of whom later joined the Church Army as staff.

Members of this society wore a distinctive uniform like the 'Sallies'; the men adopted military rank but the women were given the more subservient title of Sister, wearing veils and a nursing-style uniform to match their title.[73] A distinctive uniform was important for these women as it distinguished their role quickly in the community, opened doors which would otherwise have remained shut, saved expense on clothes and gave protection in dangerous situations.

Salvation Army women officers, Church Army sisters and deaconesses would have agreed with Sister Declan Ruffles' description of the habit as being like a 'flaunting banner which proclaims, almost with drums and trumpets that Christ is worth more than all the world'.[74]

⚜ Paving the way for future progress

The inter-war period was ostensibly disappointing in its progress towards gender equality in the church. The cataclysm of World War I, followed so soon after by the scourge of the Great Depression, appeared to dampen down the cause of female leadership, compared with the heady days of the 1880s and 1890s. However, the quiet but tenacious work of women in orders was paving the way for later recognition for women and their gifts.

Single professional churchwomen continued to prove themselves, creating a splendid record of service in schools, nursing and social work, as well as in parish work. Their numbers increased, they specialised daringly in medical and educational fields and, by their dedication and efficiency, they challenged the male hierarchy to think again about its divine right to assume leadership and to limit freedom of ministry.

10

Out of the cocoon

THE ROLE OF LAYWOMEN BETWEEN THE WARS

'Women are doing by far the major part of the work of the laity. The more freedom and scope and expansion is given to womanly and manly service in conjunction, the richer will society and the church be.'

Bishop Geoffrey Cranswick of Gippsland (1925)

'She hath put her hand to strong things.'

Motto of the Catholic Women's Social Guild
founded in Melbourne in 1916

'Isn't it strange that, though the impetus towards woman's emancipation came from Jesus Christ, the church which bears his name has lagged behind the state in giving her equality with men?'

Winifred Kiek, ordained in Adelaide in 1927

ALTHOUGH THE INTER-WAR PERIOD WAS in many ways a stagnant one for the average laywoman seeking to extend her role in the church, there were signs of startling change which was to find its fulfilment — and, in at least one church, its suppression — in the years following World War II.

In the Nonconformist churches, the first woman was ordained to the ministry and the cure of souls in Australia. This was Winifred Kiek, who was officially accepted as a Congregational minister in 1927 after a period of effective ministry in a new housing area of Adelaide. In the Anglican Church, there was growing recognition of the possibility of an expanded role for women: the English feminist preacher Maude Royden was invited to enter the pulpit of St Mark's Church, Darling Point, in 1928 — the first woman to do so in the Church of England in Australia.

Bishops, especially missionary and rural bishops, became heavily reliant on amateur and professional women workers to extend and maintain their flocks.

In the Roman Catholic Church, where feminism was spreading amongst laywomen, arguably as a result of their convent education, there was a flowering of women's organisations like the Catholic Women's Social Guild and the Grail Movement, which endeavoured to set up a women's lay apostolate. Most of these bodies fell foul of the Catholic hierarchy which was suspicious of their independence and, in some cases, even worked towards their dissolution.

As has been already remarked, World War I brought about a setback to the women's movement both within the church and in society at large. The masculine ideology and imagery of war, which was based on man as the warrior and protector, was also predicated on woman as the passive sufferer who sacrificed her children to the conflict. These concepts spilled over into peacetime and man returned to act as breadwinner and economic leader in society, while woman retreated into her 'place' in the home to fulfil the role of wife and mother, as the church sanctioned.

In vain did the co-founder of the Catholic Women's Social Guild, Dr Mary Glowrey, warn the women of the period:

Do mothers never realise that duty does not require —
nay, rather forbids — them to become slaves to their
husbands and children?[1]

Women were thoroughly exhorted by the church and
media of the day to avoid taking jobs from the men and this
concentration on domesticity became all the more inevitable
when the unemployment of the Great Depression arrived.

The Anglican Mothers' Union in 1922 voiced its disapproval of those women who were taking men's jobs. They
declared that while some women could do men's work, men
could not fill women's jobs. The hearth was the place for the
ideal woman and this view was reinforced by the Archbishop
of Melbourne, who said that home duties were a joy if offered
up to 'Christ as creditor'.[2]

Despite this discouragement of their married sisters and to
some extent themselves, single professional women began to
enter the workplace between the wars and, amongst their most
distinguished achievers, were devout laywomen.

To name but a few, there was the pioneer of women's
medicine, Constance D'Arcy, who was a member of the senate
of the University of Sydney from 1919 and was a leader of the
Catholic Women's Association. The devout Methodist, Kate
Cocks, pioneered the women's police force in South Australia
for the benefit of women and children in that state. Victorian
Catholic lawyer, Anna Brenan, worked for equal rights for
women before the law, and numerous pious laywomen gave
a lifetime of service to education in this period.

Church feminism was probably strongest amongst single
women in the inter-war period for reasons of time alone.
Family responsibilities and lack of domestic help prevented
most married women — if they were interested — from
actively supporting the women's movement. As in previous
stages of the women's movement, education was the key to

liberation and the increasing access of women to tertiary education was basic to independent female expression.

Even more significant a factor was the expansion of church secondary education for girls. Only a minority of boys, much less girls, could go to university, so it was at secondary level that education was important. There had been a massive growth of convent schools since the turn of the century and, as has been observed, the professed nun prized her independent role and was inclined to pass on her views to her students.

Thus, some commentators attribute the clash between lay Catholic women's groups and the male hierarchy which took place mid-century to the influence of convent education.[3] Others attribute Catholic feminism to such social factors as the excessively heavy burden laid upon mothers who had large families to bring up and sometimes an alcoholic or a gambling husband to contend with.

Daughters with education usually vowed never to follow in their embattled mothers' footsteps. They viewed with dismay the sympathy of the Catholic priest for the 'poor father having to bring up all those children' while the mother's plight was ignored.[4] This experience of the role of women could also account for the large majority of Catholic women I interviewed who asserted that the church was male-dominated.[5]

Protestant interviewees answering the same questions were not convinced that the church was male-dominated, but this might have been because most of them were married. Single deaconesses were closer to their Catholic sisters in orders in their sense of grievance at the hierarchy's exercise of power, but they seldom gave expression to their frustration in ministry.

It is possible that male-female confrontation was avoided in non-Catholic churches as a result of the role of the clergy wife. It was an onerous task for her, but she usually succeeded in acting as a bridge between clergy and female laity. Not only did she interpret her fellow women's actions and aspirations for her husband, but she also worked alongside both parties in a semi-professional capacity. There is much testimony as to the efficacy of a clergyman's ministry being enhanced or lowered by his wife's contribution.[6]

✠ Problems confronting women

In order to assess the role of the laywoman between the wars, it is necessary to look at the problems which confronted her in the society of her day. Apart from the economic turmoil of much of the period, there were issues of morality and ideology which confronted her and needed a response.

First, there was the problem of population growth and birth control. The increasing affluence of Australia by the turn of the century, particularly amongst the working classes, had not led to a rising or even a stable birthrate. The birthrate had dropped from 42.6 per thousand head of population in 1860 to 16.6 in 1935.[7]

Unquestionably, women were choosing to limit their fertility by artificial means and this was contrary to the teaching of the Roman Catholic Church; it was also opposed by the Church of England in the first decade of this period. The Lambeth Conference of 1920 opposed contraception, but ten years later the bishops abandoned their stance. Other Protestant churches followed suit or else had no public policy on the matter.

Churchwomen were conspicuously silent about the issue — except that the Mothers' Union condemned somewhat prudishly advertisements for contraceptive devices in the press. Even the journals of the new Catholic women's societies preferred to concentrate on strengthening the family and on gaining equality for women rather than discussing such problems as venereal disease or backyard abortion. There were few churchwomen as bold as the ardent Methodist, Dr Katie Ardill Brice, who opened the first birth control clinic in Sydney in 1933, arguing that prevention was better than abortion:

> Are we to believe that the whole edifice of Christian morality will fall to the ground if we remove the buttress of fear? Is fear of the Lord as naught to the fear of the risks? The ignoble safeguard of fear must make way for a morality founded on our duty towards our neighbour and a noble conception of sex love. Let us abandon the morality that has made morality synonymous with dullness and seek a sane morality more worthy of the enthusiasm of youth.[8]

Women's church groups were united in their encouragement of the family unit as the God-given basis of society. Not a meeting of the Mothers' Union, the Legion of Mary, the Presbyterian Women's Association or the Methodist Mothers Club went by without a statement, a prayer or a poem read in praise of motherhood and the family. They took comfort in the findings of the Royal Commission on the Basic Wage, which recommended in 1920 that married women should be discouraged from working and that their duty to the state lay in running their homes as thriftily as possible.[9]

Thus, government supported the churches in their view of the role of women and this was not surprising, given the success of the conjugal family in settling and building up the colonies over 130 years.[10]

Churchwomen were active in promoting the welfare of mothers and children in more specific ways after World War I, as in the creation of the District Nursing Association in Milton, Queensland by the Mothers' Union. They did not flock in such numbers as before to non-denominational movements like the WCTU, although they tacitly supported its efforts in achieving six o'clock closing of hotels in 1919. Fashions in philanthropy change, even in churches, and the WCTU gradually declined.[11] The euphoria of the 1890s had been replaced by a reticence and a lack of confidence in political action.

Second, there were problems for women in the workforce. Only the Catholic women's groups were really interested in a policy towards women in the workforce. At this point, women were earning a mere 55% of what men were being paid for commensurate work. Muriel Heagney of the Catholic Women's Social Guild in Victoria campaigned actively for equal pay for women and she also set up a training centre for girls in Melbourne.[12] Exploitation of women was noticeable even in education where married women teachers were often posted to the country with their teacher husbands before single ones, as it was expected that the wife would help her husband with classes in an honorary capacity.

Protestant groups were also silent about the passing of the Married Women (Lecturers and Teachers) Act in 1932 when 220 women from the permanent staff of the Department of Public Instruction in New South Wales lost their jobs. From then onwards until 1947, women were obliged to resign from the permanent teaching staff when they married.[13] With the exception of Katie Ardill Brice, women's church groups failed to address the problem of abortion which was forbidden by the Crimes Act in this period, nor did they protest when illegitimate children were excluded from child endowment payments.[14]

In these uncaring reactions to difficult realities, women's church groups were reflecting the attitudes of a society which was still under the influence of Victorian concepts of propriety and marriage. However, there is no doubt that they did much good work in strengthening families and providing a constructive social outlet for housebound women. The domestic emphasis in their work also mirrored the concerns of the day, for the inter-war period witnessed a strong emphasis on home-making. Reiger postulates the appearance of an 'ideology of housewifery', whereby all things domestic were seen as part of women's natural need for 'nest-building'.[15]

Furthermore, it was now seen as important to the nation that such traditional tasks as cooking, sewing, cleaning and caring for others should be approached scientifically. Thus, domestic science was put into the school curriculum for girls, and labour-saving devices were patented in increasing numbers. Magazines concentrating on domesticity, like the *Australian Women's Weekly*, were established and quickly prospered as new inventions created greater leisure time within the home.[16]

✠ Anglican laywomen's response to developments in society

Anglican women, who were mostly drawn from the middle classes, responded to these developments in society in the following ways: first, they joined or encouraged two female societies which had been founded some thirty years earlier in Australia — the Mothers' Union and the Girls' Friendly Society.[17]

Second, they supported various societies at diocesan level, usually by membership of an auxiliary. For example, the Ladies' Home Mission Union was set up to raise funds for the Home Mission Society which worked to help the poor, sick and needy in the community. However, once the women raised these funds, it was the male executive committee of the society which determined how those funds should be spent.[18]

Third, Anglican women were able to employ their energies in a proliferation of activities at the parish level — Sunday school teaching, district visiting, singing in the choir, fundraising, hospitality and decorating and cleaning the church. Every priest had a female army of helpers at his disposal.

Fourth, as we have seen in previous chapters, they were able to volunteer for full-time ministry either as sisters in an order, deaconesses or missionaries. Although the Mothers' Union was never large in numbers — its membership reaching by 1930 only 10 000 out of an estimated one million Anglican women in Australia — it was nevertheless influential in the community, particularly through its magazine, *Mothers in Australasia*. It received unqualified support from the establishment — the Commonwealth President being the wife of the Governor-General, the President for NSW being either the wife of the Governor or of the Archbishop of Sydney. Its council consisted mainly of clergy wives and leading laywomen who were more concerned with moral issues than social prestige.

The Mothers' Union was perceived as a bulwark of society as it sought to strengthen marriage. In practice, it ran devotions for women at parish and diocesan level and provided a social club which allowed single women to join, but not divorcees. It tried to combat the rise in illegitimate births and venereal disease which had followed the Great War by advocating more thorough sex education, the setting up of good hostels for women and the appointment of a woman censor to vet 'picture films'. The government refused the last request, so they set up their own censorship group — the Good Film League — to report regularly on the cinema and any material they deemed indecent.[19]

The Mothers' Union's chief foray into social welfare was their work in the children's courts. They undertook the follow-up of Protestant girls who had been brought before the courts in New South Wales, following a request from the Chief Magistrate. It was estimated that one third of the 3000 children charged annually were Anglican. Girl offenders were fewer than boys, who were assigned for follow-up to representatives of the Church of England Men's Society.

At first, one deaconess was appointed by the Union to help these girls who were neglected or who had 'fallen into sins of immorality'.[20] By 1925, there were three full-time visitors employed by the Mothers' Union and 270 girls were passing annually through the courts and into the probationary care of the church. They were placed in homes in fifty-seven locations, visited weekly and encouraged to find a suitable job and to keep in touch with the church.[21]

The Mothers' Union commissioned members who were social workers, sending them out as visitors to maternity hospitals, mental hospitals and state and church children's homes. It employed trained staff to run three homes for unmarried mothers in New South Wales. It also cooperated with the Anglican Christian Social Union in setting up the Church of England District Nursing Association in Brisbane and then in other capital cities. These associations became non-denominational and were finally taken over by the state, but not before much valuable work had been done amongst the sick poor of the inner city, including those who could not afford obstetric care at a hospital.[22]

The Mothers' Union had its negative side insofar as it reflected the views of the church it represented: it opposed the widening of grounds for divorce and, in 1933, the NSW branch sent a delegation to the Minister of Justice opposing the Marriage Amendment Bill, which increased the grounds for divorce to include insanity and seven years' separation.

Thus, the Mothers' Union was a conservative body which worked hard for the concepts of companionate marriage and caring homes for children, whilst being to some degree reactionary and disapproving about a section of society with which they rarely came in personal contact.

Another Anglican body of conservative outlook was the Girls' Friendly Society (GFS), first founded in Britain in 1874 and then imported into Australia in 1879 to help young, single women migrants find work and homes.[23]

It was particularly strong in Perth where it was under vice-regal patronage. Its aims were, first, to band together in one society women and girls as associates and members for mutual help, sympathy and prayer and, second, to encourage such qualities as purity of life, dutifulness to parents, faithfulness to employers, temperance and thrift. Together with representatives from the Mothers' Union, GFS members would meet boats arriving from Britain and help any 'women or girls who needed a friend'. By the 1930s, it was operating mainly in city hostels and as a fellowship group for girls in parishes.[24] Its stress on thrift as being one of the attributes of Christian womanhood echoed that of the Mothers' Union: 'By wise economy, every woman can help to balance the national budget.'[25] The church was thoroughly behind the government in its thrift drive which was initiated in Victoria and copied by the Federal government in its National Thrift Week.[26]

✠ Nonconformist women's church involvement

Equally thrifty in outlook was the Presbyterian Women's Association with their efficiently run stalls and secondhand clothing shops which raised money for home and overseas missions. As with the Mothers' Union, their funds were particularly directed towards the support of deaconesses and overseas women missionaries.

The Methodists were also scrupulous in their administration of the Dorcas Society and the Mothers' Club. The Methodists ran a Thrift Bank which encouraged children to bank a penny at a time. The Pirie Street Methodist Dorcas Society in Adelaide boasted that 104 children had lodged pennies in its Thrift Bank in 1930, so that interest now stood at 15 pounds.[27]

The Pirie Street Methodist Church was known as the 'Cathedral Church' of South Australian Methodism and in its heyday was attended by up to 1100 women, as opposed to 400 men.[28] It was one of the first Methodist churches to appoint a deaconess — in 1891 — and its Dorcas Society, which commenced in 1843, was an active and powerful body in its 130 years of operation. The committee of the Pirie Street Dorcas Society consisted of a president, four vice-presidents, a treasurer, a secretary, a cutter-out, a buyer and a valuer; meetings attracted upwards of sixty-five people.[29]

Methodist ladies in Adelaide were not lazy in this period, nor were they expected to be. They handed in 240 new garments for sale in the financial year 1930 to 1931 and thirteen patchwork quilts. They conducted wood, soap, sugar and jam drives and collected cast-off clothing to cut down or redistribute. Their funds paid for a sister to visit the unemployed, hospitals and offices and to run a mothers' meeting each week. She reckoned on making over a thousand visits a year.

The scrupulous account books of this branch of the Dorcas Society create the impression that one female trustee might have been appointed to the all-male administration of this church without detriment to its efficient execution of duties.[30]

Rural Methodist women worked as hard as their city counterparts to raise funds for their church. They produced bottled fruits, jams, pickles and sauces, dried fruits, cakes, cured hams, butter, honey, embroidery, dressmaking, knitting, crochet, patchwork quilting, flower arrangements and even paintings — and all in the spirit of comradeship such as is particularly found in the country. Their funds were particularly directed towards upkeep and improvement of country churches and parsonages.[31]

✠ The roles of Anglican women at the parish level

Apart from the activities of diocesan organisations, Anglican laywomen played a multitude of roles in individual parishes. Not many were as active as Mrs Harriet Patton of St Hilary's Church, Kew, in Victoria; she lived in the parish for most of her ninety years (1893–1982). A graduate of Melbourne University, she taught at the CMS school in Colombo, Sri Lanka, before returning to Melbourne to marry.

She was an active lobbyist for the Women's Christian Temperance Union, representing them on the League of Women Voters, the Status of Women Committee of the United Nations Organisation and the Howard League of Penal Reform. She led the three Girl Guide troupes active at St Hilary's. She was an active member of the church choir and trained the children's choir in the 1940s. She encouraged the church to retain its archives and preserve its history. All her fellow parishioners held her in the highest respect.[32]

A study of the records of a rural and an urban Anglican church gives some idea of the key role played by women in this period, even though they were not promoted in the hierarchy. Looking at the Anglican Church of Belair outside Adelaide, a church with four and later five branches, there is an occasional promotion of a woman to a significant leadership role when there were absolutely no men available. In 1927, for instance, women were allowed to act only as visitors in the parish. There was one Sunday school superintendent out of the five who was a woman — a Mrs Ougden — but her role as a caterer was obviously more welcome to the rector: 'Fifty-five sat down to tea in the parish hall. . . Mrs Ougden and her assistants are to be congratulated as "providers".'[33]

The following year, a woman was appointed as organist at one of the branches, but layreaders, synodsmen and churchwardens were steadfastly male — despite the ruling in Britain in 1919 that women could be elected churchwardens.[34] In 1929, history was made at Belair and a woman warden was appointed to the outlying branch church of Eden Hills. She does not survive to the following year, so the appointment must have been temporary.[35]

The next seven years of parish magazines reveal that women remain the backbone of the Sunday school, the fete committees, the Comforts Guild, the Missionary Work Party and, of course, the Parish Hall Entertainment Committee. They are asked to bring the inevitable 'supper basket' to evening meetings and they decorate the church for services.[36] Then at last comes a break with tradition and Miss C. Maag is appointed people's warden for Coromandel Valley in May 1937.[37]

Looking at the whole picture, by 1938, out of the 207 parishes in the Diocese of Adelaide, there are sixteen female church wardens, four deaconesses and seventy-seven Sunday school superintendents. The upper echelons of the hierarchy were totally male.[38]

The church choir, a feminine domain: St Andrew's Church of England, Summer Hill, Sydney, 1937

Equally unbalanced in terms of gender is the listed hierarchy of the large Sydney parish of St Andrew's, Summer Hill. Parish magazines and annual reports reveal that the congregation is at least two-thirds female and the lower echelons of its workforce are overwhelmingly female. The choir numbers upwards of twenty-five women and ten men; the Sunday school of approximately 300 children has a majority of women teachers, but only one of them is listed in the parish hierarchy and she is the Sunday school librarian.

Women are allowed to act as treasurers of small church organisations like the Young People's Union; they never become churchwardens. Women are allowed to collect funds for the parochial fund which financed parish needs (apart from the rector's stipend which came from the Sunday collection), but they are not allowed a voice in spending these funds.

These twenty-odd collectors or 'district visitors', as they were known, were a formidable band of mainly middle-class ladies who acted as part of the rector's vanguard. Hatted and gloved, they would set out across the parish distributing parish papers and collecting for the parochial fund, but they also

The rector's army': parish district visitors, Summer Hill, Sydney, about 1930

reported to the rector cases of sickness and trouble in families which put him on the alert and increased the outreach of the parish. Up to 200 donations were made via the district visitors each year, most being between ten shillings and one pound.[39]

The parish also supported three missionaries, all of them women: Miss Booth working in China, Miss Acland with the Aborigines in the Northern Territory, and Sister Dowling with the Bush Church Aid in South Australia.[40]

❊ Why laywomen accepted a subsidiary role

There seems to have been almost universal acceptance by laywomen of their subsidiary role in parish life. None of the surveyed Protestant laywomen, who were active in church work at this stage, felt that the church was too male-dominated — although the deaconesses were in agreement with the Catholic nuns on this issue.

Laywomen accepted their role as Indians rather than chiefs and there are several possible explanations for this. First, the church — and particularly the Church of England — was a conservative body which often clung to the patriarchal *status quo* in society. It did produce radicals, but they often left its ranks.

Second, women of this period were conditioned by their upbringing and education into accepting a subordinate role in the church. Church schools were particularly conservative in their view of education for girls: girls should be prepared for marriage before all else — like oysters being plumped for the table, was the comment of one writer.[41]

Third, they were often nervous about speaking and leading meetings, through lack of experience and also because the media often portrayed women philanthropists and missionaries as figures of fun.

Finally, it would appear from the survey and from data

available in parishes that the subsidiary role of the clergy wife was a model for other women.

✖ The role of the clergy wife

This role was crucial in the success and happiness of the parish. The clergy wife acted as a bridge between her husband and the women of the parish. If she were a worker and a person of sympathy, she usually carried the parish with her.

For example, the wife of Canon Sydney Langford Smith, rector of Summer Hill throughout the inter-war period, was commended by the parish council for: 'Her quiet Christian spirit. . . she has been a friend in the true sense of the word to so many in Summer Hill, especially in times of illness, trouble and bereavement. . . she will indeed be sadly missed.[42] This lady led a women's Bible class in the parish for twenty-one years as well as chairing the Mothers' Union and attending numerous meetings. It was a relentlessly public life and was often complicated by her role as peacemaker between warring parties or as buffer between her husband and the parishioners.

The significance of the role of the clergy wife has been further underlined by Kenneth Dempsey's research into the wives of Methodist ministers. In a study of six ministers from a particular NSW country town (called 'Barool' for the purpose of the survey), it was found that those who had wives who persistently deviated from traditional expectations left the town early or else resigned from the ministry prematurely.[43] Two-thirds of the wives in the Methodist survey presided over one or more of the women's organisations in the church, plus Sunday school, youth work, involvement in fetes and flower rosters and so on. Advantages for the clergy wives — since the position was not materially rewarding — were, first, the sense of leading a vicarious career plus the companionship of engaging in a joint enterprise. Second, the wives felt caught up in their husband's work anyway because of its very proximity. Finally, there was the companionship of the laywomen amongst whom they worked.

Protestant laywomen of this period interviewed by the writer consisted mainly of clergy wives whose husbands commenced ministry in the 1930s. Not many of these women survive, but there is no reason to suspect that their experience does not mirror that of their counterparts in orders. Of five Anglican ministers' wives and one clergy daughter who responded, not one would agree that the church was male-dominated or that they would have had their lives of sacrifice any other way. Five out of six nonconformist church ministers' wives were of the same opinion, while two out of the three deaconesses felt that the church was weighted too far in favour of the men.

These responses lead me to believe that clergy wives played an invaluable bridging role in parish life — representing both clergy and laity. It was a life of drudgery — the concept of helpmeet being carried to the nth degree — but it was also for many a vocation with its own rewards.

The nine semi-professionals of this period appear to have had no regrets. 'We all loved to help', was the comment of the oldest interviewee when asked if expectations of clergy wives were too high. Another wrote: 'I was happy to be a helpmeet, but I was never a doormat.'[44]

✠ Catholic laywomen

The Catholic laywoman in the inter-war period played for the most part a passive role which was acceptable to the male hierarchy. As girls, many had been members of pious societies like the Children of Mary. This sodality met every month on a parish basis; its members attended Mass together, wearing a badge, white veil and blue cloak and carrying banners. Older women could join such sodalities as the Sacred Heart Sodality or the Legion of Mary and these societies were encouraged by the hierarchy.

An emotional Marian piety, reinforced by the Fatima vision of 1917, was the basis of ecclesiastical expectations of women. In practice, the parish priest relied upon his lay-women to help with church housekeeping, to raise funds by means of fetes and balls and to arrange accommodation for immigrants: 'Devout laywomen were the backbone of the church. . . [they] did everything to facilitate the easy working of a parish and its school.'[45]

Most women gladly accepted the role of parish auxiliary and their work was usually appreciated by the priest, but it was a different matter when women elected to join one of the more radical Catholic laywomen's societies which began to spring up in the twentieth century. The latter came to be regarded by the male hierarchy as unpredictable and, at worst, subversive so that coexistence on each other's terms became largely impossible.

The chief reason for the misunderstandings which arose was, as we have seen, the gap between the orthodox images of Catholic women as held by the hierarchy and the actual experiences of the laywomen themselves. A great gap was fixed between the image of the Blessed Virgin Mary and the image of Eve in Catholic mythology. If you were a Bride of Christ rather than a bride of man, you were more likely to fall into the first category rather than the second and vice-versa.

The hierarchy refused to trust women, first, because of their perceived sexual frailty. 'Impurity was bad enough in a man, but in a woman — of course, it is fatal'[46] wrote the Jesuit Father John Churnock in 1910. Many priests suspected women of practising birth control, thus causing divorce. Sally Kennedy argues that the position of lay Catholic women in the eyes of the church was 'negligible'; their brief was to work hard in the home.

Furthermore, because it was felt by the hierarchy that women were not sound enough moral guardians of their children, a massive school system run by the religious was set up to fulfil this task. In 1933, Archbishop Duhig told a gathering of laywomen that their role in the church must of necessity always be secondary to that of the nuns: 'We must never forget that in the forefront of women's work in Australia, there are 10 000 consecrated Virgins of Christ.'[47]

Thus, an active role for laywomen outside the home and a narrow circle of parish activities was frowned upon by the hierarchy in this period. However, the very lack of trust shown in the female laity by the clergy seemed to spur on certain women of education and spirit to higher expectations of their role in the church.

In 1913, a meeting of lay Catholic women bent on inter-parish dialogue drew up a constitution for the Catholic Women's Association (CWA) in Sydney and asked the arch-bishop for his approval. He gave it on condition they established a hostel for Catholic girls in the city — it was thought that this new body must have a useful moral function. Such outstanding Catholic laywomen as Constance D'Arcy, the pioneer doctor and member of the university senate, were early members. The following year, the Catholic Women's League was founded in South Australia, principally to integrate Catholic women into the war effort.[48]

The other states followed suit and in 1916 the Catholic Women's Social Guild (CWSG) was founded in Victoria. It was to prove a lively feminist body which promoted a vigorous role for Catholic women in terms of social and political reform. One of the reasons for the strength of this society was the strength of its leaders — Mary Glowrey, Anna Brenan and Julia Flynn were all outstanding professionals in their own right.

Mary Glowrey, as we have seen, was a doctor who began baby clinics for new mothers in Victoria in 1917 before going to India as a missionary. Anna Brenan was a fine lawyer who worked to establish equality of women before the law and Julia Flynn overcame male opposition to become Chief Inspector of Schools in Victoria in 1924.[49] The dynamism of this group was reflected in the motto they chose from the Book of Proverbs for their society — 'She hath put her hand to strong things'. Before long, they were affiliating with the National Council of Women (NCW), since this seemed to be the best tactic for women to achieve equity in the workplace across the country.

However, the hierarchy in the form of Cardinal Mannix strongly opposed links with a supposedly secular body and the CWSG yielded and broke its ties with the NCW in 1920. Anna Brenan and several others then left the CWSG and its membership steadily dwindled until the minutes of 1927 recorded: 'It was remarked by all that the opposition of the parish priests made it almost impossible for women, no matter how enthusiastic, to do any Guild work.'[50]

As a more compliant body, the Catholic Women's Association in New South Wales had a harmonious relationship with the hierarchy, at least on the surface. Its most politically active members, the Golding sisters and Kate Dwyer having left in the early 1920s, the CWA drifted along under the conservative leadership of Mary Barlow, but played a valuable role during the Depression years with its soup kitchens and fundraising for the poor. After Mary Barlow's death, the more radical Kate Egan took over. Work amongst the blind commenced and an effort was made to reach out to the unemployed and Aborigines after 1935. By the end of the

1930s, the CWA was a vigorous and optimistic society, but difficulties were ahead: within a few years, the Sydney hierarchy would clip its wings irrevocably.[51]

Meanwhile, the CWSG had been working quietly in Victoria setting up sex education lectures and physical education classes in the parishes, but relations with Cardinal Mannix continued to be uneasy throughout the Depression. The CWSG would not abandon its political agenda in the 1930s; it continued to champion the underdog, particularly if they were women. The September 1929 issue of their magazine, *Horizon*, commenting on the Depression, pointed out that:

> Public sympathy has not been given [to the woman] as readily as to the man, probably because the unemployed man is always pictured as a distressed father of a family of helpless and starving children.

The hierarchy did not want to hear when *Horizon* pointed out that it was not the low birthrate, but the sweating of labour, bad housing and unemployment which were the great problems in society. Likewise, the 7 000 members of the CWSG did not want to hear when Archbishop Duhig depicted women as 'moral tamers of society' and suggested that they found a Legion of Decency in 1937. It never eventuated.[52]

The Catholic hierarchy was further bemused by the advent of two more Catholic women's societies in this period. These two were exotic organisations, the St Joan's Social and Political Alliance, which arrived from England in 1936, and the Grail Organisation, which came from Holland in the same year.

Both were strongly feminist in outlook; the former, consisting mainly of single intellectuals, gained instant prestige from the appointment of the prime minister's wife, Dame Enid Lyons, as first president. Their prime aims were equal rights for women and social justice for all. The Alliance attacked romantic Victorian views of women and stressed that women should define their own roles in the light of modern society. It was not a large group, but it was politically active, developing strong ties with non-Catholic organisations like the WCTU, NCW and the Federation of Mothers' Clubs. It was particularly active in campaigning for the rights of Aboriginal women and children in Western Australia and the Northern Territory.[53]

The Grail Organisation began with the arrival of five Dutch lay Catholic women in Sydney to a welcome from Archbishop Kelly. It was to base itself more firmly in Sydney, while the St Joan's Alliance was strongest in Melbourne. It also promulgated a politically active role for women, but not in terms of the feminism of the 1890s. The Grail attacked the first wave feminists because they 'conceived of equality on a masculine pattern'; it was wrong to attempt a 'slavish imitation of men'. Their criticism of the first wave feminists was arguable, since they were children of their own generation and the feminists of the 1930s would not have had the suffrage but for the feminists of the 1890s.

The Grail Organisation was delightfully idealistic — 'Women should lead the revolution to improve the world' — but they were politically naive. Archbishop Kelly was kind to them, hoping they would mobilise Catholic youth in an age of mass youth movements. However, the majority of the hierarchy were suspicious and waited for the Grail to make a false step. Their first error was to refuse the offer of a chaplain; their next was to attack the Legion of Mary as narrow, parochial and unbalanced theologically.

The Irish clergy were instantly alienated as the Legion was one of their favourite organisations. The aim of the enthusiastic Grail members was to harness the potential of women so that they formed a lay apostolate within the church. They gave lectures; they organised summer schools, tennis parties and hikes; they encouraged drama and music, organising pageants in which the children wore uniforms and badges.

By the end of 1939, there were 1 000 active members of the Grail in twenty-five parishes across Sydney and a group at the university. The bishops approved of their lay apostolate, but not of much else. To the men, so much of their talk was emotional waffle and they seemed dangerously independent in the context of war.

By 1941, the new Archbishop Norman Gilroy had virtually suppressed them; he appointed a chaplain to keep an eye on them and to censor their publications. He imposed repressive control over the CWA by appointing a chaplain with sweeping powers. He gave the hierarchy's stamp of approval to the Legion of Catholic Women as the acceptable organisation for laywomen. He kept the St Joan's Alliance out of NSW till 1946 and he constantly obstructed the Grail members in their administration of the Catholic Central Library, where they had been working without tenure or responsibility since 1950. When after seven years they had failed to resign, he told them they need no longer run the library. Thus, a sad episode in the history of male-female relations in the church ended.[54]

✖ The ordination of women

One of the most important issues facing the post-war Australian church was to be the question of the ordination of women. The issue barely surfaced in the inter-war period, but there were foretastes of the struggle to come as Australia's first ordination of a woman to the cure of souls took place as early as 1927.

Attitudes towards change and especially towards female leadership differ greatly from church to church. The most hierarchical churches — the Roman Catholic, Orthodox and Anglican were the most resistant to change because of their patriarchal organisation and long history. The Non-conformist churches have proved to be the most ready to adapt to cultural change because of their emphasis on the democratic rights of the individual. Hence, the Congregationalists, Methodists and Presbyterians were the first to adopt the principle of the ordination of women, followed by the Baptists; but the Congregationalists were the only ones to do so in this period. The Salvation Army and the Quakers had always accepted equality of function in their churches, the latter adhering to the prophetic tradition of inspiration and therefore eschewing any form of ordination.

It has been in the Anglican Church that the most bitter division has arisen over the ordination of women and this is because of that church's divided, if comprehensive, nature. The Anglican Church has always been made up of the Catholic, Broad and Evangelical traditions and, although supporters of female ordination have come from all three of these strands, at least two of them, the Catholic and the Evangelical, have provided some ardent opponents of the ordained woman. However, this division was still in the future at the end of the 1930s: Florence Li Tim Oi was not to be ordained by the Bishop of Hong Kong for another six years. Apart from the visit of Maude Royden in 1928, Australia appeared to be well cocooned from the inroads of Anglican feminism in the inter-war period.[55]

After World War I, the bishops of the Church of England were forced to address the question of female leadership as a result of the formidable record of women in philanthropic work and in overseas missions. Moreover, nearly twice as many women attended Anglican services as men by this time.[56] In 1919, the Archbishop of Canterbury appointed a committee of both sexes to study the ministry of women. It reported that:

Much of the immense expansion of activity and of the efficiency of ministry [was due] to the mainly voluntary efforts of women. . . hundreds of wives, widows and daughters of clergymen, and of single women, who in obscurity have dedicated their lives and substance to the promotion of the kingdom of God in our own country and in heathen lands.[57]

However, the Lambeth conference of bishops which met the following year made scant acknowledgement of the contribution of women. Although it affirmed the spiritual equality of the sexes, women still 'needed to redeem the fallen nature in procreation' — in other words, 'virgins and mothers were still the only categories for respectable women'.[58] The conference came to the conclusion that 'in the last resort' authority belonged to man and that although the order of deaconesses were the same diaconate as the men's, ordination to the priesthood for women was 'out of the question'.[59] There was, however, one small reform for Anglican women: they were now permitted to join church councils.

Ten years later, the next Lambeth conference was to reverse their attitude to deaconesses and to declare that they were not in holy orders, but were 'distinct from and complementary to the historic Orders of the Faith'.[60] The cause of female ordination seemed more doubtful than ever. Nevertheless, feminism in the Anglican Church began to strengthen during the 1920s and many churchmen, including Archbishop Temple (privately), were being won over.

The leader of the church feminist cause was Maude Royden and her visit to Australia in 1928 was significant in awakening an awareness of female leadership in a church asleep to that possibility. Maude Royden had impeccable credentials in English society and these unsurprisingly helped her to gain an entree into Australian society and crowded lecture halls in

1928. Daughter of a respected baronet, educated at Cheltenham and Oxford, suffragette and parish worker amongst the poor in Liverpool, she lectured at Oxford and established a reputation as a public speaker. During World War I, she accepted an assistant preachership at the City Temple in London; it was a Congregational Church. There, her preaching drew large crowds and she was licensed to baptise.

Maude Royden, first woman to occupy an Anglican pulpit in Australia: 1928

She was the first woman to preach at an Anglican service — at St Botolph's, Bishopsgate — in 1919.[61] The Bishop of London was opposed to her occupation of one of his pulpits, but the Archbishop of Sydney was perfectly agreeable in June 1928 during her Australian visit, when she accepted an invitation from the rector to preach at St Mark's, Darling Point.[62] This invitation was probably at the insistence of Jessie Street, who was a leading parishioner as well as an activist in the women's movement. Reform in the Anglican Church has not infrequently emanated from the laity. An Adelaide observer who called himself 'A Mere Man' wrote of Royden's visit to that city:

The cathedral pulpit and in it a little, quiet, unassuming figure in a plain dress. . . holding every single person in that crowded building hanging on her every word. Transparent sincerity. . . wonderful power of expression. . . varied intonations. . . quiet. Never at a loss for words. Great psychological insight. . . simple naturalness. There is no doubt that Miss Royden is in her right place in a pulpit, cathedral or any other.[63]

Maude Royden attracted such large crowds in Sydney that the police usually had to be called to control them. She was a complete novelty to conventional Sydney society and her residing at Government House did her no harm either. Her lectures covered such subjects as psychology, evolution, sex, as well as theology. 'The process called evolution,' she declared, 'was after the mind of God.'

Archbishop Wright asked her to speak to clergy at the Chapter House on the subject of 'The Divine Mystery of Sex'.[64] The extreme Protestants in his diocese grumbled and the arch-Protestant *Church Record* sniffed:

Frankly, we don't like her all-inclusive outlook and many of her fundamental positions we straitly disagree. In certain directions, she has exercised power for good and desires, according to her lights and temperament, to aid the cause of righteousness.[65]

However, more liberal members of her audience like Canon W.G. Hilliard were deeply impressed and were won over to a supportive view of women's ministry. Later, as Coadjutor Bishop, he told the all-male Sydney Synod that one of the best addresses he had ever heard was given by Maude Royden. He then defied 'any member of Synod to say he was not controlled by a woman, his mother, his lover or his wife'. There was dead silence at this and no-one took up his challenge.[66] Life in Australia resumed its peaceful tenor after the departure of Maude Royden, but the seeds of questioning tradition had been sown.

Her books, *Woman's Nature* and *Sex and Commonsense*, continued to be read. They were a mixture of lofty expression:

> Women respond with passionate gratitude to Christ because of his sublime preaching that every human soul was made for God and that no part or section of society, no race, no class and no sex, was made for the convenience of another.[67]

and bold controversy:

> I conceive it much better to use contraceptives than to bear unwanted children; I conceive it also better to use them than to be cruel to others or become neurotic oneself; but that it is an ideal I do not believe.[68]

In her view, there were five reasons why the Anglican Church rejected the priesthood for women:

1. Subordination of women was necessary because of their physical weakness
2. The taboo of uncleanness [some clerics feared women entering their pulpits because of menstruation]
3. The bearing of children
4. Sexual attraction
5. Ecumenical considerations [the Roman Catholic Church would be offended].[69]

These reasons did not influence the Congregational Church in South Australia when they decided to ordain Winifred Kiek in 1927. Born to a devout Quaker family in Manchester, she imbibed ardent pacifism and strict teetotalism from her background. A prodigious worker and a fine intellect, she gained a first class degree at Manchester University. She began teaching in the slums of her native city before marrying Sydney Kiek, an Oxford theologian and Congregational minister. His views on women were years ahead of his time; he did not expect his wife to be domesticated, but felt that anyone with intellectual gifts should be developing them for the service of God and man.[70]

Sydney Kiek applied for the principalship of the Congregational Theological College in Adelaide and was accepted. The family arrived in 1920 and two years later Winifred became the first woman to gain a Bachelor of Divinity degree from an Australian university (Melbourne University). She began lecturing in Old Testament and continued her studies. In 1926, she began work as a probation officer, juvenile delinquents being passed on to her from the children's court.

Winifred Kiek at the time of her ordination in Adelaide: 1927

She had preached on a number of occasions in England, including once before a thousand men at the Halifax Brotherhood 'and never once felt that I was a mere woman. A spirit of comradeship prevailed between men and women and this is how it should be'.[71]

So when she offered to preach once a Sunday in 1926 at the new housing area of Colonel Light Gardens, the Congregational Church in Adelaide which was short of ministers readily accepted. The Congregational Church in Britain had been ordaining women to full ministry since 1918. Winifred Kiek began by arranging pulpit supplies, delivering her sermon and visiting those in need. The church soon applied to the Union for the ordination of their new minister. Permission was granted and, on 13 June 1927, she was ordained, the Reverend L.C. Parkin, Chairman of the Congregational Union, presiding at the service. Amongst the hands on her head were those of her husband.[72]

There was opposition from some quarters to her ordination. When she was invited to preach at one Adelaide Presbyterian church, one of the elders protested in the following terms: 'You might as well have the devil in the pulpit as a woman. If she comes, I'm resigning!'[73]

She was invited back twice to that church and there was no evidence — apart from this elder — of men leaving the congregations to which she ministered. Outside her Sunday commitments was her involvement in care for the needy, particularly during the Depression. At one stage, all but one of her deacons were unemployed. So she organised collections and clothing, fundraising for the poor, soup kitchens and work for the unemployed.

Winifred Kiek received encouragement from overseas women church leaders, most notably Maude Royden and the Reverend Dorothy Wilson who was President of the Society for the Ministry of Women in the USA. She urged the importance of sex education for Australian children and attempted to help divorcees, migrants and Aborigines at their point of need. Her feminism was tempered by strong views as to children's need of mothering:

> Say what you like about the equality of the sexes, a woman must stay at home to nurse her babies through their childhood. A creche, no matter how scientifically conducted, is no substitute for a mother's arms.[74]

Kiek was idealistic in her pacifism, in her opposition to gambling being licensed by the state and in her proposed reforms of the children's court. Yet she was realistic in her feminist philosophy:

> One cannot deny that there is difficulty in the notion of equality as no two people are really equal and no one can have complete freedom.

and gentle in her reproach to a discriminatory church:

> Isn't it strange that, though the impetus towards woman's emancipation came from Jesus Christ, the church which bears his name has lagged behind the state in giving her equality with men?[75]

It was ten years before the church could pluck up the courage to break again with tradition. The next woman to be ordained in Australia was another Congregational minister, the Reverend Isabella Merry. After this took place in 1937, Isabella Merry ministered in a number of churches in Melbourne, before becoming one of the country's first full-time hospital chaplains.[76]

The Methodist Church was the next to consider seriously the ordination of women, but there was enough indifference and opposition to delay its approval by the General Conference for forty years. In 1929, the Reverend Dr Alex McCallum brought a resolution to the annual Victorian and Tasmanian Conference calling for the ordination of women. It was deferred and, to keep McCallum quiet, he was put in charge of a committee to draw up recommendations. This committee reported that:

(a) Any unmarried woman believing herself to be called should be able to offer herself for the ministry like the men
(b) The training and ordination of women should be the same as for the men.
(c) If they married, they must resign as marriage is a separate vocation.

Again, the matter was deferred by Conference, but in 1935 a proposal was put forward for Methodist deaconesses to replace the former largely untrained 'sisters of the people'. They were to work principally in women's areas and were to be subject to a two year training course in theology and general subjects. Very few women applied; the new deaconesses were allowed only one year on a circuit, except in special circumstances, and their ministry was not officially accepted by General Conference until 1941 when manpower was short in time of war.[77]

Other denominations did nothing about the ordination of women in the inter-war period. Like the history of churchwomen themselves, it was a hidden issue waiting for braver souls to take it up.

⊞ The extent of change for laywomen in the inter-war years

The interval between the Great Wars witnessed greater involvement of women than ever in the life of the church and its related activities — mainly because of the retreat of so many into their homes and away from the paid workforce, where it was decreed that men must have priority.

Yet a distinction grew between the actual role of women within the churches and the place assigned them by the churches. Women had been conditioned to look after the spiritual and moral side of the church, while the expansion and administrative building side was taken up by the men. As Australia became less of a pioneering society, feminine images increased in the churches; women outnumbered men more substantially in the congregations and laywomen provided the largest unpaid workforce in the parishes.

At the behest of the hierarchy, Catholic sisters in vast numbers had established a massive school system across the continent. Yet even convent education inculcated an independence and a feminism which was to spill over into a proliferation of new Catholic women's societies.

The male hierarchy for the most part failed to read the signs of the times. There were exceptions like Bishop Geoffrey Cranswick of Gippsland who pointed out that the teaching and prophetic gifts of women were not sufficiently recognised and that educated women might have more time for study than their clergy. He was delighted with the spiritual contribution of women in his outback diocese and felt that:

> The more freedom and scope and expression is given to womanly and manly service in conjunction, the richer will society and the church be.[78]

This concept of leadership as servanthood based on principles of equality was largely absent in the more authoritarian churches of the period. They favoured a clerical caste which mediated a 'word' or a 'grace' from above to lower orders in the hierarchy. Under this concept, women were obliged to be passive in role when interacting with traditionally male authority. Nor were the majority unhappy with their lot until later in the century when society's expectations changed.

However, when the more venturesome sought to break out of this cocoon of passivity, they were often deeply hurt. It was a process which would intensify as the century unfolded.

11

An era of greater freedom and creativity

WOMEN IN ORDERS, 1939 TO THE 1990S

'I do feel a lack of freedom. . . we [religious] are frequently criticised for being forthright, demanding of equality and challenging in our thinking and expression.'

Sister Maureen McGuirk, RSM (1996)

'Women have to take their place by reason of their gifts and abilities.'

Eva Burrows, elected General of the Salvation Army in 1986

'I hope that, in the future, unity between men and women can help them achieve equality at every level. Equality means mutuality, a sharing from different angles. And when that happens, then you'll get a marvellous blend of creativity going on.'

Sister Angela Solling, after her ordination in 1992

T HE CHANGES WHICH HAVE TAKEN place in Australian society over the past half century have not escaped women in orders. World war and the return to peace, the arrival of second wave feminism, technological change and the growth of secularism have demanded a response from church and society. The result has been a shrinkage in vocations and, at times, an uneasy relationship between professional churchwomen and the hierarchy. However, out of the turbulence of change has come a greater creativity and greater freedom for feminine gifts to be exercised.

For women in orders in the Roman Catholic Church, the greatest internal changes took place as a result of the Second Vatican Council, which met from 1962 to 1965. This conclave of clerics did not include any women, but some were invited as observers in the later stages. The reforms which they initiated arose out of a background of general socio-economic change which could no longer be ignored.

✠ Factors leading to a climate of change for women in orders

The first factor that led to this climate of change was the general increase in democratic sentiment following the defeat of absolutism on most fronts in World War II. Australian and other Western societies began to move away from rule by hereditary privilege and, in the process, were questioning traditional hierarchies.

This shift in values had implications for church order. Equality is the badge of democracy and so inequality in male-female relations gradually became unacceptable, even in so traditional a body as the church. As one *Quadrant* writer put it: 'If the deepest value of the democratic age is equality, how can one accept inequality between man and woman?'[1]

A second factor leading to change for women in orders in this period was the extension of equality in education; university and theological courses were now open to women as never before. This not only enabled women to develop their talents more fully, but it also impelled them to seek broader avenues for the expression of those gifts. One of Vatican II's greatest reforms was to encourage women in orders to go out of their communities and seek further education.

In practice, this meant that Catholic women religious, often at great cost to their health, undertook part-time university courses after heavy teaching or nursing commitments during the day. Before long, they were better educated than the majority of parish priests and this tended to widen the gap between religious and the hierarchy.[2]

Most degrees achieved since 1965 have been in arts, science and social work, but some religious like Margaret Doyle, vicar of the Sisters of Mercy at Parramatta, gained law degrees. Doyle has since been appointed chief conciliator of the Human Rights and Equal Opportunity Commission.[3]

A third factor leading to change is the women's movement, which has been a potent force in shaping the responses of women in orders. Whereas once they might have accepted the social and political limitations of their calling, they now sought wider job opportunities and greater self-fulfilment. This sense of freedom and independence was imparted to their students, but it was difficult to pass on any enthusiasm for vocations to the religious life amongst the young in the climate of the 1970s and 1980s.

Blame for this can be laid at the door of both feminism and secularism but, whatever the cause, the emphasis on obedience and commitment which undergirds a religious institute began to appeal less and less to potential candidates. A former Josephite sister, Colleen Malone, commented:

> Religious vocation no longer has meaning or appeal. The mission of the church can be part of the everyday life of the person. Celibacy is not attractive.[4]

After 1950, the demands of the Catholic education system

in Australia began to place an intolerable burden on women religious which increased their discontent with the *status quo*. Post-war immigration of large numbers from Catholic countries in Europe led to overcrowded schools and inadequate resources. Classes exceeding forty were not uncommon.

Margaret O'Sullivan of the Sisters of Charity writes of being 'stretched to the utmost' in her first years as a religious in the 1960s: she began a Leaving Certificate class at one school and led the school to registration; she shared in the running of school sports, visited the elderly, wrote items for the parish paper, organised some of the school cleaning — all while teaching a full day, with extra hours for Honours classes plus playground duty.[5]

Maureen McGuirk of the Sisters of Mercy argues that many religious developed a strong aversion to teaching as a result of this pressure and opted to become health and social workers as soon as it was possible. By 1988, more were engaged in social welfare than in the traditional sphere of education for which their orders had been initially recruited by the bishops. This meant greater autonomy for religious as they handed over responsibility for schools to lay teachers who could be employed on salaries as a result of the introduction of State Aid from the 1960s onwards.

The downside of this change for orders was that religious developed a visibility problem: by 1980, most children in Catholic schools were no longer being taught by nuns, and traditional personal relationships based on friendship and role modelling were not being formed between pupils and religious. Of this, Maureen McGuirk says:

> The possibility of religious life as an alternative is not now considered by young women; parents are dubious about the suitability of religious and priestly life as a happy alternative for their children. . .[6]

The falling off in numbers of religious must not obscure the contribution they have made to Australian society both before and since World War II. The vast state of Western Australia in particular owes much to the work of the Presentation Order in education and the Sisters of Mercy in education and medicine. The St John of God Order from their mother house in Broome provided a civilising and caring influence in the remote area of the Kimberleys. The full saga of the achievements of religious women in the development of the country has yet to be told.

With the changes since Vatican II, most sisters have welcomed the freedom to diversify their role and respond to fresh areas of need. Thus, a Josephite sister goes out each day nursing AIDS patients in their own homes, a Sister of Charity specialises in palliative care rather than hospital administration, a Sister of Mercy trains unemployed youth to set up a coffee shop for young people lacking in morale and purpose.[7]

The Mamre Project: Mary-Louise Petro of the Parramatta Sisters of Mercy training unemployed youth in the hospitality industry

Religious are now able to pinpoint need and use their own initiative, while still relying on the sustenance of community. They are cheerful about the decline in numbers, recognising that society is now less in need of the old pioneering imperatives.

✠ Vatican II, 1962-1965:
a watershed for the church

The importance of the Vatican II Council, convened by the reforming Pope, Pope John Paul I, cannot be overemphasised. The Council, in a series of sessions, marked a watershed in the development of roles within the church for both lay and religious. No longer were lay men or women to be regarded as inferior in status to religious, 'but rather, the faithful of Christ are called by God from both states of life, so that they might enjoy this particular gift in the life of the church'.[8]

Thus, Catholic laity were able to become more articulate and autonomous and greater dialogue with Protestant churches could be undertaken.

Religious orders were also reformed. There was to be no watering down of the threefold vow of poverty, chastity and obedience, but religious were encouraged to reconsider their vocations and to expand their biblical and theological knowledge.[9] Changes in habit and greater recognition of gifts were permitted and overseas travel and study were authorised.[10] Some orders as a result rewrote their rule: in Australia, the Brigidines carried this out in 1977 and the Josephites in 1986. Enclosure of orders was considerably relaxed and religious were encouraged to take responsibility for their own lives.

Many of them did this by leaving. Some married. Within two years, 400 priests and 3 000 religious had left their vocation across the country.[11] For many Catholic women, both inside and outside the orders, the *Humanae Vitae* decree of Pope Paul VI in 1968 against artificial contraception prompted further disillusionment with the church. It is impossible to say how many would have left because of it; it is more likely that women ignored the hierarchy and remained as Catholics who were determined to limit their family as they saw fit. Women religious tended to side with their sex in this matter. They could not forget the stress experienced by their mothers in bringing up large numbers of children.[12]

Women religious now express mixed reactions to the reforms of Vatican II. Most rejoice in the discarding of outdated regulations and in the greater freedom to serve outside traditional parameters. Some declare that it makes no difference to the basic hierarchical structure of the church.

Colleen Malone expressed reservations:

> I have certainly studied its documents — [but] what difference? I am not sure it has made all that difference in terms of the official structural church, but at the grassroots level it has given us some freedoms. These freedoms, however, have walked hand in hand with the women's movement and have been mightily influenced by it.[13]

One of the most beneficial of its effects has been the liberalisation of community life through greater education of superiors. Inflexibility, narrowness and gullibility were gradually put to flight. The hard conditions for women religious before Vatican II were now relaxed so that fewer of the unhappy and overworked remained in communities. Most religious entered henceforth into an atmosphere of family affection where trust rather than coercion prevailed. As one American observer at Vatican II commented:

> There are perhaps few groups who have as much cause to resent the advice to become as children, as we sisters, because often it has been real infantilism which has been expected of us.[14]

This did not mean that all unhappiness was eliminated within orders by the reforms of Vatican II. Those who did not take advantage of the new freedoms often remained discontented and even oppressed by the decrees of canon law as most recently revised in 1917, as one correspondent has said:

> The church in reality does little for religious in practice, except to bind them by canon laws that are outside the jurisdiction of civil laws. . . Most lawyers would not even take on cases, no matter how unjust by civil standards, because of the Church's jurisdiction. They have tied things up very cleverly — in the name of Christianity.[15]

Financial arrangements within orders can be viewed as restrictive and discriminatory in comparison with conditions for workers in the secular world. Nuns in Catholic schools do not receive wages like lay teachers, but a stipend which is paid to the congregation rather than the individual. On retirement, pensions are also paid straight into the convent account and sisters are allotted a small sum to pay for all personal expenses. Details of the financial resources of orders are difficult to obtain, but it is certain that they are asset-rich. The option to leave the order for middle-aged nuns is not viable financially as they have been unable to save in their professional life thus far.

Thus, a sense of grievance for some is inevitable. For those who are happy to soldier on in accordance with their vow of poverty, such complaints would be unspiritual, but others feel both trapped and unrewarded for years of toil.

Religious engaged in hospital work like the Sisters of Charity at St Vincent's Hospitals in Sydney and Melbourne and the Sisters of Mercy at the Mater Hospitals in Brisbane and Sydney (not to mention a string of regional hospitals) have always presented strong images of control both within and outside the convent. The old style fundraising of fetes and art unions to finance hospitals was replaced by negotiations with government which required both toughness and professionalism. Hospital religious were constantly dealing with adults, whether patients, police or prostitutes.

Relations with medical staff were often problematical, especially for nurses and women doctors. The latter found the nuns of the 1950s very hard to deal with; they were ordered about like junior nurses, with scant recognition of their professional training. The mindset of the novitiate died hard. For nursing religious, a return to the quiet of the convent was refreshing after the hurly burly of hospital wards. However, they were disappointed with the church hierarchy for its lack of recognition of the importance of the ministry of health care within the church's mandate.[16]

Since Vatican II, therefore, a constant decline in the numbers of religious in Australia has taken place; membership has dropped from its peak in 1966 in NSW of 14 622 to a little over half that figure by 1990 — or at a rate of fourteen per cent every five years. Across the state's eighty-five orders — fifty-six of whom are female and twenty-nine male — the average age of religious in 1990 was estimated at sixty by the Conference of Leaders of Religious Institutes. Thirty years earlier, it was below fifty.

'We are on a downward curve of religious life,' said Sister Angela Cameron, president of the Conference of Leaders of Religious Institutes in 1995. 'How can we attract young women today when they are going to be living with their grandmothers?'[17]

The church and the orders are philosophical about the decline in vocations — which, of course, have not totally dried up. Religious are still optimistic about a role for younger women and are prepared for further changes in lifestyle and emphasis, as Sister Emma Trotter suggests:

I think we have done much to rethink our training programs very seriously to meet the needs of the times. Vocations are coming to mission committees and to contemplative committees, because young people and not so young are seeing real purpose in their work. . . we will all have to follow a radical pattern. . . take a few risks and, if they don't work — well, at least we have tried.[18]

Admittedly, this optimism issues from an order which is based on annual vows which naturally allow greater latitude for its members. It would seem, too, that more alternatives for lay involvement in ministry have arisen since Vatican II. Such service organisations as the Paulian Association and, more latterly, the enthusiastic lobby group, Women in the Australian Church, have provided an outlet for women seeking an autonomous role. These do not require changes in lifestyle and limitations resulting from vows and yet they have been found to be fulfilling for members.

✠ Convent education and feminism

It is an inescapable fact that convent education has produced the majority of articulate women leaders in Australian society since 1970. Catholic education has been responsible for such political leaders as Susan Ryan, Ros Kelly and Carmen Lawrence in federal politics and Kerry Chikharovski in state politics. In the arts and media, Germaine Greer, Anne Summers, Wendy McCarthy and Geraldine Doogue were taught by Catholic orders.

Feminism and Catholicism appear to have been inextricably linked in the Australian context, the record of Protestant schools in producing leading feminists being slight by comparison. Although academic standards were no lower — indeed, possibly higher than those at Catholic schools post 1960 — the emphasis in Protestant secondary education was on preparation for marriage rather than on a career.

There are several possible reasons for the connection between Catholicism and feminism. First, whether orders were under the control of bishops or not, they were run by women for women. At all times, orders presented an image to their pupils of women leading, working, organising and building without the manifest presence of men. The image of a strong, independent and resourceful woman was for the most part passed onto children for emulation. Most religious women were articulate and competent, thus providing good role models for those with leadership potential. Often without adequate resources, they became very creative in overcoming obstacles and developing alternatives.[19]

Sister Pauline Rae has said:

> I think I was personally affected by this. I left school with the sense that I could do anything I set my mind to. It never occurred to me that I would be thought less capable because I was a woman.[20]

Geraldine Doogue also attributes feminist consciousness to her convent upbringing:

> We saw women in control of their own lives and world: we saw much richness and complexity. They expected a lot of us and got it back. . .[21]

Opinions of convent education were not universally favourable, however. Many pupils in the pre-Vatican II era resented the saturation effect of convent education as well as its attempts to inculcate political attitudes. Daily masses, evening rosaries (if a boarder), Hail Marys, frequent confession, indulgences, sodalities, holy pictures and warnings about sex often put students off religion, as did the anti-Communist propaganda of the 1950s.[22]

The historian, Katharine Massam, has prepared a study of the way in which Catholic Action used the orders to inculcate an anti-communist stance in pupils against the background of the Cold War. Devotion to the Blessed Virgin Mary was stressed as a weapon to be used in a cosmic struggle against the communist threat.[23]

'They brainwash their students in Soviet Russia,' declared one of the nuns in a history class in the late 1950s. 'Isn't that what you are doing to us?' asked one of the class innocently — for which she was instantly banished from the room.[24]

In linking Catholicism with feminism, Maureen McGuirk and Pauline Rae attribute the independent streak bred in convent girls to Irish roots. As a matriarchal society, the Irish expected a strong role from women and, as a society with a history of oppression, the Irish transmitted to Australia their inclination to question the *status quo*. When the women's movement emerged in the late 1960s, 'convent girls' simply applied their tendency to question to another element in the *status quo*, as their consciousness of gender inequality was raised.[25]

Whatever the flaws of convent education in terms of narrowness and suspicion of students, most graduates register gratitude for the devotion and standards of teaching nuns: 'They taught me a love of learning' was the simple comment of one who had attended a remote rural convent.[26]

The contribution of these schools in encouraging the value of women as leaders in family and community in the second half of the twentieth century has without doubt been immeasurable. More than their Protestant counterparts, they adapted to changing roles for women and especially to the entry of married women into the workforce after 1970. 'Our convent education had prepared us for the fight. The nuns had taught us discipline and tenacity and a pride in ourselves.'[27]

❈ Anglican orders

A similar spirit of independence was bred in schools run by Anglican orders, although they were far fewer in numbers. Perth College, run by the Sisters of the Church, but staffed principally by laity, concentrated on a strong chapel life, high academic standards and a flexible attitude to the role of women in a changing society.

Although vocations were diminishing in the Society of the Sacred Advent in Queensland, numbers having fallen from thirty in 1945 to twelve by 1988, there was a deliberate policy of encouraging independence as well as spirituality in the girls of St Margaret's Albion, St Anne's Townsville, St Gabriel's Charters Towers and St Mary's Herberton. Falling vocations and parlous finances (religious never knew when or if they would be paid) forced the closure of St Mary's in the 1960s and the transfer of St Anne's and St Gabriel's to the Diocese of North Queensland in the 1970s.

The Brisbane school continues to flourish side by side with the convent and chapel, but most sisters have moved from the classroom to hospital chaplaincy, parish work, retreats and life vows.[28]

Retreat work is also carried out by Sister Angela of the Clare Community at Stroud, NSW. Born Wendy Solling, she became a sculptor of international renown before entering a convent in Britain in 1957. She returned to Australia with three other sisters in 1975 at the invitation of the Bishop of Newcastle. Four years later, land was given to her community on the outskirts of Stroud and, with the help of volunteers, sixteen mudbrick buildings were put up on that land. A monastery followed, over 2000 attending the opening ceremony in 1980.

Sister Angela's spirituality is based on a knowledge of God as parent — both mother and father — and, as a Franciscan, she identifies strongly with nature. A wide variety of people come to Stroud for retreats, counselling and healing as well as to worship in the chapel. In 1988, Bishop Holland decided to ordain Sister Angela as a deacon and this was followed four years later by her ordination to the priesthood. After celebrating her first Mass in the community chapel, she was swept by a great sense of liberation:

> Women are out and running and there's no way women are going to be held back now. They're no longer willing to be swept under the carpet. . . A woman's badge of office is the love in her heart and her priestly dancing with people. It's a different way of looking at the whole ministry.[29]

Perhaps the largest and best organised of the Anglican orders in Australia is the Community of the Holy Name (CHN) which is based in Melbourne. Until the death of its founder, Sister Esther, in 1938, the order had staffed schools, hospitals, hostels and children's homes. Like the Clare Community at Stroud, it stressed a love of nature and animals. Its numbers never exceeded sixty at any one time, the early 1960s being the high point in vocations — as in Roman Catholic orders. By 1986, its numbers had fallen to the low twenties, but it had achieved a proud and varied record of service in Victoria and beyond, while maintaining an Anglo Catholic centre of spirituality.[30]

This order was fortunate in its funding in that it was supported by a wealthy middle-class parish in Melbourne which did not attempt to interfere with its running. Thus, religious were able to concentrate on their work without the grinding poverty of such orders as the Society of the Sacred Advent which in some cases owed its members years of arrears.

The founder's successor as superior in 1938 was Sister Ida.

A practical and authoritarian leader, she spent much of her time coping with administration and the financial pressures of running so many institutions both during and after World War II. She was first obliged to close the House of Mercy orphanage in 1946 for lack of funds. Flourishing hospitals like St George's were found to be too complex and expensive to run in the brave new post-war era. St George's was handed over deep in debt to the government in 1949 and St Ives Private Hospital was sold to the government in 1954.

The order then decided to turn its attention to aged care, opening a home for elderly women in 1950. It was able to staff for some years branches in Goulburn and Auckland and to send sisters to Dogura in Papua New Guinea, ostensibly to work in the diocesan girls' school there. The three sisters who went were disappointed to find that the bishop apparently wanted them as quasi hostesses for himself and missionaries passing through.[31]

One of the most difficult problems faced by home missions, whether run by orders or by a diocese, was that of governmental control. As governments gradually assumed financial responsibility for church welfare and medical institutions, so they gained control of policy. In the case of the babies' home at Darling, the order felt that they were unable to exercise a ministry there because the home had become 'a clearing house for wards of the Social Welfare Department'. So in 1967, after only thirteen years of operation, they reluctantly decided to sell it.[32]

A trickle of departures from the community in the late 1960s corresponded with the larger stream issuing from Roman Catholic orders at the time. By 1974, the novitiate had collapsed as socio-economic changes meant that vocations were much rarer. Two years later, the CHN was forced to withdraw from New Guinea. By the 1980s, the order realised that more adaptation to a changing world was needed and a smaller, leaner community was learning to rely on dialogue and consultation rather than the old dogmatism. Older members of the order were nervous about their future, but they were ready to adapt: 'We're fringe dwellers in a sense. . . we've got a lot of good things going for us. We've got freedom in a way. . .'[33]

Although their work in indoor relief is now at an end, the CHN sisters are engaged in a number of ministries such as chaplaincy to AIDS victims and running the retreat program. A strong contingent attended the first ordination of women deacons in Melbourne in 1986 and it was agreed that any sister called to the priesthood would receive full support from the community.[34]

✠ Migrant women

Some migrant women played a valuable part in the post-war era by ministering to their own people through membership of an order. Migrant women normally expressed their devotion to the church by exercising the traditional roles of hospitality and care of church fabric. In the Orthodox churches, however, some took their vows as religious and played an active role in social welfare among their own people.

Sister Kaliniki: Australia's first Greek Orthodox nun

One of these women was Sister Kaliniki of the Greek Orthodox Church in Sydney. Born Coralia Christides in Cairo in 1907, she was educated in a French convent and taken to the island of Patmos, where her aunts and cousins were nuns. She and her family migrated to Australia at the outbreak of World War I, where she founded a charitable organisation for women — the Christian Ladies and Girls Greek Orthodox Society of Australia. The society was active in fund-raising and visiting the sick, aged and lonely.

Following the death of her husband, she was encouraged by Sister Dorothea of the Catholic Mercy order to take vows. In 1971, in the Redfern Cathedral, she was ordained a sister of the Greek Orthodox Church. Two nuns from the Russian Orthodox Church supported her throughout the service. Before her death in 1989, she ministered tirelessly to the aged, particularly at the St Basil's Home for the Aged and the Lourantos Village in NSW.

⛨ Deaconess orders

Deaconess orders continued to play a valuable, if problematic role in the post-war Australian church. Although their theological and pastoral training was upgraded in the Anglican Church in Melbourne in 1970 to a level comparable to that of male candidates for the ministry, yet paid employment in the church was difficult to find, as was security of tenure.

Openings in parish work in Sydney were even harder to find; Deaconess Narelle Jarrett was forced to support herself in parish ministry for fifteen years from 1970 to 1985, despite excellent theological qualifications. The principalship of Deaconess House was the first paid employment in the church that she was able to find.[35]

However, the Diocese of Melbourne attempted to treat men and women candidates in an egalitarian manner as far as financial assistance and placement were concerned. By 1982, stipends for deaconesses were raised to a level comparable with those of the clergy.[36]

However, lack of status and meagre income did not deter some very outstanding women from serving as hospital chaplains and missionaries in Gippsland and remote parts of New South Wales following their training at the Melbourne or Sydney deaconess institutions.

Marie Kingston worked on islands in the Bass Strait, like the Furneaux group and King Island. She pastored churches, ran services and preached, being made rural dean of the area. Dorothy Genders pioneered much welfare work amongst Perth's poorest during World War II. Aborigines, abused wives, prisoners and prostitutes owed much to this 'tiny figure, scarcely five feet tall, wearing a grey frock and cape, a small black hat and veil and carrying a string bag of magazines and books.'[37]

Mildred Symons, who also trained at Deaconess House in Sydney, initiated a significant enterprise in the care of the aged and sick.

Mary Andrews on the day of her ordination as a deaconess: 1946

Following her ordination in 1946, she worked on foot amongst the poor of Redfern and Surry Hills. She realised that her nursing training would be more effective if private transport were available and also if a hostel could be built for those who could not be cared for in their own homes.

After five years of working in her 'time off', she was able to save for the first car to be used by the Anglican home nursing service. Helped next time by a church auxiliary, she was able to establish in 1952 the first of the Chesalon nursing homes, which provided full nursing home care for those in need of it. There was no government help with the Home Nursing Service, but Mildred Symons was delighted with the government initiative of a deficit financing scheme to provide for non-profit nursing homes so that fees were not raised above the pension rate.[38]

The first bishop to raise the parochial status of deaconesses above the level of ecclesiastical 'hewers of wood and drawers of water' was Archbishop George Appleton of Perth who authorised three deaconesses in 1967 to baptise, preach and teach and to administer the chalice in Holy Communion. In his view:

> The average congregation today has three or four times as many women as men. I believe a dedicated woman could minister more effectively to women members of the congregation. I will not hide my own hope that in future our church will accept women for ordination to priesthood. It is increasingly recognised that there is no real difference between the ordination of men and women — only a conservative dislike.[39]

It is in Victoria that the most positive steps have been taken to redefine the status of the deaconess order and, with it, the role of a professional female ministry. In 1980, a commission on women's ministry reported that there was no long-term future for deaconesses as a separate order and that women should join the diaconate alongside men, as part of the historic threefold order of bishops, priests and deacons. This was followed up five years later by a Melbourne Diocesan Committee's recommendation for a diaconate separate from the priesthood and containing both men and women.

Most deaconesses in the diocese then applied for ordination as deacons on the ground of their similar training to the men and similar calling to that experienced by New Testament deacons. On 9 February 1986 at St Paul's Cathedral Melbourne, eight women were ordained deacons, seven of whom were deaconesses. The other dioceses followed suit. The traditional deaconess order was thus more under threat than ever, but it was a development which most of them desired. Indeed, the vast majority of them did not want to stop at the diaconate, but wanted to have the option of the priesthood as well.

In Nonconformist churches, deaconesses have become practically extinct since 1980, following the availability of ordination to women seeking professional ministry. However, this should not obscure the notable achievements of such women as Laura Francis and Kay Edwards. Sister Laura Francis, as she was known, gave sterling service to the Central Methodist Mission in Sydney in the 1940s and 1950s as a lay evangelist and hospital visitor. Her stipend was paid by the Methodist Women's Home Mission League.

A key figure in the Methodist Church in the 1960s and 1970s was Deaconess Kay Edwards, who worked tirelessly amongst migrants, Aborigines and homeless people. Like Eva Holland, her mission field was Woolloomooloo and Kings Cross and she frequently assisted the Reverend Ted Noffs in his Wayside Chapel venture. She was particularly interested in helping city Aborigines and helped to establish the Foundation for Aboriginal Affairs.[40]

As in the Anglican Church, deaconesses suffered from lack of recognition by both clergy and leading laity, though the poor valued their work. A very strong character was necessary for a deaconess, for she was ill-paid and often treated as an inferior in church circles, while being unable to benefit from a strong community, like her Catholic sisters.

Salvation Army officers

Women officers in the Salvation Army, on the other hand, operated from a position of strength, both philosophically and numerically. Their egalitarian status had been assured as a result of the work of the founder's wife, Catherine Booth, who wrote and preached about the equality of women in ministry alongside men.

Women have traditionally outnumbered men as trained army officers in the twentieth century; by 1988 in the Eastern Territory (consisting of NSW, Queensland and Papua New Guinea), women officers on active service numbered 379, while the men numbered 320. Numbers of fully trained officers have declined, but slightly compared with other women in orders, to a rate of just under two per cent annually for women. In 1995, women officers numbered 343 and men 289 and in this year married women officers were allowed to drop the title Mrs and retain their rank rather than taking their husband's, provided their years of service were longer.[41]

In 1986, Australia was honoured in the appointment of the second woman General of the Salvation Army (the first was Eva Booth, daughter of William and Catherine). Eva Burrows was to serve for seven years as spiritual and administrative leader of the Army's worldwide constituency of two million members, 27 000 officers and cadets and 15 000 corps.

She was in charge of 4 000 institutions, schools and hospitals across the world, operating in 116 different languages.

Eva Burrows, General of the Salvation Army worldwide: 1986–1993

During her period of leadership, she improved the status of officer wives, endeavouring to ensure meaningful appointments for them alongside their husbands. She did not cut across the domestic role, but regarded both as equally significant. Although she found it difficult to promote women through the upper echelons of the Salvationist bureaucracy — because this was largely a territorial responsibility — she managed to advance women through missionary service, as she herself had risen to prominence.[42]

A period of greater freedom, but a decline in numbers

The period 1938 to 1988 has witnessed immense changes for women in orders. As in wider society, an egalitarian paradigm was beginning to replace an hierarchical paradigm in church structures and polity. Vatican II succeeded in conferring greater equality on women from above but, in doing so, it was responding to deeper currents of change which had been released by war and the spread of education.

Significant numbers of women religious applied for release from their vows and vocations fell away markedly. Lay involvement in a variety of ministries then began to come into its own. Non-Roman Catholic orders also declined in numbers after 1970, as the possibilities of ordination and autonomous decision-making in the church began to open up.

12

An influence out of all proportion to their numbers

WOMEN MISSIONARIES, 1939 TO THE 1990S

'When we arrived, Sister Pennell was holding the fort in her white veil and uniform. . . she had been there something like twelve months. She stayed on for seventeen months and it must be recorded that she never had one day off in the whole of that seventeen months.'

Daisy Alma Fleming, Baptist missionary
in the Northern Territory (1950–1975)

'My ministry has always been intimately tied to my professional capacity, in a more holistic approach to a person in need; I have always felt my Christian ministry to my family to be my first priority.'

Dr Annette Britton, missionary
in Nepal (1978–1989)

'The whole concept of mission has become an exchange between local churches.'

Pauline Rae SMSM, missionary in
Melanesia (1965–1973)

WOMEN CONTINUED TO PLAY a dominant role numerically and professionally in postwar mission work. The challenge and sublimation offered by overseas and Aboriginal missions continued to attract the adventurous soul. Once on the field, overwork and staff shortages failed to deter the majority of women missionaries. Missionary societies made no attempt to alter the ratio of female to male applicants, while retaining a strongly male hierarchy on mission boards and the staff of missionary training colleges.

However, by the end of the 1980s, the gender imbalance in both areas was easing as ordination became a valid option for women seeking a full-time vocation and as overseas fields traditionally dominated by women workers were no longer an option. At the same time, appreciable numbers of women began to receive offers of membership of mission boards and appointments to university and Bible college faculties. Greater acceptance by society of the administrative gifts possessed by women was beginning to infiltrate church attitudes.

Australian missionaries, both male and female, were confronted by immense change throughout the half century after 1938. First and foremost was the impact of World War II, which convulsed and devastated whole communities, followed by the threat of nuclear holocaust. Second, the consequent breakdown of the British and other European empires restricted the traditional freedom of operation enjoyed by missionaries, although it was to ease indigenous perceptions of them as imperialist fellow travellers.

The third main ingredient of change arising out of the war and, in some cases, preceding it, was the emergence of nationalism in developing countries. As independence came to these countries, a complete overhaul of missionary policy took place. Mission boards hastened to build up the indigenous church so that the traditional role of missionaries could be modified and personnel could be withdrawn. A partnership between churches across the cultures was the ultimate aim and, indeed, by the end of the period, Australia was regularly receiving missionaries from churches it had once proselytised.

This interchange was particularly noticeable in the case of South Pacific missions where the warmth and piety of the island churches contrasted sharply with the nominalism of Australian Christianity.

This evolution of mission to partnership was well illustrated in Solomon Island churches, which had found their origin in the work of women missionaries. Such was the efficacy of Florence Young's South Sea Evangelical Mission, which started in 1907 amongst the former headhunters of the Solomon Islands, that by 1936 the work was self-propagating.[1] In 1968, with the granting of independence, the South Sea Evangelical Church was founded and, by 1995, mission and church had merged into a mutual relationship entitled 'South Pacific Partners'.[2]

In the case of the historic Marist missions to the South Pacific which date back to 1845 and the pioneering work of Francoise Perroton on the islands of Wallis and Futuna, there was steady progress to an indigenous church until '. . . by 1990, the whole concept of mission is an exchange between local churches. It is no longer just home and mission now. They send to other cultures now.'[3]

As the post-war decades unfolded, missionaries found that they were required to display ever-increasing sensitivity to indigenous cultural heritage. Whereas in the past they may have operated from a supposition of cultural superiority, by the 1970s they were approaching cultural barriers with ever-increasing delicacy.

The Lausanne Congress of World Missions meeting in 1977 proclaimed a theology of indigeneity whereby missionaries would work for the autonomy of the overseas church and, in so doing, prepare for their own redundancy. Studies in missiology were prescribed as essential for those preparing for missionary service.[4] This subject, a *melange* of theology and anthropology, took its place in the curriculum of missionary training colleges. These included St Andrew's Hall in Melbourne, established in 1964 for Church Missionary Society (CMS) candidates, the Columban Institute for Catholic missionaries, and the Bible College of Victoria, the Sydney Missionary and Bible College and the Bible College of Queensland — the latter three for Protestant missionaries.

Eight of the ten women missionaries interviewed for this study either read anthropology at university or else missiology at Bible college or mission institute. The two exceptions were doctors who were undertaking extra training in tropical medicine prior to departure. Nine out of the ten undertook study of the indigenous language, the one exception being a doctor in the Northern Territory; the same nine found the most difficult aspects of the alien culture to be the lowly status of women in that culture. Thus, the caste system in India, the dowry system in Africa and the practice of polygamy in the Southern Pacific area were found to be demeaning for indigenous women — or even downright oppressive. In this respect, the modern woman missionary was no different to her counterpart of the 1890s.

✠ Women missionaries in war

The outbreak of World War II immediately put the lives of women missionaries in danger. Those who were married were usually evacuated with their husbands and children. Over 300 male and female missionaries perished in Indonesia during the Japanese invasion and occupation. Most were Melanesian nationals or members of Catholic orders working in Timor.[5]

Mary Andrews was one who remained behind in the traditionally hazardous field of China. She worked in the mountainous province of Chekiang, which was for the most part behind enemy lines. She even undertook the dangerous task of nursing back to health five American airmen who crash-landed in the area in 1942. Her serenity was remarkable:

> Travelling in China is certainly not like Australia. There are pirates, shells, bombs and guerillas to contend with, but anywhere He leads me I am not afraid.[6]

However, wartime missionary service did take its toll on another Australian missionary working in the same province, Elizabeth Varley. She was a veteran of twenty-three years service with CMS and was in charge of the mission compound in the township of Chuki. She handled the invasion of her compound by Japanese soldiers with great fortitude, saving the lives of a number of Chinese Christians from death by bayonet. For six terrible days when the city was put to the torch and 2000 people died, she gave sanctuary to fifty-seven refugees. It is no wonder that she was invalided home after the Japanese moved on.

When the mission doctor reached her several weeks later, he commented: 'Patient has been through some very nerve-wracking experiences during the past few months. . . Advise complete rest for at least six months.[7] Such had been her ordeal that she was never able to return to her beloved China.

As a younger woman who was stronger in health, Mary Andrews was able to remain at her post for much of the war. She trained her Biblewomen to go out into the villages with the good news. She preached each Sunday in the city church, nursed in the hospital when needed and taught illiterate children to read and write.[8]

She also endured a Japanese invasion of her city in April 1942. Her first step was to approach the Japanese commander, clutching her English-Japanese dictionary, and ask him for protection of all citizens. He agreed on one condition: as she frantically scanned the dictionary, she realised that he wanted her to organise the making of Japanese flags for her children to wave when the Japanese airforce flew in triumph over the city next day. The soldiers departed the following day, leaving a trail of destruction behind them. The vacuum was filled by an influx of Chinese looters, who made the population even more miserable.

Even more trying for missionaries in wartime was the fact that communication with home was impossible. Mary Andrews received no letters from outside China for two years and it was not till she made her escape across enemy lines to India in September 1944 that she was able to have any news of family at all.[9]

There was much evidence of close cooperation between missionary societies in a wartime context. Mary Andrews noted that the close links between China Inland Mission (CIM) and CMS personnel doubled the effectiveness of the work.

Irene Neville was a young Australian nurse with CIM who worked in China from 1936 to 1951 when the Communists assumed power. Even before the Japanese invasion, she survived two bandit raids, the bandits being 'under the impression that she who controlled the medicine also controlled the money'. Her sense of humour constantly came to her aid. When asked how it felt to be held at gunpoint, she replied: 'The things of earth grow strangely dim. . . when you are looking down the barrel of a gun!'[10]

She was often obliged to ride on horseback for many hours in order to reach patients. 'Your wonderful missionary has just slept her way through an entire sermon!' she wrote after returning from a ride of forty miles through rough terrain to treat a patient in emergency. Her courage and humour assisted her to remain in China until the CIM was finally expelled by the Communist government in 1951.[11]

Most of the 121 CIM missionaries from Australia and New Zealand who remained at work in so-called Free China were able to avoid invasion by the Japanese. However, those working near the coast were captured and interned. Seventeen of the CIM internees were women and nine were men, six families having their children interned with them.[12]

Not as fortunate in surviving Japanese invasion were five representatives of the Australian Board of Missions (ABM) who met their deaths in 1942 in north-east New Guinea in controversial circumstances. The New Guinea Martyrs, as they were subsequently known, consisted of one Englishman, Father Vivian Redlich, and four Australian women. Two of the latter were May Hayman, who was in charge of the mission hospital at Gona, and Mavis Parkinson, who supervised the school on the same compound. These women were often the only white missionaries in the area, receiving sporadic visits from bishop and priest. Further inland at Sangara were two other women missionaries, Margery Brenchley, a nurse, and Lilli Lashmar, a schoolteacher. Vivian Redlich was the priest in charge of this mission station.

ABM was a body which represented the High Anglican arm of the church. It had a history of martyrdom going back to the demise of the Tractarian missionary bishop, John Coleridge Patteson, in the New Hebrides in 1871. As an organisation, it was generally impoverished and it therefore attracted celibate missionaries who were able to live on next to nothing. Anglo Catholicism also traditionally encouraged a celibate ministry, as expressed in Australia by the Brotherhood of the Good Shepherd and the Society of the Sacred Advent.

At the head of the mission at the outbreak of war was Philip Strong, the bachelor Bishop of Dogura, who had won the Patteson Scholarship at Cambridge. The theology of the ABM was strongly incarnational and its policy equally paternalistic, the bishop often referring to the Papuans as 'children'. Strong believed firmly in the religious vocation and that 'the call' should be worked out by the individual believer, regardless of military strategy or political events.[13]

By the end of 1941 when Pearl Harbour had been bombed, the Papua New Guinea Administration ordered the evacuation of all white women from New Guinea. The Methodist Overseas Mission Board obeyed this ruling and their missionaries prepared to leave New Guinea and the surrounding islands. Such pragmatism, however, was foreign to the idealistic Strong. He vacillated between telling the women missionaries that 'they should be free to make their own decision regarding evacuation'[14] and ignoring the Japanese bombs already falling on New Guinea, to make the following broadcast to his missionaries on 31 January 1942:

> We could never hold up our faces again if, for our own safety, we all forsook him and fled when the shadows of the Passion began to gather round him in his spiritual body, the church in Papua. . .

He went on deliberately to appeal to his female staff:

> . . .our Papuan women. Our influence is just beginning to tell with them. How would they fare if all our women missionaries left?. . . No, my brothers and sisters, fellow workers in Christ, whatever others may do, we cannot leave. . . We shall stand by our vocation.[15]

His plea met a ready response from the four women missionaries who were determined to stay at their posts. 'What will the children do if I go?' asked Mavis Parkinson. 'I only want to be a good soldier of Jesus Christ,' wrote Lilli

Lashmar in her last letter to her mother.[16]

Although Strong subsequently changed his mind a few months later and advised (but not ordered) them to move to a safer place, it was too late. Mavis Parkinson and May Hayman were betrayed by indigenous people and executed by Japanese bayonet on the beach at Gona in August 1942. The following month, Lilli Lashmar and Margery Brenchley met a similar death with Father Vivian Redlich on the beach of Buna.[17]

Strong was no coward, braving strafing attacks in his mission boat; nor was he hard-hearted, noting in his diary how 'nervy' and 'depressed' he felt when he left the women for the last time.[18] However, he was safely residing at Government House in Port Moresby when the news came through of the death of his missionaries. On receiving news of the second martyrdom, he wrote that he was 'much tormented in mind' — and well he might have been, since a simple command from him in March would have saved their lives. It was all very well to scorn the Methodist missionaries for joining the evacuation: 'They are apparently going to desert their work. . .'[19] Ignorance about the nature of Japanese militarism and a naive, triumphalist theology had cost the lives of five servants of the mission. The family of Mavis Parkinson have not forgiven Bishop Strong to this day.[20]

The exigencies of war also impacted upon the lives of women missionaries in the Northern Territory. Margaret Somerville was the daughter of a Methodist minister who felt constrained to offer help at the Methodist Croker Island mission in 1939. She had no formal training for her work and so was accepted on a 'temporary basis' in 1939. Little did she realise it would be a lifetime association, lasting until 1965.[21]

In the early years of the war, she worked with ninety-five children of mixed descent, using a pedal radio for contact with the outside world. When Darwin was bombed in 1942, resulting in the death of 240 people, a general evacuation of women missionaries was ordered. With four others, she took most of the children down to Otford on the outskirts of Sydney for the duration of the war. They returned to Croker Island in 1946, where Margaret resumed her work in charge of stores, the bakery and the laundry.

This mission was the first in the Northern Territory to adopt the cottage system, as opposed to the dormitory system, which made for a happier, less institutional lifestyle for the children placed there under the government's policy of assimilation. It was a hard but happy lifestyle for Margaret who commented on the great bane of the missionary — the lack of leisure time: 'We were always petitioning God (and the mission) to send us someone to take our place during furlough. . .'[22]

The other problem which confronted her — as with most other single women missionaries who have to contend with isolation in various forms — was a desire for marriage, but the opportunity did not arise:

> The word 'sublimation' came into my mind and I felt as though I learnt what sublimation was. And I just believed that God sublimated my desire to be married and have children because never after that was it any problem to me. And yet I went up north and had more children than most had. . . about thirty children [went] through my cottage. . . a wonderful time in my life. . . I think it was all in God's plan for my life. . .[23]

The changed world of postwar mission

After the war, missionary enterprise appeared to resume on the same terms as prewar work; however, it soon became clear that the colonial era had passed and with it special conditions for missionaries. The British left India in 1947 and in the next decades proceeded to divest themselves of all but the smallest outposts of empire. Missionaries could still benefit from such aspects of the Pax Britannica as the prevalence of the English language and, in certain countries, of English laws and customs. But the disadvantages of the imperial connection for the Western missionary far outweighed the advantages as the century progressed.

It was not till the 1980s that the image of the missionary as an imperialist fellow traveller was finally put to rest. This can be illustrated by the changing definition of the word 'missionary' in the North Korean dictionary: in 1981, 'missionary' was defined as 'an agent of aggression in the guise of religion sent by imperialists, such as the USA, under the pretext of propagating and promoting Christianity.' In the 1992 edition of the dictionary, the definition was 'a person sent abroad on a mission to promote and propagate Christianity'.[24]

With the rise of nationalism and the granting of independence to numerous former European colonies, missionaries found that they were obliged to tread ever more carefully in cultural matters.

Mary Andrews relinquishes her congregation at Shaohsing, China: in 1951

In Africa, for example, they could not now interfere in social customs, like bargaining in dowries — which often precluded Christians from marrying each other — or in the calling of political meetings in school during class time.[25]

Furthermore, male and female missionaries found it increasingly difficult to obtain visas. China closed its doors to all foreign missions in 1951 and the CIM was forced to change its name to the Overseas Missionary Fellowship (OMF) and direct its personnel to the Chinese diaspora in East Asia. No longer could missionaries put 'missionary' as their occupation on visa applications if they wanted to gain access to developing countries. Both husband and wife — if possible — should be qualified in a profession useful to the host country. The Church Missionary Society ruled in 1953 that husbands and wives were equally missionaries in their own right.[26]

Openings for missionaries further contracted in the postwar era when Islamic countries like Malaysia and Indonesia forbade Christian missionary work amongst Muslims. However, they did permit limited access to those wishing to work amongst Chinese and tribal peoples. It was particularly difficult for women missionaries working in such countries as Pakistan. Despite the fact that they were working amongst minority Christian and tribal groups, they found that they were unable to move freely outside the home because of the strict Islamic dress code.

Teenage daughters of missionaries especially faced harassment.[27] Conversely, missionaries were obliged to avoid misunderstanding and offence and respect indigenous protocol at all times, otherwise their message was viewed as hollow and patronising. Hence, missiological training became increasingly important postwar if cultural boundaries were to be crossed.

✠ The postwar gender missionary ratio

The prewar ratio of three female workers to every male missionary continued in the first post-war decades. Such denominational missions as CMS and the Australian Baptist Missionary Society sustained this trend, as did OMF and smaller independent missions, such as the Borneo Evangelical Mission.

This pattern continued into the 1970s as can be assessed by looking at the *Protestant Missions Handbook of 1977*, which lists nine major denominational and nine interdenominational missions (covering those with fifty or more overseas members).[28] These missions were staffed by an average of 60–66% women. Presbyterian and Methodist missions had the lowest ratio of women (46% and 47% respectively) because of a more clerical and institutional emphasis in their work.

At the other end of the scale were interdenominational missions concentrating on rural evangelism like OMF, staffed by 64% women, the African Inland Mission (74%) and the Sudan Interior Mission (83%). Australian CMS in that year boasted a proportion of 64.5% of women working overseas and in the Northern Territory. Of these, sixty were single women and sixty-five were married. Most were engaged in nursing and teaching; others varied in role from doctor to student or literature worker. They worked alongside sixty-eight men in all.[29]

The only area in missionary endeavour in which there was no sharing until the end of our period was executive administration. Federal CMS did not admit women to its council until 1943, positions mainly being taken by clergy and returned male missionaries.[30] By 1986, however, five women had taken office on the council alongside thirty men; by 1990, the number of women had grown to twelve, compared to twenty-four men.

✠ OMF's attitude to women as administrators

The Overseas Missionary Fellowship remained exclusively male in administration until 1980, despite its history of female predominance overseas. The mission historian, Val Griffiths, points out that Hudson Taylor used to advise women to exercise power unostentatiously, citing a letter to Miss Faulding which suggested that she should guide the church in his absence 'without actually appearing to do so'.[31]

The issue of female administration on the field, so earnestly requested by the field director since 1920, dragged on for the next two decades (see pages 239–240 above). Finally, it was ruled in 1945 that women could not become regular members of mission councils, but 'a special ladies committee might be helpful when considering the cases of women candidates'.[32] This women's committee then met for the first time at the end of 1945 under the direction of the chairman's wife and was able to assist gingerly in the interview of female candidates.

Council policy regarding female power sharing was, of course, not only guided by a particular interpretation of scripture, but also by such pragmatic considerations as fear of alienating 'devoted supporters at home'. Furthermore, it must be acknowledged that women did not sit on the boards of business or church in the 1940s or 1950s, so that their prominence on the mission field was many decades ahead of events at home. However, by 1980 women were admitted to membership of the Council of OMF and by 1988 their numbers were over forty per cent of its membership.

✠ The Bivocational missionary comes into her own

One of the most notable trends of postwar mission has been the burgeoning of the bivocational or 'tentmaker' missionary. Men and women from the various professions needed in developing countries, support themselves by working for a foreign employer, usually a government, and then fit in their evangelism after they have finished work. This option of bivocational ministry goes back to St Paul and was adopted by the Moravians in the early eighteenth century. It has gained impetus since the closure of Muslim and Hindu frontiers, in particular, to those who nominate 'Christian missionary' as their occupation on passports.

Possibly the most acclaimed Australian missionary in this category is Dr Catherine Hamlin, who has worked as a gynaecologist for the Ethiopian government since 1959. She and her husband left senior positions in Royal Adelaide Hospital to serve for a limited period in Addis Ababa. The Hamlins were dismayed at the plight of rural women who had suffered obstructed childbirth, causing a tear of fistula in the vagina — and in the bladder and bowel wall as well. The subsequent stench of dripping urine and sometimes faeces meant that these unfortunate women were discarded by their husbands and became leper-like outcasts from the community. Scarcely more than children, having been married off at puberty, their bodies were too small for normal childbirth.

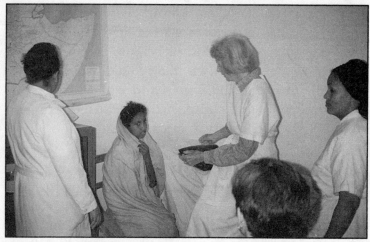

Dr Catherine Hamlin working at the Fistula Hospital, Ethiopia

They often spent months walking from the countryside to the hospital for treatment, as they did not have the bus fare.

The Hamlins set about fundraising in church and government circles in Australia, Britain and the USA and were able to found a fistula hospital in Addis Ababa in 1974. This fifty-bed hospital now carries out some 800 bladder repairs each year and has never closed its doors, despite three episodes of civil war.

This observation of Catherine Hamlin's indicates something of the value of the work:

> You would be touched if you could see these little girls; they come to us with nothing but faith and hope and urine-soaked clothes. After three weeks, we can send them home with a new dress, their bus fare and a second chance in life. . .[33]

Although in her seventies, Catherine Hamlin still carries on this work despite her husband's death. She remains at her post training indigenous women surgeons to take over eventually.

Another feature of post-war missions has been the unprecedented degree of mobility enjoyed by more highly skilled women in developing countries. From the 1950s onwards, Doctors Grace Warren and Audrey Halloran from NSW were in keen demand for their surgical skill in Asia and Africa respectively. Grace Warren was associated principally with the Leprosy Mission, gaining an international reputation for her medical management and reconstructive work on leprosy patients. From 1975 to 1990, in her capacity as adviser in leprosy, she ran in-service training courses in ten Asian countries. On her visits home, she acted as consultant to eight Australian hospitals.

Also engaged in constant travel has been Audrey Halloran; after a period with the Australian Inland Mission, she joined a

Dutch Reformed mission in Zimbabwe. In addition to her medical work, she helped to establish churches and various works of mercy in needy parts of Africa, flying from Capetown to Madagascar without a qualm in order to achieve her objectives.[34] There was no limit to the scope of the work available to the highly qualified missionary in the post-war era, provided they were prepared for a nomadic life.

✠ Work amongst Aborigines

Missionary work amongst Aborigines since the war has been spearheaded by women nurses and teachers who have either worked for the Northern Territory government or else in decreasing numbers after 1970 for Protestant missions.

Catholic orders have had a strong presence in other parts of outback Australia. In Western Australia, the Benedictines and Josephites carried out educational and institutional work at New Norcia, while the St John of God and the Queen of Apostles Sisters worked in the Kimberleys. The order founded by Mother Teresa in Calcutta, the Missionary Sisters of Charity, established an outpost in Bourke in 1969 to minister to needy Aborigines.

Missions were obliged to implement and, in most cases, mitigate the policy of the Commonwealth government which had set out to assimilate mixed race children after 1940. Homes were set up by churches and missions across the outback and even on the outskirts of large cities.[35] Aboriginal missions were generally marginalised in church strategies and so often received less in terms of resources and personnel, compared with exotic missions.

Aboriginal attitudes towards missions have been ambivalent, ranging from gratitude for protection offered against secular white depredation to the following statement of displeasure at cultural insensitivity often shown by missionaries:

Many types of preachers came around to convert us. They were evangelists, Inland Mission and every type of missionary. They did not try to teach us carefully and gently. There was no discussion and we had to accept everything they told us. Our own religious beliefs were a subject for ridicule.

On the other hand, the same commentator wrote:

I had always felt at home at the mission; I liked being among my own people and had suffered enough. . . To be settled. . . at the mission would spare me having to listen to those remarks about blackfellows.[36]

Those missionaries who were more sensitive to Aboriginal spirituality were clearly more effective in their outreach, but this was often an impossible criterion for staff who were limited educationally themselves and, above all, limited in time and personnel.

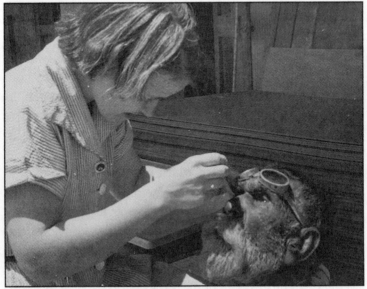

Sister Mary Chenoweth treating a patient's eyes, Central Australia

As Daisy Alma Fleming testified of the Baptist mission at Yuendumi: 'Sister Pennell. . . never had one day off in the whole seventeen months.'[37] Daisy Fleming and her husband, who ran this mission of 1000 people in Central Australia from 1950 to 1975, also rarely took furlough, much less a day off. In her view, 'the strength in the (Aboriginal) church was among the women'.[38]

The Aborigines themselves commented shrewdly on the power imbalance modelled by Christian missions:

> The men are the presidents and councillors [on church committees], but the majority of the church attendance is made up of women and children. The Anglican Church has a group called the GFS and the Mothers' Union. From my observation, these are caterers for church functions. They are workhorses and they do a very good job, but somehow I feel the task should have been shared by both sexes equally.[39]

✠ Women in Catholic missions

With the encouragement of Pope Pius XII, women's institutes began to send increasing numbers of their members overseas to take part in the worldwide task of post-war reconstruction. New communities of missionary orders began to appear in Australia and long-established orders started to send out missionaries from Australia in response to a particular need. By 1964, the Catholic Church had more than 60 000 missionaries working overseas — a figure which includes nationals.[40]

Teaching, health and social care were the main concerns of congregations of missionary sisters. Longer established Australian orders like the Mercies, Josephites, Charities, Dominicans and Presentations set up communities in New Guinea and various Pacific Islands.[41] Marist sisters continued their historic work in Melanesia and the Society of the Sacred Heart likewise in Japan.

The main emphasis of Catholic missions was to create an indigenous church chiefly by training nationals in Australian institutes so that they could return to positions of leadership in their own countries. The orders also stressed a holistic approach, sending out trained medical staff when needed in times of war or famine. The Sisters of Charity, for instance, sent a team of intensive care staff from St Vincent's Hospital in Melbourne to help in 1971 during the Vietnam War. Some of the same order joined with the Irish Sisters of Charity to teach in Africa and three sisters worked as requested amongst refugees in Kampuchea and Rwanda in the 1990s.[42]

Australian Josephites laboured amongst street children and the rural poor in Peru, Sister Irene McCormack being martyred by guerillas at Huasa-Huasi outside Lima in 1991. Her leadership in combating illiteracy and teaching villagers to grow their own food and fend for themselves economically was resented by the Shining Path guerillas, who dragged her out of the convent and executed her in the town square alongside five Peruvian laypeople.[43]

✖ An overview of the role of women missionaries

As with their forerunners, postwar women missionaries revelled in the freedom of opportunity to serve in another culture.

Of the ten women interviewed from a variety of mission backgrounds, the average period of service was nineteen years. Three were married when overseas and their period was of necessity shortened (to an average of ten years) for the sake of their children's education. Some families did remain overseas for life, but this was the exception rather than the rule.

Most wives accepted roles outside family commitments, even when their children were young, the most significant being the duty of hospitality. Most missions paid a living allowance to missionary families rather than a salary. If the wife happened to earn any money professionally when overseas, it was expected that the family would receive a lower allowance from the sponsoring society.[44]

The postwar period witnessed a consolidation of the practice of women missionaries preaching and leading services. Mary Andrews had preached and led services in wartime churches in Chekiang province in China. She usually alternated with Chinese pastors and sometimes with the bishop if he was passing through.[45] Of the ten other missionaries surveyed, only one — a doctor in her eighties — was not in the habit of preaching on the mission field.

It was a different matter on their return to Australia. Sometimes, they were asked to speak about their work informally; occasionally, they were asked to preach (usually in the Uniting Church), but rarely were they asked to lead a service. One missionary who had been recently ordained deacon found that she was asked to do far less than her customary deputation work on her return to the Anglican Diocese of Sydney because of her new ecclesiastical status.

All ten of those interviewed were in favour of the ordination of women, having observed the efficacy of joint leadership on the field. As one of them said:

> The witness of women exercising godly leadership with men in the church has a profound impact in all cultures, but particularly where the place of women in society is low.[46]

✠ The decline in the number of women missionaries by the 1980s

By the late 1980s, a decline was evident in the number of working missionaries of both sexes. Terms were now shorter. Single women going out with CMS dropped from fifty-five in 1980 to twenty-four in 1985. The total missionary slump in that period was from 190 to 115, which indicates that a number of single women missionaries had retired and were not being replaced by younger women.[47]

The process of empowerment of the indigenous church was clearly a major reason for declining numbers of Western missionaries. Indigenous bishops were now the rule rather than the exception, overseas evangelists were no longer required to establish churches and increasing numbers of developing countries were now in a position to train their own nurses and teachers.

The decline in demand for Western missionaries was accompanied by the reverse trend of visits to Australia by missionaries from long-established mission areas, like the South Pacific and Korea. In India alone, over 9 000 Indian missionaries now work in different language areas on the subcontinent.[48]

Thus, the decline in the number of Australian women missionaries — and, indeed, missionaries in general — is explicable in terms of changing needs in the host country. As far as the decline in numbers of single women candidates is concerned, it would appear that the women's movement has opened up more challenging career paths for young women at home.

The feminism of the late nineteenth century which had fuelled the missionary surge of the Victorian era had given way to a more political and consciously egalitarian movement, which wished to reform the church before going out to serve it. Many of those who might have felt a vocation to the field (or to an order) are now in a position to take up the option of ordination. Mission directors feel that new methods of recruitment are probably needed to attract staff of quality.[49]

Some would blame the secularism and inertia of the home church in the late twentieth century for the decline in missionary numbers. Certainly, there has been a decline in women's missionary auxiliaries across state branches of the Protestant churches, which coincides with the general decline of traditional laywomen's organisations. For example, the CMS women's missionary councils or fellowships in the various states have dwindled as younger members cannot be found.

A specific example illustrating the decline in missionary interest is the fate of the CMS Women's Outreach Committee in Victoria. This was launched with high hopes in 1972 by the wife of Bishop Alfred Stanway, whose diocese was in Tanzania. Its aim was to 'reach out to women with the gospel and to foster an interest in missions'. By the mid-1980s, the committee was struggling as the support of younger members failed to materialise. In 1990, it went out of existence.[50]

Whatever the causes of the decline in women's church organisations at the close of this millennium, be they socio-economic or philosophical, the record of Australian women missionaries since 1938 has been an illustrious one. Their influence in peace and war has been out of all proportion to their numbers. Though they have made mistakes at times in their approach to other cultures, they have done significant work in raising the status and health of women in developing countries. These women have preached and taught alongside men in mission areas without, for the most part, being accorded the same privilege on their return.

Recognition of this ministry has not come easily. Yet they have resisted the temptation to become a power bloc within the church by way of response. However, women missionaries have always been in the vanguard of change, having gained confidence and initiative from their experiences in other cultures. Not for the first time, they find themselves at the cutting edge of theological change at home.

13

Towards freedom, ecumenism and leadership

LAYWOMEN IN THE CHURCH: 1939 TO THE 1990s

'I think things are moving so fast it is going to be impossible for the church to stand out against a social revolution. . . all I can say about the movement to free women is that the church is fighting tooth and nail to prevent it.'

Submission to the Enquiry into the Status of Women in the Church, Australian Council of Churches (1974)

'It is for freedom that Christ has set us free.'

Galatians 5: 1

THIS PERIOD HAS WITNESSED THE MOST FAR-REACHING changes experienced by women in the two hundred years of European settlement in Australia. Social, economic and ideological change has left many bewildered and the church scrambling to catch up.

For centuries, the church had been able to categorise women in auxiliary roles as helpmeet and housekeeper or, more gloriously, as saintly virgin. Few women dared to step outside these perceptions of themselves. However, the growth of tertiary education for both men and women, added to the upheavals of war and technological advance, have conspired to revolutionise postwar society and, with it, the role of women.

Nor has the study of theology or history escaped the emergence of gender as a central mode of analysis. Women have now become recognised as significant agents in the historical process — whether in spearheading the schooling of Australian children or in deciding to limit their families, thus leading to the introduction of massive postwar immigration.

Since 1970, courses in women's studies have appeared in the fare offered by Australian universities; they cover a range of disciplines, from history and anthropology to law and economics. Theologians have been slower to incorporate a feminist strand in their hermeneutics, but the interdenominational Sydney College of Divinity offers such courses as Feminism and Mission to increasing numbers of students.

The chief reasons for the appearance of a feminist perspective in Australian scholarship and society are first of all the complex social change which arose out of World War II. Second, women were able to regulate their fertility and therefore their lives to their own chosen pattern following the introduction of the pill. Third, the iconoclasm of the 1960s, which questioned traditional authority and institutions in general and Australia's involvement in the Vietnam War in particular, went hand in hand with the more radical feminism of the campus.

Most churchwomen avoided espousal of such causes at the outset, especially if they belonged to conservative churches. However, as the prevailing culture altered, they too began to modify their stance on a variety of issues.

The outbreak of war in 1939 was to result in a far more active participation by women than had occurred during

World War I. Women were allowed to enlist and serve overseas in the newly formed Australian Women's Army Service, Women's Australian Auxiliary Air Force and the Women's Royal Australian Navy Service. By 1944, more than 45 000 had enlisted. The church was apprehensive about the social and moral implications of the presence of so many women in a predominantly male community and so applauded the appointment of Major Kathleen Deasey as liaison officer between the women's services and the chaplain's department. The feared breakdown in morals in the services did not eventuate.[1]

Most servicewomen welcomed the experience of serving overseas, especially for the self-confidence it engendered. Indeed, war was to transform the role of women, especially in the realm of leadership, as army sister Margaret Murchison suggests:

> My service as a nurse with the AIF did have a tremendous bearing on my entire life. . . you had to accept the fact of being put in a position of trust and that you had to have guts and stick to those standards. . . As a woman, the experience was a liberation. You were no longer just a housewife. . . and it lifted your self-confidence.[2]

The outbreak of World War II also revolutionised the lives of those Australian women who stayed at home. Six thousand signed up to work away from home in the Women's Land Army. Their brief was to sow and harvest crops and to tend stock in the place of countrymen who had gone off to war. Despite the scepticism of older people and the farmer's wife in particular, they proved themselves willing and apt workers.

However, the largest contingent of women was employed in munitions factories and other heavy industry, earning wages between 60 to 100% of those earned by men. Trade unions were nervous that men's jobs would be supplanted by cheap female labour, but the Curtin government assured them that the *status quo* would return after the war.

Judge Alfred Foster of the newly-formed Women's Employment Board commented:

> To all of us, it was a revelation to see women who were yesterday working in beauty salons or who had not previously worked outside their own homes. . . who now stood behind mighty machines, operating them with a skill and mastery that was little short of marvellous.[3]

Together with their newfound economic freedom, younger women also experienced greater social mobility and sexual freedom, particularly with the advent of large numbers of American troops in Australian cities.

⌘ Protestant views of the roles of women in the 1940s

The churches' response to such changes was muted as they — or at least the Protestant denominations — had always observed a sharp delineation between the sacred and the secular. They concentrated instead on supporting those involved in the war effort and marshalled their full complement of women volunteers to raise funds for servicemen and their families and to take part in such para-military organisations as the Red Cross. The churches, through such bodies as the Catholic United Service Auxiliary, carried out a sustained voluntary effort during the war years.

In Sydney, Archbishop Mowll and his redoubtable wife set up the Church of England National Emergency Fund to care for soldiers on leave. They supervised the building of substantial huts in the Cathedral grounds, where a thousand meals were served each day at nominal cost and soldiers could find rest and recreation. Dorothy Mowll personally supervised the rostering of volunteers for this mammoth work.[4]

Dorothy Mowll

At this point, tribute must be paid to the remarkable leadership of Dorothy Mowll (1890–1957), both as a missionary in China and later as wife of the Archbishop of Sydney from 1934 to 1957. Her creativity and enthusiasm were boundless; not only was she chiefly responsible for CENEF, but she also helped to pioneer youth work and geriatric care in her husband's large diocese. 'The frontiers of the kingdom of God were never advanced by men and women of caution,' she wrote in her diary.[5]

Elected Fellow of the Royal Geographical society for her work in mapping Western China, she took a vital interest in social, economic and political strategies both inside and outside the church. She knew all her clergy wives and children personally and her pastoral care of them was at least partly responsible for their general contentment when interviewed. She was a worthy successor to Frances Perry and Jane Barker, the other great episcopal wives in Australian history, being described by the Archbishop of Canterbury at Lambeth in 1960 as 'one of the most remarkable women in the Anglican Commission'.[6]

With such notable exceptions, the church was generally tardy in the sphere of social action where the needs of women were concerned. Middle-class values were the touchstone in the Protestant churches of this period. The wartime trend of establishing childcare centres, to enable working women to combine motherhood and paid work, was generally not acclaimed by the church which believed that the health of society was predicated on the wife and mother remaining at home to care for the children.

When the new Widows' Pension Act was introduced in 1943 by the Federal government, which allowed for de facto wives to be eligible for a pension, the Mothers' Union protested that this payment was 'a reward for immorality'.[7] However, the bill was scarcely prodigal in its provisions — such recipients should have lived a minimum of three years with a man, be fifty years of age, have dependent children and be in need of financial help.

The Mothers' Union did not comment on another significant event for women in that year and that was the entry of Australian women into Federal parliament for the first time. As a result of the work of the Women for Canberra movement, Dame Enid Lyons was elected to the House of Representatives and Dorothy Tangney to the Senate. It was not that they were opposed to political representation by women; rather, they were so accustomed to male dominance in public life that it took them some time to adjust to this new departure. A change of attitude was evident by 1964, when they expressed delight at the five women senators who had entered Federal parliament.[8]

There was, however, one notable voice of dissent amongst

Mothers' Union members in the war years who proposed reforms decades ahead of her time. This was Norma Coughlan, a clergy wife who, together with her husband, founded the Christian Social Order Movement (CSOM), a small but articulate group which worked for social justice, particularly in the context of postwar reconstruction.

Norma Coughlan was a regular columnist in the Mothers' Union magazine, *MIANZA*, which circulated nationally in Australia and New Zealand. She deplored 'band-aid' methods of social welfare and asked such awkward questions as, 'Would they let Jesus into Australia?' when opposing the White Australia Policy. She pleaded for trained leaders in social welfare, for sex education for young people, for marriage guidance classes and for community-based education.[9] She attacked the competitive society for its materialism and divisiveness:

> Life is loaded against most folk from birth and even before that quite often. . . we must plan that the community at large must save and plan by regular contributions to meet necessary human need.[10]

Her reformism attracted the wrath of the Bishop of Willochra, who chided her for advocating a handout mentality in society:

> There is a real danger that in the desire to set life free of every sort of inconvenience, so that we shall have everything we want. . . we shall adopt a sub-Christian standard and disregard the apostolic advice to endure hardness as a good soldier of Jesus Christ.[11]

Norma Coughlan and her husband William received little appreciation from clerical circles who thought their views were too liberal, although Howard and Dorothy Mowll tried to encourage them, until the CSOM ran out of funds in 1951 and was obliged to close down. It had made a positive contribution to church thinking on postwar reconstruction and the Coughlans now turned their considerable energies to marriage guidance programs.[12]

✠ The 1950s for churchwomen

The 1950s were a time of stability and growth for the churches in which women played a part which was little different to that of their forbears a century before. They entered orders in large numbers; they staffed Sunday schools, sang in choirs, raised funds for missions and social welfare, tended the fabric of the church and catered for church functions.

Laywomen joined the staffs of church schools only to find that their salary was less than that of the male gardener employed by the school![13] Again, the churches never commented on the disparity between male and female wages, the female wage having been raised from 54% to 75% that of the male wage in 1949. It was left to individual Catholic laywomen, like Kate Dwyer (1861–1949), to represent the church unbriefed in working for greater equality for women in the workplace.

Church affiliation was strong in the 1950s, 89.4% of Australians professing allegiance to Christian denominations in the census of 1954. Thirty-three per cent of those canvassed claimed to be regular churchgoers. It was also an age of mass religious demonstrations: 150 000 Roman Catholics flocked to a Family Rosary Crusade in the Melbourne Botanical Gardens in 1953. Father Patrick Peyton was the eloquent leader of this movement which attracted large crowds across the country using the motto, 'The family which prays together stays together'.

The National Eucharistic Congress in the same year attracted 24 000 marchers through the streets of Sydney; amongst them were female religious from fourteen orders, who were allowed to march in public for the first time.[14]

The Methodist Church attracted many thousands of listeners through its Mission to the Nation, led by the Reverend Alan Walker in 1956. Large gatherings were peculiarly suited to the urban culture of the day, when almost eight out of ten Australians were living in the capital and provincial cities. Prestigious dissenting churches, like St Stephen's Presbyterian Church and the Central Methodist Mission, boasted large regular congregations which both supported and were fed by the Mission to the Nation.

Other factors which assisted the growth of churches — while not particularly encouraging change for women — were the political homogeneity of the day, where the Cold War and the Korean War united Australians in an anti-Communist outlook. Also, the Menzies policy of stressing family values and the importance of the home chimed in with church attitudes. The introduction of television in 1956 had not yet begun to erode congregational attendance or attention spans in church!

The close of the decade witnessed the largest religious crusade of all with the visit of the popular American evangelist Dr Billy Graham to Australia. Carefully planned and superbly organised, the Graham Crusades attracted huge attendances night after night and registered 130 000 commitments across the country, three-fifths of whom were from women.

Historian Stuart Piggin points out that such crusades were largely masculine in execution. Women were able to sing in the choir and counsel enquirers, but the only executive position a woman could specifically occupy was that of vice-chairman of the prayer committee.[15]

�֍ Changes for churchwomen in the 1960s

The 1960s opened with the same certainties as the 1950s, but changes in society and church were soon apparent. Girls' church schools retained their customary Spartan or Puritan standards — or both — for their pupils. Dorothy Knox, the redoubtable headmistress of PLC Pymble in NSW, proclaimed that 'leisure time for women can bring about self-destruction'. She recommended church, the Red Cross, Girl Guides and study as the best ways for her girls to occupy their time.[16]

For the Catholic schoolgirl in particular, every moment should be dedicated to God and bodily modesty should be observed at all times. When the students at Melbourne's Genazzano Convent were found talking about sex, such punishments were prescribed as reading about the sufferings of St Teresa of Avila.[17]

Music was one sphere in which women dominated in church worship. They had taken part in church choirs since the early years of the nineteenth century and it was a woman, Cathleen Fitzpatrick, who organised the first Catholic choir in Sydney, even before the arrival of the first official priests in 1820. From 1880 onwards, choirs in Anglican parish churches were mostly sustained by women singing alongside trebles. The result was a softening of the starkness of previous Anglican worship. Women also played an integral part in Methodist choirs and Salvation Army evangelistic music after 1880.[18]

Church music, therefore, became an outlet for women not in the paid workforce, as well as for the single woman. It was fulfilling socially and artistically as well as spiritually. However, few women in Protestant churches became choirmasters until the late twentieth century, most choirs working under the firm direction of two men — the director and the rector!

Tempers occasionally flared, as in the parish of St Mary's Anglican Church, Waverley, Sydney, in the 1930s, when the women in the choir were forbidden to sit in the choirstalls with the men. They went on strike for a month until the rector relented.

Women were invited in the 1960s to join the choir at St James, King St, also in NSW, but again the condition was that they must not be seen by the congregation. After months of being penned up in the 'chicken coop' — as the enclosure was called — they finally prevailed upon the rector to allow them to join the rest of the choir.[19]

After 1960, the heyday of the parish choir began to pass. Choir numbers, especially amongst younger women, began to decline. By 1988, only a handful of choirs remained in suburban churches (less than ten in Sydney Anglican churches). This trend — for many, symptomatic of a general decline — was due to the modernisation of traditional liturgy in an attempt to reach a younger, more secular culture.

The 1960s witnessed the emergence of a youth culture as a basis of society. The so-called 'generation gap' and an increasing sophistication in a society not threatened by war or depression helped to produce a decline in parish activities. The parish was no longer the social centre of the district, as young people found more to interest them in secular pursuits and clubs. Sunday schools declined in number and braver women shifted to the more difficult task of teaching scripture in government schools. Gradually, women assumed a more ecclesiastical role in churches, leading Bible studies and even worship in smaller congregations.

Hans Mol in his survey of Australian religious belief, *Religion in Australia*, published in 1971, found that church attendance had declined five per cent over the decade and that women were more regular attenders at church than men — but only by a factor of seven women to six men amongst Catholics and Methodists, and seven women to five men amongst Anglicans and Presbyterians.[20] Female predominance in Australian congregations had been a feature of church life since the earlier days of the colonies, but the time was coming when numerical predominance was not to be enough; women were ready for more prominent roles in church polity and worship than their predecessors.

Social changes, added to increased educational opportunities for women, both in secular and theological studies, resulted in the movement towards ordination for women in the various churches.

✠ Second wave feminism and the church's response

As if to accelerate the changing role of women in church and society came the exuberant force of second wave feminism at the close of the 1960s. Few churchwomen identified with such a secular movement, linking it with the increased sexual permissiveness of the 1960s which, in its turn, was blamed on the introduction of the pill as an easy means of birth control.

Most were shocked by the bawdiness and wilfulness of Germaine Greer's book, which burst upon the world in 1970. *The Female Eunuch* gained instant attention in the media as it exhorted women to reject every institution and assumption affecting their lives. It was deliberately subversive in its approach to what Greer saw as the sentimentality and hypocrisy which had surrounded women up to that point. Radical feminism on the campus was delighted with the furore and reassessment caused by the book. From the other side, the Mothers' Union recorded the objection of the vast majority of its members at the Federal government's proposed grant to Germaine Greer to produce a television series on reproduction and mothercraft.[21]

The incisiveness of Greer's pronouncements — which few

men found palatable — forced women to re-examine their lot as determined for them by society. The status of women in the workplace was palpably unequal — advertisements were gender specific and rates of pay varied sharply between men and women. Working mothers were thought to be victimising their latchkey children. Divorced women could get the single mother's pension only if they were the 'innocent party' in the breakdown of the marriage. Apart from continuing their traditional social welfare policies, the churches took some time to find an answer to these problems, having for so long relied on their doctrine of the home as the panacea for society.

However, by 1976 change was becoming evident as leaders in the Mothers' Union asked, 'How can we help to promote the integrity of the home and give new and realistic status to the place of the wife and mother?' After 'endless discussion', a decision was made to reverse their traditional policy of excluding divorced women from membership.[22]

As women began entering the workforce in ever-increasing numbers after 1970, there was a further challenge for churches to retain their laywomen. The Mothers' Union under Dorothy Mowll had sensibly initiated a Young Members' Department in 1951, which began founding Young Wives' groups five years later in the Diocese of Sydney. Other dioceses followed suit, as did many Presbyterian and Methodist churches.

These groups had considerable success in so-called 'Bible Belt' areas, often splitting into smaller units to meet in homes. Some meetings were held at night, hoping to attract younger women in paid employment, but most of these women were too tired to take on such a commitment.

✵ The decline in numbers in women's groups and its effects

The flow of women into the paid workforce became an irresistible tide and the Mothers' Union found by 1980 that numbers of members and groups were declining perceptibly.[23] In 1960, there were 3 386 members in approximately 100 branches. By 1988, this had declined below 2 000 in fewer than eighty branches. More disturbing for some members was the emerging concept, both inside and outside the church, that education, rather than marriage, was the key to economic independence and self-worth. In reply, laywomen's groups strongly opposed any idea that the status of women choosing to remain in the home lacked dignity.

Despite falling numbers, the Mothers' Union and the Presbyterian Women's Association were determined to play a constructive spiritual role in Australia's development in the 1970s and 1980s. Attempts were made to integrate the large numbers of postwar migrants in the country by supporting the work of the Good Neighbour Council. Delegates were sent to the government's Co-ordinating Committee for Overseas Students in 1974 and a home tutor scheme for non-English speaking migrants helped to ease the isolation of women in a new culture.[24]

In 1978, the trend towards cooperation with the state continued, when church groups were asked to contribute information and suggestions to the newly formed Women's Advisory Committee, which was linked to the Premier's Department. The Mothers' Union attempted to tackle such difficult social issues as delinquency, pornography and domestic violence by setting up family crisis centres and by making recommendations to government through its Social Action Committee (founded in 1973).[25]

There were positive aspects to the decline in numerical

strength of laywomen's organisations in the church: one was a far greater ecumenism amongst members and a closer relationship in particular with the Roman Catholic Church. For instance, Mothers' Union members of the parish of St Mary's Narromine joined with the women of St Augustine's Catholic Church and St Andrew's Uniting Church in birthday celebrations in 1982.[26] Since Vatican II, most Catholic parishes have joined with other denominations in the Women's World Day of Prayer.

The Mothers' Union magazine, *Mia Mia*, reprinted a wide-ranging article from the *Catholic Weekly* in 1984 which attacked Marxists for their desire to abolish the family, the Wran Government for its legalisation of homosexual acts, and certain radical feminists for supporting pedophiles.[27]

✠ Women's groups in the Nonconformist churches

Women's groups in nonconformist churches also suffered a decline in numbers and an ageing membership after 1980. The Presbyterian Women's Association, which was more avowedly fundraising than the Mothers' Union, continued to run jumble stalls, and sew and cook in support of social service programs.

Postwar Methodist guilds also concentrated on homecrafts in their tasks of fundraising for the church. They also garnished the church, polished the brass and provided meals and flowers whenever needed. Fiona Clarke, in her study of Methodist women's voluntary groups in South Australia after 1945, points out that women duplicated the work they were already carrying out in their own homes and, in so doing, became 'housewives of the church'.[28]

It is true that for rural women in particular, auxiliary groups provided company and stimulation for the isolated and therefore membership reaped its own rewards; yet at the same time, there was a lack of consultation with the women as to where their funds might be spent and certainly a lack of female representation on church property trusts which were made up exclusively of men. Even by 1975, only 13.1% of the Methodist Conference in South Australia were women.[29]

The Australian historian, Beverley Kingston, recalls the endless ingenuity and thrift of her grandmother, who was a member of the Presbyterian guild in Innisfail:

> I learnt some of the ways in which a 70 lb bag of sugar could be stretched into lollies, by the addition of the coconuts she collected throughout the year from the tree in the fowlyard.[30]

The fabled *Presbyterian Women's Cookbook* bears eloquent testimony to the creativity of these women in the service of the church.

✖ Providing greater support in a changing world

Patience and thrift, however, were not qualities that were greatly prized by society in the 1980s. Technological advances leading to the electronic revolution, ecological strategies to reclaim an environment ravaged by thoughtless exploitation of resources, and the accelerated pace of life with its stress on instant gratification left people grasping for certainty amid the change.

These changes encouraged a return to private devotional life, a shift to small groups meeting in homes and to large pentecostal gatherings — the last two being perceived as offering warmth and emotional support in greater measure than traditional churches whose membership declined further. Home churches were generally egalitarian in their attitude to female leadership, since they did not believe in ordination anyway. Charismatic churches varied in their use of female prophetic gifts, but male leadership was predominant.

Since the 1960s, women had sought emotional and spiritual support increasingly through programs of Bible study. One interdenominational group which was particularly successful in reaching women in Australia and then overseas was the Christian Women's Convention movement. Sensing that the church was 'not particularly relevant' to the modern woman, they started day and weekend conventions for women using women speakers and Bible study courses. Broadcasts, seminars, workshops and coffee mornings were only part of their armoury. They began a magazine called *Christian Woman*, which had 12 000 subscribers by 1972.[31] 'Safari' teams of women travelled many thousands of miles in the north of Australia, advertising by poster their meetings in both English and Aboriginal languages. Christian Aboriginal women assisted on teams and in the translation of addresses.

The movement has spread to such European countries as Holland, Switzerland and the UK and to developing countries like Zimbabwe, Peru and Papua New Guinea. Its success in attracting such a following can be attributed to a mildly feminist strand — it is led only by women for women — and to what its leaders describe as the 'enabling freedom' which results from studying the scriptures.[32]

Two of the most notable speakers in this work should be identified, both originally of Brethren background: one was Ada Chambers who, even into her ninth decade, was particularly gifted in Bible exegesis, as well as in the answering of difficult questions without notice in front of a thousand women.

The other woman was Irene Young, an early graduate of the London School of Economics, whose energy and humour were legendary. She played an invaluable role in a host of interdenominational societies at university and school level, operating at a pace which left her family gasping. Possibly her most strategic work was with the Overseas Christian Fellowship. Under the Colombo Plan, students from Africa and Asia began arriving in Australia in the early 1950s to study. As the Inter Varsity Fellowship representative on the Australian Council of Social Services, she was deputed to meet students coming in by plane and ship. It meant being at the airport or wharf, particularly at 5.00 a.m. on a Sunday morning, when the government could never get people to meet incoming students. A steady stream of these students, who are now leaders in their own countries, found their way to the Young household at weekends where they encountered friendship and hospitality.[33]

Clergy wives

Before turning to the role of Catholic laywomen, it is necessary to assess the role of clergy wives in the late twentieth century — especially in the light of the social and ideological change which had emerged in the 1960s. In conservative churches like those of the Anglican Diocese of Sydney, there appeared to be little change from traditional roles of helpmeet and bridge between clergy and congregation.

Thirty Anglican clergy wives were interviewed in 1991 by Catherine West as part of a university survey. Only two of them were engaged in full-time work; fourteen worked part-time. In total, one-third of the subjects worked in some form of paid employment, as opposed to the national average of 53.2%.

There was little evidence of role-sharing by husband and wife, the wife being confined to traditional nurturing and housekeeping roles as well as leadership or participation in women's groups in the parish. Most found the lack of privacy in living in a rectory difficult, but none objected to being incorporated in the husband's job — obviously having counted the cost first! All expressed opposition to the ordination of women to the priesthood on theological and subjective grounds. West found that the ideology underlying the structure of clergyman with wife as helpmeet was so strong, it was almost impossible for a wife to deviate from her allotted role: 'It is easier to give into strong personalities than to risk ill-feeling. . .' and 'they expect me to do what I do. . .' were two representative comments.[34]

Similar findings had occurred in Kenneth Dempsey's survey of Methodist wives in a NSW country town in the 1950s and 1960s, where most ministers' wives accepted the cultural expectation that they should put their husband's work before their own interests. The maxim that a clergy wife will 'make or break' her husband's work is probably a realistic one, but it places pressure on the clergy wife to conform to lay expectations. One clergy wife said: 'I would not marry a minister again if I had to choose. It broke my health, the criticism got inside me and we were always fighting debt.'[35]

It can be argued that the role of the clergy wife — up to 1975 at least — had not altered since European settlement. It was assumed (perhaps because a residence and a car allowance were supplied) that parish ministry was a joint enterprise and that the husband's career was also vicariously the wife's. However, in Dempsey's more recent survey of Methodist/Uniting clergy in a Victorian town taken in the 1970s and 1980s, wives registered a declining commitment to their husband's work.

Some felt a reduction in traditional roles was not incompatible with their husband's image and efficacy. Others had undertaken university study or paid employment for economic reasons or to satisfy the need for increased privacy. None went so far as the minister's wife in her submission to the 1974 Enquiry on the Status of Women in the Church, who exclaimed:

> I feel it wrong for a wife of a minister to be obliged to accept demands made upon her time by the congregation. If a Session wishes to have the full-time services of the minister's wife, then they should pay a double stipend.[36]

It would appear that expectations of clergy wives have been lowered to more realistic levels since the 1970s, largely as a result of the women's movement. Younger women, who are in part or full-time employment themselves, recognise the need for clergy wives to seek an outlet beyond the parish. Older women parishioners and certain clergy of unbending disposition often retain absurdly high expectations of the minister's wife, but a growing proportion of clergy wives are now engaged in work outside the parish for both economic and professional reasons.

The very withdrawal of the clergy wife from the epicentre of parish affairs allows the appointment of trained deaconesses and women clergy to assist the minister. Hence, the employment of ordained women, as in the Uniting Church and certain Anglican dioceses, has released clergy wives from traditional pressures.[37]

❋ The Commission for the Status of Women

The setting up of a Commission on the Status of Women (under the presidency of Marie Tulip) by the Australian Council of Churches in 1973 was a milestone for women seeking greater freedom of ministry in the church. The need to redefine the role of women in the church had become more urgent in the context of a society in flux. Submissions were received from three sources — church executives, women's church groups and from women themselves. Two hundred submissions were received from eleven different denominations, mainly in NSW.

The unsurprising conclusion that arose from the enquiry was that, although women made up the large majority of the congregation and raised much of the funds to support church activities, they were still barely represented on decision-making bodies. For example, in the Sydney Anglican Synod, there were three women representatives out of a total of 600. No woman could serve on the Church Property Trust and none on the Glebe Administration Board. A general licence to preach was not granted to women.[38]

There seemed to be less bias against women in executive positions in country dioceses — where perhaps qualified men were fewer than in the metropolis. For instance, in the Diocese of Bathurst, the Diocesan Registrar was a woman and this was the case also in Grafton and Riverina.[39]

In Nonconformist churches, only eleven out of eighty-nine lay representatives in the Methodist General Conference of 1972 were women and in the Presbyterian General Assembly of 1973 in NSW only eight out of 226 elders were women. Clearly, these gender ratios were set to alter over the next two decades, as the church gradually began to reflect the changes which were taking place in the society in which it was set down. By 1988, there were ninety-two female representatives in the Uniting Church's General Assembly of 220 members, of whom thirty-seven were ordained ministers and fifty-five were lay.[40]

Even in the synod of the most conservative and wealthy Anglican diocese of all — Sydney — the number of female synod representatives had risen to 101 by 1988, an improvement of 3 400% on the figure of 1973! However, the powerful Standing Committee of that diocese still had only one woman representative to forty-eight men.[41] By 1996, this figure had actually crept up to five women out of a total of fifty.

Even in such an egalitarian church as the Congregational Union, no woman served on the Finance Council in 1974 and only one on the Ministry Council out of a total of membership of twelve. The vice-president of the Congregational Union, the Reverend Lilian Wells, affirmed that all offices in the Union were open to women and it was only personal diffidence or reluctance which had held women back from applying for particular posts. The Salvation Army reported to the Enquiry that 650 of its officers out of a total of 900 in Australia were women. A comparison of ranks on a gender basis was not given, however.

Perhaps the least discriminatory of all denominations, the Quakers, pointed out that they had no women's church groups, thereby declaring gender a non-issue in their church.[42]

✠ Catholic laywomen

The response of the Roman Catholic Church to the 1973 Enquiry was a long and guarded explanation by a member of the hierarchy — rather than a laywoman or woman in orders — which outlined official acts of the church governing its organisation. The code of canon law as decreed in 1917 governed the discipline of the church, but the status of women had altered since then, he wrote.

The greatest modification had occurred since the Second Vatican Council of 1962–1965. This body had declared the essential equality of men and women and declared that women should be free to acquire education or 'cultural benefits equal to those recognised for men'.[43] At its third session, the council actually admitted women as 'Auditores'. Of the fifteen women allowed to attend, eight were religious and seven were laywomen. By 1967, an Australian laywoman, Rosemary Goldie, was appointed joint-assistant secretary of a new Council for the Laity, as constituted by Pope Paul VI.[44]

Following Vatican II, further committees were set up by Paul VI in 1973 to deal with the role of women. The Committee for the Family was to deal primarily with marriage and the family and eleven out of its eighteen members were lay. However, only five of the laity were women — a miserly proportion when it is considered where the burden of sustaining a family lay. The new Commission on Women in Society and Church was made up of twenty-five members, women predominating for the first time by fifteen to ten. In according women such an improved status, they were still not granted permission to regulate their own fertility and thereby ensure personal freedom.

As far as the role of women in worship was concerned, the Vatican made few concessions at this stage. A woman was now able to baptise in an emergency when an ordained minister was not available (and presumably a male layman). She could read prayers in the liturgy. Ordination was, of course, out of the question.[45]

Present-day Catholic laywomen vary in their assessment of the reforms achieved for women through the Second Vatican Council. Some accord it but modest praise: 'It did move women through to the present century' was the comment of one.[46] A more laudatory opinion of Vatican II comes from the pen of commentator Geraldine Doogue: 'It led to a "targetted" compassion and thoughtfulness and a new culture of creativity.'[47]

The role of the Catholic laywoman in Australia has gradually expanded since the war years. For many, there was the psychological barrier of not possessing the canonical status granted to women religious, which tended to place the single woman in particular in a position of inferiority vis-a-vis the orders. Those laywomen with a strong desire to serve God outside a religious community and outside the official church umbrella of the Catholic Women's League often involved themselves in politics as an avenue of service.

This could be a disillusioning experience, particularly for a woman unaccustomed to male bargaining and factional deals. Some managed to battle on and ignore the inevitable contumely, but others became involved in new lay societies like the Paulian Association.

Founded in 1956 in the Catholic Archdiocese of Sydney, the association has been directed by Mary Gilchrist since 1986. It has worked in the field of further education in spiritual matters and in social action. Laywomen have found a particular gift in piloting small groups of enquirers into a firm Christian commitment. Lay missionaries have also been trained and sent out as volunteers to assist churches and agencies in Third World countries. Mary Gilchrist herself served in Zimbabwe for several years and found overseas service 'a liberating experience'.[48]

The Catholic Women's League (CWL) has been the chief official organisation for laywomen in the Catholic Church since the war years. Like the Mothers' Union, it is basically conservative in outlook, because of its hierarchical patronage. Again like the corresponding Protestant bodies, it has striven to uphold the family and Christian values in society, expressing grave concern also at the divorce boom of the 1960s which had followed the marriage boom of the 1950s.

Politically, its most sensitive function was that of fundraising, as it was this issue which had particularly caused friction with the hierarchy in the past. CWL members were aware of the harsh treatment of their predecessor, the Catholic Women's Association, by Cardinal Gilroy in 1941 when he disbanded the CWA and channelled their hard-earned funds into the training of priests.[49] A series of battles then occurred between 1940 and 1960 between Catholic women and the hierarchy in which a number of younger women left the fold.

Cardinal Gilroy did his best to control the laywomen of Sydney by setting up the Legion of Catholic Women in 1941 as a parish-based organisation recruited by and under the control of the local priest. There was an ominous note in its charter for the laywoman of independent mind:

> The parish priest will be in complete control and each parish branch and the whole movement will be under the complete direction of the archbishop. All funds will be pooled with the headquarters administration. All assets will belong to the diocese.[50]

Nor was the Legion allowed autonomy in policy matters. This was to be the province of the Director of Catholic Action who was a male. Although numbers rose to 17 000 by 1948, there was a steady decline thereafter and active laywomen transferred their commitment to the Catholic Women's League. The growth of an educated middle class amongst Catholic adherents in this period meant that laywomen were less likely to submit to the *fiat* of the hierarchy, particularly in financial matters.[51] A decline in sectarianism also gave Catholic women more confidence to develop ecumenical initiatives with women's groups from other churches.

After 1960, there gradually emerged a distinctive voice for laywomen and a modification of hierarchical control in the Catholic Church. In responding to the 1973 Enquiry of the ACC into the status of women, the CWL was able to note its financial autonomy and its right to take part in the election process for bishops — a privilege not entirely available to women of the synodically governed Protestant churches.[52]

A positive relationship had also developed after 1960 in the Diocese of Tasmania between the Catholic Women's League and the hierarchy under the far-sighted Archbishop Guilford

Young. In response to Vatican II, Young formed a Diocesan Pastoral Council in 1967 and two CWL members were elected to it.

The humorous bishop remarked at the 1972 conference of this body that 'Vatican III will be attended by bishops and their wives and Vatican IV by bishops and their husbands!' Tasmania was one of the first states in Australia to permit women to read the liturgy in worship. The following year, the CWL Conference at national level passed a motion that women should be permitted ordination to the ministries of both lector and acolyte.[53]

Since the 1970s, there have been a flurry of appointments of women laity to church boards and a proliferation of new associations set up by the Vatican to initiate change and, hopefully, give women a greater voice. The Council for the Laity, the Catholic Commission for Justice and Peace, and Diocesan Pastoral Councils all contained women members. Many laywomen, however, are sceptical about the degree of power-sharing that has been allowed and feel that even as late as the 1990s the hierarchy is still window-dressing.[54]

The Catholic Women's League, for its part, has continued to lobby government on such issues as pornography, euthanasia and abortion. Although it contains members of varying shades of opinion, it tends to be cautious in policy like its Protestant counterparts, opposing radical feminism and the Women's Electoral Lobby for its perceived humanism. It has not pronounced strongly in the matter of artificial contraception, nor would it have been heeded if it had.

Catholic women had decided to use the pill and similar contraceptive methods to those employed by the rest of the community. In 1966, married Catholic women aged between thirty-five and thirty-nine had an average of 3.18 children, compared with 2.91 per family across all religions. In 1991, the average family size for Catholic women between thirty and thirty-four was 1.73 children, compared with 1.7 children across all religions.

The primary cause of this plummeting of the Catholic birthrate was clearly a rejection by women of the church's teaching on contraception.[55] Not all women abandoned Catholic doctrine on birth control, but the overwhelming majority claimed the right of private judgment while remaining, for the most part, within the church.

✳ Aboriginal women

The last two decades of this century have seen Aboriginal women come into their own as church leaders. Despite experiencing domestic subjection, they have generally enjoyed a teaching and prophetic role amongst their own people in spiritual matters, mainly because of their strong oral skills. Hence, as we have seen, their valuable work as advisers to Bible translators on mission stations.

Missionaries also tended to depute to indigenous women leadership of services in the 1950s and 1960s. When revival occurred amongst Aboriginal people at the Uniting Church Mission at Elcho Island in 1979, two of the most remarkable changes for women occurred: first, they were treated with unaccustomed kindness by their husbands; and second, they were able to share their leadership of the church with the men.[56]

Some Aboriginal laywomen identified more strongly with European churches than others, particularly if they came from or had worked in southern states. Ellen Campbell Atkinson, wife of the Reverend Edwin Atkinson and aunt of Pastor Doug Nicholls, was noted for her leadership. In 1957, she and her husband were given the cure of the Church of Christ in Mooroopna, Victoria.[57]

Rosalie Kunoth-Monks, better known for her leading role in the film *Jedda*, served for a time as a novice in the Community of the Holy Name in Melbourne. She worked in gaols, hospitals and children's homes while she tested her vocation:

> I specialised in child care; I don't know how many kids went through my little hands — hundreds of them. . . I was trained to care for them.[58]

Women missionaries often commented on the spirituality of Aboriginal laywomen. Mrs Daisy Fleming, who worked at the Baptist Yuendumi Mission in Central Australia in the 1950s, spoke of her impressions of Rosie Ngumbi: 'She took to Christian doctrine and seemed to understand more readily than any of the others. . . The strength of the church was among the women.'[59]

The confidence placed by missionaries in indigenous female leadership has been rewarded in the acceptance of several women for ordination since 1990. The interdenominational theological college in Darwin — Nungalinga College — has provided theological training for Liyapidiny Marika, who was ordained into the Uniting Church at Yirrkala in 1991, and for Gloria Shipp, prior to her ordination in the Anglican Diocese of Bathurst in 1996. The college had already instituted women's studies courses in 1983 for wives of pastors from outlying communities who needed help with English and for town Aborigines who wish to renew their cultural roots.

Thus, Aboriginal laywomen have played a leading part in the development of the indigenous church, because of their oral skills and spiritual sensitivity.

❖ A greater religious commitment by women than men

The growth of statistical surveys in the postwar period have revealed more of the habits of women churchgoers in the last half century. Gender has now become a category with modern sociologists like Gary Bouma and Hans Mol. In his first survey of religion in Australia, published in 1971, Mol had included women as part of the male response, but the advent of the women's movement altered that.[60] These surveys confirm what has always been obvious — that women are more avowedly religious than men.

Despite sociological change, women remained more 'religious' than men in the 1980s: 64.75 of females identified themselves as religious, as opposed to 51.1% of men, whilst 20.4% of women prayed on most days, as opposed to 13% of men. The gap between men and women in church attendance has narrowed in the 1980s, probably because of the increasing involvement of women in the paid workforce.[61]

The churches themselves have commissioned a report which attempts to assess roles undertaken by church attenders: the National Church Life Survey has found that teaching, lay leadership and ministry roles are more often carried out by females (57%), while the majority of administrators are men (54%). The women in question were more likely to be under forty years of age, while the men were over forty. This distribution was explained as a matter of 'gifts'; questions of hierarchy and executive power-sharing were not raised.[62]

❖ Progress towards freedom, ecumenism and leadership

The post-World War II era has seen marked changes in the role of laywomen in the Australian church. Apart from the ideological change accompanying the women's movement which has brought greater freedom and individualism for women inside and outside the church, there has been greater ecumenism and cooperation across the denominations.

The Women's Inter-Church Council (WICC), founded in 1938, for example, has gradually embraced representatives from all churches — including the Roman Catholic Church in 1969 — as Christians realise that what unites in a secular and pluralistic society is more important than what divides. Even at the height of World War II, the WICC invited a Lutheran laywoman, Mrs Regina Stolz, to attend the conference unofficially as a gesture of solidarity amongst churchwomen. This gesture would never have been countenanced during World War I. The WICC has supported such important initiatives as the Women's World Day of Prayer and the Asian Church Women's Conference, which sponsors young women from overseas for professional training.[63]

Apart from the issue of ordination, which must occupy a chapter on its own, there has been a continuing trend since World War II for women to gain a voice in the councils of the church. Whereas their mute support had always been taken for granted in terms of filling pews and teacups, it was inevitable that their ascension to leadership roles in the community at large would ultimately be reflected in that most conservative of bodies — the church.

14

The struggle for a share of leadership

THE ORDINATION ISSUE: 1939 TO THE 1990s

'A feminist on the warpath is a terrible thing to behold.'

Rt Rev. John Hazlewood, Bishop of Ballarat, 1986

'The ordination of women is a means to an end; it is not an end in itself. . . Those who support it are striving to transform the church into a more just, more caring, less hierarchical and, I think, in many ways a less pompous organisation.'

Dr Janet Scarfe, 1989

'I have learned that when women preach or administer the sacraments, or lead worship, or counsel, or listen, or encourage within the community of faith, people experience the risen Christ as surely as when a male priest does the same.'

Rev. Colleen O'Reilly, 1987

IN 1944 IN WAR-WRACKED CHINA, there occurred a ceremony which was to have profound implications for women

in the Australian church forty years later. A Chinese woman
— Li Tim Oi — was ordained priest by the Bishop of Hong
Kong.

Bishop R.O. Hall had been deeply impressed by her lone
ministry to the Anglican congregation in Macau and so he
decided that her people should not be left rudderless. He did
not, however, consult Canterbury and, as soon as the war was
over, the church decided to deal with this 'irregularity'. Pressure was brought upon her to resign her orders. The bishops
at Lambeth in 1948 and 1958 argued over the niceties of her
case. Meanwhile, she continued to teach and pastor in Communist China under great difficulty.

The decades passed, bringing about a massive change of
attitude in Western countries to the role of women. In 1984,
the bishops gathered again, this time in Westminster Abbey,
in order to celebrate her priesthood and long years of service
under persecution. Li Tim Oi had become the icon of the
women's ordination movement.[1]

The 1980s were a revolutionary decade for women and the
church. The church's notable tradition of public service had
been based through the centuries on the voluntary work of
women. No government could afford to pay for the labour
of this female army. It was now realised that society owed
them a debt and, in the context of the women's movement,
that debt should be paid by a recognition of equality and a
willingness to share power. However, it was the promotion
of women to the hierarchy that the larger conservative
churches found so difficult.

At first, the church attempted to ignore the possibility of
a changed role for women, so women were obliged to found
their own societies to gain a voice. The Catholic orders
founded Women in the Australian Church in 1986, which
attracted several hundred members eager to define and work

for an inclusive church. From this body arose the Ordination of Catholic Women in 1993, which affiliated with similar groups worldwide who wanted the admission of women to the ordained ministries of the Catholic Church. Anglican women (and men) founded such bodies as the Movement for the Ordination of Women (1983) and Men, Women and God (1987).

These groups were also affiliated with organisations with similar names in Britain and the USA. They were encouraged by the fact that living, working models of their goal already existed in other countries. Women had been ordained in the Episcopalian Church of the USA since 1974, in the Anglican Church in Canada since 1976 and the Anglican Church in New Zealand since 1977. Most Australians who had worshipped in these churches when overseas returned home persuaded by the pragmatic argument:

> I have learned that when women preach or administer the sacraments, or lead worship, or counsel, or listen, or encourage within the community of faith, people experience the risen Christ as surely as when a male priest does the same.[2]

Another factor influencing a change in attitude amongst rank and file church people was the example of the Uniting Church which had ordained women since its formation in 1977. Since 1970, the Methodist and Presbyterian churches had moved towards the ordination of women and, in 1974, the general and state assemblies and the presbyteries finally approved the proposal.

The Congregational Church had been ordaining women since Winifred Kiek in 1927. So when the Uniting Church of Australia was formed in 1977, it inherited thirty-six women clergy from its three constituent members — the Methodists,

Presbyterians and Congregationalists. By 1988, this number had risen to 138 and in 1994 the number stood at 265. This 200% increase for women was remarkable in such a short period.[3]

Apart from the moral support lent to Anglican and Catholic women seeking ordination, the Uniting Church also led the way in campaigning for affirmative action in church committees and inclusive language in a reformed liturgy. The state of Victoria also saw the first women to be ordained in the Churches of Christ and the Baptist Church — in 1973 and 1978 respectively.[4]

❖ Women's ordination and the Anglican Church

It was to be from Victoria (and the Diocese of Melbourne, in particular) with its strong tradition of voluntarism that the most forceful push for ordination of Anglican women was to come.

Ranged against Melbourne was its traditional rival, the conservative evangelical Diocese of Sydney. The Diocese of Melbourne was also largely evangelical, but its interpretation of scripture was more liberal than that of the older diocese. The leadership of Archbishop, David Penman, until his untimely death in 1989, was crucial in marshalling support for ordination of women in Melbourne, first of all to the diaconate in 1986 and ultimately to the priesthood.

On the other hand, Sydney's archbishops and many of her clergy had either taught or been taught at Moore Theological College, with its proud tradition of conservative scholarship going back over a century. Their appeal was to scripture — and as literal an interpretation of it as possible. Various arguments were adduced from certain Pauline scriptures that women should not have leadership in the church.

For instance, the injunction in I Timothy that women

should not teach or speak in church was quoted as a basic principle of church order.[5] Some male theological students at Moore College were to carry this to extremes on one occasion, when they walked out of class rather than be taught by a female lecturer.

The next argument to be used by opponents of women's ordination was that the God-given order since creation was that the man was the 'head' of the woman as Christ was the 'head' of the church.[6] Therefore, it was reasoned, a woman could not exercise any authority in church over a man.

Sir Marcus Loane, Archbishop of Sydney from 1966 to 1982, had spoken strongly against the ordination of women at the Lambeth Conference in 1968, using these arguments amongst others. He also ruled that women should not speak in church from the pulpit in his diocese: special permission could be applied for by clergy to have a deaconess or a returned woman missionary speak from the chancel steps. Some clergy ignored the caveat and invited gifted women speakers like Jean Raddon and Deaconess Andrews to preach but, on the whole, the prohibition was observed.[7]

The next archbishop, Donald Robinson, a former vice-principal of Moore College, was similarly opposed to the concept of ordaining women, but he did relent in the matter of the diaconate and, to the surprise of many, the first women deacons were ordained in a packed St Andrew's Cathedral in March 1989. However, on the question of ordaining women to the priesthood, Archbishop Robinson was adamantly opposed.

Thus, the conservative nature of Sydney's theological education and of subsequent political groupings in the diocese meant that the struggle to ordain women across the Australian church would be a battle royal. As the largest diocese, Sydney could command the majority of votes in general synod and thereby veto any change for the Anglican Church in Australia.

A warning of its intentions had already come from the principal of Moore College, Dr Broughton Knox, in 1977. He appended a minority report to the general synod's Doctrine Commission, which had found no doctrinal objection to the ordination of women. The basis of his argument was the 'eternal principle of relationship' between the headship of man and the subordination of woman as mirrored in the headship of Christ over the church.[8] Knox was later to attack the women's ordination groups for their militancy and 'status-seeking'.[9]

The final argument, used by leaders of the Diocese of Sydney as events in the late 1980s moved to a climax, was that to ordain women was to depart from 'the apostolic authority as attested by the New Testament'.[10] Archbishop Robinson wrote in no uncertain terms:

> For my part, I do not regard the ordination of women to the priesthood as a negotiable matter, since I hold that our church's constitution commits us to the apostolic tradition concerning the 'mind of Christ' and the 'commandment of the Lord'.[11]

In enunciating this policy, Robinson was allying himself with the Anglo-Catholic and the Roman Catholic traditions. Sydney's old tradition of attacking Rome was suddenly being set aside in the interests of keeping women in their place. He found himself in agreement with Graham Leonard, the Anglo Catholic Bishop of London, and Father John Fleming of Adelaide, both of whom threatened to leave the Anglican Church if their respective synods voted in women priests. Fleming finally carried out his threat in 1987 and became a Catholic layman.

Robinson also warned of the possibility of schism if women were admitted to the priesthood and he did not preclude going to the secular courts if it were necessary to thwart such an undesirable outcome.

The chief support lent to Sydney's stand came from the country dioceses of Ballarat, Murray, Armidale and Wangaratta. It was Bishop John Hazlewood of Ballarat, an ardent Anglo-Catholic, who was most critical of women's ordination, announcing that it was an assault on the church and an overturning of 2 000 years of tradition.

The saga of the progress of Anglican women towards ordination has already been told in great detail by Muriel Porter in her *Women in the Church: The Great Ordination Debate*[12] and in its 1994 postscript, *The End of the Great Debate: The 1992 General Synod Decision on Women Priests*.[13] A journalist and historian who acknowledges bias,[14] she gives an eyewitness account as a member of both Melbourne and general synods at the height of the drama. Another account which delves into the theological and legal aspects of the struggle is Stuart Piggin's perceptive study, *Evangelical Christianity in Australia: Spirit, Word and World*.[15]

Both these accounts of the events which stretched from the Melbourne synod of 1976 through numerous diocesan and general synods to the climactic general synod of November 1992 are difficult to put down. It was an epic which gripped the man and woman in the street and divided the churchgoers. High emotion was generated on both sides and the press was quick to capitalise on the vision of an oppressive male hierarchy denying justice to downtrodden women.

The church, with some justification, believed that it was the victim of a media-driven campaign. Public disenchantment occurred as the church was revealed as a highly political body, often manipulating synod elections and proceedings. As the religious correspondent for the *Sydney Morning Herald*, Alan Gill, wrote in 1981: 'When it comes to artful manoeuvring,

Brisbane's first Anglican women priests, following their ordination: 1992

churchmen leave Canberra for dead.'[16]

Nor was the opposition free from politicking. The vigour with which the Movement for the Ordination of Women (MOW) pursued its cause was to arouse disquiet even among those who supported its aims.

The fact that Australian women were part of a worldwide struggle for recognition in the church added to the intensity of the debate. When the age-old citadel of male exclusivism was toppled on 11 November 1992 and the Church of England voted to admit women to the priesthood, there was wonderment and rejoicing in Australia. Surely, the Australian church and the Diocese of Sydney must perceive that the writing was on the wall?

The laity were showing signs of a change of mind, but not so clerical Sydney. They believed that they were the 'guardians of the deposit', come what may. Archbishop Robinson threatened impaired communion amongst the dioceses if the measure was passed in Australia, but it was not enough to prevent general synod from following the English precedent ten days later.[17] The women's ordination canon was passed, despite fierce opposition from Sydney delegates, by just two votes.

By the end of the year, ninety women had been ordained priests of the Anglican Church of Australia.[18]

The die was cast, but not all dioceses were prepared to ordain women immediately. Furthermore, the bitterness engendered as a result of the false steps taken on both sides threatened the Constitution of 1962 and would cause distrust for years to come. For instance, Sydney was outraged at the unilateral decision of Archbishop Carnley to ordain the first women priests in March 1992, without waiting for the stalemate in the Appellate Tribunal to be resolved. Carnley argued that he had consulted his diocesan synod and lawyers; besides, Perth had always led the way in this matter from the time his predecessor Archbishop Appleton had licensed deaconesses to preach and distribute the sacraments in 1968.

Sydney had already acted in the Supreme Court of NSW to restrain Bishop Owen Dowling of Canberra-Goulburn from ordaining women priests as early as February 1991. Now, it sought an overturning of Carnley's procedure from the same court, but it was ruled out of order. The case against Bishop Dowling dragged on for twelve months; Anglicans were generally distressed at the resort to secular courts and especially at the spending of a six figure sum on lawyers. This money was, of course, available for the litigants on both sides, but Dowling declined to accept it.

Muriel Porter argues that the court case against Bishop Dowling was 'a more significant and urgent catalyst for General Synod' than the Perth ordination, which was largely ignored once it was over. 'The Perth ordination offended a minority of church people; the public liked it.'[19] The proposed ordinations in Goulburn Cathedral aroused much more sympathy amongst the general public, because of the wide media coverage given to the rejected women. The more protracted the battle to ordain these women, the greater was the support of the general public for their cause.

When warned by the primate, Dr Keith Rayner, in February 1991 that he must go back to the Appellate Tribunal and not ordain unilaterally, Dowling at first complied for the sake of church unity. When, however, the tribunal could give no firm answer after fourteen months of deliberations, Dowling felt he could not wait and announced that he would ordain the women on 2 February 1992. He now had the backing of five other diocesan bishops. His opponents obtained an injunction in the Supreme Court of NSW to restrain him from going ahead.

With a fine sense of theatre, Dowling led the women, robed ready for priesting, through the service up to the point of ordination — whereupon he ordained only the male candidates. Public sympathy, fanned by the media, was solidly with Dowling and the women. It was vindicated when the NSW Court of Appeal finally dismissed the case on 3 July 1992.[20]

The other main error made by the opponents of women priests was their threat of schism. This made the smaller rural dioceses feel insecure. They were particularly dependent on a unified national church, representing, as many did, far-flung and often impoverished dioceses.

Archbishop Rayner was in a difficult position. He could not encourage unconstitutional behaviour, but he felt the unity of the church was all-important; on the other hand, the will of the people could not be ignored:

If the general synod is not able to find a way forward. . .
then, we face an extremely serious threat to the order and
unity of our church. . . There are now about 150 women
deacons in Australia, the majority of whom are convinced
that God is calling them to the priesthood. All of the
evidence suggests that the overall support for the ordination
of women to the priesthood is of the order of 2 to 1.[21]

In his presidential address to the fateful Anglican General
Synod of July 1992, Rayner again stressed: 'It is vital that this
general synod finds a way forward.'[22] He found support from
Archbishop Hollingworth of Brisbane who warned against the
church lapsing into 'ecclesiastical tribalism' and that the world
was watching the events of synod 'with a critical eye'.[23] Then
unexpected support came from Bishop Peter Chiswell of
Armidale — an opponent of women priests — who noted that
'the publicity of the previous six months has brought us into
disrepute'. The other country dioceses took note.[24]

Thus, on the basis of unity above all, the legislation was
passed narrowly and it needed only the convening of one more
meeting four months later to confirm the decision. In less than
a decade, the battle had been fought and won and the speed
of events, bewildering as it was to many traditional church-
people, confirmed to others that the hand of God was at work.

❈ Pressure groups involved in the Anglican ordination issue

First and most prominent of the bodies working for the change
was the Movement for the Ordination of Women. The MOW,
as it was known, began in 1983 in Melbourne, a city which
was historically more attuned to feminist causes than other
parts of the country. However, it was with the appointment
of a Sydney woman, Dr Patricia Brennan, as president in 1985,
that MOW began to take off.

An evangelical and a former missionary in Nigeria, Patricia Brennan poured her not inconsiderable energies into the Movement for five years. With her forthright — some would say, abrasive — approach, she attracted much media attention, including her own ABC programs for a time. She mobilised support from Uniting Church women and also from Catholic women. Marie Louise Uhr, the first convener of OCW — the Ordination of Catholic Women movement — attended MOW conferences, as did Sister Veronica Brady, the Loreto nun and Perth academic.[25]

The MOW, which attracted over forty men and women to its conferences from a much larger mailing list, concentrated on four strands of action. Significantly, the first was political action — the means by which change could be achieved: lobbying, demonstrations and contact with the media. Second was the nurture of all members, particularly of those seeking ordination. The third was education, involving lectures, literature and a members' library. Finally, MOW encouraged regular worship together, which included experimentation with liturgy and inclusive language.[26]

In the former activity, they were inspired by their Catholic members; in the latter, by their Uniting Church members. Inclusive language was already entering Anglican liturgy and hymnody anyway through the work of early women members of the Doctrine Commission, such as Deaconess Margaret Rodgers.

Members of MOW, who were mostly middle-class professionals, could afford to pay for the visits of overseas women clergy, who inspired them to greater efforts. The first to be brought out was the Reverend Alison Cheek, an Australian who was working in a parish in Boston. Another was Bishop Penny Jamieson of the Diocese of Dunedin in New Zealand, who first visited in 1991. Both women were forbidden 'hospitality' (the right to celebrate communion) by the church in Sydney and some other dioceses, but later visits were not so restricted.

More controversial were the visits of Elizabeth Schussler-Fiorenza, a radical American theologian. Her first visit to the MOW Conference in August 1989 signalled an explicitly feminist approach to theology, which appealed to a section of the membership. These members were generally associated with the radical magazine *Women-Church*, the publication of a group of mainly Catholic women who had first banded together in 1985. This biennial journal stressed the role of God as Father and Mother and tended to be equivocal about the position of Jesus since he was male.[27]

MOW literature, however, gave surprisingly little space to the utterances of *Women-Church*, nor to the emphasis of Elizabeth Schussler-Fiorenza, much as the members respected her and looked forward to her visits. The chief strength of MOW was its success in capturing the attention of the media: they were always available for comment and their statements were clear and apposite.

Nevertheless, some Anglicans who also wanted an inclusive church found MOW to be too strident and political. Moderates in Sydney founded a society in 1987 known as Men, Women and God: Christians for Biblical Equality. MWG, as it came to be known, was piloted by leading Sydney laity, Gerald and Rosemary Christmas, but it also received support from a number of clergy.

This group endeavoured to act as a think-tank for those contemplating the role of women in the church. Its stress was on partnership between men and women as the essence of ministry. Articles by notable evangelical church leaders who favoured women's ordination, such as F.F. Bruce, John Stott and Larry Crabb, were included in its newsletters, along with biblical and pastoral material.[28]

MWG lacked the drive of MOW and its nationwide network, being almost exclusively Sydney-based. However, it argued in such a way as to appeal to both liberal and conservative Anglicans. Its emphasis was on persuasion rather than confrontation and, for this reason, it attracted less attention than MOW in the eight years of its existence.

MWG differed from other pro and anti ordination groups in that it set out to be more holistic in its approach. It tapped into other issues which had been taboo or skated over by the church — damaged relationships in Christian marriages, spiritual injury of various kinds, physical and sexual abuse, and the treatment of women as second-class citizens in church circles. In this sense it was ahead of its time:

> We see the partnership model of relating as being more biblical than the traditional hierarchical one. We are not just a one-issue organisation pushing for women's ordination. The ordination issue is part of our total concern for healthy and balanced relationships in church, home and society.[29]

Turning to the women's groups which opposed female ordination, the earliest was Women Against the Ordination of Women, started by conservative Melbourne laywoman, Phyllis Boyd, in 1987. This group made little headway despite the high profile of its leader in synod affairs. It was later absorbed by the Association for Apostolic Ministry.

Better organised was the Equal but Different group which did not mobilise until the last minute — the week before the 21 November 1992 meeting of General Synod, when ordination was to be decided upon once and for all. Amongst the 1800 names drawn from across Australia, which appeared in the press and were handed out to delegates by women demonstrating in MOW style, were those of numerous clergy wives, most lobbying for the first time in their lives. Their document called upon members of general synod '*not* to give into pressure to ignore God's commands in order to conform to current social trends'.[30]

The clergy wives who were signatories had enlisted the names of laywomen in their parishes to swell the numbers. It is doubtful that many of these clergy wives were responding to uxorial pressure in allowing their names to go forward. On the other hand, many would have felt insecure about their role — should an ordained woman be in ministry partnership with their husbands? As has been shown, deaconesses often felt uneasy vis-a-vis clergy wives in a parish situation. In the event of women priests, whose preserve would be whose?

Opposition to women's ordination amongst men in the church was chiefly led by a society known as the Association for Apostolic Ministry (AAM), which was founded in London in 1987 as an international body — chaired initially by the Bishop of London, Graham Leonard, and the Archbishop of Sydney, Donald Robinson. Its chairman in Australia was Dr Ian Spry, a Melbourne QC. Within six months, it had been joined by fourteen Australian bishops and its total Australian membership numbered 2 000 — more than MOW and MWG put together.[31] It was an impressive show of support for the *status quo* and yet, in less than two years, the AAM would be defeated and its membership decimated.

The AAM depicted itself from the beginning as the bastion of the age-old true church; it was obsessed with the evils of feminism, which it blamed for all the social ills of the day. Women priests would bring about the destruction of the church, proclaimed its advertisements in the religious media.[32]

Two books were published in this period which supported the views of AAM. One was edited by the Melbourne academic, David Wetherell, the other written by a Melbourne priest, M. T. Gilchrist. The former, entitled *Women Priests in Australia?*, was an exploration of the case against the ordination of women by nine contributors, following the 1986 Melbourne ordination of women deacons. Wetherell himself argued that the move to ordain women was totally secular in origin:

> The origins of the political philosophy on which the women's movement seems based has only the most trifling connection — if there is any connection at all — with the religion of the incarnation, death on Calvary and events of Easter. Thus, the origins of the present agitation for women priests and bishops do not lie within what might be called authentic Christian culture, past or present.[33]

The response of the apologists for the other side was that women were vitally involved in all three of these major events and why should the women who were first and last to handle Jesus' earthly body now be excluded from doing so at the Eucharist today?[34]

More strident in its opposition to the priesting of women was M.T. Gilchrist's polemic, *The Destabilisation of the Anglican Church*, which appeared in 1991 when threats of schism were strongest from the AAM and from individual clergy in the Diocese of Sydney. The small continuing Presbyterian Church had already voted to discontinue the ordination of women in four out of its six assemblies. Gilchrist attacked the Uniting Church as 'a secularised model which has acted as a pressure group' in the move to ordain women.[35]

He seized upon the more extreme writings of the radical journal *Women-Church* to label the full gamut of the ordination movement. This journal, which had sponsored with the Catholic group WATAC the 1989 National Conference of MOW, had earlier expressed such notions as:

The time has come to call the Great Mother back from the edge of existence. . . A maternal theology would affirm those qualities symbolised by the Great Mother, an assertive, whole motherhood in all human beings. . .[36]

In such a volatile atmosphere labels could stick, but the MOW was careful not to depart from theological orthodoxy in its literature. It might have invited Elizabeth Schussler-Fiorenza to Australia, but most did not readily embrace her view of God as 'She'. It might have admired the erudition of the unorthodox scholar Barbara Theiring, but it did not publicise or support her views. Indeed, it was possible that the Catholic Church contained a stronger feminine and maternal approach to theology — derived from a reaction to the male hierarchy as much as from its Marian tradition. Thus, the newsletters of MOW and MWG stressed the principle of biblical equality rather than the 'gender' of God.

Such caution was valuable in winning the support of both laity and clergy. They were further reassured by the moderate nature of Dr Janet Scarfe's statement on her election in 1989 as first national president of MOW:

The ordination of women is a means to an end; it is not an end in itself. . . Those who support the ordination of women are striving to transform the church into a more just, more caring, less hierarchical and, I think, in many ways a less pompous organisation.[37]

For the handful of extremely able women who had been ordained in the Presbyterian Church, the ruling of the General Assembly against female ordination in September 1991 was a terrible blow. The NSW Assembly, which represented over half the continuing Presbyterians in Australia, had voted in favour of women ministers five months earlier. They were, however, outpolled at national level by the creation of numerous small presbyteries in Queensland. Current women ministers were not stripped of their office, but it was ruled that no more were to be ordained.

Following this ruling, the reverend Theodora Hobbs who had ministered at Abbotsford in NSW for nearly six years wrote to her congregation:

> You might wonder why I do not leave the church, whose power structures have comprehensively rejected women. My first and greatest reason for staying has been the parish where I have worked; your support, your acceptance of someone different from the norm, and your understanding that gender has nothing to do with the call to serve God have upheld me in some very difficult times. . .[38]

The remnant of Presbyterian women clergy find parish ministry particularly rewarding, but comment on the prejudice against women in orders and even women elders which is manifested by many male clergy and their wives. Also, like many Anglican women priests and deacons, they are dismayed at the general lack of employment opportunities for women clergy. 'It is painful to be regarded as inferior and unworthy of office because of one's gender.[39]

The Catholic perspective on the ordination issue

Tertiary-educated Catholic men and women were increasingly supportive of the concept of the ordination of women from 1880 onwards. The Catholic Church in Western countries faced a crisis of manpower as fewer men were prepared to train for the priesthood and more were leaving, chiefly because of the prescription of celibacy. Despite the evidence of opinion polls, such as the Morgan-Gallup poll of June 1987 which revealed that 49% of Catholics were in favour of women priests, as against 32% opposed, the church refused to countenance either married or women priests.[40]

Thus, Catholics faced apparently insuperable odds in changing the mind of their church. There were no synods or assemblies where laity could influence the direction, much less the implementation of church policy. Such is the hierarchical structure of the Roman Catholic Church and so enmeshed are its counsels in the toils of canon law that reformers face a Sisyphean task. Women seeking reform were especially dashed by the content of the 1988 Papal edict *Mulieris Dignitatem*, which stressed the traditional role of women as being the only one acceptable to the church.

However, calls still emanated from the USA, Holland and Austria in particular for the church to reconsider its views on the ordination of women. Australian women religious, while not pressing strongly for women priests, had become increasingly dissatisfied with the failure of the hierarchy to consult women. So in 1982, a conference of the women religious of Australia set up a body known as Women in the Australian Church. This was to be open to lay and religious, men and women, Catholic and Protestant. Its aim was to promote 'a change in the understanding of the role of women in Australian church and society'.[41]

Although it was opposed initially to the idea of women deacons and priests, WATAC linked up with MOW from 1986, both sending delegates to each other's conferences and mutually encouraging each other. Finally, a WATAC member, Marie Louise Uhr, who was a Canberra scientist and academic, founded the Ordination of Catholic Women Movement (OCW).

Commencing in 1994, OCW quickly attracted 200 members and the encouragement of certain priests, particularly of Jesuit background. However, it received a heavy blow with the publication of the apostolic letter *Ordinatio Sacerdotalis* in

1994, denying the admissibility of women to the ministerial priesthood. When this was questioned by theologians and women as to whether the ruling belonged to the 'deposit of faith', it was followed up by a pontifical *Responsum ad Dubium* which held that the ruling definitely belonged to the 'deposit of faith'.[42] Under the doctrine of papal infallibility, that seemed to be that.

However, the voice of protest was still raised in such quarters as the English Catholic journal *The Tablet*, encouraging Catholic women not to give up:

> Such an implicit admission [the Vatican's invocation of infallibility] that the Vatican's theological case has not been found compelling will not help those theologians and campaigners for female ordination, who may now find themselves faced with a dilemma of conscience. . . But for the great majority in the church. . . the Vatican's latest statement probably changes nothing. They are aware that there is no prospect of women priests under this pontificate anyway. . .[43]

A similar conclusion was reached by Fr Edmund Campion, the Sydney historian, when launching the OCW pamphlet, 'Women in the Catholic Church — A Gospel to be Proclaimed', in August 1995. He pointed out that, since 1570, documents that were 'immutable, irrevocable and never to be changed' were in fact changed or added to in due course, when conditions demanded it.

OCW, meanwhile, resolved to explore the possibility of working towards admission of women to the diaconate, as their Anglican sisters had done. Married men were already being admitted to the permanent diaconate; why should women not be also?[44]

✠ Views of churchwomen on the ordination issue

Turning to the views of active churchwomen in the 1980s and early 1990s, it is clear that, with the exception of Sydney clergy wives, the vast majority of those surveyed were in favour of the ordination of women. Women missionaries (twelve in all interviewed) were overwhelmingly in favour, having exercised similar ministries themselves when away from home. One former missionary, now in parish work in Sydney, wrote:

> Ordination is a post New Testament construct, but inasmuch as it is the 'system' in the Anglican Church for validating leadership, I think it is entirely appropriate that suitable women should be recognised for leadership roles. I do not think the Bible forbids women exercising leadership and teaching ministries (because of Jesus' recognition of women by entrusting them with the good news of the resurrection and Paul's citations of women co-workers and prophets).[45]

Another missionary returned from Pakistan commented that the Muslim view of women as stated in the Koran is that they are equal, but different. She noted that this was the very title taken up by women opponents of female ordination in Sydney since 1992.[46]

The general impression during the survey was that the younger the interviewee, the more they were likely to be in favour of ordination — and, in particular, daughters of interviewees were quoted as being strongly in favour of women's ordination. One clergy wife wrote:

> I'm very comfortable, but I know that my daughters find much to criticise. [They seem to be saying that] if they express opinions other than mainstream or orthodox, they are ignored. Young, university-educated women are keen to address social justice issues and feel that the church conveniently ignores them.[47]

Of ten leading laywomen I interviewed in the Protestant and Catholic churches, seven were in favour of women's ordination, two were ambivalent and one — the oldest interviewed — was opposed. One who was ordained in the Uniting Church commented: 'The authority of the priesthood lies in servanthood — washing feet — not in headship.'[48]

Eight women from a variety of Catholic orders were asked their views on the ordination of women. None was opposed, although two were not in favour of it for themselves. 'Women who become honorary male priests are not the answer. . . The priesthood is an elite cut off from the rest of the community.'[49] Most were enthusiastic and positive about the benefits of women's ordination to the church:

> The church would benefit greatly from a feminine perspective on its decisions, structures and ministry. This would be reflected in a less dogmatic, less hierarchical and more compassionate church.[50]

Some argued that the move to ordain women was a God-driven initiative:

> I think this new direction could be the work of the Holy Spirit today and a sign of the time. The expression of church is changing dramatically and so the expression of priesthood must change with it.[51]

However, none of the Catholic sisters interviewed was optimistic about an early breakthrough in the drive to ordain women priests. One said:

> Married priests will come first (particularly with the precedent of the Greek Orthodox communion); Rome will not be persuaded to ordain women priests because of any concept of a shortage of priests. [Instead] they will import some from Asia and Africa.[52]

All Catholic interviewees agreed that it was important for the other churches to demonstrate the efficacy of women priests over a considerable period before their church would move in the matter.

✠ The state of the ordination issue by the early 1990s

The 1980s and early 1990s witnessed a radical change in perceptions of the role of women in the church. No longer were women hiding in history; instead, they were front page news. From 1986 to 1992, their quest for ordination was constantly featured in electronic as well as print media. Members of other denominations watched as the Anglican Church was convulsed by the women's struggle for a share in leadership in that church. If the Anglican Church capitulated, where would that leave the even more conservative Catholic and Orthodox churches?

In the end, a typical Anglican compromise was reached in November 1992: those dioceses which were ready to ordain women could; the others need not. The church was still intact, although divided between the view that the last decade had been an aberration in its history and the conclusion that change had been wrought by the Holy Spirit.

The ordination issue had without a doubt caught the church on the wrong foot. For centuries, it had neglected women in assigning significant roles to its members. It was suspicious of the women's movement for its secular origins, although close scrutiny would reveal that such churches as the Catholics and Quakers had played their part in bringing about second wave feminism.

For an increasing number of both men and women, the struggle for ordination had become a justice issue. Should church order continue to reflect first century society? Should the church use women as leaders in primitive situations, but not in established society?

The speed of change was also a problem for the church. Events certainly moved at a bewildering pace in the 1980s and 1990s — far too quickly for the Anglican Church, but agonisingly slowly for those women who were convinced of the reality of their calling.

Conclusion

THE TAPESTRY IS COMPLETE. The richness of its fabric reflects the depth and variety of the contribution of women to the Australian church over two centuries. Yet there is a dark thread of oppression and pain interwoven thoughout. Not only have the gifts of women been frequently overlooked by the church they have served, but the work and aspirations of women religious, missionaries, clergy wives and laity have been unsung for too long. This is an attempt to redress that imbalance.

Conditions for the church and its women members varied widely over the period 1788 to 1988. Australia grew from a penal colony with a chaplain from the established Church of England to a pluralistic nation of seventeen million people. Within that time span, Aboriginal dispossession aside, women began as pioneers and ended largely as members of a comfortable urban society. The churches were also transformed from primitive bodies working in makeshift conditions to powerful and, in many cases, wealthy institutions with agencies in every part of society.

Where did women fit into this pattern of expansion? In the earliest days, because of the shortage of clergy, they were allowed to assume roles which were normally the province of men — preaching, taking services and catechising. This was also common practice on the mission field from the 1880s onwards. Thus Georgiana Molloy was the founder of the church at Augusta, Western Australia, and its pastor, while Ellen Arnold and Katie Miller played a like role in Bengal and Tanzania respectively. Once the trail was blazed, however, a male hierarchy emerged to take over the reins of government.

Furthermore, although the workforce and membership of the church came to be predominantly female by the early twentieth century, women were excluded — except in the smaller Nonconformist churches — from power-sharing. They were expected to be foot-soldiers in the church militant, but never in command.

The strongest tension between men and women during the consolidation phase of the church was between the orders and the Catholic hierarchy. Women's orders prized their independence of state and, at times, of church; their allegiance was first to a heavenly Master and then to their own community. However, the hierarchy needed them if the church were to grow. Their numbers were also greater than parish clergy and men religious put together, which made the masculine need to control them more imperative. The question of *authority* lay at the root of the struggle between the orders and the hierarchy: braver souls began to question the assumption that power should always reside with the male.

The chief impulse for feminism within the church emanated from the Catholic orders and from the Quakers who had consistently led the way in matters of social action. However, until the 1970s, the majority of laywomen were far from being feminists. They worked quietly in their parishes and church societies, fundraising, visiting and looking after the church fabric. For some time, they had comprised the larger part of the congregation. They undertook honorary teaching and welfare roles in the name of the church. However, as they looked about, they could see very few to succeed them in the work.

Socio-economic change was now fast overtaking the church and its voluntary army. The majority of married women entered the paid workforce. At the same time, tertiary education became widely available to women and, with it, an open door into the professions. With the advent of second wave feminism, younger women began to seek an ecclesiastical role in the church. This quest was seen as part of the ascent of women generally to executive roles in the wider community.

However, it was at this stage that the church drew back. In a context of social change, it had always tended to trail rather than to set agenda. The decades of opposition to the abolition of slavery by devout nineteenth century Christians, the reluctance of the church to allow women property rights or freedom from a violent marriage — all bore witness to the stubborn conservatism of the church.

Even good women of high principles, like the early members of the Mothers' Union, believed they were doing God's will in excluding divorced women from their membership. Those seeking a fairer role for women could not detect any link between the church's attitude and Jesus' affirming behaviour towards women, although there were exceptions like Bishop Geoffrey Cranswick and certain missionary clergy.

The decision of many churches in the last decades of the twentieth century to exclude women from equality of ministry was to cause much distress to those who believed they were called to an ordained ministry. The church appeared hypocritical in its willingness to allow women to found and lead churches overseas, but to deny them that right when they returned to their own country. The resistance of a number of clergy and their wives in the Anglican and Presbyterian churches made the issue appear to be a political rather than a spiritual one. The equal sharing of the priesthood could pose a real threat to clergy tenure. Too many took refuge in 'proof texts' without reflecting sufficiently on the tenor of scripture and the exhilarating attitude of Jesus towards women. The injunctions of St Paul against women speaking in church must be balanced against the manifesto of Galatians 3: 28, which declares against sexism, racism and slavery.

The refusal of Rome even to allow debate on the ordination of women has been a cause of dismay for many Catholics. Neither the rapid decline of male ordinands for the priesthood, nor the frustration of women religious and laity wishing to expand their ministry has made any difference to the intransigence of the church hierarchy. The issue will not go away; neither will the pain it has caused.

'Sometimes I feel the church puts structures before the movements of God's Holy Spirit in life and the ministry of the church. . .'[1] commented Mary Andrews in 1970, and it is certain that the church has yet to grasp the vision of the joy of ministry in which men and women are complementary and unfettered and in which the whole emphasis is on service rather than roles.

Women in the Australian church have come a long way since penal days, but full emancipation is still not theirs. 'Daughters of freedom' they may be theologically, but in many churches they are still constrained.

Endnotes

Chapter 1

1. M. Kiddle, *Caroline Chisholm*, Melbourne University Press, 1950, pp.51–53
2. A. Summers, *Damned Whores and God's Police*, Melbourne University Press, 1975, pp.225–290
3. Miriam Dixson, *The Real Matilda: Women and Identity in Australia, 1788–1975*, Penguin, 1976, p.32
4. Submission of the Sydney Anglican Diocese to the Royal Commission on Human Relationships (1975) in Dixson, *op. cit.*, p.49
5. Rachel Henning to Etta Henning, 17 September 1864, in *Letters of Rachel Henning*, D. Adams (ed.), *Bulletin*, 1952, p.77
6. Women, Class and History, E. Windschuttle (ed.), Fontana, 1980, p.43. See also J. Roberts, *Maybanke Anderson*, Hale & Iremonger, 1993, pp.73 and 96
7. A term for the early, native-born children in the colony.
8. Margaret Reeson, *Currency Lass*, Albatross, 1985, pp.109, 129–131, 176 and 227
9. Cited in O. Thorpe, *Mary MacKillop*, Principal Press, 1982, pp.7–8
10. Letter of Catherine Booth to William Booth, cited in Flora Larsson, *My Best Men Are Women*, Hodder & Stoughton, 1974, p.15
11. Sr Cathleen O'Carrigan, historian for the Sisters of Charity. Interview, June 1991
12. D.P. McCann and C.R. Strain, *Polity and Praxis: A Program for American Practical Theology*, Winston Press, 1985, in S. Piggin, *From Independence to Domesticity: Masculinity in Australian History and the Female Ordination Debate*, Studies in Australian Christianity, Vol.2, M. Hutchinson and E. Campion (eds), Centre for the Study of Australian Christianity, 1994, p.151

13. B. Taylor, *Eve and the New Jerusalem*, Virago, 1983, pp.124–126, and L. Davidoff and C. Hall, *Family Fortunes: Men and Women of the English Middle Class, 1780–1850*, Hutchinson, 1987, pp.25 and 78

14. F.K. Prochaska, *Women and Philanthropy in Nineteenth Century England*, Oxford, 1980, pp.42–43

15. J. Ruskin, *Sesame and Lilies* (first edition 1893), Ward Lock, 1911, pp.xviii and 108

16. J. Godden, 'Philanthropy and the Woman's Sphere in Sydney, 1870-1900', PhD thesis, Macquarie University, 1983, p.ii

17. Caroline Chisholm, *Emigration and Transportation Relatively Considered* (1847), in Summers, *op. cit.*, pp.301–302

18. Sir Henry Parkes to NSW Legislative Assembly, 14 August 1866, V. and P., NSW Legislative Assembly, ML

19. Sabine Willis, *Homes Are Divine Workshops*, E. Windschuttle (ed.) *op. cit.*, pp. 173–191

20. I. McCorkindale, *The Old Order Changeth*, WCTU, 1938, ML

21. Summers, *op.cit.* pp.40–60

22. *Ibid*, p.323

23. J. Tregenza, *Professor of Democracy: The Life of Charles Henry Pearson*, Melbourne University Press, 1968, p.46

24. J.A. Hone, 'The Movement for the Higher Education of Women in Victoria in the later 19th Century', MA thesis, Monash, 1966, p.37

25. W.V. Mole and A.H. Treweeke, *The History of the Women's College within the University of Sydney*, Halstead, 1953, p.33

26. Summers, *op. cit.*, p.333

27. *Ibid*, p.402

28. S. Willis, *op. cit.*, p.187

29. *Ibid*, pp.99–102 and 116–122. See also S. Judd and K. Cable, *Sydney Anglicans*, AIO, 1987, pp.175–191

30. Carmel Shute, 'Heroines and Heroes: Sexual Mythology in Australia, 1914–1918' in *Hecate*, January 1975, p.7, in Summers, *op. cit.*, p.382

31. Summers, *op. cit.*, pp.380–385

32. M. Gilding, 'Gender Roles in Contemporary Australia', in *Contemporary Australian Feminism*, K.P. Hughes (ed.), Longman Cheshire, 1994, p.106

33. K. Reiger, *The Disenchantment of the Home*, OUP, 1985, p.56

34. Jackson, *op. cit.*, pp.120–142

35. For a study of clergy wives in a NSW and a Victorian town covering the period 1905–1985 which reveals changing attitudes towards their role, see K. Dempsey, 'Ministers' Wives: Continuity and Change in Relation to their Husbands' Work', in *The Force of the Feminine*, H. Franklin (ed.), Allen and Unwin, 1986, pp.81–99. See also C. West's contrasting study of Anglican ministers' wives in the Diocese of Sydney

conducted in 1991, Women's Studies Seminar project, University of Sydney.

36. R. McGinley, 'Catholic Women's Religious Institutes in Australia, 1830–1940: Some Considerations', in *Long, Patient Struggle*, E. Campion and M. Hutchinson (eds), Centre for the Study of Australian Christianity, 1994, pp.89–111

37. See chapters 11 and 13.

Chapter 2

1. Some of the marines had brought their wives with them and these women landed with their husbands a few days later at Camp Cove, according to Watkin Tench, *Narrative of the Expedition to Botany Bay*, London, 1789, p.6, cited in Portia Robinson, *The Hatch and Brood of Time*, OUP, 1985, p.70.

2. Eliza Marsden to Mary Stokes, 1 May 1796, in *Some Private Correspondence of the Reverend Samuel Marsden and Family, 1794–1824*, G. Mackaness (ed.), D.S. Ford, 1942, p.14. Also in Hassall Correspondence, ML, A1699\2

3. Richard Johnson to Henry Fricker, 30 May 1787, Letters of Richard Johnson, ML, MSS Ajl\5

4. Sheila Wright, 'Quakerism and Its Implications for Quaker Women: The Woman Itinerant Ministers of York Meeting, 1780–1840', in *Women in the Church: Studies in Church History*, W.J. Sheils and Diana Wood, Blackwell, 1990, p.404. See also G. Eliot, *Adam Bede*, J.M. Dent, 1976, especially chapter 2.

5. William Bull to John Newton, December 1786, in J. Bonwick, *Australia's First Preacher*, London, 1898, p.61. Newton was vicar of St Mary Woolnoth, London, at the time and a leader of the Eclectic Society, a small group of evangelical churchmen who agitated for the appointment of a chaplain to the new colony.

6. 'From her company I derive neither pleasure nor profit,' said Elizabeth Macarthur of Mary Johnson, in Portia Robinson, *Women of Botany Bay*, Macquarie Library, 1988, p.307. Eliza Marsden to Mary Stokes, 13 December 1794, praises the kindness of Mary Johnson, *Correspondence of the Reverend Samuel Marsden. . .*, op. cit., p.8, and Hassall Correspondence, 1699\2, ML, p.14.

7. Of those convicted in the trial years of 1782 to 1787 and transported to Botany Bay, over two-thirds came from London, according to P. Robinson, op. cit., List A1, pp. 281–282.

8. Richard Johnson to Henry Fricker, 15 November 1788 and 9 April 1790, Ajl\7–8

9. Neil McIntosh, *Richard Johnson, Chaplain to the Colony of New South Wales*, Library of Australian History, 1978, p.47

10. Richard Johnson to Henry Fricker, 9 April 1790, M.L., MSS Ajl\8. The Moravians sold themselves into slavery in order to win the galley slaves to Christianity.

11. Neil McIntosh, *op. cit.*, p.42

12. *Ibid*

13. John Newton to Richard Johnson, 1794, in Neil McIntosh, *op. cit.*, p.83

14. Marsden boasted of feeding a total of eighty mouths on his many establishments, Samuel Marsden to Henry Williams, 5 January 1829, Marsden Papers, ML, MSS C44, also in A. Yarwood, *Samuel Marsden: The Great Survivor,* Melbourne University Press, 1977, p.88 and Mary Cover Hassall to Rev. Thomas Hassall, January 1817, Hassall Correspondence, 1813–1828, ML, MSS A280.

15. Neil McIntosh, *op. cit.*, p.43

16. Hazel King, *Elizabeth Macarthur,* Hodder, 1984, p.4

17. Marsden Diary, 2 March 1794, in A. Yarwood, *op. cit.*, pp.29–30

18. 'Ann Marsden to Mary Stokes, 18 June 1813, 4 March 1816 and 20 August 1820', in *Correspondence of the Reverend Samuel Marsden. . .*, *op. cit.*, pp.48–49, 57–59 and 76

19. Eliza Marsden to John Piper, *loc. cit.*

20. Eliza Marsden to Mary Stokes, 7 November 1812, in *Correspondence of the Reverend Samuel Marsden*, *op. cit.*, p.47. Marsden also took his daughters — Mary in 1830 and Martha in 1837 — with him to New Zealand to help him in declining years. His only surviving son, Charles, was not a reliable person.

21. Margaret Reeson, *Currency Lass,* Albatross, 1985, pp.15–16

22. *Ibid*, pp.36–37

23. Anne Marsden to Mary Stokes, 20 August 1820, in *Correspondence of the Reverend,* Samuel Marsden, *op. cit.*, p.76

24. *Ibid*, and also Beverley Earnshaw, *Fanned into Flame: The Spread of the Sunday School in Australia,* Diocesan Board of Education, 1980

25. Margaret Reeson, *op. cit.*, pp.109, 122–131

26. *Ibid*, p.176

27. *Ibid*, p.99

28. *Ibid*, p.227 and also Stuart Piggin, *Helpmeets and Heroines: Women and the History of Australian Evangelicalism,* Wollongong Mothers' Union, 1988

29. Margaret Reeson, *op. cit.*, pp.249–251. It was in the bearing of this child in distant England that she died at the age of twenty-six.

30. Alexandra Hasluck, *Portrait with a Background: A Life of Georgiana Molloy,* OUP, 1955, pp.1–33. The Molloy Correspondence is to be found in the Western Australian Archives and the Battye Library, Perth.

31. *Ibid*, p.5

32. *Ibid*, p.73 and also S. de Vries-Evans, *Pioneer Women, Pioneer Land*, Angus & Robertson, 1987, pp.176–196

33. *Ibid*, pp.76 and 93

34. Sabina Molloy was later to marry Matthew Hale, Notebook — Journal of Georgiana Molloy, 1836, MSS Collection, Battye Library

35. S. de Vries-Evans, *op. cit.*, pp.190–194

36. One plant was named after her — the *boronia molloyae*. *Ibid*, p.195

37. *Christian Advocate and Wesleyan Record*, 19 December 1867, p.123

38. Elizabeth Windschuttle (ed.), *Women, Class and History*, Fontana, 1988, p.59

39. Samuel Marsden to J.T. Bigge, 18 March 1821, Bonwick Transcripts, Box 27, ML, in *loc. cit.*, pp.60–61

40. *Ibid*, p.62 and also Helen Heney, *Australia's Founding Mothers*, Nelson, 1978, p.203

41. John Ritchie, *Lachlan Macquarie: A Biography*, Melbourne University Press, 1986, pp.88–135

42. E. Windschuttle, *op. cit.*, pp.63–64. Also B.H. Fletcher, *A Governor Maligned.*, OUP, 1984, p.309 and D. Peyser, *A History of Welfare Work in Sydney from 1788–1900*, JRHS, Vol. 25, pp.119–120

43. *Sydney Gazette*, 21 June 1826 and 12 May 1827

44. Report of the Board of Management of the Female Factory, 19 January 1829, HRA 1, xiv, p.657

45. B.H. Fletcher, *op. cit.*, p.310

46. Fanny McLeay complained that Eliza had appointed her Treasurer and Secretary of the new school against her will. *Ibid*, p.311

47. E. Windschuttle, *op. cit.*, p.46

48. Published by James Tegg, Sydney, 1837, ML

49. *Ibid*

50. Eliza Darling to Henry Dumaresq, 20 May 1820, Letters 1820–1835 (Allport Library, Hobart), in B.H. Fletcher, *op. cit.*, p.31

51. B.H. Fletcher, *op. cit.*, p.313

52. *Sydney Gazette*, 26 April 1826

53. In B.H. Fletcher, *op. cit.*, pp.307–308

54. Eliza Darling to Edward Dumaresq, 13 November 1847, in B.H. Fletcher, p.313

55. *Ibid*

56. Eliza Darling to Edward Dumaresq, 20 March 1849, in Allport Library

57. Elizabeth Fry to Jane Franklin, in Frances J. Woodward, *A Portrait of Jane: A Life of Lady Franklin*, Hodder & Stoughton, 1951, p.197

58. F.J. Woodward, *op. cit.*, pp.213–217

59. *Ibid*

60. Jane Franklin to Elizabeth Fry, 3 August 1841, *Letters of Sir John and Lady Jane Franklin*, G. Mackaness (ed.), Vol. 2, Review Press, 1977, p.22

61. F.J. Woodward, *op. cit.*, p.247

62. The Illawarra Diary of Lady Jane Franklin, 10–14 May, 1839. Michael Organ (ed.), Illawarra Historical Publications, 1985, p.8, indicates her close friendship with the Rev. Matthew Devenish-Meares and also with the devout Captain Robert Westmacott.

63. F.J. Woodward, *op. cit.*, p.211

64. 'Jacqueline Eales, Samuel Clarke and the Wives of Godly Women in Seventeenth Century England', W. Sheils and D. Wood (eds), *op. cit.*, pp.374–376. Lady Mary Vere was a devout patron of clergy in late seventeenth century England, who worked indefatigably for the church and its expansion.

65. James Waldersee, *Catholic Society and New South Wales, 1788-1860*, University of Sydney Press, 1974, pp.36, 218 and 259

66. For example, the Sykes correspondence, treated by Alexandra Hasluck in *Unwilling Emigrants: A Study of the Convict Period of Western Australia*, OUP, 1959

Chapter 3

1. For a treatment of evangelicalism and its influence on Victorian church and society, see G.R. Balleine, *A History of the Evangelical Party in the Church of England*, CBR Press, 1951. Also W.O. Chadwick, *The Victorian Church*, Vol.I, A. & C. Black, 1966, pp.468–476 and D.W. Bebbington, *Evangelicals in Modern Britain: A History from the 1730s to the Present Day*, Unwin Hyman, 1989. For evangelicalism in Australia, see S. Judd and K. Cable, *Sydney Anglicans*, AIO, 1987, pp.111–121 and 150–153.

2. Findings of Kenneth and Leonie Cable in compiling their Register of Australian Anglican Clergy, 1788-1952

3. Published in London by Holdsworth and Ball, ML

4. *Ibid*, p.3

5. James Hassall, *In Old Australia*, R.S. Huws & Co., 1902, pp.16 and 170 in A. Yarwood, *op. cit.*, pp.201–202 and 264

6. Nonconformist clergy wives often had to rear large families alone or with the help of one Aboriginal girl, because of their husband's meagre stipends.

7. Mrs Edward (Janet) Millett, *An Australian Parsonage or The Settler and the Savage in Western Australia*, 1872, pp.128–146

8. *Ibid*, p.345

9. *Ibid*, p.63. See also pp.246–268 and 360

10. James Hassall, *op. cit.*, p.82

11. James Cameron, *Centenary History of the Presbyterian Church*, Angus & Robertson, 1905

12. Margaret Reeson, *Currency Lass*, Albatross, 1988, p.77. It was the policy of WMMS that its missionaries had to be unmarried in their first term. See S. Piggin, *Making Evangelical Missionaries*, Sutton Courtenay Press, 1984, p.121, n. 86.

13. Interview [January 1990] with Mary Conti, daughter of Rev. William Mcllwraith, Presbyterian minister at Dunoon, Clunes and later Grafton from 1909. Her mother, Margaret, was one of the first women graduates of the University of Sydney, but was never able to exercise any other role but that of helpmeet.

14. A. Cambridge, *Thirty Years in Australia*, M. Bradstock & L. Wakeling (eds), NSW University Press, 1989, Vol. 1, pp.220–224 and Vol. 2, p.30. See also Audrey Tate, *Ada Cambridge, Her Life and Work: 1844 to 1926*, Melbourne University Press, 1990

15. A. Cambridge, *op. cit.*,Vol. 1, p.226

16. A. Cambridge to E. Turner, 7 August 1896 in Ada Cambridge, *Some Episodes*, n.d., typescript, ML, MSS C842

17. A. Cambridge, *Thirty Years in Australia*, Vol. 2, p.70

18. From a sermon entitled, 'The Wife: A Mirror of Maidenhood', in the *Christian Advocate and Wesleyan Record*, September 1859, ML

19. Douglas Pike, *A Paradise of Dissent*, Longmans, 1957, pp.300–303, 310–311, 331, 381–386 and 493

20. The *Weekly Advocate*, August-September 1888

21. The *Baptist Recorder*, May 1924, quoted by Mrs Lorna Ollif in her paper, 'Women's Place in the Baptist Church'. Read to the Baptist Historical Society of NSW on 21 February 1980.

22. Interview with Mary Conti [January 1990], daughter of Margaret Mcllwraith.

23. Interview with Helen Sharpe [March1990], daughter-in-law of Constance Sharpe, wife of the Reverend George Sharpe, whose missionary home was in Ryde, NSW

24. Diary of Jessie Newth, 15 August 1890, Journal of the Hungerford and Associated Families Society, Vol. 2, No.1, May 1993

25. *Ibid*, 23 August 1890

26. D. Hulme-Moir, *The Edge of Time*, Christian Outreach Book Service, 1988. Contains extracts from the diaries.

27. *Ibid*, pp.183–184 and xi of introduction.

28. For example, the protection of Archbishop Wright when W.G.Hilliard fell foul of his churchwardens over churchmanship issues in 1916 in Ashfield parish saved a certain resignation. See Janet West, *Innings of Grace: A Life of Bishop W.G. Hilliard*, Standard, 1987, pp.44–49.

29. *The Lady's Realm*, 24 vols, 1896–1908, Vol.1, 1896, pp.288–289. For these portraits of English bishops' wives, I am indebted to Robert Withycombe's witty paper entitled, 'No Place for Mrs Proudie: The Role and Expectations of the Colonial Bishop's Wife', read to the Ecclesiastical History Society's Conference, York, July 1989

30. *Ibid*, Vol. 6, 1899, p.146

31. Janet West, *The Early Life and English Background of Bishop W.G. Broughton: First Bishop of Australia*, MA thesis, University of Sydney (1972), pp.28–29

32. *Ibid*, p.82. See also G.P. Shaw, *Patriarch and Patriot: William Grant Broughton, 1788–1853*, Melbourne University Press, 1978, p.182.

33. *Selections from the Prayers and Private Devotions of Mrs Sarah Broughton*, Sydney, 1849, ML. See also James Hassall, *op. cit.*, p.64.

34. Frances Perry's account of the overland journey of Bishop Perry and herself in February 1849 is in the Reverend G. Cox, *Notes on Gippsland History*, No. 38, M.L. See also *Contributions to an Amateur Magazine in Prose and Verse*, Richard Perry (ed.), Booth, 1857, pp.73–121.

35. Mrs Perry's Journal, *loc. cit.*, p.79

36. *Ibid*, p.140

37. *Ibid*, pp.143–165

38. *Ibid*, p.168. See also Patricia Clarke, *The Governesses: Letters from the Colonies, 1862–1882*, Hutchinson, 1985, pp.64, 65 and 134.

39. A. de Q. Robin, *Charles Perry: Bishop of Melbourne*, University of Western Australia Press, 1967, p.20. See also 'Barbara Darling: Some Leading Women in the History of the Anglican Church in Australia' in *Australian and New Zealand Religious History: 1788–1988*, R.S.M. Withycombe (ed.), 1988, p.145

40. D. Foskett, *John Harden of Brathay Hall: 1772–1847*, Kendal, 1974. An account of Jane Barker's family and upbringing. Aunt Rankin was a product of the Scottish Revival.

41. K.J. Cable, *Mrs Barker and Her Diary*, JRAHS, 1968, Vol. 54, part I, pp.67–105.

42. The *Melbourne Messenger*, 13 April 1876, ML. See also the *Australian Churchman*, March 1876.

43. A.E. David to R.T. Davidson, February 1904, Davidson Papers, Vol. 90, f.206. Quoted in Withycombe, *op. cit.* p.11.

44. H.H. Montgomery to R.T. Davidson, February 1904, Davidson Papers, Vol. 90, fols. 236–237. Quoted in Withycombe, *ibid.*

45. *Goulburn Herald*, 30 November 1898

46. *Goulburn Herald*, 28 November 1898

47. B. Montgomery, *A Field Marshal in the Family*, Constable, 1973, pp.114–116

48. M.M. [Maud Montgomery], *Bishop Montgomery: A Memoir*, SPG, 1933, pp.29–31. Quoted in Withycombe, *op. cit.*

49. Diary of Archbishop J.C. Wright, 13 December 1909. In the possession of the family.

50. Interview with Marie Moore [daughter of the Presbyterian minister, the Reverend John Christian, minister at Campbelltown, NSW, in the 1930s], 18 March 1995

Chapter 4

1. *Exploring Women's Past: Essays in Social History*, Patricia Crawford (ed.), Allen & Unwin, 1984, pp. 15 and 30–32

2. The Society of the Sacred Heart schools at Elizabeth Bay and Rose Bay attracted the children of the wealthy in NSW and expected high and cultivated standards of education from them. However, music and drawing had already been part of the syllabus offered by the Sisters of Charity at St Vincent's College (founded in 1858).

3. 'The love of Christ constrains us' (2 Corinthians 5: 14)

4. L. Dilly and C. Jones, *The Daughters of Charity of St Vincent de Paul* (unpublished), 1990, pp.1–4

5. She was assisted in this task by the Jesuit priest, Robert St Leger. A copy of the constitution is to be found in the Archives of the Religious Sisters of Charity of Australia, A102/1. See also G. Davis, *Annals of the Sisters of Charity* (unpublished), 1903, ASC

6. *History of the Sisters of the Church in Australia* (unpublished), p.12, ASC. See also C. O'Carrigan, *The Spirit of the Pioneer Sisters of Charity*, (unpublished), Potts Point, 1976

7. M.M.K. O'Sullivan, *A Cause of Trouble? Irish Nuns and English Clerics*, Crossing Press, 1995, p.15

8. Polding to Murray, 4 October 1841, Irish Archives of the Sisters of Charity, in M.M.K. O'Sullivan, *op. cit.*, p. 59

9. *History of the Sisters of the Church in Australia*, op. cit., p.14, ASC

10. For a thorough treatment of the sisters' financial position, see chapter 5 of M.M.K. O'Sullivan, *op. cit.*

11. Polding to Murray, 4 October 1841

12. Murray to Polding, 14 November 1840, in M.M.K. O'Sullivan, *op. cit.*, p. 61; and O'Brien to Aikenhead, 16 October 1844, *ibid*, p.64

13. *History of the Sisters of the Church in Australia*, op. cit., pp.58–60

14. *Ibid*, pp.62–65

15. They arrived in 1847 and carried out similar work to that started in Parramatta. Shirley King, 'Quietly, Without Fuss: Catholic Religious Sisters in Tasmania' in *Women, Faith and Fetes, op. cit.*, pp. 80–81

16. Expressed in 1846 and recalled by Alicia De Lacy in a letter to Mother M.F. McCarthy, 25 May 1859, ASC

17. O'Sullivan, *op. cit.*, pp.193–194

18. People outside the order, especially in this case businessmen and doctors, some of whom were Protestant. D. Birchley, *John McEncroe: Colonial Democrat*, Collins Dove, 1986, p.154

19. History of the Sisters of the Church, *op. cit.*, pp. 115–120 and *Sydney Morning Herald*, 4 March 1859

20. Moira O'Sullivan feels that the Bible incident may have been engineered by Gregory. He certainly made the insulting accusation that the trustees of the hospital would profit financially from their position. See Moira O'Sullivan, *op. cit.*, pp.195 and 218

21. Sister A. Baptista De Lacy to Sister M. Clare Dunn, 10 April 1875, ASC

22. Interview with Sister Gerard McGlynn, Good Samaritans Archivist, St Scholastica's Convent, Glebe, 22 November 1991

23. M. McEwen, *A Living Stream: Sisters of the Good Samaritan, 1857–1924* (unpublished), p.110. See also *Memoirs of M.M. Dorothea Hanly* (unpublished), AGS

24. M. McEwen, *op. cit.*, p.112

25. *History of the North Sydney Foundation of the Order of the Sisters of Mercy*, with Letters of M. Ignatius McQuoin (1865), S. Price (ed.) (unpublished), 1987, pp.1–2, ASM

26. *Ibid*

27. *op. cit.*, pp.2–4. The Marist Fathers, it must be noted, suggested the exchange because they regarded the convent building as sub-standard and were in a better position financially to renovate it. In exchange, they offered to build the sisters a chapel and refectory in their new quarters. See J. Hosie, *Challenge: The Marists in Colonial Australia*, Allen & Unwin, 1987, p.242

28. S. Price, *op. cit.*, pp.4–5

29. *Ibid*, p.6

30. J.T. Reilly, 'Reminiscences of Fifty Years Residence in Western Australia' (1903), in N. Turner, *Catholics in Australia*, Collins Dove, 1992, Vol. 1, p.130

31. M.A. Gaudrey, *Mercy from Generation to Generation* (unpublished), p.11, ASM

32. M.O'Donoghue, *Mother Vincent Whitty: Women and Education in a Masculine Society*, Melbourne University Press, 1972, pp.30–82

33. *Ibid*, pp.90–121

34. *History of the North Sydney Foundation. . .* , *op. cit.*, p.2

35. M. Ignatius McQuoin to 'My dear child', 23 October 1879, *op. cit.*, p.29

36. Mary Kavanagh, *The Educational Work of the Presentation Sisters in Victoria, 1873-1960*, MEd thesis, University of Melbourne (1965)

37. B.T. David and S. Tearle, 'Centenary of the Wagga Wagga Presentation Sisters' in *Australian Catholic Historical Society Journal*, Vol. 6, 1918-1980, pp.36–39

38. M. Purcell, 'The Original Sin, Submission as Survival: Women Religious in the Early Maitland Diocese', S. Willis (ed.), *op. cit.*, pp.197–203

39. Interview with Sister Leila Barlow, SSH, 31 May 1991

40. In D. Cave, *The Pedagogical Traditions of the Religious of the Sacred Heart in France and Australia*, Melbourne Studies in Education, 1985, p.34

41. The foundation of Sancta Sophia College and the achievements of the SSH in Japan will be treated in chapters 8 and 9.

42. M. Foale, *The Josephite Story*, St Joseph's Generalate, 1989, pp.2–3

43. O. Thorpe, *Mary MacKillop*, Principal Press, 1982, pp.7–8

44. D.Lyne, *Mary Mackillop: Spirituality and Charisma*, Edward & Shaw, 1984, pp.86–88

45. O.Thorpe, *op. cit.*, p.13 and pp.65–68. For Woods' dream of an institute for the poor, see Woods to MacKillop, 23 August and 12 and 19 September, in M. Foale, *op. cit.*, p.19

46. Woods to MacKillop, 23 August 1870, in M. Foale, *op. cit.*, p.18

47. MacKillop to Woods, 5 March 1870, MacKillop Correspondence, ASJ

48. MacKillop to Monsignor Kirby, 13 November 1873, ASJ

49. MacKillop to Woods, 21 October 1871, in O. Thorpe, *op. cit.*, p.107

50. O. Thorpe, *op. cit.*, pp.160–164

51. Notes taken from Bishop J. Quinn's sermon, given on 30 November 1879 at St Joseph's, Kangaroo Point, in D. Lyne, *op. cit.*, pp.147–148

52. In O. Thorpe, p.164

53. *Ibid*, p.169. Those sisters of St Joseph's who decided to remain behind in Queensland and Bathurst under diocesan control adopted a black habit and were known as Black Josephites.

54. Even Cardinal Moran in December 1889 attempted to treat the Josephites as a diocesan institute. See M. Foale, *op. cit.*, pp.177–179

55. *Ibid*, p.234

56. M. Sophie McGrath, *These Women? Women Religious in the History of Australia: Sisters of Mercy, Parramatta, 1888-1988*, University of NSW Press, 1989, p.5

57. Anne McLay, 'The Feminisation of Structures in Religious Orders', in *The Force of the Feminine: Women, Men and the Church*, M.A. Franklin (ed.), Allen & Unwin, 1986, pp.149–153

Chapter 5

1. M. Vicinus, *Independent Women: Work and Community for Single Women, 1850–1920*, Virago, 1985, pp.1–3

2. In 1890, 54% of the population attended church in Victoria as opposed to 14% in 1851. In W. Phillips, 'Statistics on Churchgoing and Sunday School Attendance in Victoria: 1851–1901,' Australian Historical Statistics Bulletin, No. 5, May 1982, p.36, in H. R. Jackson, *Churches and People in Australia and New Zealand: 1860–1930*, Allen & Unwin, 1987, p.104

3. The opinion of an early Victorian clergyman, quoted in F.K. Prochaska, *Women and Philanthropy in Nineteenth Century England*, Clarendon, 1988, p.21

4. Ruth Teale, 'Matron, Maid and Missionary: The Work of Anglican Women in Australia' in *Women, Faith and Fetes*, S. Willis (ed.), WCC, Dove, 1977, p.120

5. *Ibid*, p.119. See also A. Cambridge, *Thirty Years in Australia*, Methuen, 1903, pp.88–89 and 123

6. Address of the Rev. H.D. Sealy-Vidal to the Bathurst Synod, *Bathurst Times*, 23 July 1906, in Ruth Teale, *op. cit.*, p.118

7. F.K. Prochaska, *op. cit.*, p.66

8. The more extreme Protestants referred to Catholic bazaars as 'gambling hells', *Baptist Magazine*, 1 March 1911, in R. Broome, *Treasure in Earthen Vessels*, UQP, 1948, pp.149–150

9. Sir James Stephen, *Essays in Ecclesiastical Biography* (2 vols), London, 1849, i, p.382, in F.K. Prochaska, *op. cit.*, p.28

10. Sydney City Mission Annual Report: 1870–1871, ML

11. Benevolent Society of NSW, Annual Report 1879, ML

12. Testimony of G. Williams, February 1991

13. Lorna Ollif, *op. cit.*, p.5

14. *Ibid*

15. C.H. Pearson, 'The Higher Culture of Women,' address given in Melbourne 1875, Australasian Pamphlets, ML

16. F.K. Prochaska, *op. cit.*, p.21 and D. Pike, *A Paradise of Dissent*, Melbourne University Press, 1967, p.373

17. Matthew 25: 40 and 45

18. M. Kiddle, *Caroline Chisholm*, Melbourne University Press, 1950. Also R. Flynn, *The Emigrants' Friend*, MacMillan, 1991; J. Bogle, *Caroline Chisholm: The Emigrants' Friend*, Dove, 1992. The fullest treatment is M. Hoban, *Fifty-one Pieces of Wedding Cake*, Lowden Press, 1973.

19. C. Chisholm, *The ABC of Colonization in a Series of Letters*, 1850, p.22

20. G.P. Shaw, *op. cit.*, p.209

21. E. MacKenzie, *Memoirs of Mrs Caroline Chisholm*, Webb, Millington & Co., 1852, pp.28–33, in N. Turner, *op. cit.*, Vol. 1, p.122

22. J. Godden, *op. cit.*, pp.82–86

23. *Ibid*, pp.82–86

24. Letter of H.A. Harding to Judith Godden, 6 August 1977. In the latter's possession.

25. *Ibid*

26. Letters of Eliza Pottie to Sir Henry Parkes, 4 December 1873, 29 April 1879 and 13 November 1890, Parkes Correspondence, Vol. 30, pp.87–88, 109–110 and 123–126, ML

27. In J. Godden, *op. cit.*, p.402

28. View of her nephew, H.A. Harding, in letter cited above

29. Helen Jones, Mary Colton in *Two Hundred Australian Women*, H. Radi (ed.), Women's Redress Press, 1987, pp.20–21

30. N. Mackenzie, *op. cit.*, pp.6–7; A. Summers, *op. cit.*, pp.317–320; R. Teale, *op. cit.*, pp.121–122; and B. Jackson, *op. cit.*, p.143

31. R. Teale, *op. cit.*, p.123. See also *Well Played: A Short History of the Mothers' Union* (unpublished), M. Hawken (ed.), 1976, p.11

32. Mrs H. Dangar, Vice-President's Address to Annual General Meeting, Sydney, 1903, Mothers' Union Reports, ML

33. In L. Strahan, *Out of the Silence: A Study of a Religious Community for Women*, The Community of the Holy Name, OUP, 1988, p.27

34. R. Teale, *op. cit.*, pp.126–127. See also chapter 3.

35. S. Willis, 'Homes Are Divine Workshops', in *Women, Class and History, op. cit.*, p.181

36. *Ibid*, pp.177 and 182

37. R. Teale, p.124

38. J. Seymour, *A Century of Challenge, 1888–1988*, GFS, 1988, pp.7–10; S. Judd and K. Cable, *op. cit.*, p.193; J. Godden, *op. cit.*, p.90; B. Harrison, *For Church, Queen and Family: The Girls Friendly Society, 1874–1920*, in *Past and Present*, No.61, pp.109–138

39. *The White Ribbon Signal*, November and December 1892, ML; A. Hyslop, 'The Women's Christian Temperance Union of Victoria', in *Women, Faith and Fetes, op. cit.*, pp.44–46

40. *The White Ribbon Signal*, 7 November 1892

41. A. Hyslop, *op. cit.*, pp.57–58

42. W. Lawton, 'The Better Time to Be', PhD thesis, 1986, University of NSW

43. Newscuttings on Women's Suffrage, Rose Scott (ed.), ML, 396/3

44. Australian Women's Franchise Society Leaflets, MLQ 32V3/1

45. I. McCorkindale, *The Old Order Changeth*, WCTU, 1938, p.1

46. *Uphill All The Way*, K. Daniels and M. Murmane (eds.), UQP, 1980, pp.246–247

47. Jean Beadle in an address given at the Labour Church, Melbourne, 1899, *ibid*

48. *Adelaide Advertiser*, 17 March 1893, in S. Magarey, *Unbridling the Tongues of Women*, Hale & Iremonger, 1983, p.14

49. 'Mia Mia: Commemorative Issue, 1876–1976,' p.12, Mothers' Union Papers, ML

50. Menie Parkes to Sir Henry Parkes, 18 January 1865, in *Letters From Menie*, A.W. Martin (ed.), Melbourne University Press, 1982, p.47

51. B. Kingston, *My Wife, My Daughter and Poor Mary Ann: Women and Work in Australia*, Nelson, 1975, p.118

52. *Ibid*, pp.81–88

53. See Patricia Clarke, *The Governesses: Letters from the Colonies, 1862–1882*, Hutchinson, 1985

54. B. Kingston, *op. cit.*, pp.74–79

55. 'The Role of the Church in the Education of Girls and Women', *The Force of the Feminine*, M. Franklin (ed.), p.19

56. C.H. Pearson, *The Higher Culture of Women*, Mullen, 1875, ML

57. *The Force of the Feminine, loc. cit.*

58. W.N. Oats, *A Question of Survival: Quakers in Australia in the Nineteenth Century*, UQP, 1985

59. A. Summers, *op. cit.*, p.331

60. J. Nelson and L. Walker, *Women of Spirit*, St Marks, 1989, p.46

Chapter 6

1. M. Hill, *The Religious Order*, Heinemann, 1973, p.11

2. M. Rodgers, *Deaconesses in the Church of England in the Nineteenth Century: with special attention to the Bethany Church of England Deaconess Institution*, BD Hons thesis, University of Sydney, 1977, pp.29–30

3. In M. Hill, *op. cit.*, p.276. See also *Colonial Tractarians*, B.M. Porter (ed.), Joint Board of Christian Education, 1989, pp.145–155

4. M. Hill, *op. cit.*, p.278

5. *A Valiant Victorian*, The Life and Times of Mother Emily Ayckowrn: 1836–1900, anon., Mowbray Press, 1964, p. 61

6. *Ibid*, p.124

7. Sister Phyllis to Mother Emily Ayckbowm, 1895, *ibid*, p.129. See also *Some Memories of Emily Ayckbowm, Mother Foundress*, Church Extension Association, 1914, p.126.

8. Proceedings of the Second Session of the Ninth Synod of the Diocese of Sydney, NSW, 8 August — 16 August 1893, p.25, MCA

9. Australian Church Record, 7 January 1893, 21 January 1893, 4 February 1893, 11 March 1893, 22 April 1893 and 29 April 1893, MCA

10. *Some Memories of Emily Ayckbowm*, p.138

11. 'Esther: Mother Foundress of the Community of the Holy Name' (unpublished), p.103, archives of the Sisters of the Church, Glebe. See also L. Strahan, *Out of the Silence: A Study of a Religious Community for Women, The Community of the Holy Name*, OUP, 1988, pp.21–26

12. Barbara Darling, 'Some Leading Women in the History of the Anglican Church in Australia,' Australian and New Zealand Religious History 1788–1988, R. Withycombe (ed.), 1988, pp.147–152

13. D. Ryan, *An Examination of the Development of the Educational Policies of the Sisters of the Society of the Sacred Advent in the Years 1892–1900*, BEd thesis, University of Queensland (1971)

14. *A Short History of the Society of the Sacred Advent*, 1892–1934, Roberts and Russell, 1955, pp.1–11

15. *Ibid*, pp.12–14

16. M. Hill, *op. cit.*, p.12

17. See Romans 16: 1 and 1 Timothy 3: 10–11

18. J.S. Howson, *The Diaconate of Women in the Anglican Church*, 1886, in M. Rodgers, *op. cit.*, p.6. See also M. Hill, *op. cit.*, p.276

19. M. Rodgers, *op. cit.*, p.3

20. R. Teale, *op. cit.*, p.125

21. M. Rodgers, *op. cit.*, pp.14–15

22. *Ibid*, pp.20, 45-49

23. M. Archdall, address given at the Hobart Church Congress, 1894, in H.K. Archdall, *Mervyn Archdall: A Memorial*, Angus & Robertson, 1922, pp.109-117

24. Ibid, pp.x-xx

25. R. Teale, *op. cit.*, p.125 and M. Rodgers, *op. cit.*, pp.117–124

26. *Ibid*, p.130

27. M. Rodgers, *op. cit.*, p.107

28. Ruth Sturmey, 'Anglicanism and Gender', *Religion in Australia: Sociological Aspects*, A.W. Black (ed.), Allen & Unwin, 1991

29. The Methodists did not generally use the term 'deaconess' till 1930, preferring 'sister' till then.

30. John Flynn, *The Inlander*, Gordon and Gotch, 1914, pp.88–89

31. B.R. Keith, *Lives of Frank Rolland*, Rigby, 1977, pp.27–30

32. Report of the Committee on Social Service, Proceedings of the Presbyterian Assembly of 1917, p.138. See also Proceedings of 1918 and 1920, PCA (NSW).

33. The Eva Holland Chapel, 107 Stanley Street, East Sydney, dedicated on 2 November 1991

34. Proceedings of the Presbyterian Assembly of 1909, Women's Missionary Association Report, PCA

35. Proceedings. . . , 1910, *loc. cit.*

36. Proceedings. . . , 1917, *loc. cit.*

37. Proceedings. . . , 1931 and 1939, *loc. cit.*

38. Report on Sisterhoods, Laws of the Methodist Church of Australasia, 267 A, Uniting Church Archives, North Parramatta

39. *Ibid*

40. M. Porter, *Women in the Church: The Great Ordination Debate in Australia*, Penguin, 1989, pp.26–28

41. 'Women Evangelists in Early Victorian Britain', *Women in the Church: Studies in Church History, op. cit.*, pp.415–420

42. J. Godden, *Philanthropy and the Women's Sphere in Sydney, 1870–1900*, PhD thesis, Macquarie University, pp. 200–201

43. Sydney City Mission Minutes, 16 August 1900, ML

44. J. Godden, *loc. cit.*

45. R. Collier, *The General Next to God: The Story of William Booth of the Salvation Army*, Collins, 1965, pp.36–37

46. Barbara Bolton, *Booth's Drum: The Salvation Army in Australia*, Hodder & Stoughton, 1980, p.149

47. R. Collier, *op. cit.*, p.39

48. *Ibid*, p.40

49. *Ibid*, p.57

50. Barbara Bolton, *op. cit.*, p.150

51. R. Collier, *op. cit.*, p.109

52. F. Coutts, *No Discharge in this War*, Hodder & Stoughton, 1974, p.23

53. Barbara Bolton, *op. cit.*, pp.151–153

54. In Barbara Bolton, *op. cit.*, p.153

55. *Ibid*, pp.154–155

56. F. Coutts, *No Discharge in the War*, Hodder & Stoughton, 1974, p.27

57. J. Godden, *op. cit.*, p.261

58. Central Methodist Mission Annual Report, 1906–1907, in J. Godden, *op. cit.*, p.275

59. Archives of Deaconess House, Sydney

60. B. Heeney, *The Women's Movement in the Church of England, 1850–1930*, Clarendon, 1983, p.17

61. *Ibid*, p.19

Chapter 7

1. E. Stock, *A History of the Church Missionary Society*, CMS, 1899, Vol. 1, p.38

2. *Ibid*, pp.107–108. See also A. K. Davidson, 'Missionary Propaganda — Its Early Development and Influence with Respect to the British Missionary Movement and India', annual lecture to the Presbyterian Historical Society, New Zealand, 1974, p.14

3. See chapter 2, footnote 24

4. *Ibid*, footnote 28

5. J.W. Burton, *Modern Missions in the South Pacific*, LMS, 1949, pp.82–84. See also J. Gutch, *Beyond the Reefs*, Macdonald, 1974

6. Methodist Overseas Missions Records, Register of Missionaries to 1916, Item 216, ML

7. Journals of John and Esther Thomas, 1826–1859, Methodist Overseas Mission Papers, ML. See also Diary of Mrs John Polglase, August 1850—January 1859, MOM, Item 138, ML

8. Janet Cosh to Maggie Frame, Pango Efate, 3 August 1868. Letter in possession of David Denne, Killara.

9. T.W. Leggatt and J.& R. Parlane, Agnes C.P. Watt, *Twenty-five Years of Mission Life on Tanna*, New Hebrides, p.90, ML

10. *Ibid*, p.210

11. Hassall Papers, A280, ML, p.328

12. C.F. Pascoe, *Two Hundred Years with the SPG, 1701–1901*, SPG, 1901, p.617

13. C.F. Hayward, *Women Missionaries*, Collins, n.d., pp.226–230

14. E. Daniel Potts, *British Baptist Missionaries in India, 1793–1887*, Cambridge University Press, 1967, pp.122–123

15. Sarah Potter, *The Social Origins and Recruitment of English Protestant Missionaries in the Nineteenth Century*, PhD thesis, University of London, 1974, p.222

16. Testimony of Dr Clarke, in R. Lovett, *A History of the London Missionary Society*. Vol.2, Froude, 1899, pp.235–236,

17. F. Timms, *Mary MacLean: A Memorial*, Robert Day & Sons, 1943 and the *New South Wales Presbyterian*, 3 February 1943

18. D.F. Mitchell, *Ellen Arnold: Pioneer and Pathfinder*, Baptist Publications, 1932, p.11. See also *The Missionary Heritage of Australian Baptists*, Australian Baptist Foreign Missions, n.d., pp.1–28

19. Lecture of Rosalind Gooden to the Baptist Historical Society of NSW, Morling College, 10 April 1992

20. D.F. Mitchell, *op. cit.*, pp.12–23

21. *Ibid*, pp.17–18

22. *Ibid*, pp.29–30

23. CMS Register of Missionaries (Clerical, Lay and Female) Native Clergy, 1804–1904, Friendship House, London, p.260

24. K. Cole, *A History of the Church Missionary Society in Australia*, Church Missionary Publications, 1971, p.55

25. E.Stock, *op. cit.*, Vol. 3, pp.188–289

26. *Ibid*, pp.674–675

27. S.M. Johnstone, *A History of the Church Missionary Society in Australia and Tasmania*, 1925, p.251. The house was known as 'Cluden' and was situated in Frederick Street, Ashfield. A fine photograph exists in CMS Archives of Eliza Hassall and her trainees outside the house in 1892.

28. *Ibid*

29. *St Catherine's: A Pictorial Record*, 1976. Also various records in the Archives of St Catherine's Waverley.

30. S.M. Johnstone, *op. cit.*, p.344 and St Catherine's Archives

31. E.K. Cole, *Sharing the Mission: A Centenary History of the Victorian Branch of the Church Missionary Society*, 1882–1982, Bendigo, 1992, p.110

32. Minutes of the Ladies' Committee of CMA of NSW, 1893–1894, CMS Archives, Sydney. Amongst NSW records for CMS, only the ladies' committee minutes remain intact as the others were destroyed by a fire in 1921. The secretary of the ladies' committee always kept her minutes in a suitcase which she carried with her.

33. M.L. Loane, *The Story of the China Inland Mission in Australia and New Zealand from 1890 to 1964*, CIM/OMF, 1965, pp.21, 151 and 162. See also *East Asia's Millions*, Centenary Edition, 1989–1990, OMF Publications.

34. *China's Millions*, 1889, p.103, Overseas Missionary Fellowship Archives, Epping

35. Mary Reed, *Death and Life*, CIM booklet, n.d., OMF archives

36. Mary Reed, *By Boat and Barrow in China*, CIM booklet, ML, pp.7–13

37. *Ibid*, pp.14–17

38. V. Mathews, *A Life on Fire: The Life Story of Alice MacFarlane*, Marshall, Morgan & Scott, 1945. See also E.H. McIntyre, *High Privilege*, Kemp and Peterson, 1922

39. *East Asia's Millions*, 1989–1990, pp.6–7

40. J. Kerr, *Southern Sugar Saga: A History of the Sugar Industry in the Bundaberg District*, Bundaberg Sugar Company, Queensland, Oxley Library, n.d., p.17

41. M.L. Loane, *op. cit.*, pp.12 and 33–34 and Florence Young, *Pearls from the Pacific*, Marshall, 1926, pp.42–49

42. *Ibid*, pp.70–111

43. *Ibid*, pp.112–120 and M.L. Loane, *op. cit.*, p.28

44. The Katoomba Convention began at Khandala, the home of C. Ernest Young, Florence's brother. Like Keswick, it strongly emphasised practical holiness and missionary outreach.

45. F. Young, *op. cit.*, pp.160–172

46. G. White, *Thirty Years in Tropical Australia*, SPCK, 1918, pp.224–225. Also J.W.S. Tomlin, *Australia's Greatest Need*, SPG, 1914, pp.216–218.

47. E.C. Dawson, *Heroines of Missionary Adventure*, Seeley, 1909, pp.325–338

48. Egerton C. Long, *Retta Jane Long* (unpublished), ML. See also Retta Long, *Providential Channels* (1936) and *In the Way of His Steps* (1937), both unpublished, ML

49. Testimony of Barbara Cummings, a graduate of the Retta Dixon Home, now known as Karu Park, in *Fighters and Singers: The Lives of Some Aboriginal Women*, I. White (ed.), Allen & Unwin, 1985, p.145

50. Methodist Overseas Mission (MOM), items 218 and 302, ML

51. MOM, Minutes of the Board, 17 April 1903, item 203

52. MOM, Minutes 8 April 1918 and 7 February 1920, item 206

53. *Ibid*, 4 October 1918

54. Australian Christian Commonwealth, 14 July 1905, MOM, item 218, ML

55. Anon., *Hamari Mataji — With Hannah Dudley in India and Fiji.*, S. & A. Wheeler, 1951

56. MOM, item 302, ML

57. J. Colwell, *A Century in the Pacific*, W.M. Beale, 1914, p.554; A.H. Wood, *Overseas Missions of the Australian Methodist Church*, 4 vols, Aldersgate Press, 1975. See Vol. 3 for the solitary chapter, MOM, items 216 and 218, ML

58. CMS Register of Missionaries (Clerical, Lay and Female) and Native Clergy, 1804–1904, Friendship House, pp.260–474

59. International Review of Missions, J. Oldham (ed.), January 1913, No.5, pp.148–164

60. Entry in *Australian Dictionary of Evangelical Biography*, Evangelical History Association of Australia (1994), p.172

61. China's Millions, CIM, 1 May 1899

62. W.J. Lawton, *The Better Time To Be*, University of NSW Press, (1990), pp.30–34 and 73–75

Chapter 8

1. A. Tippet, *Introduction to Missiology*, William Carey Library, 1987, pp.94–153; S. Neill, *A History of Christian Missions*, Penguin, 1979, pp.249–258

2. These are statistics for Australia and New Zealand and are to be found in M.L. Loane, *op. cit.*, p.49

3. The diaries of Katie Miller — thirty-nine in all — are a terse but fascinating record of life as a pioneer missionary in Africa from 1905 to 1944. They are in the possession of the Short family.

4. K. Miller, diary, 22 April 1915

5. *Ibid*, 4 September 1916

6. On 21–26 July 1918. See Papers of Katie Miller.

7. Confidential agenda in Papers of Katie Miller

8. George Brown Memorial Training Home, Minutes for 4 October 1920, MOM, ML, MSS 278

9. *Missionary and Bible College Quarterly*, April 1928. See also various prospectuses composed by the founder and principal, the Reverend C. Benson Barnett, under such picturesque titles as *The Girdle. . . His Faithfulness* (1918), *Ebenezer* (1921), *The Right Way* (1927), Sydney Missionary and Bible College Archives.

10. M.L. Loane, *op. cit.*, pp. 55 and 70–71. The Angas College became the Adelaide Bible Institute in 1924.

11. *Ibid*, pp.65–80

12. A.J. Broomhall, *Hudson Taylor and China's Open Century*, Hodder & Stoughton, 1981, pp.232–235

13. V. Griffith, *The Role of Women in the History of Missions*, OMF Bulletin, March 1979, p.11

14. Minutes of the Australasian Council of CIM, 16 October 1922, Book 10, CIM Archives, BCV

15. Minutes of council meeting, 18 December 1922

16. Letter of D.E. Hoste to Council, Minutes of 9 June 1925

17. *East Asia's Millions*, April–June 1990, p.10. Christina Shaw came from New South Wales.

18. *Ibid*, p.11

19. M.L. Loane, *op. cit.*, p.85

20. *East Asia's Millions*, p.11

21. *Ibid*, p.12

22. E.H. McIntyre, *High Privilege*, Kemp and Paterson, 1924, pp.35–77

23. S.M. Johnstone, *op. cit.*, pp.142–144

24. M.L. Loane, *op. cit.*, pp.15–16

25. S.M. Johnstone, *op. cit.* pp.142–145

26. Interview with Deaconess Andrews, November 1989 and *Book of Dedications*, International Biographical Centre, Cambridge, p.3

27. K. Miller, diary entries for March and April 1919

28. *Ibid*, 19 November 1925, 5 February 1930, 28 February 1934

29. *Ibid*, 18 Oct. 1929

30. *Ibid*, 25 December 1930, 17 April 1938

31. Interview with Bishop Kenneth Short, 12 October 1992

32. 'Bibi' is a Swahili term of respect and endearment, meaning 'Grandmother' or 'female leader'. K. Miller, diary, entries for 10 August 1927, 10 September 1933, 16 April 1937.

33. Narelle Bullard's Papers are an extremely thorough archive of one life. They are housed in the Mitchell Library, although her original wish was that they be preserved in the Library at Dar-es-Salaam. As Tanzania did not have the resources to preserve them, her family decided they should go to the Mitchell. See Narelle Bullard Papers, 1905–1982, ML, MSS 5090/1–5.

34. Narelle Bullard Papers, ML, MSS 5090/3

35. She also completed a tropical medicine course and the Tresillian mothercraft course in 1932–1933 on her first furlough. *Ibid*.

36. J.W. Ferrier, General Secretary of CMS, to Narelle Bullard, 21 March 1928. *Ibid*.

37. Letter to Esme Bullard, 20 March 1929, Bullard Papers, ML, MSS 5090/1. All letters are to her sister, Esme, unless otherwise stated.

38. Letters of 7 April and 22 July 1929 *Ibid*.

39. Letter, 19 September 1929

40. Letters of 23 July 1928 and 23 September 1929

41. Interview in the *Sydney Morning Herald*, 1952 (cutting without full date), Narelle Bullard Papers, ML, MSS 5090/2

42. Address given at St Aidan's Church of England, Blackheath, in 1938, Narelle Bullard Papers, ML, MSS 5090/4

43. Letters of 14 September 1930, 5 October 1930, 23 August 1931

44. Letter, 23 August 1931

45. Interview with Timothy Wynn Jones, 2 December 1992

46. Narelle Bullard, diary, 22 January 1980, ML, MSS 5090/3

47. The Minton Taylor letters and papers are part of a larger collection preserved by the Wynn Jones family and kept in their private possession. Ruth married Bill Wynn Jones in 1933. In 1947, Bill followed Bishop Chambers as Bishop of Central Tanganyika, but died prematurely three years later.

48. G.A. Chambers to R. Minton Taylor, 13 January 1929, Wynn Jones Papers

49. R. Minton Taylor to H. Minton Taylor, 26 October 1931, Wynn Jones Papers

50. K. Miller, diary, 10 September 1937 and 29 July 1933 and Narelle Bullard, diary, 5 October 1930, ML, MSS 5090/2

51. Missionary sermon preached by Narelle Bullard at Constable Lee, UK,

27 June 1937, ML, MSS 5090/4

52. I am indebted to Rosalind Gooden, Baptist historian, for these statistics.

53. See chapter 7 for the work of Ellen Arnold and chapter 5 for the sexism prevalent in Baptist churches at home.

54. U. Clinton, *An Australian Medical Nun in India*, Advocate Press, 1960, pp.9–17

55. The pamphlet was entitled 'Dr Agnes McLaren' by Mary Ryan (B 226, Catholic Truth Society, 1915.), *ibid*, p.18

56. It was thought by the priestly hierarchy that the practice of midwifery would encourage sexual desire in nuns. Interview with Sr O'Carrigan, RSC, 12 November 1992.

57. U. Clinton, *op. cit.*, pp.16–18

58. In Clare Percy-Dove, 'A Gust of Epic — The Life of Mother Mary Sheldon', *Women, Faith and Fetes*, S. Willis, (ed.), *op. cit.*, p.143

59. *op. cit.*, pp.130–151

60. Appendices in each of the 4 volumes of A.H. Wood, *op. cit.*

61. Methodist Overseas Mission Board Minutes, Box 208, p.271, ML

62. MOM, Box 206, 8 April 1918 and 3 February 1920

63. MOM, Report in Minutes of 4 October 1918, Box 206, p.129

64. *Ibid*, p.130

65. *Ibid*, p.131

66. Executive Minutes of MOM, 28 February 1919 to 3 April 1925, Box 212, ML

67. A.H. Wood, *op. cit.*, Vol. 4, p.54

68. B.R. Keith, *The Lives of Frank Rolland.*, Rigby, 1977, pp.28–29; W. Scott McPheat, *John Flynn: Apostle to the Inland*, Hodder & Stoughton, 1965, pp.132–133

69. The *Inlander*, John Flynn (ed.), Vol. 1, No.2, Gordon and Gotch, 1914, p.93

70. *Ibid*, p.96

71. B. James, *No Man's Land: Women in the Northern Territory*, Collins, 1989, p.98; J.C. Finlayson, *Life and Journeyings in Central Australia*, Arbuckle Wardell, 1925

72. E. Burchill, *Innamincka*, Hodder and Stoughton, 1960, pp.40, 41 and 84

73. S.J. Kirkby, *These Ten Years: A Record of the Work of BCA, 1920–1930*, Edgar Bragg, 1930

74. See also T.E. Jones, *These Twenty Years: A Record of the Work of BCA for Australia and Tasmania, 1919–1939*, Edgar Bragg, 1939

75. Daisy Bates to Senator G.F. Pearce, 1 August 1920, in *Women in Australian Society, 1901–1945: A guide to the holding of the Australian Archives relating to women*, Janet Reed and Kathleen Oakes (eds)

76. Mounted Constable William Willshire, in J. Harris, *One Blood: Two Hundred Years of Aboriginal Encounter with Christianity*, Albatross, 1990, p.237

77. *Ibid*, pp.563 and 578–579

78. K.Cole, *Oenpelli Pioneer: A Biography of the Founder of the Oenpelli Mission*, Rev. A.J. Dyer, CMS Historical Publications, 1972, pp.43–45

79. Diary of Mrs H.E. Warren, 17–27 April 1915, ML, MSS 872/CY482, item 7

80. Journal of Mrs Warren, May 1915—December 1917, pp.225 and 229, ML, MSS 872/CY, item 8

81. Interview with Leonard Harris in J. Harris, *op. cit.*, p.840

82. N.Bullard to E. Bullard, 22 July 1929, ML, MSS 5090/1

Chapter 9

1. C. Shute, 'Heroines and Heroes: Sexual Mythology in Australia, 1914–1918' in *Hecate*, 1975, p.7

2. M. Lake, 'The Politics of Respectability: Identifying the Masculinist Context' in *Australian Historical Studies*, Vol. 22, 1986–1987, pp.438–441

3. Interview with Sister Ellen Mary Nolan RSM in July 1991 regarding parish life in the 1930s

4. M. Sophie McGrath, *op. cit.*, p.4

5. Report of the Royal Commission on the Basic Wage, Commonwealth Parliamentary Papers, 1920–1921, Vol. 4, in M. Lake, *op. cit.*, p.130

6. Sister M.G. McGlynn, 'The Growth of a Religious Institute: Some Lists and Statistics Relating to the History of the Good Samaritan Sisters OSB, 1857–1937' in *Tjurunga 39* (September 1990), pp.94–95, AGS

7. Statistics provided by Sister Paula Ziesing, Loreto Order, Ballarat

8. Statistics provided by Sister Evelyn of Sisters of St Joseph Archives, North Sydney

9. Statistics provided by the archivist, Sisters of Mercy, Monte Sant' Angelo, North Sydney

10. Curial Directive: Act of Nursing Orders, 11 February 1936, which modified Canon 139#2 forbidding religious to practise medicine or surgery without an indult from the Holy See. Interview with Sister Moira O'Sullivan RSC, November 1994.

11. Sister Veronica Brady, 'A Quixotic Approach to the Women's Movement in the Church in Australia' in *Knowing Otherwise: Feminism, Women and Religious*, E. White and M. Tulip (ed.), David Lovell, 1991, p.142

12. See Appendix II.

13. Testimony of Deaconess Dorothy Harris, 26 April 1991

14. P.J. O'Farrell, *The Catholic Church and Community in Australian History*, University of NSW Press, 1985, p.259

15. *Ibid*, p.255

16. The view of Cardinal Moran, *ibid*, p.254

17. M. Purcell, *The Original Sin; Submission as Survival: Women Religious in the Early Maitland Diocese* (unpublished MSS), p.205, Dominican Archives, Strathfield

18. For, example, the testimony of Sister Etienne Flynn RSM, 1990. See also 'Survey of the Life of Sister Clare Slattery SGS, 1900–1980', AGS

19. Testimony of Sister C. O'Carrigan RSC, 1990

20. Testimony of Sister Dominica Conaghan OP, 1990

21. The Daughters of Charity of St Vincent de Paul, *op. cit.*, pp.3–5

22. M. Foale, *op. cit.*, p.195

23. C. O'Carrigan RSC, *The Sisters of Charity and Maternal Care at St Vincent's* (unpublished), 1981

24. In C. O'Carrigan RSC, *Sisters of Charity Take Steps to Inaugurate a Medical Hospital* (unpublished), 1983

25. Sister Marie McGlynn SGS, *op. cit.*, pp.94–98

26. *Ibid*

27. *Ibid*, pp.98–99. See also R. MacGinley, *op. cit.*, pp.104–105

28. Utterances of Father J. Brophy and Mr P.W. Grove of Brisbane, P.J. O'Farrell, *op. cit.*, pp.254–255

29. Archbishop Kelly in 1911, in P.J. O'Farrell, *op. cit.*, p.261

30. D. Cave, *op. cit.*, see chapter 4

31. B. Cosgrove, *The Will to Rebellion: A Study of the Movement for a Catholic Women's College within the University of Sydney* (unpublished), 1982, pp.6–8

32. O'Reilly to Kelly, 1 April 1919, St John's College Archives, in B. Cosgrove, *op. cit.*, p.9

33. *Ibid*, p.5

34. Sally Kennedy, *Faith and Feminism: Catholic Women's Struggles for Self Expression*, Manly, Studies in the Christian Movement, 1985, p.65

35. Hilary Carey, *Truly Feminine, Truly Catholic: A History of the Catholic Women's League in the Archdiocese of Sydney, 1913–1987*, University of NSW Press, 1987, p.29

36. S. Kennedy, *op. cit.*, p.68

37. L. Barlow, *Living Stones: The Convent of the Sacred Heart Rose Bay, 1882–1982*, Kincoppal-Rose Bay, 1982, p.63

38. Cited in B. Cosgrove, *op. cit.*, p.12

39. *Ibid*, p.13

40. Cited in B. Cosgrove, *op. cit.*, p.14.

41. Kelly to Sheldon and Egan, 13 March 1924, Sancta Sophia Archives, in B. Cosgrove, *op. cit.*, p.15

42. *Ibid*

43. O'Reilly to Salmon, 2 December 1924, St John's College Archives, in B. Cosgrove, *op. cit.*, p.17

44. O'Reilly to MacRory, 24 March 1925, St John's College Archives, in B. Cosgrove, *op. cit.*, p.18

45. *Ibid*, pp.10 and 21

46. O'Reilly to Egan, 12 October 1928, St John's College Archives, in B. Cosgrove, *op. cit.*, p.24

47. Sister Rosalie, Perth College, 1902-1952, University of Western Australia Press, 1958, pp.3-6

48. Statistics for vocations to the Sisters of the Church were provided by Sister Margaret Mae CSC, St Michael's Convent Richmond, UK, October 1993

49. Ruth Frappell, *The Anglican Ministry to the Unsettled Rural Districts of Australia c.1890-1940*, PhD thesis, University of Sydney (1991), pp.327-328

50. Barbara Darling, *The Church of England in Melbourne and the Great Depression, 1929-1935*, MA thesis, Melbourne University (1983)

51. L. Strahan, *Out of the Silence: A Study of a Religious Community for Women, The Community of the Holy Name*, OUP, 1988, pp.56-76 and 109-115

52. *Ibid*, p.99

53. Sister M. Declan Ruffles RSM [entered the Mercy Order in 1930] — Personal Notebook, p.147, ASM

54. *The Sister Alice Mary, Society of the Sacred Advent: A Memoir by the Bishop of North Queensland*, T. Wilmott and Sons, 1928, p.5

55. *Ibid*

56. *Ibid*, pp. 5-13. See also North Queensland Jubilee Book, J.O. Feetham and W.V. Rymer (eds), McGilvray and Co., 1929, pp.18-19 and 82-92

57. *Sister Rosa of the Society of the Sacred Advent: An Appreciation by the Bishop of North Queensland* (unpublished), pp.4-5. See also *A Short History of the Society of the Sacred Advent, 1892-1954* (anon.), Roberts and Russell, 1955

58. *Ibid*

59. See chapter 5

60. M. Porter, *Women in the Church: The Great Ordination Debate in Australia*, Penguin, 1989, p.27

61. Statistics gleaned from N. Tress, *Caught for Life: A Story of the Anglican Deaconess Order in Australia*, Mission Publications, 1993, pp.171-204

62. *Ibid*, p.10
63. Interview with Dorothy Harris, 26 April 1991
64. R. Teale, *op. cit.*, p.120
65. Papers in the possession of Dorothy Harris
66. D. Harris, *God's Patience*, The Book Printer, 1990, pp.26–30
67. Answer to questionnaire, 11 July 1991
68. N. Tress, *op. cit.*, p.167
69. Interview of 11 July 1991
70. B. Bolton, *Booth's Drum: The Salvation Army in Australia*, Hodder & Stoughton, 1980, pp.156–157
71. Interview with Colonel O. Allitt, 20 April 1991
72. B. Bolton, *op. cit.*, p.159
73. A.W. Batley, *The Boomerang Returns: The Story of the Church Army in Australia*, Tyrrell House, 1955, in various places; the *Pioneer*, Church Army Magazine, 1955–1965, numbers 44–68, ML
74. See footnote 53.

Chapter 10

1. Sally Kennedy, *op. cit.*, p.21
2. Address entitled 'Christ and Home Duties: Mothers in Australia', Journal of the Mothers' Union, 1 June 1924, , ML. See also S. Willis, 'Homes are Divine Workshops', in *Women, Class and History, op. cit.*, p.188
3. For example, Sally Kennedy, *op. cit.*, pp.65-68
4. Interview with Sister Moira O'Sullivan RSC, 12 November 1993
5. Ten out of fourteen women in orders and two out of four Catholic laywomen
6. For example, Easter Report of Vestry of St Andrew's Church Summer Hill, 1937
7. N. MacKenzie, *Women in Australia*, Melbourne, Cheshire, 1962, p.6
8. Katie Ardill Brice in 1932, quoted in K. Daniels and M. Murmane, *Uphill All the Way*, UQP, 1980, pp.154–155
9. K. Reiger, *The Disenchantment of the Home*, OUP, 1985, pp.68–70
10. The role of the family in Australian society is explored in P. Grimshaw and G. Willett, 'Women's History and Family History' in *Australian Women and Feminist Perspectives*, N.Grieve and P. Grimshaw (eds), OUP, 1981, pp.134–155
11. J. Smart, 'The Panacea of Prohibition, the Reaction of the WCTU of Victoria to the Great War' in *Women, Faith and Fetes, op. cit.*, pp.164–183
12. Sally Kennedy, *op. cit.*, p.31

13. *Uphill All the Way, op. cit.*, pp.237–255
14. A. Summers, *op. cit.*, p.392
15. K. Reiger, *op. cit.*, p.56
16. The *Australian Women's Weekly* was founded in 1932
17. See above, chapter 5.
18. R. Teale,'Matron, Maid and Missionary: The Work of Anglican Women in Australia', in *Women, Faith and Fetes, op. cit.*, p.121
19. The League was led in NSW by active laywoman, Mrs Cecil Hoskins, Mothers' Union Annual Reports, Diocese of Sydney, 1932–1933, ML.
20. Report of the Mothers' Union, June 1920—June 1922, ML
21. *Women, Faith and Fetes, op. cit*, pp.184–185
22. R. Teale, *op. cit.*, p.124
23. See above, chapter 5.
24. Mothers' Union Report, 1924–1925, ML. See also B. Harrison, *op. cit.*, in various places.
25. Mothers' Union Newsletter of 1930, Mothers in Australasia, ML
26. Introduced in 1921. K. Reiger, *op. cit.*, pp.65–66
27. Report of the Pirie Street Methodist Dorcas Society 1930–1931, Mortlock Library.
28. J.D. Everett, The Pirie Street Methodist Church, Adelaide, SA, Methodist Historical Society, 1973, p.26
29. Report of the Pirie Street Dorcas Society, 1930–1931, Mortlock Library
30. Account Books of the Pirie Street Dorcas Society, 25–35, Mortlock Library
31. M. Reeson, *Certain Lives*, Albatross, 1989, p.358
32. History of St Hilary's Anglican Church, Kew (n.d.), p.98
33. 'The Church News', Parish of Belair, South Australia, November, 1927
34. *Ibid*, November 1928
35. *Ibid*, July 1929
36. *Ibid*, issues for 1933 to 1936
37. *Ibid*, May 1937
38. Year Book for the Diocese of Adelaide and Willochra, 1938–1939, Anglican Archives, Adelaide
39. Easter Reports of the St Andrew's Parish Council for 1926, 1928 and 1937 and parish magazines for the same period
40. St Andrew's Parish Souvenir Booklet, 1881–1937
41. The comment of a former student of MLC Melbourne, *The Half-Open Door*, P. Grimshaw and L. Strahan (eds), Hale & Ironmonger, Sydney, 1982, p.56
42. Easter Report of the Parish of St Andrew's Summer Hill for 1937

43. K. Dempsey, *Conflict and Decline*, Methuen, 1983, p.96. See also P. Glasner, *Practice and Belief*, Allen & Unwin, 1983, pp.25–42 and Janet Finch, *Married to the Job: Wives of Incorporation in Men's Work*, Allen & Unwin, 1983, in various places.

44. Interviews of July 1990

45. Interviews with Sister C. O'Carrigan RSC, July 1990 and with Sister Dominica Conaghan OP, July 1990

46. In Sally Kennedy, *op. cit.*, pp.xii–xiii

47. *Ibid*, p.xiv. For Marian piety and its application see K. Massam, *The Blue Army and the Cold War*, AHS, Vol. 24, pp.420–422. Also Veronica Brady, 'We Are Such Stuff. . .' in *Sweet Mothers, Sweet Maids: Journeys from Catholic Childhood*, V. and D. Nelson (eds), Penguin, 1986, pp.27–30

48. *Ibid*, pp.4–10 and P.J. O'Farrell, *op. cit.*, pp.248–249

49. *Ibid*, pp.10–13

50. Sally Kennedy, *op. cit.*, pp.40–45

51. *Ibid*, pp.78–89

52. P.J. O'Farrell, *op. cit.*, p.379

53. Sally Kennedy, *op. cit.*, pp.93–104

54. Sally Kennedy gives an excellent description of the vicissitudes of the Grail Movement in her book, *Faith and Feminism*, *op. cit.*, pp.108–165

55. Brian Heeney's posthumous study of Anglican feminism is illuminating — *The Women's Movement in the Church of England, 1850–1930*, Clarendon Press, 1988, Vol. 2, p.222

56. O. Chadwick, *A History of the Church of England*, Vol. 2, A. & C. Black, 1971, p.222

57. *The Ministry of Women: A Report by a Committee Appointed by His Grace the Archbishop of Canterbury*, SPCK, 1919, p.22, MCL

58. The comment is from Muriel Porter, *Women in the Church: The Great Ordination Debate in Australia*, Penguin, 1989, p.16

59. *Report of the Lambeth Conference of Bishops*, SPCK, 1920, MCL

60. *Report of the Lambeth Conference of Bishops*, SPCK, 1930, MCL

61. B. Heeney, *op. cit.*, p.90

62. The *Sydney Morning Herald*, 4 June 1928, p.4

63. The *Adelaide Church Guardian*, 8 July 1928, p.9, ADA

64. The *Sydney Morning Herald*, 18 June 1928, p.12

65. The *Australian Church Record*, 26 April 1928, MCL

66. Recollection of Deaconess Mary Andrews, written on 10 August 1992

67. M. Royden, *Sex and Commonsense*, Paternoster Press, 1921, p.29

68. Ibid, p.192

69. M. Royden, 'Woman's Nature' in B. Heeney, *op. cit.*, pp.132–133

70. M. Knauerhase, *Winifred*, Lutheran Publishing House, 1978, pp.3–18

71. *Ibid*, p.37

72. *Ibid*, p.36

73. *Ibid*, p.38

74. *Ibid*, p.37

75. *Ibid*, pp.107–110

76. At Queen Victoria Hospital, Melbourne. M. Porter, *op. cit.*, p.25

77. *Ibid*, pp.25–27

78. Bishop G. H. Cranswick, *The Ministry of Women: Official Report of the Ninth Australian Church Congress, May 1925*, Gippsland Diocesan Registry, 1925, p.194

Chapter 11

1. A. Manne, 'Children in the New World Order', *Quadrant*, June 1995, p.130

2. Testimony of Sister Maria Cunningham RSC, February 1996

3. Profile, Sisters of Mercy, *One Heart and Mind*, Sisters of Mercy pamphlet, December 1995

4. Testimony of Colleen Malone, formerly RSJ, March 1996

5. Testimony of MMK O'Sullivan RSC, December 1995

6. Maureen McGuirk, *loc. cit.*

7. Instances observed in New South Wales since 1985

8. *Religious Life in the Light of Vatican II*, St Paul's Publications, Philippines, 1968, p.24

9. 'Religious obedience is and must remain a holocaust of one's own will which is offered to God', address of Pope Paul VI to all religious, 23 May 1964, *ibid*, p.157

10. 'Decree on Adaptation and Renewal of Religious Life', n.17, *ibid*, p.377

11. P.J. Gearon, *The Wheat and the Cockle*, Britons Publishing Company, 1969, in Breward, *op. cit.*, p.165

12. Venetia Nelson in V. & D. Nelson (eds), *Sweet Mothers, Sweet Maids, Journeys from Catholic Childhood*, Penguin, 1986, p.208

13. Colleen Malone, formerly a Josephite sister, interview March 1996

14. Sister Mary Emil IMM, Amherst College, 3 November 1967; *Religious Life in the Light of Vatican 2, op. cit.*, p.220. See also A. Lohrey, in V. & D. Nelson, *op. cit.*, pp.223 and 231

15. Letter from unnamed sister to author, 19 December 1994

16. Sister Maria Cunningham RSC, March 1996

17. P. Fray, 'Shrinking Orders', the *Sydney Morning Herald*, 19 September

1995. See also R. McGinley, 'Catholic Women's Institutes, 1830–1940: Some Considerations' in *Long, Patient Struggle*, M. Hutchinson and E. Campion (eds), Vol. 2, CSAC, Sydney, 1994, p.104

18. Sister Gemma Trotter DC, April 1996

19. Sister Maria Cunningham RSC, March 1996 and Colleen Malone, formerly RSJ, April 1996

20. Sister Pauline Rae MMS, February 1996

21. Geraldine Doogue, March 1996

22. V. Nelson, *op. cit.*, p.200

23. K. Massam, 'The Blue Army and the Cold War: Anti-Communist Devotion to the Blessed Virgin Mary in Australia in *Australian Historical Society*, Vol. 24, pp.420–428

24. Testimony of Betsy Conti, a student at Monte Sant' Angelo College NSW, given in June 1995

25. M. McGuirk and P. Rae, *ibid*

26. Testimony of Anne-Louise Pociask, now a secondary school teacher, who had been educated at the Josephite Convent, Lochinvar, NSW interview, 16 May 1996

27. Lilyan Staniforth, 'Slipping the Knot', V. & D. Nelson (eds), *op. cit.*, p.163

28. Interview with Sister Eunice SSA, Brisbane, 28 August 1995 and letter from Jean Myers, formerly SSA, 1 January 1994

29. D. Selway, *Women of Spirit*, Longman, Melbourne, 1995, pp.44–60. Also letter from Sister Angela to author, February 1996

30. L. Strahan, *Out of the Silence: A Study of a Religious Community for Women, The Community of the Holy Name*, OUP, Melbourne, 1988, pp.5–12

31. *Ibid*, pp.141–149

32. *Ibid*, p.171

33. *Ibid*, p.297

34. *Ibid*, pp.291 and 301–302

35. Testimony of the Reverend Narelle Jarrett, March 1996

36. N. Tress, *op. cit.*, p.84

37. *Ibid*, pp.102–104 and 116–118

38. *Ibid*, pp.34–36

39. The *Western Australian*, 20 July 1967, in N. Tress, *op. cit.*, p.117

40. D. Wright and E. Clancy, *op. cit.*, p.204

41. Numbers supplied by the Public Relations Department of the Salvation Army, Eastern Territory Command, 29 April 1996

42. H. Gariepy, *General of God's Army: The Biography of Eva Burrows*, Victor Books, 1993, pp.18, 191–192 and 239–240

Chapter 12

1. See chapter 7 above.

2. A. Griffiths, *Fire in the Islands*, Harold Shaw, 1977, pp.37–116

3. Pauline Rae SMSM, director of the Columban Institute, April 1996

4. S. Neill, *A History of Christian Missions*, Penguin, 1979, p.518; A. Tippet, *Introduction to Missiology*, William Carey Library, 1987, pp.46–64

5. A. Tippet, *op. cit.*, p.276

6. M. Lamb, *Going It Alone: Mary Andrews, Missionary to China*, Aquila, 1995, p.45

7. *Ibid*, p.95

8. *Ibid*, pp.99–112

9. *Ibid*, pp.133–144

10. *China's Millions*, Centenary Edition, April—June 1990, OMF, p.16

11. *Ibid*

12. M.L. Loane, *The Story of the China Inland Mission*, CIM, 1965, p.98

13. *The New Guinea Diaries of Philip Strong*, D. Wetherell (ed.), MacMillan, 1981, pp.i–x

14. 18 December 1941, *ibid*, p.66

15. *Ibid*, Appendix B, p.222. See also L.C. Rodd, *The Road from Gona*, Angus & Robertson, 1969, p.28

16. 'The Good Shepherd', sermon preached by Sir Philip Strong at the Festival of the New Guinea Martyrs, 2 September 1981, St Peter's Eastern Hill, Melbourne, pp.3–4

17. L.C. Rodd, *op. cit.*, pp.45–58

18. Entry for 6 March 1942, *The New Guinea Diaries of Philip Strong, op. cit.*, p.89

19. Entry for 27 January 1942, p.75

20. Letter to writer by Adrienne Ellis who is closely associated with ABM personnel in Brisbane, 19 February 1996

21. Interview with Margaret Somerville, December 1991 to February 1992, TS 713, Northern Territory Archives, pp.5-6

22. *Ibid*, T 3, p.3

23. *Ibid*, T 2, p.8

24. Observation of Deaconess Margaret Rodgers, Anglican Media, March 1996

25. Interviews with Margaret Lawry Brain and the Rev. Pauline McCann, formerly Australian CMS missionaries working in Tanzania, April 1996

26. CMS Federal Council Minutes, Octobeer 1953 and letter of General Secretary to Federal Secretary, 11 March 1954, CMS Archives, Sydney

27. Testimony of Catherine Thew, whose parents were CMS missionaries in Pakistan, May 1996

28. *Protestant Missions Handbook* (1977), Association of Church Missions, Pasadena, p.14

29. CMS Diary for 1977, CMS Archives

30. The first woman on the CMS Federal Council was Mrs Harold Bragg of Sydney. She was followed by Sophie Edwards from Victoria (1945) and Rene Jeffreys from South Australia (1946). CMS Archives

31. V. Griffith, *The Role of Women in the History of Missions*, OMF Bulletin, March 1979, p.11

32. Minutes of CIM Council Meeting, 16 December 1945, Archvies, BCV

33. BBC audio visual, 'Walking Back to Happiness'. Interview with family (John and Sheila Knox) and the *Sydney Morning Herald*, 26 January 1995, p.8.

34. Testimony of Kathleen McCredie and Jean Rixon

35. For example, the Marella Mission which was linked with the Anglican Church, founded at Kellyville outside Sydney (1949–1986). This home for Aboriginal children was run as a farm by Keith and Gwen Langford Smith and an indefatigable secretary, Norma Warwick, who has left voluminous records for future students.

36. *A Life Together, A Life Apart: A History of Relations Between Europeans and Aborigines*, B. Attwood (ed.), Melbourne University Press, 1994, pp.15–18

37. Interview with Daisy Alma Fleming (1988), TSS 208, p.9, Northern Territory Archives

38. *Ibid*, p.29

39. *A Life Together. . .* , *op. cit.*, p.86

40. S. Neill, *op. cit.*, pp.457–458. By 1958, approximately 43 000 Protestants worked in overseas missions, including 27 733 Americans.

41. R. McGinley, *A Dynamic of Hope; Institutes of Women Religious in Australia*, Crossing Press, 1996, p.316

42. 'Only If We're Asked', address by Margaret O'Sullivan to the CSAC Conference on Mission, July 1996

43. M. Le Breton, *Tribute to Irene McCormack*, Josephite Archives

44. Interview with the Rev. David Claydon, Federal Secretary of CMS, May 1996

45. M. Lamb, *op. cit.*, pp.160, 180, 193, 202

46. A woman missionary who served in Tanzania for twenty-three years from the 1970s onwards ·

47. CMS Year Books for 1980 and 1985

48. Interview with David Claydon, May 1996

49. *Ibid*

50. K. Cole, *Sharing in Mission: Centenary History of the Victorian Branch of CMS, 1892–1992*, Keith Cole Publications, 1992, p.136

Chapter 13

1. *MIANZA* (Journal of the Mothers' Union in Australia and New Zealand), 1 December 1944, ML

2. Margaret Murchison, army sister with the 2/6 Australian General Hospital in the Middle East, 1940–1941, the *Australian*, 10 September 1995

3. Marilyn Lake, the *Australian*, 18 March 1995. See also M. Lake, 'Female Desires: The Meaning of World War II' in *Australian Historical Studies*, Vol. 24, No.95, October 1990, pp.267–268

4. Monthly Reports of the Mothers' Union, October and November 1941, ML

5. Diary of 1957 in M.L. Loane, *Archbishop Mowll*, Hodder & Stoughton, 1960, p.249

6. *Ibid*, p.248

7. Report of 1 February 1943, ML

8. *Mia Mia*, Commemorative issue, November — December 1976, p.12, ML

9. *MIANZA*, May 1945, pp. 103–104, ML

10. *Ibid*

11. *Ibid*, 1 February 1946, p.72

12. *Ibid*, 1 March 1951, p.103

13. MLC Melbourne Centenary History, 1882–1982, pp.268–269, in J. McCalman, *Journeyings: The Biography of a Middle Class Generation*, Melbourne University Press, 1900, p.128

14. S. Piggin, *Spirit, Word and World: A History of Evangelicalism in Australia*, OUP, 1996, p.127 and D. Hilliard, *God in the Suburb: The Religious Culture of Australian Cities in the 1950s*, AHS, Vol. 24, No.97, October 1991, pp.399 and 416

15. S. Piggin, *op. cit.*, p.156

16. D. Knox, *Time Flies: The Memoirs of Dorothy Knox*, Rigby, 1982, p.327

17. J. McCalman, *op. cit.*, p.100

18. J. Mansfield, 'Music: A Window on Australian Christian Life' in *Re-visioning Australian Christianity*, M. Hutchinson and E. Campion (eds), Centre for the Study of Australian Christianity, 1994, pp.115–116 and 132–133

19. Conversation with Pauline Thomas of the Royal School of Church Music, March 1996

20. H. Mol, *Religion in Australia*, 1971, pp.15–16

21. Annual Report of the Mothers' Union, 1976, ML

22. *Mia Mia*, November — December, 1976, p.14, ML

23. Annual Report of the Mothers' Union, 1981, ML

24. Reports for 1977 and 1981

25. Reports for 1977 and 1978

26. *Mia Mia*, November 1982, p.14

27. *Ibid*, July 1984, p.6

28. F. Clarke, '"She Hath Done What She Could", Methodist Women's Voluntary Groups in South Australia, 1945–1977' in *Long Patient Struggle*, Centre for the Study of Australian Christianity, 1988, p.133

29. *Ibid*, p.134

30. B. Kingston, 'Women and the History of Churches in Australia', in S. Willis, *op. cit.*, p.27

31. Interview with Jean Raddon, 29 February 1996, the first full-time worker with the Christian Women Communicating International

32. G. Collins and J. Raddon, *Beyond Expectations: The Story of Christian Women's Convention International*, Bell, 1993

33. Letter from Irene Young to the writer, 14 March 1995

34. C. West, *A Sociological Study on the Role of the Clergyman's Wife in the Sydney Anglican Diocese*, University of Sydney Social Work Department (1991), p.10

35. K. Dempsey, *Conflict and Decline*, Methuen, 1983, p.140. See also K. Dempsey, 'Minister's Wives, Continuity and Change in Relation to their Husbands' Work', in *The Force of the Feminine*, M. Franklin (ed.), Allen & Unwin, 1986, pp.83-84 and 91

36. Commission on the Status of Women, Australian Council of Churches (1974), p.73

37. Interview with Kay Clark, assistant parish minister at St Matthew's, West Pennant Hills, NSW, February 1996

38. Report of the Registrar of the Church of England in Australia, John Denton, *loc. cit.*, p.11

39. *Ibid*, pp.13–15

40. Recent figures supplied by Peter Bentley, archivist of the Uniting Church in Australia

41. Yearbook of the Diocese of Sydney (1988), pp.212–232, and Yearbook of the Diocese of Sydney (1996), p.29

42. Commission on Status of Women, ACC, pp.23–24

43. The Catholic submission was made by the Rev. P.L. Murphy, past chairman of the Archdiocesan Commission for Ecumenism, *ibid*, p.25

44. *Ibid*, p.26

45. *Ibid*, pp.28–30

46. Interview with Mary Gilchrist, 27 February 1996

47. Testimony of Geraldine Doogue, 25 February 1996

48. Interview with Mary Gilchrist, 27 February 1996

49. H. Carey, *Truly Feminine, Truly Catholic: A History of the Catholic Women's League in the Archdiocese of Sydney, 1913–1987*, University of New South Wales Press, 1987, pp.1–5 and 40–44

50. *Ibid*, p.63

51. S. Kennedy, *Faith and Feminism: Catholic Women's Struggles for Self Expression*, Studies in the Christian Movement, 1985, pp.xv–xvi

52. ACC Enquiry Report, pp.45–47

53. A.R. Nuss, *Women of Faith and Action: A History of the Catholic Women's League of Tasmania, 1941–1983*, Southern Holdings, 1986, pp.33 and 83–111

54. Interview with Colleen Malone, 25 March 1996

55. Study conducted by K, Betts, P. Miller and K. Diener, 'People and Place (1992)', Monash University, in the *Sydney Morning Herald*, 18 December 1995

56. M. Hart, *A Story of Fire: Aboriginal Christianity*, New Creation Publications, Blackwood, SA, 1988, p.50f., in S. Piggin, *op. cit.*, p.198

57. *Fighters and Singers: The Lives of Some Aboriginal Women*, I. White (ed.), Allen & Unwin, 1985, p.175

58. Interview with Rosalie Kunoth-Monks, April 1988, TS 501, Northern Territory Archives

59. Interview with Mrs Daisy Fleming, 16 September 1988, TS 208, Northern Territory Archives

60. H. Mol, *Religion in Australia*, Nelson, 1971

61. H. Mol, *The Faith of Australians*, Allen & Unwin, 1985, p.181. Also G.D. Bouma and B.R. Dixon, *The Religious Factor in Australian Life*, Zadok, 1986, pp.198–200

62. *Winds of Change: The Experience of Church in a Changing Australia*, P. Kaldor, J. Bellamy, R. Powell, M. Correy, K. Castle (eds), Lancer, 1994, pp.121–122

63. M. Andrews, *A History of Australian Church Women*, ACC (NSW Unit), 1991, pp.3–4

Chapter 14

1. T. Harrison, *Much Beloved Daughter. The Story of Florence Li*, Moore-house-Barlow, 1985, various references

2. Rev. Colleen O'Reilly, MOW Newsletter, July 1987, ML

3. Statistics supplied by Peter Bentley, archivist to the Uniting Church Assembly, 29 March 1996

4. M. Porter, *Women in the Church: The Great Ordination Debate*, Penguin, 1989, p.34. Also, R. Dalziell, *Indispensable but Marginalised: Women in the Australian Church*, Zadok, Series I, Paper S49, Canberra

5. 1 Timothy 2: 12–15

6. Genesis 2: 18 and Ephesians 5: 22

7. Testimony of Jean Raddon, March 1996 and Deaconess Mary Andrews, September 1991

8. The Ministry of Women: A Report of the General Synod Commission on Doctrine, 1977

9. *MOW Newsletter*, August 1985

10. *Church Scene*, 12 December 1986, in M. Porter, *op. cit.*, p.124

11. *Southern Cross*, March 1985 and February 1992

12. Published by Penguin, Melbourne, 1989

13. *Long, Patient Struggle*, M. Hutchinson and E. Campion (eds), CSAC, Sydney, 1994, pp.161–182

14. *Ibid*, footnote 1, p.182

15. OUP, 1996, pp.203–221

16. The *Sydney Morning Herald*, 1981, in M. Porter (1989), p. 94

17. The voting was House of Laity (99 members) 69 for and 30 against; House of Clergy (99 members) 67 for and 32 against; House of Bishops (22 members) 16 for and 4 against, 2 informal. MWG *Meeting Place*, December 1992

18. I. Breward, *A History of the Australian Churches*, Allen & Unwin, 1993, p.209

19. M. Porter, *op. cit.* (1994), p.180

20. *Ibid*, pp.166 and 173

21. *Southern Cross*, February 1992, p.5

22. Presidential Address at the Ninth Ordinary Session of the General Synod. . . 9 July 1992

23. *Church Scene*, 27 November 1992, in M. Porter, *op. cit.* (1994), p.174

24. *Ibid*, p.175

25. *MOW Newsletter*, June 1987 and *MOW National Magazine*, November 1995, p.39

26. *MOW Newsletter*, April 1985. For inclusive language in the Uniting Church, see 'Women in the Uniting Church in Australia: Report of the Social Responsibility and Justice Committee', April 1988, pp.54–56

27. *Women — Church*, No.I, pp.25–26

28. *Meeting Place: Newsletter of Men, Women and God, Christians for Biblical Equality*, 1–20, 1988–1994, ML

29. *Meeting Place*, No. I, September 1988

30. *Ibid*, November 1993

31. *AAM Newsletter*, in S. Piggin, *op. cit.*, p.210

32. *Church Scene*, 26 June 1992

33. D. Wetherell, *Women Priests in Australia? The Anglican Crisis*, Spectrum, 1987, p.78

34. J. Nelson and L. Walter, *Women of Spirit. Woman's Place in Church and Society*, 1989, p.158

35. M.T. Gilchrist, *The Destabilisation of the Anglican Church*, 1991, pp.24–25

36. *Women-Church*, No.1, pp.25–26, in M.T. Gilchrist, *op. cit.*, p.9

37. The *Age*, 21 August 1989, in M.T. Gilchrist, *op. cit.*, p.58

38. Letter of Rev. Theodora Hobbs to the parish of Abbotsford, 17 October 1993, *The Tower*, Abbotsford Parish Paper

39. *Ibid*

40. The *Bulletin*, July 1987, in J. Nelson and L. Walter, p.161

41. WATAC Manifesto (1995)

42. OCW News, Vol.2, No.3, December 1995, p.1

43. The *Tablet*, 22 November 1995, pp.1495–1496, in *loc. cit.*, p.5

44. *Ibid*, p.6

45. Testimony of Kay Clark, February 1996

46. Testimony of Cathryn Thew, March 1996

47. Testimony of Jan Livingstone, March 1996

48. Testimony of the Reverend Dorothy McCrae–McMahon, Uniting Church National Director for Mission, April 1996

49. Testimony of Colleen Malone, April 1996

50. Testimony of Sister Maria Cunningham RSC, April 1996

51. Testimony of Sister Maureen McGuirk RSM, May 1996

52. Testimony of Sister Moira O'Sullivan RSC, February 1996

Bibliography

Abbreviations

AIM	Australian Inland Mission
ASC	Sisters of Charity Archives
ASM	Sisters of Mercy Archives
ASSA	Society of the Sacred Advent Archives
ASSH	Sisters of the Sacred Heart Archives
AGS	Good Samaritans Archives
ASJ	Sisters of St Joseph Archives
BMS	Baptist Missionary Society
BCA	Bush Church Aid Society
BCV	Bible College of Victoria
CIM	China Inland Mission
CMS	Church Missionary Society
LMS	London Missionary Society
MOM	Methodist Overseas Mission Papers
OMF	Overseas Missionary Fellowship
MCL	Moore College Library
ML	Mitchell Library
PCA	Presbyterian Church Archives
UCA	Uniting Church Archives

Primary sources

Anglican Church, General Synod Papers, Ninth Ordinary Synod, July 1992 and Ministry of Women: A Report of the General Synod Commission on Doctrine, 1977

Australian Women's Franchise Society Leaflets. Q32V3/1. ML.

Barker, Jane. In Memoriam addresses, April 1876. A920.7. ML.

Belair, South Australia. Records of the Anglican parish, 1918–1938.

Bullard, Narelle. Papers. 5 boxes. ML MSS 5090/1–5.

China Inland Mission Archives. Minutes of Federal Council, 1922–1955. BCV.

Church Missionary Association. Minutes of Ladies Committee, 1893–1894. CMS Archives. Diaries. Minutes of Federal Council. CMS House, Sydney.

Church Missionary Society Register of Missionaries (Clerical, Lay and Female) and Native Clergy, 1804–1904. Friendship House, London.

Cosh, Janet. Letters from Tonga. In possession of the Denne family.

Hanly, M.M. Dorothea. Memoirs. AGS.

Hassall Correspondence, 1813–1828. ML MSS A280.

Historical Records of Australia. Vol. I, xiv. 1829. Report of the Board of Management of the Female Factory, 19 January 1829.

Johnson, Richard. Letters. ML MSS Ajl.

de Lacy, Alicia Baptista. Letters. ASC.

Mackillop, Mary. Letters. ASJ.

Marsden Papers. ML MSS C44.

Methodist Church of Australasia. Laws. 267A. UCA.

Methodist Overseas Mission. Records and Register of Missionaries to 1916. ML MSS. MOM 1–311.

Miller, Katie. Diaries, 1905–1944. Thirty nine in all. In possession of the Short family.

Molloy, Georgiana. Papers. Battye Library and Western Australian Archives, Perth.

Mothers Union Papers. Reports and AGMs, 1895–1984. ML.

Northern Territory Archives. Transcripts 2, 3, 208, 501, 713.

NSW Legislative Council, Votes and Proceedings, 1866. MDQ 328.9106. ML.

Parkes, Sir Henry. Correspondence. Vol. 30. ML MSS A900.

Perry, Frances. Journals. 1849-1856. Found variously in Notes on Gippsland History, G. Cox (ed.), No. 38 and Contributions to an Amateur Magazine in Prose and Verse, R. Perry (ed.), 1857. 982/P. ML.

Pirie Street Methodist Church, Adelaide. Reports and Accounts of Dorcas Society. Mortlock Library.

Presbyterian Assembly. Proceedings. 1909, 1910, 1917, 1918, 1920, 1931 and 1939. PCA of NSW.

Purcell, M., *The Original Sin: Submission as Survival. Women Religious in the Early Maitland Diocese.* Unpublished MS. Dominican Archives, Strathfield.

Ruffles, M. Declan. Personal Notebook. ASM.

Summer Hill. Parish of St Andrew's Anglican Church, NSW. Records 1917–1938.

Sydney City Mission. Minutes, 16 August 1900. 279/1S No.38. ML.

Sydney Diocese. Proceedings of the Ninth Synod, August 1893. MCL.

Sydney Missionary and Bible College. Prospectuses and Reports.

Warren, Ellie M. Diary and Journal, 1915–1917. ML MSS 8-215B. Items 7 and 8.

Women in the Uniting Church in Australia. Report of the Social Responsibility and Justice Committee, April 1988.

Wright, John Charles. Diary 1908–1916. In possession of the Wright family.

Wynn Jones Papers, containing letters of Ruth Minton Taylor and her future husband who became Bishop of Central Tanganyika. In possession of the Wynn Jones family.

Secondary sources

A Life Together, A Life Apart: A History of Relations between Europeans and Aborigines, B. Attwood (ed.), Melbourne University Press, 1994

Andrews, M., *A History of Australian Church Women*, Australian Council of Churches (NSW), 1991

Anonymous, *Hints for a Clergyman's Wife*, Holdsworth & Ball, 1832, ML

Anonymous, *History of the Sisters of the Church in Australia* (unpublished)

Anonymous, *A Valiant Victorian, the Life and Times of Mother Emily Ayckbowm, 1836–1900,* Mowbray Press, 1964

Anonymous, *Some Memories of Emily Ayckbowm, Mother Foundress,* Church Extension Association, 1914

Anonymous, *History of St Hilary's Anglican Church, Kew, Victoria* (n.d.)

Anonymous, *Esther, Mother Foundress of the Community of the Holy Name* (unpublished)

Anonymous, *A Short History of the Society of the Sacred Advent, 1892–1954,* Roberts & Russell, 1955

Anonymous, *Mataji Hamari, with Hannah Dudley in India and Fiji*, S. & A. Wheeler, 1951

Archdall, H.K., *Mervyn Archdall: A Memorial*, Angus & Robertson, 1922

Australian Women and Feminine Perspectives, N. Grieve and P. Grimshaw (eds), OUP, 1981

Balleine, G.R., *A History of the Evangelical Party in the Church of England* (new edition), CBR Press, 1951

Barlow, L., *Living Stones: The Convent of the Sacred Heart, Rose Bay, 1882–1982*, ASSH

Batley, A.W., *The Boomerang Returns: The Story of the Church Army in Australia*, Tyrrell House, 1955

Bebbington, D.W., *Evangelicals in Modern Britain: A History from the 1730s to the Present Day*, Unwin Hyman, 1989

Birchley, D., *John McEncroe, Colonial Democrat*, Collins Dove, 1986

Bishop of North Queensland, *Sister Rosa of the Society of the Sacred Advent: An Appreciation*. (unpublished)

Bishop of North Queensland, *The Sister Alice Mary, Society of the Sacred Advent: A Memoir*, T. Wilmott & Sons, 1928

Bogle, J., *Caroline Chisholm: The Emigrants' Friend*, Gracewing, 1992

Bolton, B., *Booth's Drum: The Salvation Army in Australia*, Hodder & Stoughton, 1980

Bonwick, J., *Australia's First Preacher*, 1898, ML

Bouma G.D. and Dixon B.R., *The Religious Factor in Australian Life*, Zadok, 1986

Breward, I., *A History of the Australian Churches*, Allen & Unwin, 1993

Broomhall, A.J., *Hudson Taylor and China's Open Century*, Hodder & Stoughton, 1981

Broughton, S., *Prayers and Private Devotions*, 1849, ML

Burchill, E., *Innamincka*, Hodder & Stoughton, 1960

Burton, J.W., *Modern Missions in the South Pacific*, 4 vols, LMS, 1949

Cambridge, A., *Thirty Years in Australia*, M. Bradstock & L. Wakeling (eds), NSW University Press, 1989

Cameron, J., *A Centenary History of the Presbyterian Church*, Angus & Robertson, 1905

Carey, H., *Truly Feminine, Truly Catholic: A History of the Catholic Women's League in the Archdiocese of Sydney, 1913–1987*, University of NSW Press, 1987

Chadwick, W.O., *The Victorian Church* (2 vols), A. & C. Black, 1971

Chisholm, C., *The ABC of Colonisation in a Series of Letters*, 1850

Clarke, P., *The Governesses: Letters from the Colonies, 1862–1882*, Hutchinson, 1985

Clinton, U., *An Australian Medical Nun in India*, Advocate Press, 1960

Cole, K., *A History of the CMS in Australia*, Church Missionary Publications, 1971

Cole, K., *Oenpelli Pioneer: A Biography of the Founder of the Oenpelli Mission, the Reverend A.J. Dyer*, CMS Historical Publications, 1972

Cole, K., *Sharing in Mission: Centenary History of the Victorian Branch of CMS, 1892–1992.*, CMS Publications 1992

Collier, R., *The General Next to God: The Story of William Booth of the Salvation Army*, Collins, 1965

G. Collins and J. Raddon, *Beyond Expectations: The Story of Christian Women's Convention International*, Bell, 1993

Colwell, J., *A Century in the Pacific*, W.M. Beale, 1914

Colonial Tractarians, B.M. Porter (ed.), Joint Board of Christian Education, 1989

Commission on the Status of Women, ACC, 1974

Connell, R.W., *Gender and Power: Society, the Person and Sexual Politics*, Allen & Unwin, 1987

Coutts, F., *No Discharge in This War*, Hodder & Stoughton, 1974

Cranswick, G., The Ministry of Women, Official Report of the Ninth Australian Church Congress, May 1925, Diocesan Registry, 1925

Creusen, J., *Religious Men and Women in Church Law* (6th English edition, revised by Adam J. Ellis), Bruce Publishing Co., 1958.

Daly, M., *Beyond God the Father*, Beacon Press, 1973

Daniels, K., *So Much Hard Work: Women and Prostitution in Australian History*, Fontana Collins, 1984

Darling, E., *Simple Rules for the Guidance of Persons in Humble Life, More Particularly for Young Girls Going Out to Service*, James Tegg, 1837

Davidson, A.K., *Missionary Propaganda — Its Early Development and Influence with Respect to the British Missionary Movement and India*, Presbyterian Historical Society of New Zealand, 1974

Davis, G., *Annals of the Sisters of Charity* (unpublished), 1903, ASC

Dawson, E.C., *Heroines of Missionary Adventure*, Seeley, 1909

Dempsey, K., *Conflict and Decline*, Methuen, 1983

Dilly L. and Jones C., *The Daughters of Charity of St Vincent de Paul* (unpublished), 1990

Dixson, M., *The Real Matilda: Women and Identity in Australia, 1788–1975*, Penguin, 1976

Earnshaw, B., *Fanned into Flame: The Spread of the Sunday School in the Sydney Diocese*, Anglican Board of Education, 1980

Eliot, G., *Adam Bede*, J.M. Dent, 1976

Ensor, R.C.K., *England, 1870–1914*, Clarendon, 1949

Everett, J.D., *The Pirie Street Methodist Church. Adelaide, SA*, Methodist Historical Society, 1973

Exploring Women's Past: Essays in Social History, P. Crawford (ed.), Allen & Unwin, 1984

Fighters and Singers. The Lives of some Aboriginal Women, I. White (ed.), Allen & Unwin, 1985

Finch, J., *Married to the Job: Wives of Incorporation in Men's Work*, Allen & Unwin, 1983

Finlayson, J.C., *Life and Journeyings in Central Australia*, Arbuckle Wardell, 1925

Fletcher, B.H., *A Governor Maligned*, OUP, 1984

The Force of the Feminine, M. Franklin (ed.), Allen & Unwin, 1986

Foskett, D., *John Harden of Brathay Hall, 1792–1847*, Kendal, 1974

Gaffney, E., *Autobiograph: Somebody Now*, Aboriginal Studies Press, 1989

Glasner, P., *Practice and Belief*, Allen & Unwin, 1983

Griffiths, A., *Fire in the Islands*, South Sea Evangelical Mission, 1990

Harris, D., *God's Patience*, The Book Printer, 1990

Harris, J., *One Blood: Two Hundred Years of Aboriginal Encounter with Christianity*, Albatross, 1990

Harrison, T., *Much Beloved Daughter: The Story of Florence Li*, Moorehouse-Barlow, 1985

Hart, M., *A Story of Fire: Aboriginal Christianity*, New Creation Publications, 1988

Hasluck, A., *Portrait With a Background: A Life of Georgiana Molloy*, OUP, 1955

Hasluck, A., *Unwilling Emigrants: A Study of the Convict Period of Western Australia*, OUP, 1959

Hassall, J., *In Old Australia*, R.S. Huys & Co., 1902

Hayward, C.F., *Women Missionaries*, Collins, n.d.

Heeney, B., *The Women's Movement in the Church of England, 1850–1930*, Clarendon, 1933

Heney, H., *Australia's Founding Mothers*, Nelson, 1978

Hill, M., *The Religious Order*, Heinemann, 1973

History of the North Sydney Foundation of the Order of the Sisters of Mercy (unpublished), S. Prince (ed.)

Hoban, M., *Fifty-One Pieces of Wedding Cake*, Lowden, 1973

Hulme-Moir, D., *The Edge of Time*, Christian Outreach Book Service, 1989

The Illawarra Diary of Lady Jane Franklin, 1839, M. Organ (ed.), Illawarra Publications, 1985

Jackson, H.R., *Churches and People in Australia and New Zealand, 1860-1930*, Allen & Unwin, 1987

James, B., *No Man's Land: Women in the Northern Territory*, Collins, 1989

Johnstone, S.M., *A History of the CMS in Australia and Tasmania*, 1925

Jones, T.E., *These Twenty Years: A Record of the Work of BCA for Australia and Tasmania, 1919-1939*, Edgar Bragg, 1939

Judd, S. and Cable, K.J., *Sydney Anglicans*, Anglican Information Office, 1987

Keith, B.R., *Lives of Frank Rolland*, Rigby, 1977

Kennedy, S., *Faith and Feminism, Catholic Women's Struggles for Self-Expression*, Studies in the Christian Movement, 1985

Kiddle, M., *Caroline Chisholm*, Melbourne University Press, 1950

King, H., *Elizabeth MacArthur*, Hodder, 1984

Kingston, B., *My Wife, My Daughter and Poor Mary Ann: Women and Work in Australia*, Nelson, 1975

Kirby, S.J., *These Ten Years: A Record of the Work of the BCA, 1920-1930*, Edgar Bragg, 1930.

Knauerhase, M., *Winifred*, Lutheran Publishing House, 1978

Knox, D., *Time Flies: The Memoirs of Dorothy Knox*, Rigby, 1982

Knowing Otherwise: Feminism, Women and Religions, E. White and M. Tulip (eds), David Lovell, 1991

Lamb, M., *Going It Alone: Mary Andrews, Missionary to China*, Aquila, 1995

Lambeth Conference of Bishops of 1920, Report., SPCK, 1920, MCL

Lambeth Conference of Bishops of 1930, Report, SPCK, 1930, MCL

Lawton, W.J., *The Better Time To Be*, University of NSW Press, 1990

Larsson, F., *My Best Men Are Women*, Hodder & Stoughton, 1974

Leggatt, T.W. and Parlene, J.& R. and Watt Agnes C.P., *Twenty Five Years of Mission Life on Tanna, New Hebrides*, ML

Letters from Menie, A.W. Martin (ed.), Melbourne University Press, 1982

Letters of Rachel Henning, D. Adams (ed.), Penguin, 1969

Loane, M.L., *The Story of the CIM in Australia and New Zealand from 1890 to 1964*, CIM/OMF, 1965

Long, E.C., *Retta Jane Long* (unpublished), ML

Long, Patient Struggle: Studies in the Role of Women in Australian Christianity, Vol. 2, M. Hutchinson and E. Campion (eds), Centre for the Study of

Australian Christianity, 1994

Lovett, R., *A History of the London Missionary Society* (2 vols), Froude, 1899

Lyne, D., *Mary MacKillop: Spirituality and Charisma*, Edwards & Shaw, 1984

McCalman, J., *Journeyings: The Biography of a Middle Class Generation*, Melbourne University Press, 1990

McCorkindale, I., *The Old Order Changeth*, WCTU, 1938

MacKenzie, N., *Women in Australia*, Cheshire, 1962

McEwen, M., *A Living Stream: Sisters of the Good Samaritan, 1857–1924* (unpublished), AGS

MacGinley, M.R., *A Dynamic of Hope: Institutes of Religious Women in Australia, 1838–1939*, Crossing Press, 1996

McGrath, M.S., *These Women? Women Religious in the History of Australia: Sisters of Mercy, Parramatta, 1888–1988*, University of NSW Press, 1988

McIntosh, N., *Richard Johnson, Chaplain to the Colony of New South Wales*, Library of Australian History, 1978

McIntyre, E.H., *High Privilege*, Kemp & Paterson, 1922

McPheat, W. Scott, *John Flynn: Apostle to the Inland*, Hodder & Stoughton, 1963

McQuoin, Mother Ignatius, *Early History of the Mercy Foundation* (1865), S.Price (ed.), ASM

Mathews, V., *A Life on Fire: The Life Story of Alice MacFarlane*, Marshall, Morgan & Scott, 1945

Mill, J.S., *Essay on Liberty with The Subjection of Women*, Cambridge University Press, 1989

Millett, Mrs Edward, *An Australian Parsonage or The Settler and the Savage in Western Australia*, 1872

Millett, K., *Sexual Politics*, Bantam Books, 1969

Ministry of Women: A Report by a Committee Appointed by His Grace the Archbishop of Canterbury, SPCK, 1919, MCL

Mitchell, D.F., *Ellen Arnold, Pioneer and Pathfinder*, Baptist Publications, 1932

Mol, H., *Religion in Australia*, Nelson, 1971

Mole, W.V. and Treweeke, A.H., *The History of the Women's College within the University of Sydney*, Halstead, 1953

Montgomery, B., *A Field Marshal in the Family*, Constable, 1973

Neill, S., *A History of Christian Missions*, Penguin, 1979

Nelson, J. and Walker, L., *Women of Spirit*, St Mark's Library, 1989

The New Guinea Diaries of Philip Strong, D. Wetherell (ed.), MacMillan, 1981

Newscuttings on Women's Suffrage, Scott Rose (ed.), ML 396/3

North Queensland Jubilee Book, J.O. Feetham and W.V. Rymer (eds), McGilvray & Co., 1929

Nuss, A.R., *Women of Faith and Action: A History of the Catholic Women's League in Tasmania, 1941–1983*, Southern Holdings, 1986

Oats, W.N., *A Question of Survival, Quakers in Australia in the Nineteenth Century*, UQP, 1985

O'Brien M., *The Politics of Reproduction*, Routledge & Kegan Paul, 1981

O'Carrigan, C., *The Spirit of the Pioneer Sisters of Charity* (unpublished), ASC

O'Donague, M., *Mother Vincent Whitty: Women and Education in a Masculine Society*, Melbourne University Press, 1972

O'Farrell, P.J., *The Catholic Church and Community in Australian History*, University of NSW Press, 1985

Pascoe C.F., *Two Hundred Years with the Society for the Propagation of the Gospel, 1701–1901*, SPG, 1901

Piggin, S., *Making Evangelical Missionaries*, Sutton Courtenay Press, 1984

Piggin, S., *Helpmeets and Heroines: Women and the History of Australian Evangelicalism*, Mothers Union, 1988

Piggin, S., *Spirit, Word and World: A History of Evangelicalism in Australia*, OUP, 1996

Pike, D., *A Paradise of Dissent*, Longmans, 1957

Porter, M., *Women in the Church: The Great Ordination Debate in Australia*, Penguin, 1989

Potts, E. Daniel, *British Baptist Missionaries in India, 1793–1887*, Cambridge University Press, 1967

Presbyterian Women's Association, Historical Booklet for Presentation to PWA Conference, Brisbane 1988 (unpublished), ML

Private Correspondence of Sir John and Lady Jane Franklin (2 vols), G. Mackaness (ed), Review Publications, 1977

Prochaska, F.K., *Women and Philanthropy in Nineteenth Century England*, Clarendon, 1980

Reed, M., *Death and Life*, CIM booklet (n.d.), OMF Archives

Reed, M., *By Boat in China*, CIM booklet (n.d.), ML

Reeson, M., *Currency Lass*, Albatross, 1985

Reiger, K., *The Disenchantment of the Home*, OUP, 1985

Religion in Australia: Sociological Perspectives, A.W. Black (ed.), Allen and Unwin, 1991

Religious Life in the Light of Vatican Two, St Paul's Publications, Philippines, 1968

Re-visioning Australian Colonial Christianity: New Essays on the Australian

Christan Experience, 1788-1900, Vol. 1, M. Hutchinson and E. Campion (eds), Centre for the Study of Australian Christianity, 1994

Ritchie, J., *Lachlan Macquarie: A Biography,* Melbourne University Press, 1986

Roberts, J., *Maybanke Anderson: Sex, Suffrage and Social Reform,* Hale & Iremonger, 1993

Robin, A. de Q., *Charles Perry, Bishop of Melbourne,* University of WA Press

Robinson, P., *Women of Botany Bay,* Macquarie Library, 1988

Robinson, P., *The Hatch and Brood of Time,* OUP, 1985

Rodd, L.C., *The Road from Gona,* Angus & Robertson, 1969

Rosalie, Sister CSC, *Perth College,* University of Western Australia Press, 1958

Royden, M., *Sex and Commonsense,* Paternoster Press, 1921

Ruether, R., *New Woman, New Earth,* Dove Communications, 1975

Ruskin, J., *Sesame and Lilies,* Ward Lock, 1911

St Andrew's Summer Hill: Souvenir Booklet, 1937 (unpublished)

St Catherine's Waverley: A Pictorial Record, 1976 (unpublished)

Selway, D., *Women of Spirit,* Longmans, 1995

Seymour, J., *A Century of Challenge, 1888-1988,* GFS, 1989

Shaw, G.P., *Patriarch and Patriot: William Grant Broughton, 1788-1853,* Melbourne University Press, 1978

Some Private Correspondence of the Reverend Samuel Marsden and Family, 1794-1824, G Mackaness (ed.), D.S. Ford, 1942

Stock, E., *A History of the Church Missionary Society* (2 vols), CMS, 1899

Strahan, L., *Out of the Silence: A Story of a Religious Community for Women, The Community of the Holy Name,* OUP, 1988

Strong, Sir Philip, 'The Good Shepherd'. Sermon preached at the Festival of the New Guinea Martyrs, September, 1981, Melbourne.

Summers, A., *Damned Whores and God's Police,* Melbourne University Press, 1975

Sweet Mothers, Sweet Maids: Journeys from Catholic Childhood, K. and V. Nelson (eds), Penguin, 1986

Tate, A., *Ada Cambridge, Her Life and Work, 1844-1926,* Melbourne University Press, 1990

Tench, W., *Narrative of the Expedition to Botany Bay,* n.p., 1789, ML

Thorpe, O., *Mary MacKillop,* Principal Press, 1982

Timms, F., *Mary MacLean: A Memorial,* Robert Day, 1943

Tippett, A., *Introduction to Missiology,* William Carey Library, 1987

Tregenza, J., *Professor of Democracy: The Life of Charles Henry Pearson, 1830-1894,* Melbourne University Press, 1968

Tress, N., *Caught for Life: A Story of the Anglican Deaconess Order in Australia*, Mission Publications, 1993

Turner, N., *Catholics in Australia: a Social History* (2 vols), Collins Dove, 1992

Two Hundred Australian Women, H. Radi (ed.), Women's Redress Press, 1988

Uphill All the Way, K. Daniels and M. Murmane (eds), University of Queensland Press, 1980

de Vries-Evans, S., *Pioneer Women, Pioneer Land*, Angus & Robertson, 1987

Waldersee, J., *Catholic Society and New South Wales, 1788–1860*, University of Sydney Press, 1974

West, J., *Innings of Grace: A Life of Bishop W.G. Hilliard*, Standard Publishing, 1987

Wollstonecraft, M., *Vindication of the Rights of Women*, Penguin, 1975

Women, Class and History, E. Windschuttle (ed.), Fontana, 1980

Women, Faith and Fetes, S. Willis (ed.), Australian Council of Churches, Dove, 1977

Women in Australian Society, 1901–1945, J. Reed and K. Oakes (eds), Australian Government Public Services, 1977

Women in the Church: Studies in Church History, W.J. Shiels and D. Wood (eds), Blackwell, 1990

Women in the Australian Church. Manifesto (1995).

Women Priests in Australia? The Anglican Crisis, D. Wetherell (ed.), Spectrum, 1987

Wood, A.H., *Methodist Overseas Missions* (4 vols), Aldersgate, 1975

Woodward, E.L., *The Age of Reform, 1850–1870*, Clarendon, 1949

Woodward, F.J., *A Portrait of Jane: A Life of Lady Jane Franklin*, Hodder & Stoughton, 1951

The World Moves Slowly: A Documentary History of Australian Women, B. Kingston (ed.), Cowell, 1977

Wright D. and Clancy E., *The Methodists: A History of Methodism in NSW*, Allen & Unwin, 1993

Yarwood, A., *Samuel Marsden: The Great Survivor*, Melbourne University Press, 1977

Year Book of the Diocese of Adelaide and Willochra, 1938–1939

Year Book of the Diocese of Sydney, 1893–1894, 1938–1939 and 1988–1992

Young, F., *Pearls from the Pacific*, Marshall Bros, 1926

Newspapers and journals

Adelaide Church Guardian, 8 July 1928, Anglican Archives, South Australia

The Australian, 10 September 1995

Australian Church Record, January to April 1893 and 26 April 1928, MCL

Baptist Recorder, May 1924

China's Millions, 1889 and 1899, OMF Archives

Christian Advocate and Wesleyan Record, September 1859

Church Scene, 12 December 1986, 26 June 1992, 27 November 1992

East Asia's Millions, Centenary Edition, 1989–1990, OMF Publications

Goulburn Herald, 28 and 30 November 1898

Meeting Place: Newsletter of Men, Women and God, 1988–1994

Mothers in Australasia: Journal of the Mothers' Union, 1918–1938

Movement for the Ordination of Women Newsletter, 1985–1994

Ordination of Catholic Women, News, 1994–1996

NSW Presbyterian, February 1943, PCA

Quadrant, June 1995

Southern Cross, magazine of the Diocese of Sydney, March 1985, February 1992

Sydney Gazette, 26 April 1826, 21 June 1926 and 12 May 1827

The *Sydney Morning Herald*, 4 March 1959 and 4 June.

The *Inlander*, Vol.I, John Flynn (ed.), Gordon & Gotch, 1914, PCA

The *Pioneer*, Church Army Magazine, 1955–1965, Nos.44–68

Weekly Advocate, August — September 1888

The *White Ribbon Signal*, November — December 1892

The above to be found in the Mitchell Library, unless otherwise stated.

Papers and addresses

Cave, D., 'The Pedagogical Tradition of the Religious of the Sacred Heart in France and Australia', Melbourne Studies in Education, 1985

Cable, K.J., 'Mrs Barker and Her Diary', *Journal of the Royal Australian Historical Society*, 1968, Vol. 54, Part I, pp. 67–105

Cosgrove, B., *The Will to Rebellion: A Study of the Movement for a Catholic Women's College within the University of Sydney* (unpublished), 1982

Dalziell, R., *Indispensable but Marginalised: Women in the Australian Church*, Zadok, Series I, Paper S49

Darling, B., 'Some Leading Women in the Anglican Church in Australia' in *Australian and New Zealand Religious History, 1788–1988*, R.S.M. Withycombe (ed.), pp. 147–157 (1988)

David, B.T. and Tearle, S., 'Centenary of the Wagga Wagga Presentation Sisters', *Australian Catholic Historical Society Journal*, Vol. 6, 1918–1980, pp. 36–39

Fox, B.J., 'Conceptualizing Patriarchy', *Canadian Review of Sociology and Anthropology*, 1988, Vol. 25, pp. 163–182

Gooden, R., 'Baptist Women Missionaries in Bengal'. Lecture to the Baptist Historical Society of NSW (1992)

Harrison, B., 'For Church, Queen and Family: The Girls' Friendly Society, 1874–1920', *Past and Present*, No. 61

Hilliard, D., 'God in the Suburbs: The Religious Culture of Australian Cities in the 1950s' in *Australian Historical Studies*, Vol. 24, No.97, October 1991

International Review of Missions, J. Oldham (ed.), No. 5

Lake, M., 'Female Desires: The Meaning of World War 2', *Australian Historical Society*, Vol. 24, No.95, October 1990

Levine, P., 'British Gender History: Some Thoughts on the Australian Contribution' in *Australian Historical Association Bulletin*, December 1988, pp.38–40

Massam, K., 'The Blue Army and the Cold War, Anti-Communist Devotion to the Blessed Virgin Mary in Australia' in *Australian Historical Society*, Vol. 24, pp. 420–428

Mansfield, J., 'Music: A Window on Australian Christian Life', in *Re-visioning of Australian Christianity*, M.Hutchinson and E. Campion (ed.), CSAC, 1994

McGlynn, M. G., 'The Growth of a Religious Institute. Some Lists and Statistics Relating to the Good Samaritan Order, 1857–1937' in *Tjurunga* 39 (September 1990), AGS

Newth, Jessie Hungerford., Diary, August 1890, *Journal of the Hungerford and Associated Families Society*, Vol. 2, No.I, May 1993

O'Carrigan, C., 'The Sisters of Charity and Maternal Care at St Vincent's Hospital' (unpublished), 1981, ASC

O'Carrigan, C., 'The Sisters of Charity Take Steps to Inaugurate a Medical Hospital' (unpublished), 1983, ASC

O'Sullivan, M.M.K., 'Only If We're Asked'. Address to CSAC Conference on Missions, July 1996

Ollif, L., 'Women's Place in the Baptist Church'. Paper read to the Baptist Historical Society of NSW, 21 February 1980

Pearson, C.H., 'The Higher Culture of Women'. Address given in Melbourne in 1875. Australasian Pamphlets, ML

Peyser, D., 'A History of Welfare Work in Sydney from 1788 to 1900' in

Journal of the Royal Australian Historical Society, Vol. 25, 21 February 1980

Withycombe, R.S.M., 'No Place for Mrs Proudie: The Role and Expectations of the Colonial Bishop's Wife'. Paper read to the Ecclesiastical History Society's Conference, York, UK, July 1989

Theses

Darling, B., 'The Church of England in Melbourne and the Great Depression 1929–1935', MA thesis, University of Melbourne (1983)

Godden, J., 'Philanthropy and the Women's Sphere in Sydney, 1870–1900', PhD thesis, Macquarie University (1983)

Hone, J.A., 'The Movement for the Higher Education of Women in Victoria in the later nineteenth century', MA thesis, Monash University (1966)

Kavanagh, M., 'The Educational Work of the Presentation Sisters in Victoria, 1873–1960', MEd thesis, University of Melbourne (1965)

Lawton, W., 'The Better Time To Be: The Kingdom of God and Social Reform, Anglicans and the Diocese of Sydney', PhD thesis, University of NSW (1986)

Potter, S., 'The Social Origins and Recruitment of the English Protestant Missions in the 19th Century', PhD thesis, University of London (1974)

Rodgers, M., 'Deaconesses in the Church of England in the Nineteenth Century: with special attention to the Bethany Church of England Deaconess Institution, BD Hons thesis, University of Sydney, 1977

Ryan, D., 'An Examination of the Development of the Educational Policies of the Sisters of the Society of the Sacred Advent in the Years 1892–1900', BEd thesis, University of Queensland (1971)

West, C., 'A Sociological Study on the Role of the Clergyman's Wife in the Sydney Anglican Diocese', University of Sydney, Social Work Department (1991)

West, J., 'The Early Life and English Background of Bishop W.G. Broughton, First Bishop of Australia', MA thesis, University of Sydney (1972)

Index

Picture acknowledgements

Anglican Retirement Villages, Castle Hill, NSW, p.381
Church Missionary Society archives, p.214
Crosson family, p.346
Eva Holland Chapel, p.185
Focus magazine, 21 December 1992, p.414
Knox family papers, p.368
Margaret Yarwood Lamb/Andrews family papers, pp.348, 364
National Library of Australia, pp.60, 260, 274, 371
Nungalinya College, Darwin, p.38
Order of the Good Samaritan, Glebe, pp.112, 114
Rex Nan Kivell Collection, National Library of Australia, p.60
St Andrew's Anglican Church, Summer Hill, archives, pp.138, 309, 310
Salvation Army Territorial Command, Sydney, pp.192, 193, 352
Short family papers, p.244
Sisters of Charity archives, Sydney, pp.274, 276
Sisters of the Sacred Advent archives, Brisbane, p.178
Sisters of Mercy archives, Brisbane, pp. 116, 120, 141
Sisters of Mercy archives, Parramatta, p.335
Sisters of St Joseph archives, North Sydney, p.125
Sydney Morning Herald/Mitchell Library, p.322
Sydney Morning Herald, Saturday 21 December 1996, p.39 (Palani Mohan)
Sydney Diocesan Archives, p.135
Wynn Jones family papers, p.250

Front cover painting: courtesy of the National Gallery of Victoria
Girolamo Nerli: born Italy 1860, arrived Australia 1885, died
Italy 1926
Head of a woman
oil on composition board, 46.0 x 38.1 cm
Purchased 1960

Back cover painting: Holy Trinity Church: York, Western Australia, c.1869. Original watercolour by Mrs Edward Millett.
In the possession of the church at York.